The Study of Lives

Edited by

ROBERT W. WHITE

assisted by Katherine F. Bruner

ATHERTON PRESS

70 Fifth Avenue • New York 1963

A Division of Prentice-Hall, Inc.

Published simultaneously

in Great Britain

by Prentice-Hall International

London

Frank Barron

Leopold Bellak

Anthony Davids

Erik H. Erikson

Robert R. Holt

Kenneth Keniston

Theodore C. Kroeber

Donald W. MacKinnon

David C. McClelland

The Study of Lives

Essays on Personality in Honor of Henry A. Murray

Gerhard S. Nielsen

Nevitt Sanford

Edwin S. Shneidman

M. Brewster Smith

Morris I. Stein

Silvan Tomkins

Robert W. White

Robert N. Wilson

Frederick Wyatt

THE STUDY OF LIVES
Essays on Personality
in Honor of Henry A. Murray
Robert W. White, Editor

Copyright © 1963 by Prentice-Hall, Inc.
Atherton Press, New York, New York

Published simultaneously in Great Britain by
Prentice-Hall International, Inc.
28 Welbeck Street, London W.1, England

Copyright under International, Pan American,
and Universal Copyright Conventions

Atherton Press, A Division of Prentice-Hall, Inc.
70 Fifth Avenue, New York 11, New York

Library of Congress Catalog Card Number: 63–11993
Printed in the United States of America   85896

THE ATHERTON PRESS BEHAVIORAL SCIENCE SERIES

General Editor
WILLIAM E. HENRY
The University of Chicago

To
Henry A. Murray
this book is presented
on his seventieth birthday
May 13, 1963,
· by students and colleagues
past and present
who will always remember
with excitement and gratitude
their sojourn in
the high invigorating climate
created by his infectious zest,
wide-ranging awareness,
bountiful powers of creation,
and staunch fidelity
to the increase
of human understanding

CONTENTS

Contents

PREFACE

This book of essays on personality has been given its title with a view to capturing something of the flavor of Henry A. Murray's thinking and influence on psychology. "The study of lives" is a phrase he has often used to describe his own work, and it suggests his central conviction that living beings must be studied as living wholes. Personality, he has repeatedly pointed out, is a dynamic process—a constantly changing configuration of thoughts, feelings, and actions occurring in a social environment and continuing throughout life. If small parts and short segments of human affairs have to be isolated for detailed scrutiny, they must still be understood as parts of a patterned organic system and as segments of a lifelong process. This has never meant for him that all research should take the form of collecting life histories, although his contributions along this line have been outstanding. It implies simply that isolating, fragmenting, and learning just a tiny bit about a lot of people tend to carry us away from what is most worth studying. The significant things about personality are part of the whole enterprise of living.

In his own research, Murray has followed the plan proposed in 1938 in his *Explorations in Personality*. This plan calls for stating a series of specific research problems, designing experimental situations to explore them, and using a relatively small number of subjects, whose life histories become known through other tests, interviews, and imaginative productions. Whatever the focus of interest—family relations, superego, the role of imagination, sentiments, ego strength, fitness for dangerous tasks, commitment, values, dyadic interactions—the specific findings can then be seen as aspects of lives. When several workers pool their efforts in this way, the results obtained by each enrich all the others, and there may be the additional bonus that some subject, like "American Icarus," will disclose a pattern of development not hitherto recognized. Research done according to this plan is neither rapid nor easy, but it has the supreme virtue of being adapted to the nature of its subject matter. It keeps specific findings from falling out of the life configurations that give them significance.

The essays in this book are grouped under headings that represent some of Murray's strongest interests. His conception of personality as a dynamic process is reflected in Part I, which deals with continuities and changes in the course of life. His interest in devising procedures suitable for disclosing live feelings, fantasies, and adaptations and his insistence on the necessity for an adequate taxonomy of carefully discriminated, carefully defined variables are represented in the papers of Part II. His view that creativity is a central property of human nature has contributed to the reflections and researches that make up Part III. Finally, his concern with values—the great blind spot of traditional science but so obviously a momentous problem for contemporary lives and societies —has been taken up in several different ways by the authors of Part IV.

Murray's conception of personality still awaits its final exposition by his own pen. His former student and colleague, Gardner Lindzey, made an excellent though brief summary in 1957 in a chapter of his book with Calvin Hall, *Theories of Personality.** The most pertinent excerpts from Murray's own writings are perhaps the following: the second chapter of *Explorations in Personality* (1938), entitled "Proposals for a Theory of Personality"; the introductory essay, written with Clyde Kluckhohn, to the second edition of *Personality in Nature, Society, and Culture* (1953); and the essay entitled "Preparations for the Scaffold of a Comprehensive System" in Volume III of Koch's *Psychology*, "A Study of a Science" (1959). That this last paper is held to deal only with a scaffold, and indeed only with the preparations for a scaffold, reflects Murray's sense of the incalculable immensity of that ultimate structure, the conceptual cathedral far beyond present imaginings, which could dare to be called a comprehensive system for the understanding of lives.

In contemporary American psychology, Murray's influence has been against the prevailing orthodoxy of positivistic behaviorism. In this respect, he resembles Gordon Allport, who has likewise steadfastly opposed the crude mechanisms and hedonisms—the "simple and sovereign" theories—that somehow seem to have satisfied psychologists whose principal loyalty has been to the tradition of physical science. Murray and Allport both brought to psychology a humanistic interest which undoubtedly influenced their choice of scientific models, leading them less to chemistry and physics than to biochemistry and biology. In Murray's case, as we learn from his "Preparations," a "bent of empathy and curiosity toward all profound experiences of individual men and women"

* New York: John Wiley & Sons, 1957.

led to the choice of history as a field for undergraduate concentration and of medicine as a subsequent career. Medical training led to two years of surgical practice and five of research in physiological chemistry. It was from medical practice that he drew his convictions with regard to the "multiform method" of assessment, the scientific value of detailed and systematic case histories, and the necessity for careful classification of entities and processes. But it was in chemical embryology that he found his fundamental concepts. Studying the earliest manifestations of vitality in the chick embryo, "peering through a microscope, through a little fabricated window in the egg's shell, spellbound as any libidinous voyeur, I witnessed the procession of momentous transformations that mark the hours when the embryo is no bigger than an angel perching on a pin point." The embryo manifested an inherent spontaneity of cellular activity, which resulted in a continuous sequence of orderly changes; it was *proactive* rather than merely *reactive,* and it was inherently creative.

Such observations clearly made for scepticism of the stimulus-response formula. The model for that formula, the basis of the reflex theory of behavior, was the isolated nerve-muscle preparation—a model that presupposed the reactive nature of behavior and that eliminated surgically the possibility of important proactions. It is difficult nowadays to take seriously the claim that this artifact was fundamental or that the wiring diagrams of the nervous system which grew out of it were conceptually appropriate. If one wants to establish a claim to what is fundamental, it is well to remember that the nerve-muscle preparation had to be taken from a living creature that was once an embryo by another living creature that was also once an embryo. Murray's deductions from chemical embryology are indeed fundamental to any scientific study of living processes. They establish "the necessity of including formative (constructive) processes in one's scheme of variables."

It was only after this period of medical practice and research that Murray decided to shift to psychology. One determinant of this decision was, as he expresses it, "my special interest in the dispositions and thoughts (rather than the bodies) of human beings." He was attracted by psychoanalysis, which dealt with dispositions and thoughts, including those that come earliest and are most determining. Acknowledging Freud's monumental contributions in the realms of id and superego, he set out to create an adequate psychology of the ego—years before this became popular among more orthodox analysts. In work with Jung and in Jung's writings he found "a hive of great suggestiveness," a congenial recognition of, among other things, the importance of fantasy. After three years of work with Morton Prince, Murray succeeded him as director of the Harvard Psychological Clinic and, along with teaching and a certain amount of psychoanalytic practice, began the research that came to its first fruition in *Explorations in Personality*.

Shortly after 1938, Murray and his collaborator, Christiana Morgan, gained fame among clinical psychologists for their creation of the Thematic Apperception Test. But Murray was never totally pleased with the test's reception: clinicians seemed bent on adopting it merely as a technique, or gadget, interpreting the results as they liked and paying little attention to the conceptual scheme that went with it. Over the years, nevertheless, the TAT has quietly inducted several generations of clinical psychologists into a respect for imaginative processes and an understanding of psychological dynamics; it has accomplished a vital educational mission as well as a diagnostic one. Thus it has helped turn the tide toward more penetrating and more holistic conceptions of assessment, and this cannot fail to improve the climate for similar trends in theory.

Murray's own characterization of his theoretical outlook emphasizes its relation to organismic and field theories. Personality is organismic in the sense that its functional processes are highly interdependent and are bound together through hierarchical integration. Its events and proceedings require a field interpretation because they occur in a real environment, perceived and apperceived in various ways by the subject. These generalizations are implicit in certain concepts that have been of particular interest to Murray in recent years. Among these is the dyadic system, based on the idea that a two-person relationship should be formulated as a single system with equal attention to both participants. "I use dyadic interactions," he writes, "as a test of every formulation or theoretical system," requiring of it that it provide "variables appropriate to the prediction of concrete social episodes." These interactions can be captured in the concept of "thema," which formulates a proceeding in terms of the proactor's need aims and the reactor's need responses. This insight leads Murray to describe the energic components of personality as thematic dispositions rather than general actional dispositions. In effect, this alters the earlier practice of rating people on the strength of some such need as aggression and substitutes a specification of those particular situations to which a person is supersensitive and reacts aggressively—perhaps "apperceived insults to his self-respect" or "apperceived vainglorious boastings." Murray has also introduced the concept of "serials" to represent those long-range enterprises that consist of many proceedings, occurring from day to day or from year to year, whereby such remote goals as buying a house or writing a novel are reached. To understand how serials are set in motion and carried forward, he uses the concept of "ordination," which signifies the mental processes of selecting and integrating plans of action and scheduling events.

To the student of personality who bears within him a sustained interest in "significant human feelings, thoughts, and actions," who chooses the career of psychologist because he wants to find out more about these things, Murray's work stands as a unique and inexhaustible house of treasures. Here are to be found methods and concepts suited to a task both scientific and humanistic: scientific because the spirit is one of investigating the facts as carefully and impartially as possible; humanistic because the concern remains always with what people feel to be important about themselves. It is significant that Murray's conceptual scheme has constantly expanded, thus emulating the living process it is designed to describe. His is a system admired by all who realize that the study of ever-growing lives must be an ever-growing process. It is increasingly recognized that Murray's work, with its boundless inventiveness and bold conceptualization, is one of the major forward thrusts of our time toward man's understanding of his nature.

THE CONTRIBUTORS

Frank Barron is a research psychologist at the Institute of Personality Assessment and Research at the University of California at Berkeley. In his chapter, he tells of his first contact with Murray's work. On two occasions, he has been appointed visiting lecturer at Harvard.

Leopold Bellak, whose A.M. at Harvard was followed by an M.D. from New York Medical College, is director of Psychiatric Services at City Hospital at Elmhurst, New York City, and practices psychoanalysis. He has written extensively on projective techniques.

Anthony Davids is associate professor of psychology at Brown University and chief psychologist at the Emma Pendleton Bradley Hospital. He took his Ph.D. under Murray at Harvard, where he was a lecturer and research associate before going to Brown.

Erik H. Erikson made his first stop in the United States at the Harvard Psychological Clinic before going on to positions at Yale, Berkeley, and the Austen Riggs Center at Stockbridge, Mass. He is now professor of human development and lecturer in the Medical School at Harvard and is associated with the Department of Social Relations.

Robert R. Holt took his Ph.D. at Harvard and spent several years at the Menninger Foundation, Winter Hospital, and the University of Kansas. For the past ten years, he has been director of the Research Center for Mental Health at New York University, where he is also professor of psychology.

Kenneth Keniston spent several years as a research associate in psychology at Harvard, working with Murray and also taking an active part in undergraduate teaching. He now holds a research and teaching post at the Yale Medical School.

Theodore C. Kroeber, who took his Ph.D. at the University of California at Berkeley, is now teaching at San Francisco State College. For two years, he was a research fellow working with Murray at Harvard.

Donald W. MacKinnon, professor of psychology at the University of California at Berkeley and director of the Institute of Personality Assessment and Research since its founding in 1949, took one of the first Ph.D.'s done under Murray's direction. He served as instructor at Harvard, then taught at Bryn Mawr until called to work with the Office of Strategic Services, where he succeeded Murray as director of "Station S" and contributed importantly to *Assessment of Men.*

David C. McClelland, who took his Ph.D. at Yale, taught at Wesleyan University for fourteen years and became known especially for the measurement of needs through fantasy. He was appointed professor of psychology at Harvard in 1956, directs the Center for Research on Personality (direct descendant of the Harvard Psychological Clinic), and is chairman of the Department of Social Relations.

Gerhard S. Nielsen took his doctorate at the University of Copenhagen, where he is now associate professor of psychology. He worked with Murray as a research fellow at Harvard in 1956–1957 and for short periods in 1958 and 1961.

Nevitt Sanford took his Ph.D. at Harvard and directed the Harvard Growth Study of School Children before leaving to join the staff at the University of California at Berkeley. From 1952 to 1958, he was coordinator of the Mary Conover Mellon Foundation at Vassar College. He has recently become professor of psychology and education at Stanford University and director of the Institute for the Study of Human Problems.

Edwin S. Shneidman, editor of *Thematic Test Analysis,* is associate clinical profesor at the University of Southern California Medical School and is co-director of the Suicide Prevention Center and the V.A. Central Research Unit for the Study of Unpredicted Deaths, both in Los Angeles. In 1961–1962 he was a U.S. Public Health Service special research fellow and worked with Murray at Harvard.

M. Brewster Smith is a Harvard Ph.D. who served as assistant professor at Harvard before moving on to successive positions at Vassar, the Social Science Research Council, and New York University. Since 1958, he has been professor of psychology at the University of California at Berkeley.

Morris I. Stein did his graduate work at Harvard, completing his Ph.D. in 1949 after a period of service with Murray in the Office of Strategic Services during World War II. He was associate professor of psychology at The University of Chicago in 1960, when he moved to his present post as professor at New York University and director of the Research Center for Human Relations.

Silvan Tomkins, whose Ph.D. from the University of Pennsylvania was in philosophy, was associated with the Harvard Psychological Clinic for eleven years as research associate, instructor, and lecturer. Since 1947, he has been at Princeton, where he is professor of psychology.

Robert W. White took his Ph.D. at Harvard and has taught there for twenty-five years, serving at various times as director of the Psychological Clinic and chairman of the Department of Social Relations. His present title is professor of clinical psychology.

Robert N. Wilson worked with Murray at Harvard while taking his Ph.D. in sociology. After several years of work in medical sociology, he returned to Harvard to direct the Training Program for Social Science in Medicine, from which post he went to Yale as associate professor of sociology.

Frederick Wyatt is professor of psychology and director of the Psychological Clinic at the University of Michigan. His Ph.D. was from the University of Vienna. After coming to the United States, he joined the group at the Harvard Psychological Clinic and was also associated with the McLean Hospital and Clark University.

GROWTH AND CHANGE IN PERSONALITY
Part I

Murray conceives of personality as a dynamic system. He sees it as an evolving configuration of thoughts, feelings, and actions set in a social environment with which it continuously interacts. Even when considered at a single point in time, it is plainly the outcome of a long process of growth, and by studying lives at various points in time we may be able to uncover some of the secrets of this growth. The first four chapters reflect this aspect of Murray's thinking.

Sanford's chapter deals with change observed over the four years during which his subjects were students at college. His theme is the evolution of impulse expression, a variable for the measurement of which he and his colleagues had carefully devised a questionnaire. His procedure reverses the common one whereby life histories are used as a source of hypotheses, and questionnaires are used to test the hypotheses. The life history is used here as a means of illuminating test scores and of explaining changes of scores between the freshman and senior years. The two young women described by Sanford scored high on the senior year test of impulse expression, but for quite different reasons. One exemplifies the mature freeing of impulse from adolescent inhibitions; the other represents a still somewhat defensive acting out of impulse.

The variable of impulse expression occupies an important place in present thinking about personality. It will be found to recur in several chapters of this book, particularly in those dealing with creative processes. It is present also in Bellak's analysis of Somerset Maugham's stories (Chapter 6), Davids' study of intolerance of ambiguity (Chapter 7), and Tomkins' inquiry into ideologies (Chapter 17). Impulse expression is a noteworthy problem in the life history of Inburn (Chapter 2).

The chapter on Inburn is a study of personality in the best Murray tradition. It is the life story of a college student based on an autobiography and interviews, and it searches for unifying unconscious themes by an intensive analysis of the fantasies produced in the Thematic Apperception Test. Keniston calls his subject an American Ishmael, thus offering him for comparison with the narrator of *Moby Dick* and for contrast with Murray's case study of an American Icarus.* In this chapter, the intensive case study is used as the basis for tentative generalizations about the psychological nature of "alienation." As Keniston puts it:

> In Inburn we see alienation—the rejection of the roles and values and institutions he sees as typical of adult American life—in unusually pure form; and the themes of his life can stand as introduction to and summary of comparable themes in the lives of others like him.

Though Keniston is far from disregarding the social conditions that currently encourage alienation, he points out the relevance of Inburn's childhood relations to his mother and father, finding in the satisfactions and disappointments of these relations the origin of certain persistent unconscious fantasies. It is interesting to compare this chapter with Wilson's essay (Chapter 15) on Albert Camus, for whom alienation was an important and highly conscious problem.

The third chapter in this section uses, like Sanford's, the method of comparative case studies. The two men who are its subjects were studied at two points in their lives, once when they were college students and again several years later, when the patterns of their adult lives were becoming stabilized. The theme of this chapter is the sense of interpersonal competence, which means the confidence one has established, on the basis of experience, that he can exert an influence on other people in pursuit of goals and the satisfaction of needs. As college students, the two young men differed considerably with respect to this quality, one being generally poised and self-assertive, the other deferent, uncertain, and defensive. The later studies disclosed the same differences and showed how the sense of interpersonal competence influenced the subjects' military careers, their marriages, and their choices of occupation.

McClelland's chapter on the Harlequin complex takes us to the last stage of life. It is based in part on thematic apperceptions obtained from women with fatal illnesses, aware of the approach of death. The Harlequin complex refers to ". . . the theme of death as a lover, as a mysterious dark figure who comes and takes a woman away to her death." McClelland traces the history of the mythical figure of Harlequin, showing the deep embedding of the myth in Western European culture. He thus makes it clear that thematic analysis can be usefully applied to the products of popular culture as well as to individual literary works. This chapter bears an interesting relation to Shneidman's systematic discussion of orientations toward death (Chapter 9).

---

* Henry A. Murray, "American Icarus," in *Clinical Studies of Personality,* ed. Arthur Burton and Robert E. Harris (New York: Harper & Bros., 1955), Vol. II, pp. 615–641.

1: THE FREEING AND THE ACTING OUT OF IMPULSE IN LATE ADOLESCENCE

Evidence from Two Cases

Nevitt Sanford

College seniors obtain higher scores than freshmen on a scale for measuring "impulse expression" (IE), which has been defined as "a general readiness to express, to see gratification of, impulses, in overt action or in conscious feeling and attitude."[1]

In interpreting the higher IE scores of seniors, my colleagues and I supposed that a "lifting of repression" or some other kind of liberating, or perhaps strengthening, of basic emotional impulses occurred in college and that this was sometimes a result of certain educational processes. But we could not speak with much assurance, for, although the scale has validity in the ordinary sense of the word, it seemed clear that different subjects obtained extreme scores for different reasons. The scale is of the "self-report" variety, and its items have little subtlety; it expresses personality at the level of conscious attitude; one should expect no one-to-one relations between a pattern of such attitudes and either observable behavior or deeper processes of the personality. It is not clear, then, how changes in IE scores over a period of time are to be explained.

It seemed to us that high scores on the scale could be obtained by subjects who were "impulse-ridden" or who "acted out" their impulses, being unable to control them even when they wanted to; or by subjects who were "free," in the sense that they could express their impulses without inducing serious conflicts—within themselves or with society. Subjects with low scores on the IE scale might be integrated and stable but relatively simple in personality structure, or they might be rigidly restrained by fear of external or internal punishing agents.

The concern in this paper is with patterns of personality found in young women who obtain high scores on the IE scale. I shall consider in some detail differences between a college student who seems to act out

[1] N. Sanford, H. Webster, and M. Freedman, "Impulse Expression as a Variable of Personality," *Psychol. Monogr.*, 71 (1957), 1–21.

her impulses compulsively and one whose high impulse expression seems
to be under the control of a well-developed ego.

It is a safe assumption that we best understand a structure of personality when we know the conditions and mechanisms of change in that
structure. It is well, then, that both of the young women with whom we
shall be concerned have changed rather markedly during the period in
which they were observed, that is, during four years of college. One,
Patricia, or "Pat," as she is called, was high on IE (in the top quartile
of a large sample of students just entering college) as a freshman and she
is also high, much higher in fact, as a senior about to graduate. The
other subject, Penny, was fairly low on IE as a freshman—well below
the freshman mean—but as a graduating senior she has moved into the
high quartile of our large sample of college seniors.

When we compare these two young women as freshmen, using interview material and observations by people who knew them well, we get
good pictures of what I understand as high and low impulse expression.
When Pat came to college, her school principal described her as "creative
and imaginative," a girl whose interests were "legion" and who would "always be active." Pat herself reported, after a few weeks on campus, that
"Mondays and Fridays run into week ends" and that she had already used
up all her overnights. Penny's letter of recommendation, on the other hand,
stated that she was "earnest, dependable, well balanced" and that "she
leads in a quiet way by example." Whereas Pat spent her weekends away
from school, Penny stayed on campus. She said, "I go around and see my
friends here. Get my term papers written. Have dates, play bridge, talk."
At the end of the freshman year Pat's faculty adviser said that she was
"madly and equally enthusiastic about everything," whereas Penny's adviser remarked that she was an "awfully nice girl" who had not yet begun
to "operate at full capacity." Other observations and lengthy interviews
with these students confirmed the impression of Pat as a girl who was
seeking gratification in a wide variety of overt actions and of Penny as
quiet, conventional, and rather inhibited.

When these two subjects are compared as seniors, both being high
now on IE, differences in the quality of their impulse expression become
apparent. Pat now seems to exemplify the "acting-out" type of IE,
whereas Penny appears to be moving toward genuine freedom. By examining the two cases rather fully, mainly with the use of material from
interviews, it is possible to gain some understanding of the deeper sources
of these differing patterns. And the study of the college careers of our
subjects can tell us something of the conditions and processes of personality change in this educational setting.

THE IMPULSE EXPRESSION SCALE

The items constituting the IE scale were taken from a pool of 677 verbal items of the true-false type that were being used in longitudinal studies of personality development in college students.[2] Most of these items were from the Minnesota Multiphasic Personality Inventory (MMPI),[3] the California Psychological Inventory,[4] and Maslow's Scale for Dominance-Feeling in Women.[5] The IE scale was developed by first setting up as a criterion a rationally scored scale composed of items which, according to theory, were relevant to impulse expression. These were items whose content pertained to such characteristics as rebelliousness, aggressiveness, adventurousness, assertiveness, restlessness, excitability, and unconventionality. Seventy-nine items of this kind were chosen to make up the initial criterion scale. Starting with the correlations of items in the total pool with this 79-item scale, item analyses designed to maximize item homogeneity were carried out on several classes of freshmen and seniors until a 123-item test having KR-21 reliability[6] of .90 was obtained. On the basis of content, the items in the final version of the scale could, as suggested above, be considered as expressive of one or another of Murray's Needs and Traits;[7] and they could be classified into four clusters, which are illustrated as follows:

1. *Ascendance.* "When I work on a committee I like to take charge of things." "I have often either broken rules (school, club, etc.) or inwardly rebelled against them." "I go out of my way to meet troubles rather than try to escape them."

2. *Sensation.* "I like to talk about sex." "When I get bored I like to stir up some excitement." "I get excited very easily."

3. *Endocathection and intraception.* "I have very peculiar and strange experiences." "I think I take primarily an aesthetic view of experience." "Some of my friends think that my ideas are impractical, if not a bit wild."

4. *Radical sentiments.* "We cannot know for sure whether or not there is a god." "Politically I am something of a radical." "I believe women ought to have as much sexual freedom as men."

Of the items in the IE scale, 94 are scored "true," and 29 are scored "false." If a subject's responses to all the items were in the direction of impulse expression he would, of course, obtain a score of 123. The mean score for a sample of 906 college women was 45.8, with a standard devi-

[2] *Loc. cit.*

[3] S. R. Hathaway and I. C. McKinley, *The Minnesota Multiphasic Personality Inventory* (Rev. ed.; New York: Psychological Corporation, 1943).

[4] H. Gough, *The California Psychological Inventory* (Palo Alto: Consulting Psychologists Press, 1957).

[5] A. H. Maslow, "A Test for Dominance-Feeling (Self-esteem) in College Women," *J. Soc. Psychol.,* 12 (1940), 255–270.

[6] G. F. Kuder and M. W. Richardson, "The Theory of Estimation of Test Reliability," *Psychometrika,* 2 (1937), 151–160.

[7] H. A. Murray, *Explorations in Personality* (New York: Oxford University Press, 1938).

ation of 16.0.[8] Pat's scores were 57 as a freshman, 102 as a senior. Penny had a score of 37 as a freshman, 76 as a senior. It is rare that a score below 20 is obtained, and very few college women go above Pat's 102. College men usually score about 10 points higher on the average than do college women.

The IE scale has been found in various studies to correlate around .60 with the delinquency scale and around − .27 with the responsibility scale of the California Psychological Inventory; it correlates around .60 with Maslow's Test for Dominance-Feeling. High IE scores are associated with MMPI indexes of expression (rather than of repression), of "psychopathology," and of the tendency to use "psychotic" mechanisms of defense. There are strong positive correlations between IE and a measure of femininity that accents "inner life" and between IE and a measure of developmental status based on empirically determined differences between college seniors and freshmen. In a sample of 60 college freshmen, correlations of the IE scale with the ethnocentrism (E) and fascism (F) scales of *The Authoritarian Personality*[9] were found to be − .04 and − .03, respectively.[10] A scale called social maturity, made up of items from the 677-item pool mentioned above and designed to reflect the psychological rather than the ideological aspects of authoritarianism (psychological authoritarianism reversed), correlated .21 with IE.[11] These last results have a special interest. Because of the low correlations between the IE scale and measures of authoritarianism, there will be among high scorers on IE some subjects who are high and some who are low on authoritarianism, and similarly for those who score low on IE. It may be that this is a significant basis for differentiating among subjects who are at one or the other extreme on impulse expression. This is a matter to which we shall return.

There has been one study in which scores on the IE scale have been related not merely to measures based on subjects' self-ratings but to an external criterion. In a three-day assessment of 50 women in their early forties who were given the IE scale, five psychologists independently described the subjects by means of a 600-item check list.[12] The following adjectives, listed in the order of decreasing strength of statistical association, were ascribed to high and to low scorers.

[8] For a full account of the statistics of the IE scale and for reports of various studies involving this instrument, see Carl Bereiter, "Descriptions and Analyses of the VAI Scales" (mimeographed) Urbana, Ill.: Bureau of Educational Research, University of Illinois).

[9] T. Adorno, Else Frenkel-Brunswik, D. Levinson, and N. Sanford, *The Authoritarian Personality* (New York: Harper & Brothers, 1950).

[10] Sanford *et al., op. cit.*

[11] Bereiter, *op. cit.*

[12] An account of this study may be found in R. Jung, "Analysis of Psychosocial Development: A Study of Adult, Educated Women" (Ph.D. thesis deposited in the Harvard University Library, 1962).

High scorers: big-boned, impulsive, irrepressible, angular, loud, tall, full of pep, erratic, vigorous, restless, impatient, stylish, uninhibited, excitable, outgoing.

Low scorers: retiring, silent, reliable, inhibited, reserved, stolid, humorless, shy, withdrawn, plain, faint-voiced, meek, painstaking, quiet, weary.

In various studies of college students it has been found that seniors score significantly higher on IE than freshmen. The mean for senior women is usually around 50 and that for freshman women around 40. Senior and freshman men scored about 10 points higher than the women. In one study involving 175 women who were tested as freshmen and again as seniors, it was found that IE score increased in 89 per cent of the cases, decreased in 8 per cent, and showed no change in 3 per cent.

Pat and Penny belong to a group of 78 young women who are being studied rather intensively as they go through college and into adult life. Of the 10 students who scored highest on IE as freshmen and who have been seen as seniors, all but two increased their scores, but no other by so much as Pat who now heads the list. Of the 10 students who are highest as seniors, 5 were in the high group as freshmen; 5 others, including Penny, who is now fourth from the top, have joined the ranks of the high scorers. All the 10 girls who were lowest as freshmen have higher scores as seniors, but 6 of them are still among the lowest 10.

PAT AS A SENIOR

Although Pat's freshman interviews exemplified high impulse expression, her senior interviews do so far more vividly. Furthermore, these interviews should show something of the special quality of Pat's impulse expression. If, as has been hypothesized, her impulses are acted out for purposes of defense, then we must search the material for indications of deeper needs and conflicts—some of which we should expect to be unconscious.

The discussion may be organized around the major clusters mentioned earlier: ascendance, sensation, endocathection and intraception, and radical sentiments.

Ascendance

Pat's life as a senior revolves about her work as a drama major and her plans for a career in the theater. She entered college with the idea of majoring in art, but as a sophomore she had something of a triumph on the stage and this soon led to other successes and the determination to make a career in the theater. As a drama major she had the lead in two productions and parts in four others. Comedy was her forte. The drama major is demanding by itself; it can become engrossing, and a student can get by without doing much work in other courses. The major also involves a way of life, a certain choice of friends, and characteristic ways of relating to the faculty.

When interviewed in the spring of her senior year, Pat had been accepted by a school of drama and had elaborate plans for the future, which involved close association with friends from college and capitalization on family connections.

Note some of her remarks about the central place of the drama in her life and about her expectations for the future.

The drama is everything I've gotten out of this place.

"Referring to her first success on the stage."

It was my first contact with a cheering audience. I was on a pink cloud. The first time I knew what it was like to hold a whole roomful of people in the palm of my hand.

"What do you expect to be doing five years from now?"

Heading toward the top in the theater. Heading for marriage.

"Twenty-five years from now?"

Right at the top. Have a family. Have all the financial advantages I've had, security, love. Kids will have an easy life without taking it for granted.

"What is your idea of a good life for you?"

Go into the theater, marry a man in the theater, but not an actor. Reach a certain height in theater so I can take time off without losing status. I'm not even thinking of children now.

"What would you leave behind you when you die?"

A legend.

"Can you visualize life without marriage?"

Yes, everything I wanted in the way of a career and lots of affairs. Be happy in self-responsibility—but would miss close, happy, family life.

"What do you think are your chances of succeeding at acting?"

I estimate my chances as being very high. Everything has always come my way. I have a very rare kind of talent. I need someone to write for me. I may not get anywhere until I'm older. Slapstick comedy usually involves women of thirty-five. I hope to have Mr. Y's help. My family has some connections. Being an impulsive person, I might just get married— but acting is such a part of me I couldn't drop it just like that. I could marry someone who is in the theater. . . . It never occurs to you to think you don't have it. I feel that I have it. The only thing might be my health. I run myself down. I never go to bed.

Desires for power and for recognition are plainly manifest, but such is Pat's concern to be universally liked that she very rarely shows any open or direct aggression. But when she is thwarted in her central aims —her career and the closely associated solidarity with her drama-major friends—she is very willing to use aggressive means to have her way.

> We asked for the four of us to room together senior year. Alie didn't come back—we were told we would have to get another roommate. It was the middle of August. I was livid with rage. It was really a suite for three anyway. I wrote the college. They said we'd have to move. I got my Daddy to write. Actually I wrote the letter, and they let us keep the rooms, which we had picked to be near friends.

"What would be your advice to your sister if she were about to come here to college?"

> It's harder to get in than to flunk out. You don't have to grind every day. The things you can get away with—you can overlook most social rules. I have a car up here. I have permission but anyone could have a car. It's easy to get in after hours, especially in my dorm. You can stay out overnight whenever you want. . . . Try to get away from the campus now and then . . . if depressed go off for a week.

Sensation

Sex. Pat is frankly preoccupied with sex. She wishes to be regarded as sexy, as uninhibited, and, in this sphere at least, amoral. This has raised some question in the minds of the interviewers concerning the reliability of her statements about what she has done. But all the interviewers would regard the following as a reasonably accurate summary of the sex history.

> When little we boys and girls played doctor. It was a favorite pastime around six and seven. I had insatiable curiosity. Occasionally some mother would call my mother and complain about me taking some kid into the bushes. [First sex experience of adolescence?] I had planned sex experience by practicing kissing and so forth with a large stuffed animal. First experiences were fumbled because of the boy's awkwardness. Until I was fifteen. That summer there was a boy—French kissing, mild petting. From then I didn't pet below the waist—till Fred.
> Beginning with Fred there was intercourse. I was seventeen and had known him for six months at the time, had done with him all but sleep. Then a number of fellows thereafter. I assumed fellows would try; and I assume I encouraged them without knowing. [And now?] It preys on my mind just as much, but when I'm working I don't think about it so much. I began to worry, not morally, but I just figure it is unhealthy for all relationships to have one classification—sex; but I figure, too, if I feel this way isn't it normal to give in? . . . Not so much now, but used to have fascination for pornographic literature—especially if graphic. For instance, if I read of an old man seducing a young girl—I would be revolted but at the same time shaking when I put the book down.

From the following we may get an impression of the strength and variety of Pat's sexual impulses—and of boldness, sensuousness, love of excitement, and body narcissism.

Alan reminds me of my father, a conservative covering but underneath real crazy. He makes friends, everyone likes him. He knows how to put me in my place, has the ability to step on me but compliment me at the same time. He makes me feel so good, but he doesn't spoil me. He's very kind. No sex yet, because it hasn't worked before. I become addicted to sex, and companionship suffers. I'm fearful about this, after affairs with Fred and Charlie went wrong.

"In what way would you like to change yourself?"

I would like to decrease my interest in sex. It's almost an obsession. Drama relieves some of it because of so much energy consumed. I used to think I was a nymphomaniac because I couldn't get my mind off it. I couldn't enjoy the company of a boy without thinking of sex. Most of my relationships have been physical. I have to change my emotional state.

An interviewer (life history interview) says, "S. greatly enjoys physical experience with other girls, for example, back-rubbing—more pleasurable than with boys. Sometimes feels guilty about this. Asked what would be reaction if during back-rubbing, etc., the girl made a pass at her. S. not sure of reaction. She thinks girls are really more skillful lovers than men, can give more pleasures. A good polymorphous-perverse character."

"Do you have dreams and fantasies about boys and men, romantic or overt?"

All the time. [Romantic?] Very romantic—shipwreck—lots of razors—don't like men with beards. [Overt?] Oh, yes.

It is difficult to stop when petting. [Enjoy?] Yes, reach climax easily. Really enjoy the stages leading up to it. [Masturbate?] No, used to when thirteen.

I have wanted to look like Marilyn Monroe ever since I was ten. Disappointed when not getting there fast.

I was always very pleased if a boy said I was the sexiest thing he had ever known.

There is much evidence that Pat's relations with the male faculty are sexualized. For example, concerning Mr. Y., her favorite teacher, "I'd like nothing better than to go to bed with him. There is something so animal about him. . . . He has been the biggest influence in my life."

We see in some of Pat's remarks about her sex life the element of dominance feeling, which Maslow[13] noted as a distinguishing characteristic of college women who had had sex experience. From the life history interview, we learn: "Subject also reports that she gets more pleasure in sex from observing response of the fellow than she does from what he does to her."

"Should husband or wife initiate intercourse?"

Either one. [What is a desirable frequency?] Whenever the woman wants it. Can't say, pure matter of desire.

[13] *Op. cit.*

Sentience, Excitance, Play. As taken up with sex as Pat is, she knows many other ways to have a good time and to gratify her impulses.

> I play the piano by ear. I love music. It's an important part of my life—both classical and jazz. . . . I like very much the surrealistic school of painting.

Many of the things Pat likes to do cost money. She describes herself as a "big spender," her allowance of $200 a month going mainly for "clothes, food, going to the city, transportation." For the future she wants a "small house in the country and a big apartment in town with a maid and two cars." She says her father is not concerned about her spending money, but he reproaches her for not paying her bills on time. And Pat has a good time with her friends.

> Sally and I have the same habits. Stay up till dawn. Neither of us works very hard. She's terribly funny.
> Betty is terribly amusing and most unconventional. Our favorite pastime is living in a world of make-believe.
> Sandy has the most incredible sense of the ridiculous. She's like a big, joking, lovable teddy bear. We are going abroad together. I can see us going broke in the first two weeks.

These girls were among the five friends who were asked to rate Pat (1–5 scale, 5 high) on a set of sixty-two tasks, positions, or activities. They all gave ratings of five on, among other things: 1. a girl to cheer you up if you're depressed; 2. a date for your brother; 3. someone to break the rules with.

Emotionality, Impulsion, Change, Disjunctivity.

> I will do anything to avoid an argument. I go to pieces when mad, so I avoid this by leaving the field. . . . When I'm angry, I'm angry. There are no degrees.

"What girls do you admire the most?"

> Janet. I admired her mind. I practically worshipped her. I hung on her every word. I was flattered that she liked me.
> Mother is more like me than anyone I ever met—highly emotional, nervous. Has given me a terrific amount of independence; let me do a lot. My friends can't believe we argue, can't believe she can make me mad—she is hospitable, lenient, has so much common sense. If she doesn't like something I do, she says, "You're twenty-one, I can't tell you what to do." But she nags enough so you finally give up. . . .

Pat's playfulness, emotionality, and impulsiveness, as well as her narcissism, are well-described by her friends. Several girls whom she listed as her closest friends were asked to "please indicate by a few sentences or phrases your general evaluation of Pat and your feelings toward her. Mention her negative as well as positive qualities and your negative as well as positive feelings."

She's an extremely warm person with a marvelous sense of humor, and a desire to entertain one person or fifty thousand. She is easy to talk to and has a very active mind. She's opinionated and rather "catholic" in her tastes, but she's clever enough not to get stepped on. She's romantic and adventurous and inclined to be impetuous, but her *uncanny* luck never disappoints her. She tends to be irresponsible about "people and things," but this is merely due to laziness rather than intentional neglect. She's a very independent person in many respects but is dependent on people for her audience—again one or fifty thousand. She has an extremely strong personality, very winning, and is very natural with everyone. She is adaptable to many situations, but always remains herself. She's extremely easy to live with as she is rarely annoyed by situations, although, if so, she either leaves or remains silent, which is often more effective. She is also the type of friend who remains loyal without having to constantly keep in touch, and I feel I will always be devoted to her.

I find Pat extremely loyal, affectionate, charming. I am not sure that she is so to people who aren't very close friends, because I think that she is basically completely self-occupied. I am disappointed when I see her liking someone superficially because they bring her out, but I am not otherwise affected because I have known her too long and have too much affection for her to make value judgments. She is bright, lovable, free, independent, etc.

I think it is rather apparent that I like Pat very much. However, I don't trust her to get things done—she's sort of scatterbrained. But you can forgive her because she's sort of a "dear" person—even though I think it would be a strain to live with her continually and do what she forgets to do. I don't mean to imply that I don't think a lot of her mind—she's a hard worker and I find her a perceptive and keen person in interpreting dramatic parts, books, plays, and people. I honestly suspect that Pat often forgets things she feels are not important for her and applies a very keen mind to the things she is very interested in. She gets away with this as far as I am concerned by being a very kind and interested friend. Therefore, I don't think she would be good in positions she is not interested in.

It is characteristic of Pat that she takes some of her friends more seriously than they take her and overestimates their good opinion of her. Be it noted, however, that even those who speak with the most reserve testify to her ambition and devotion to the theater and to her kindness and loyalty. But concerning this last there is a sour note; some of her friends are fully aware of Pat's narcissism, and one of them suspects that she is not generally nurturant but reserves her kindness and charm for her friends.

Endocathection and Intraception

Endocathection, according to Murray, has to do with the importance to the subject of "fantasy, reflection, imagination or abstract thought" as opposed to "practical, concrete, physical or social action [exocathection]." We have seen that action is highly important to Pat. The following excerpts from her interview protocols seem to show that fantasy and imagination loom large in her scheme of things—but not reflection or abstract thought.

Intraception is Murray's term for "the disposition to be determined by diffuse personal feelings and inclinations (intangible subjective facts)." We should let Pat speak for herself.

"Do you like writing?"

I love to. Most of it is done in letters. Most of it is humorous. I'd like to do a humorous book some day. I've kept diaries for four or five months. Then dropped it. I've labored on poetry writing but it wasn't good.

"What have been the most stressful events or situations in your life?"

Probably most distressful is my fear of the supernatural and of the dark. I don't like to sleep in the dark. It's all right if someone is in the room, even a dog. A fear of a detached hand, and a reflection in the mirror and the person is not there. This can happen even when the lights are on, for example, watching TV. I can be frozen with fear. I'm fascinated by spooky stories or plays, or hypnosis. I believe in supernatural experiences, even though I have not seen them myself. I believe because there is no proof that they don't exist, and yet there are too many stories of their happening. For me there is no such thing as a friendly ghost.

"Dreams?"

I dream every night—many dreams. There is often a fine line between what I dream at night and my daydreams. Sometimes I think it was a dream but it was really a daydream. I know I'm dreaming while I'm in it. [Color?] Yes, three fourths of my dreams are in color.

"Nightmares?"

I dreamed of a monster a few nights ago. I met him in a dark room—only light was on his face—he was horrible. Janet B. appeared and said, "You're more afraid of me than of the monster." The monster turned into a small white marble. When I dropped the marble it broke in half. Then it divided again, until there were about fifty pieces.

The terror came from anticipating something terrible. When I dream I think I can change things—make a comedy or tragedy—but sometimes I can't control it. Then I shut my eyes tight and tell myself to wake up.

"Recurrent dreams?"

Dream of a little thing that jumps out, out of a drawer or a little box. The worst sensation is that I don't know what it is. It jumps out, cackles, gets all over me. It feels like I'm in a nest of squirming snakes. For a second I'm in absolute agony. I'm being tickled to death. This wakes me up.

I enjoy jumping off cliffs or sinking under water. After a second I discover I can fly or breathe. . . . I usually win if someone is chasing me.

I seldom try to analyze them.

"Daydreams?"

> Usually I daydream about some man or other. We're stranded on a desert island—or I may be captured by cannibals and have to do a primitive dance to save the man.
>
> Often daydream about taking care of somebody who has been in a horrible accident or is crippled in some horrible way—hospital—I've always been scared of something happening to my legs, so either they or I have lost our legs. I can't control the direction. Sometimes I end up crying. [What is the meaning of this?] First, the dancing. If I couldn't dance I don't know what I'd do. Second, since I was thirteen people have been telling me what nice legs I have.

It seems that Pat is thrilled by her dreams and fantasies much as she is by her impulse-gratifying overt behavior. One might say that her unconscious processes are close to the surface and enter prominently into her experience.

In this connection it should be noted that Pat's teachers, seven of them, rated her on the average 4.29 on creativity (5 is the highest). This may be compared with a mean of 2.86 for all the subjects in the sample of seventy-eight interviewees. In this group of subjects, Pat is third from the top. The faculty had not only her work on the stage to go on; she also produced some dramatic writing, mostly skits and other humorous pieces.

But Pat is not much inclined to inquire into things, to analyze or reflect upon experience, or to seek to master events intellectually. Indeed, she seems to be somewhat anti-intellectual, or at least anti-academic.

"What advice would you give to a sister entering college?"

> Take the subjects she is interested in but not get too wrapped up in theory. . . . You have to spend two years after college unlearning some of your beliefs that are based on books.
>
> Too much introspection isn't good. So much of what is between people is illogical or irrational, but that doesn't make it any the less strong.

It appears that some of the fears and nightmarish fantasies Pat reports can be really troublesome, that she sometimes struggles to repress them, and that she sometimes succeeds. "You forget the horrible things so quickly," she says.

Radical Sentiments

Pat has a great many sentiments, tastes, and opinions that are unusual for senior college women. She shows very little feeling or involvement respecting politics, government, or international relations. She has little to say about these topics, but some of her brief remarks are interesting.

"What is your concept of the ideal society?"

> I can't think there should be absolute equality. Some are of higher

ability, and they get ahead. Everybody should have some chance. If everyone had the same amount of money, I doubt if anybody would get ahead.

"Will there be a third world war? Will the U.S. be invaded?"

Yes—always has been, always will be. [U.S.?] Yes.

"Should an avowed Communist teach here?"

That's a tricky one. Hard to answer. Yes, in that as a theory Communism
is interesting. I'd like to hear about it from him. No, because he's dealing
with impressionable young girls.

Pat thinks the majority should rule, that the government should
intervene to promote economic and social welfare "if it has to," and that
to be secure as a nation, we should put our faith in NATO, rather than
in the UN or strong national defense. She has never engaged in political
activity and classifies herself as a political conservative.

Religion seems not to have entered meaningfully into Pat's life. She
was required to go to Sunday school until she was thirteen; but she is
agnostic, does not believe in life after death, prays "only in moments of
panic." Children, however, should be brought up with formal religious
training. "When older they will be able to understand it." Asked if she
disapproved of any religion, she said, "Catholicism bothers me." Her
father was brought up a Catholic but "dropped it"; her mother, she said,
"believes in God with blind faith."

Pat says she wants to have three children, all boys.

If I get married in the late twenties, I'd want to have them right away.
If I marry early, then I'll wait two years. I'll use a diaphragm.

"Why do you want to have children?"

Good question. I'd like to have something I produced that was really
mine.

"Can you imagine married life without children?"

Yes.

"At what age would you want to have your first child?"

Twenty-six.

"What kind of childbirth?"

I don't want to know about it.

"Would you treat your children any differently from the way you were
brought up?"

Yes. Self-discipline at an early age. Piano practice, etc. Get into habit
of working at an early age. I'd like them to enjoy work. I'd be more lenient
about their safety—that is, out-of-doors activity and sports.

"What do you think should be the husband's role?"

He should administer the physical punishment. Spanking is necessary. Same role as mother. Handle the financial matters.

"What problems do you anticipate in raising children?"

Millions. I'm afraid I'll be inconsistent and take my own moods out on them. I'd try to think before I leaped. I'd apologize. I won't reason with them when they're young. There'll be problems about sex—I may develop a very moral point of view.

Pat does not seem to have a very high opinion of women, and she is willing to accept a lower status for them than for men in society.

"Is there anything that women should not do?"

Should not be crusaders, should not meddle in politics, should not be in administrative posts. [Why?] Women are so concerned with details and miss the issues.

"What significant contributions are women making to American life?"

In the arts—sexes should be equal. In education—teachers. In science—they should do more in science.

"What is the ideal position of women in our society?"

Women should be on equal grounds with men in the areas I just mentioned—the creative areas. A man runs the family, but it should be sixty-forty.

"What do you criticize in a woman?"

Confidential type; shrill voices; cliques, a group of girls talking a special language; not being able to keep a secret; people insensitive to other people's moods. I prefer a little bitch to over-goodness. I'm bored with the all-good.

"Do you foresee any change in the status of women in this country?"

Women are going to become more and more like men. Too bad. I hate to see them lose their sex completely.

"What do you know about women in other countries?"

I'd hate to be a Frenchman's wife. I don't like the idea of woman's place in the home, raising kids, and so forth. I want more out of it.

"Would you marry into a different group?"

If he was in the theater. [Economic?] I will marry a poorer person. Expect to. [Religious?] I can't see bringing up kids as Catholics, but if I was in love I would. [Jews?] That's difficult; it depends; the environment is anti-Jewish, but half my friends are Jewish. I would probably stop to think about it. If he was in the theater or arts I'd do it. [Racial?] I wouldn't marry a Negro, but I find them physically attractive. [Political?] As long as he's not a Communist.

Pat's remarks about her sexual experiences and behavior, quoted earlier, are perhaps enough to indicate that she has "radical sentiments" in the area of sexual morality. The following statements, however, are more precisely to the point.

"What are your views on premarital sex experiences?"

Morally fine with me. But I advise caution to prevent pregnancy. It's people's own business as far as I'm concerned.

"What is the value of virginity?"

No value. No, I don't resent the standard; it doesn't exist for me. [Parents?] They're very idealistic about sex. They are willing to talk freely, but they're idealistic about it. They'd be disappointed if they knew about my affairs, and I see no reason to disappoint them.

"What do you think of homosexuals?"

They don't revolt me. They're rather interesting. Just find it interesting. I can't understand it.

Although many of Pat's sentiments are "contrary to those held by a majority of respected citizens,"[14] the quotations given in this section strongly suggest that we should not expect to tap impulse expression in subjects like Pat through the use of items that express political radicalism or liberalism, or liberal views in respect to child training, family relations, the roles and status of women, or social group relations. Indeed, it seems likely that values and beliefs in these areas are independent of IE. Pat reveals here a typical authoritarian outlook, and it would be surprising if she did not have a high score on the F scale of authoritarianism. Her score of 135 is second highest among the group of interviewees. (Averages for senior women are usually around 94.) She has come down from a score of 157 as a freshman. (Freshman women have average scores of approximately 114.) But, as we have seen, IE and F are virtually uncorrelated in the larger samples. As we shall see when we come to the case of Penny, high IE may go with very low F-scale scores. Does the F scale, then, help to distinguish between the types of impulse expression found in these two subjects? This is a subtle matter that will well repay further study. There may well be subjects who are high on defensive impulse expression but very low on authoritarianism.

Interpretation

It seems that in Pat impulse expression is but poorly controlled by the conscious ego; the argument is that either her mechanisms of control are so weak that she expresses more than she likes or else that she is driven, by deeper needs of her personality, to act out her impulses—or both.

[14] Murray, *op. cit.*

It may be hypothesized that behind her intense desire to be an actress, behind her narcissism, her sexual behavior and preoccupation, her relatively low ethical standards, and her fears are self-doubt, unconscious self-contempt, and a primitive superego that is alien to her conscious self.

Pat is probably aware of self-doubt, certainly of the rather desperate nature of her need for recognition and assurance. She has told us of the vast importance of an audience, and she is able to tell us more of her need for approval.

It doesn't kill me now to hear someone doesn't like me. That used to kill me. I used to think everyone liked me. You get used to professional jealousy in the theater.

But she would probably object to the idea that her desire to be a co-medienne still has a large element of self-contempt in it. She can, how-ever, project this conception onto herself as a child.

"What were you like as a child?"

Definitely a hellion, but the kind you get mad at and laugh at, at the same time; I learned from six on that comedy was my field.

Perhaps it should have been stated earlier that Pat's attractiveness does not lie in her physical features. Indeed she is at a considerable dis-advantage in this respect, being too short and plump by ordinary stand-ards, and it was the opinion of her interviewers that her vivaciousness and winning ways were in part an effort to overcome her limitations.

One might say that in her display of irresponsibility and prodigality, in her inhibition of aggression in personal relationships, and in her will-ingness to make herself look ridiculous for the sake of a joke, she is saying in effect, to women at least, "Look at me; I am harmless, and I need you to tell me I'm all right."

Low self-esteem, mainly unconscious, may go a long way toward explaining Pat's overt narcissism. It may also be an important source of her sexual behavior. She would not want to say "no" for fear of rejection; and, in order to be called sexy for long, or consistently, she would have to act the part. Further, having lost any self-respect that might have been attached to more deliberate control of her sexuality, she would naturally decide that she might as well have the benefits of sexual indulgence. Un-conscious self-contempt is also a likely source of Pat's acceptance of a relatively low status for women in society, and for herself vis-à-vis her husband. And it can help explain her strivings for social status and the benefits of economic security. These strivings seem mainly behind her anti-Semitism and anti-Communism. She could not do anything that would threaten her social class membership.

Closely associated with Pat's unconscious idea of herself as "no good" there seems to be the idea of herself as a "bad girl." She, of course, denies any misgivings about her moral standards, but we are justified in doubting that it is pure altruism that makes her not want to tell her parents about her sexual behavior. If she were found out, *then* she would feel guilty, though very probably not before. An hypothesis that can organize much of the material Pat has given us is that her superego is relatively infantile and fairly well out of communication with her conscious self.

We may note, first, the absence from her interview protocols of anything that might suggest the presence of a superego that is integrated with the ego. This is true not only of the material cited but of her interviews taken as a whole. There is little or no inhibition of impulse through the action of inner moral conviction, little or no inclination to blame herself for moral failures, no sensitivity to moral issues, little or no inclination to act according to moral principle.

But there is a superego in the present view, one that is denied, projected, externalized, and permitted to operate consciously under special circumstances.

The absence of any admission of moral conflict and the positiveness with which Pat states her position on complex issues strongly suggest that moral feelings, which would give rise to anxiety and guilt, are being repressed. The same conclusion might be drawn from her dogged optimism and belief that her luck will see her through and from her special susceptibility to boredom. When Pat says she was bored we may take this to mean that anxiety was about to become conscious—as when she said about women that she was "bored with the all-good." It also appears that she denies guilt and anxiety through her near-delinquent behavior itself. By acting, often enough, in a way that would ordinarily arouse guilt she may prove to herself that she may do so with impunity. By acting as if she had no superego she might at least for the time being convince herself that this was true.

Then there is the idea that bad things might happen through the action of agencies outside herself. In dreams and in waking fantasies, particularly in the dark, there are threatening monsters, ghosts, evil supernatural agents, a man in a picture whose eyes follow one's movements; there is imagery of torture chambers, detached hands, crippled people. The interpretation would be that Pat's primitive superego, fashioned of her imaginings concerning the consequences of her own impulses, is projected outward. This state of affairs, originating in childhood, has persisted, owing in large part to the absence of stable identifications with parents and the consequent failure to develop a reliable social superego.

Pat may be aware of the connection between her impulses and her fears; at least she acts as if she had this knowledge. She has told us of the compulsive nature of her sexuality and of her desire for better control.

It seems that, so strong is her disposition to anxiety and so slight her tolerance for it, that she seeks external agents to hold her in check. If she were left to her own devices, the fearful projected superego would take over—better to be punished and controlled by real people. Hence the desire for a husband who will dominate her—"step on me," "put me in my place." (Someone who is more like a director than like an actor, we might say.) And hence, when this pattern of interpersonal relationships is generalized, her preference for a hierarchical ordering of society. External agencies of control—the external superego—have the great advantage that they can be got around or ignored when not needed.

Finally, we may note that Pat can take a moral stance where the behavior of other people is concerned. One might say that she joins forces with her superego when the object of its restrictive or punitive action is outside herself, particularly when some of her own impulses have been projected into that object. This is what seems to be involved when she tells us how she proposes to bring up her children, or about the threat of a Communist teacher to the "impressionable young girls" at college. In telling of her ideas about child-training Pat gives fresh evidence that she would like to have better control of herself and that she wishes she had been better controlled. She would not like her children to be like herself. At the same time, she suggests that naughty behavior in her children would tend to arouse her own anxiety—as if her own deeper impulses had gone into action—and, hence, that firm measures might be required.

But why should Pat, a talented girl whose background offered many advantages, suffer from unconscious self-contempt and from the results of failure to develop a social superego? To answer these questions it would be necessary to make a thoroughgoing study of her life history, which would be beyond the scope of this paper. We are undertaking to formulate the existing personality organization—for purposes of comparison with that of Penny—rather than to trace its development. Yet, if childhood experiences were important, traces of them must be operating now, perhaps as determinants of the unconscious processes that we have hypothesized. There is not space for more life history material, but hints are to be obtained from what has already been presented.

Pat probably sets us on the right track when she tells us that the most stressful events of her life have had to do with her persistent preoccupation with sex and that the greatest influence upon her has been her brother. We may believe her when she says that she was introduced early to genital sexuality, and that stimulation of sexual impulses was intense and consistent. There seems to have been no period of letup from the age of about six on. It is a safe assumption that modes of gratification learned so early and so well are not easily given up and that much of the overt sexual expression that we observe when Pat is a senior is continuous with her childhood pattern.

Childhood sexuality of the kind that Pat knew could hardly exist without fears of consequences, particularly if parental control were lacking. The evidence seems to be that Pat's parents, rich but relatively uneducated, were unable to supply consistent discipline or stable patterns worthy of identification. The mother seems to have been generally ineffectual, the father a rigid traditionalist unprepared for life in the modern world. They left much of Pat's upbringing to servants and to her brother. In these circumstances—very unfavorable to the development of a social superego—we should expect just those kinds of fearful imaginings that Pat has always had to contend with.

The kind of childhood sexuality we are talking about here is not only productive of fears; it is also driven by fears. This is where the brother comes in. He seems to have been not only a kind of seducer when Pat was fourteen—and he was the "chaperon" on double dates—but a companion in her earliest sexual investigations and adventures. Out of the fighting and teasing and tickling came a confusion of feelings toward this brother—love, hostility, fear, and a longing to be like him. Sexual gratification became mixed up with the idea that something bad—mutilation—might happen to the man and that something bad might happen, or had happened, to herself. Recall the dream of dancing "to save the man" and the fantasy of nursing crippled people, and recall the desire for a man strong enough to "step on me." As for happenings to herself, recall the fear of damage to her legs. But this last had to be denied if possible; hence, the "insatiable curiosity," the dreams of "a little thing jumping out," and of flying. In short, it seems reasonable to suppose that Pat's early sex experiences left her with a set of misconceptions in which sexual activity was mixed up with aggression and fears of damage to herself and to a male partner. She tried to overcome the threat, or the sense, of damage to herself by trying to be like a boy. (She says she was a tomboy and a "messy child" who didn't care how she looked.) But this did not overcome her deep sense of hopeless sexual inferiority, and this, we may suppose, is a major source of the unconscious self-contempt that we have hypothesized.

We have spoken of the superego and of primitive impulses; it may be well to add a brief discussion of Pat's ego-functioning. There is, indeed, much in the case to suggest that we are dealing with what is often called "ego weakness." There seems to be relatively little self-insight, or insight into other people; in fact, self-deception would appear to be expressed in her overoptimism and trust in her luck. She does not wish to look very closely at herself, and she is tolerant of irrationality in herself and in others. There is much evidence that she cannot bear consciousness of guilt or conscious anxiety or depression, but must act in order to ward off these feelings. There is a short time-perspective and a narrowness of interest and outlook. One might say that the personality is highly organized around present interests and plans, but one is forced to be somewhat despairing when he thinks of what it would take to enlarge or to change this structure or of what would happen should present plans fall through.

On the other hand, we ought not to speak of the weakness, or the strength, of the ego without considering the dimensions of the tasks it has to perform. Pat has had to deal with a powerful, archaic superego and with fairly riotous impulses. An ego that was largely taken up with protecting itself from these forces could hardly be expected to develop well in all its other functions. In the circumstances, one might say that acting out has proved to be an effective defensive arrangement. And, having found a socially valuable form for this major trend of her personality, Pat has been able to organize an enormous amount of energy and talent. This is an impressive achievement. Perhaps it is not so much "strength," in the sense of ability to cope, that is lacking in Pat's ego as it is "breadth," that is, the expandedness and complexity of the conscious ego that we ordinarily expect to come with general education at the college level.

PENNY AS A SENIOR

Penny, now, presents a picture very different from the one presented when she was a freshman. Although the difference in IE score is not nearly as great as in the case of Pat, it seems to express a greater change in personality. Penny is very much aware of having changed and is very much taken up with efforts to stabilize a new self-conception and a new orientation to values. Coming from an upper-middle-class, conservative family, she was groomed for college in a private school of the same sort that Pat attended and arrived on the campus with a firmly established superego and a conventional outlook that was supported by family, school, and a peer group in which she had secure membership. As a senior she has a set of beliefs that are radically different from those of her parents, a new set of friends, and comfortable, equalitarian relations with members of the faculty—and she has a full fellowship for graduate study in the social science area.

I shall argue that Penny's high impulse expression is integrated with the ego in a girl who, at the same time, has a strong and well-internalized superego. This is in contrast with the defensive acting-out seen in the case of Pat. Though we are justified in speaking of both Pat and Penny as high on IE, the fact remains that Pat is much higher; she is really extreme. This difference between Pat's extremely high score and Penny's high score is reflected in the material to be presented.

Ascendance

First to be noted in Penny at this stage is a strong element of rebelliousness. This seems to be mainly an expression of striving for independence. At the same time, it can be seen that she puts rebellious
actions in the service of what she considers to be an important principle,
such as justice for a member of the faculty. In Pat, on the other hand,
rebelliousness seemed to be a kind of temporary rejection of the external
superego—a getting around it at the moment—in the interests of desire
or comfort.

Six faculty members gave Penny an average rating of 4.5 on independence, defined as the ability to function independently without
benefit of authority or guidance by the social group. (This may be compared with a mean of 3.2, SD .90, for 78 girls so rated.) She ranks third
from the top in this group of students. On rebelliousness she is rated 3.0
on the average (group mean = 2.37) and is eleventh from the highest in
the group. (Pat ranks twenty-sixth on rebelliousness and twentieth on
independence.) But the faculty members were not inclined to hold
Penny's rebelliousness against her, for they also rated her 4.17, fourth
from the top, an "ideal student," that is, "the degree to which she is in
accord with your concept of the ideal student." The following excerpts
from the interviews show something of Penny's strivings for autonomy.
Asked about changes in her attitudes toward and relations with the faculty, she said:

> I have changed a great deal since last year. Now I am much more apt
> to say what I think to teachers. I talk more freely and am apt to be more
> critical.

"How did this come about?"

> Chiefly through Mr. A. [He is a teacher of whom we shall know more
> later.]

"Do you expect financial support from your parents after graduation?"

> I will be in graduate school and will have a fourteen-hundred-dollar
> grant. I don't know what it would cost, I would like a part-time job so I
> could be independent. [How about after marriage?] I would like to be in-
> dependent, but I could get help from my parents if I had to have it.

Asked about the ways in which she had changed since her freshman
year, Penny said,

> My values have changed a lot. I have got away from always thinking
> what others would think. I am associated with people I formerly looked
> down my nose at. I am more permissive in judging other people. I used to
> be hard on people of different backgrounds, now I am hard on persons who
> go through college like vegetables.

"What has been your parents' attitude toward your college career?"

> They think I have been getting some ideas I shouldn't. . . . I am scared
> about the future; I hate to ask them for help in going to graduate school.
> They have sent me to school for sixteen years. . . . Daddy and I differ in
> respect to politics, social questions, and income tax. On integration we are
> poles apart. I don't want the kind of life they live in Hometown.

In speaking of the change that she thought was due chiefly to Mr.
A., Penny was assuming correctly that the interviewer knew the story of
her relations with Mr. A. He was a philosophy teacher who made a great
impression on Penny and on a considerable number of other girls. He
seems to have shown her convincingly that an academic subject really
did have something to do with her own central purposes and concerns
and, through revealing himself to his students, that the intellectual life
could, after all, be carried on by human beings. He could often be seen
about the campus, in rather nonacademic settings, carrying on animated
discussion with groups of girls, of whom one was usually Penny. When
it became known that his one-year contract was not going to be renewed,
she became a leader of a group of students who circulated a petition and
fought valiantly for his retention. Her relationship with him seemed to
have opened the way to other teachers, and she actually mentioned five
others of whom she had seen quite a lot.

Some of the above material suggests what seems to be generally true,
that the aggression which Penny shows—and she shows quite a bit—is
not primarily defensive, nor is it a mere release of some ego-alien impulse; rather it is usually organized in the service of some larger purpose,
such as the defense of another person or the improvement of an existing
condition. It seems also that the aggression is differentiated. She can attack someone, but at the same time say that she owes a lot to them. These
are indications that the aggression is under the control of ego processes.
This is in contrast to Pat, who is bored and annoyed when anxiety is
aroused and "livid with rage" when she cannot have her way.

Concerning her parents, Penny says: "No matter how much I may
respect my parents now, their ethics and standards have been very important. . . ."

In speaking of faculty members and of courses, she is hard-hitting
but at the same time fair-minded. She rubs her hands gleefully when
asked to speak about the five faculty members she likes least. But then
she proceeds to give a balanced account in each case. After speaking of
the five teachers she likes most, the group headed by Mr. A., she says,
for example, with respect to Professor I., "A generally ineffectual teacher,
but I have heard she has never been the same since she had some illness."
Concerning Mrs. N., she says, "Very ineffectual, but I like her as a person."

The point to be emphasized here is that she feels free to criticize, because she can control aggression and because she is willing to give people a leg to stand on.

Concerning dominance, and dominance feelings, it seems that some of this runs through much of what Penny has to tell us, insofar as it expresses her strong sense of herself and of her intellectual power. But there is very little to suggest that she is interested in the kind of power one might get from swaying an audience. Although often called shy or reticent, Penny is often chosen by her friends and classmates for leadership roles. Using a proffered list of roles, positions, and activities, they rated her 4 or above on "judge in a juvenile court," "leader of a citizens' committee interested in good government," "representative to the state legislature," "warden of a women's prison," "Washington lobbyist for women's rights," "moderator in labor-management disputes." Her friends here are showing admiration for her mental powers and for her capacity to assume responsibility. Other roles that stand out in these ratings accent nurturance, for example, "helping refugees get settled" or "taking care of children."

The need for recognition should also be mentioned here. We find none of Pat's exhibitionism here, but there are indications that Penny really would like to do something great and to achieve fame. Several of her teachers have pointed out that she sets such a high standard for herself or has such a grand conception of what she might do that she undertakes more than she can finish, gets into a "stew," and fails to hand her work in on time. But, on time or not, she must hand in much good work, for the six faculty raters give her an average of 4.75 on intellectual capacity, second from the top, and use strong terms—"a fine mind," "tremendous reserves of ability," "outstanding performance"—to express their appreciation of her qualities and work.

The argument here is that Penny's aggression and dominance and her strivings for autonomy and recognition are in the ego. There is plenty of passion, but it is expressed in accordance with the ego's way of doing things. One might say, in fact, that in some instances the presence of ego controls favors the expression of strong feelings. Compare, for example, Penny's telling faculty members and interviewers what she thinks with Pat's withdrawal from a controversy out of fear that someone might not like her. The IE scale has a place, in the general area of ascendance, for the kind of spirit that Penny shows.

Sensation

Sex. What Penny has to say about sex exemplifies, I think, what we might understand by sexuality that is integrated with the ego; and here the contrast with Pat is particularly striking. In the life-history interview,

Penny was asked where she got sex information and she said "mostly from other girls, movies, books, very little from parents. I was fairly little when I saw a little boy go to the bathroom." Concerning menstruation, she says she was fourteen at the time of onset, had been prepared at school, and that her mother said something about it. "I was not shocked. I felt underdeveloped in my breasts and I still do." Asked about lateness of the pubertal events, she said "I was not really upset—I was not the latest— not a pressing problem. I don't remember very much."

Asked about dating she says:

> In the seventh and eighth grades dating was mostly group stuff. There was pairing off, and somebody liked somebody for about a week. At boarding school, it was a matter of week-end dating of boys I had known at home. Then, at freshman year here, there were blind dates, and they didn't work out. In sophomore year I was in the depths of everything. I wouldn't go out—I don't know what was wrong with me. Last year dating was sporadic. Never until this summer have I gone out with one boy a great deal. I have a tendency to pull back from too much involvement. I have had physical inhibitions, maybe a fear of getting hurt, but not now. I don't feel ready for marriage, I don't feel I am mature emotionally.

"What was your first sex experience?"

> You mean the first time I parked and did more than just kiss goodnight? That was in the eleventh or twelfth grade—that was the first really erotic experience. I had never gone much beyond that—I have never petted. I don't think I will go to bed with a boy before marriage. I don't condemn those who do, however; there is probably a good reason. People can't help being carried away by their emotions.

"Do you have dreams or fantasies about boys and men?"

> There are two I have daydreams about—terribly. [She laughs, but is not very embarrassed, according to the interviewer.] Yes, I think of them making love to me.

"Have your ideas about sex changed at all during college years—how? when? and why?"

> Yes, when I first came here I was quite inhibited. I don't condemn others for intercourse before marriage, but I don't approve for myself. Emotional entanglements are brought on by intercourse before marriage; also the risk is pretty great no matter what you do to minimize it.

"What are your views on premarital sex experience—if the couple is engaged?"

> It would be O.K. under the right circumstances [for her]. I would want to have my hymen stretched first, because it is fairly thick and I wouldn't want it to be a messy or bloody experience. I am not anxious to be hurt I guess, or to hurt him.

"What is the value of virginity?"

I don't think it is valuable, still I would like to be a virgin at marriage. Probably some of it is fear of pregnancy. I have pretty monogamous ideas. I don't demand the same from my husband. He may have had different needs.

"What do you think of homosexuals?"

Well, I think it is too bad. I don't condemn them, I think they are sick. I met some this summer. It is hard on one's wife. This fellow was bisexual. In some cases it can't be helped. If one approached me, I would be scared to death; but I feel sorry for them.

"If you were a bachelor girl for a few years after college, would you adopt a different standard of behavior than you now have?"

I might, I don't know. I guess I would say no now. But sure, if I don't get married I'd be very likely to change my way of living so that I could have the experience.

"At present do you feel a discrepancy between the sexual needs of your boyfriend and yourself?"

No, I don't, because I feel that we both want the same thing, but, as far as getting equally worked up, I know I can and do. [The interviewer says she blushes.]

"What is your impression of your parents' sex life?"

This is something I have always wondered about. Father is reserved, polite, doesn't like sex jokes. I have a feeling that Mother is pretty frustrated, though I could be wrong.

The interviewer rates Penny 4 on "acceptance of sexual expression," 4 on "self-estimate of sexual adequacy," and 5 on "interviewer's estimate of sexual adequacy." In the case of Pat, the ratings were 5 on "self-estimate," 4 on "interviewer's estimate." Other ratings of Penny were 2 on "moralistic, compartmentalized view of sex," 2 on "resentment or fear of male sexuality," and 3 on "husband-wife relationship viewed as dominant-submissive."

A question might be raised about the rating of fear of male sexuality, in view of what Penny says about not wanting a "messy or bloody experience." The interviewer should be permitted to defend himself:

I think this gal is highly sexed and highly conscious of her sex needs at times. Her discussion of it could interest any man, even though older and fully committed. I think she may be afraid of intercourse, not for reasons given, such as its seriousness emotionally, but because of her thick hymen, common enough in this physical type. If she gets the right male, she will have a hearty need for intercourse. Her deprivation now is reflected in her fair identity with her mother and in her belief that her father does not satisfy her mother sexually.

The interviewer addresses himself to the right question, that is, will

Penny have satisfying sexual relations in marriage? The four psychologists, including this one, who know her well believe that she will. What impresses them is her conscious acceptance of so many aspects of her sexuality, including its fearful aspects. This means that her fears are fully open to modification through the experience that a young woman of her courage and warm desire seems bound to have. This is in contrast with Pat, who can admit no fears having to do with sex or men, but who is driven by unconscious fantasies that express themselves in compulsive behavior, on the one hand, and in nightmares, on the other.

More problematic in the case of Penny is the matter of dominance-submission in husband-wife relationships. She has dominance-feelings, and these might well become stronger. This means that she might be attracted by a relatively passive and ultimately disappointing male. This outcome may be favored also by her strong nurturant feelings. These tendencies seemed to be involved to some extent in Penny's relations with Mr. A. He was a rather boyish type who got into trouble and was kicked around quite a bit and thus, perhaps, made himself very appealing to this warm-hearted girl. But, as we have seen, there was more to the relationship than this; moreover, it might be possible for Penny to find a boyish type of man who is adequate and able to take care of himself without being aggressive or high-powered. Actually, what she seems mainly to desire is a relationship of equality, in which sex takes its place among a variety of other mutually appreciated qualities and feelings. In her long interview on family, children, and the status of women, equalitarianism in husband-wife and male-female relations is a major theme; and we have seen that she has sought and attained equalitarian relationships with male members of the faculty. Most important, it seems, is a genuine relationship with a man as a person, a matter in which Penny has admittedly been backward. She tells us with respect to one of her new friends at college, "She is the first girl that I have ever really enjoyed being with." Just as her school-college friendship group can be regarded as a coming together for mutual protection of status and of an authoritarian type of personality organization, so should we regard her early dates with boys as a matter of "rating and dating." She tells us that her first enjoyable relationship with a young man came only in the summer after junior year, when she began going out with a young man who worked in the same social agency that she did. We can be reasonably sure that she will require a well-educated and sensitive man who is also an adequate lover.

The kind of sexuality that we find in Penny is well calculated to make for higher scores on the IE scale. As pointed out earlier, the scale expresses personality at the level of attitude; it is not necessary for a subject to have acted, or acted out, in order to agree with items expressive of liberality and daring. Thus, for example, Penny would certainly agree that "women should have as much sexual freedom as men," but this does not mean that she would insist on their taking advantage of this freedom or on demonstrating that she herself had done so.

Penny offers a nice example of sexuality that is in the ego. It is not merely that sexual behavior is under the ego's control; more important, she is striving to make sexuality a part of her conscious self, and to a considerable extent she has accomplished this. She has conscious sexual fantasies of an explicit sort (see below), is aware of the emotions that normally accompany sexual feeling, and is prepared to take responsibility for her actions. Pat, for all her "experience," could not convince her interviewers that she had this kind of familiarity with the psychological implications of sex. One might say that Penny is trying to arrange things so that when she gives herself sexually it will be indeed her *self* that she gives. It is this that gives the impression of strong sexuality, for, when sex is fully integrated with the ego, it can be a channel for the expression of a rich assortment of feelings and emotions. Such integration also means, of course, that sex experiences can now become a means for the further development of the personality; like other important experiences, it can take its place within an expanding structure of integrated processes. It is because girls in college are usually quite well-developed in their ego functioning that they find it less difficult than is commonly supposed to inhibit overt sexual behavior. The broader the life-space, the less the chances that sex will assume overriding importance; more than this, there is now a large organization of conscious needs and purposes that has become the basis for self-respect and that can be set in opposition to any particular desire.

The argument can, of course, be made that a college senior who has not yet integrated sexual gratification with the ego is a bit late. It does appear that Penny has been delayed in her development by her strict superego, as reinforced by her school and her friendship group. On the other hand, if a girl takes it upon herself to build an identity that includes the developmental advances that a college education can bring, and if, in the most favorable developmental sequence, identity should precede intimacy, then she would appear to be justified in taking her time.

Emotionality, Disjunctivity, and Change. There are few manifestations of exhibitionism or the desire for excitement. Emotionality, however, seems to be freely displayed in her relations with people. This is particularly striking in what Penny says about the complexities of her relationships with the girls from whom she had to break away during the course of her college years. And it is manifest in what her friends and some faculty members say about her. One of her teachers, for example, says she is "gentle, kind, affectionate, and warm." Various of her friends say she is "kind, understanding, has strong feelings, is loyal, responsive"; "dependent on her friends, very helpful, highly emotional"; "genuinely sympathetic, tolerant, demands a lot of her friends." Apparently she is high on succorance as well as on affiliation and nurturance. Her dependence is shown particularly in her fear of being rejected by the friends with whom she came to college. But the tendencies that we see expressed in her relations with people are ego needs. There is little here that would make for a high score on the IE scale; rather the opposite, for the scale accents narcissism rather than object relations. Impulsiveness not under ego control does display itself when Penny feels that she has been or is about to be rejected. This is very probably what lies behind the withdrawal and "moodiness" of which she tells us and behind the "ill-temper" and the "bluntness and curtness" of which her friends have sometimes complained.

There is evidence that Penny is sometimes disorganized and irresponsible. Some of her friends say, for example, that she is "not very responsible about paying bills"; that she is "kind of unorganized and worries too much about details"; that "one wouldn't go too far in trusting her responsibility when it comes to decision-making." Her teachers have noted these same tendencies. One of them says, after pointing out that she has tremendous reserves of ability and great critical intelligence:

> She seemed to lack confidence in her own ability to achieve a standard of performance living up to her high expectations. The written work came through with an outstanding performance, but in group discussion she was often inarticulate and confused.

Here we see some effects of a strong superego that is not fully integrated with the ego. Underlying conflicts involving strivings for perfection, fear of failure, and a desire to leave the field give rise to manifest disjunctivity. Penny's friends see this as irresponsibility. She tends to do so herself; and some of this kind of tendency is expressed in the IE scale.

Endocathection and Intraception

In this area the picture is mixed. Penny displays both of these tendencies—and their opposites. She is low on fantasy but high on reflection and abstract thought. She says that during periods of her college years she did nothing but sit around and think. This was often the case in her sophomore year, when she suffered an agony of indecision concerning her friends and turned to religion. But when faculty members and interviewers describe her as a "thoughtful girl," they have in mind activity of a more intellectual sort—the sort that leads to good academic work. But we cannot say that there is the kind of closeness to the unconscious that we noted in the case of Pat. She dreams very little, barely remembers her dreams, does not know whether she dreams in color or not, does not have nightmares, and can think of no unusual experiences, such as extra-sensory perception. But she says it would be fun to dream if one could, and she does produce some daydreams. Concerning conscious fantasy she says,

> A lot grow out of immediate experience—wanting to impress people—and there are some sexual ones. Some have been morbid and violent, and I used to have one of being raped, or hurting people I don't like. Sometimes I have sexual dreams in the night that wake me up—or, after I wake up in the morning, it's a daydream then.

The main impression is of strong controlling and inhibiting ego processes that tend to transform quickly anything coming from the un-conscious. It seems, however, that there are self-awareness and acceptance in consciousness of things that would cause anxiety in Pat. This relative breadth of consciousness is shown in what Penny says about bringing up her children:

> Sure there will be problems, emotional and otherwise; I always wonder if you will remember how it was when you were a child.

In general, the accent is on intellectualization and efforts at rational mastery rather than on the direct expression of unconscious fantasies.

In this light, it is particularly interesting that seven faculty members rated Penny 4.3 (mean = 2.86) and second from the top on creativity. This is the more striking when one considers that in most studies of creativity it is the art students who walk off with the highest ratings. Penny seems to be participating in the prevailing stereotype when she remarks, "I'd love to have a creative talent, but I don't." We should probably give the faculty members credit for being able to see and to ap-preciate the use of imagination in social science work—though they are no doubt expressing here their general appreciation of Penny's ability. And we should credit Penny with being able to transform her unconscious processes into intellectual products.

There is evidence, then, of endocathection; but there is also evi-dence of the opposite, for Penny is heavily involved with people and ac-tions, particularly actions of a humanitarian kind. A rater who knew her well would probably try to give a picture of balance on this variable. But there is enough endocathection to favor acceptance of the items in this part of the IE scale.

In respect to intraception and extraception, the picture is also mixed. Certainly, Penny is often determined by diffuse personal feelings, but at the same time she is very often credited by teachers, friends, and inter-viewers with being a sharp observer who can be sensible and even hard-headed in dealing with many kinds of problems.

Radical Sentiments

It was discovered in the case of Pat that being a nonbeliever in religion practically guarantees that one will answer a number of scale items in the direction of higher IE. Pat was rather indifferent toward religion, whereas Penny as a senior is definitely antireligious. This might be in part an expression of her rebelliousness and in part an effort to overcome the shame that she still feels because of her display of fox-hole religion when she was a sophomore.

> In my sophomore year I turned to religion as a big crutch. I just don't have any religious beliefs now. I just don't buy it.

"In your thinking does man's evolutionary development mean he is anything more than an animal who has invented culture?"

> No, there is no great purpose in life. I came to that conclusion a few months ago when I was thinking about my thesis. What difference does it make anyway? It doesn't make very much.

This sort of effort at intellectual analysis and the effort to be somewhat hard-boiled about it is characteristic of Penny. It makes for a high score on the radical sentiments of the IE scale.

In respect to sex morality, we have seen that Penny is to be credited with the kind of relativism that is typical of senior women and that helps to differentiate them from freshmen on IE. I am also arguing that she has a kind of acceptance of sexuality, a kind of spirit about the whole thing, that helps to make her higher than the average senior on the scale.

Then, of course, she is well indoctrinated in the liberal, democratic, antiethnocentric political and social views of most college social science teachers today. She says, half seriously, that "we ought to secede from the South" and, quite seriously, that in our international relations "we have got to get away from the idea that our way is the only way." The development of this outlook was a foregone conclusion, once she had formed her relationship with Mr. A., gained her new friendships with more intellectual girls, and separated herself psychologically from the roommates of her freshman year. She rejects, however, the idea that she might have thoughtlessly taken over a whole platform: "At times there is a conformity of liberalism, especially in the classroom. If you know the students well, you know they are not all that liberal."

In view of the above it would be very surprising if she were not low on the F scale. Her score is 61, down from a freshman score of 96. She is in the low quartile for our group of college seniors. Hers is a kind of militant antiauthoritarianism that is quite in keeping with her spirit of rebellious independence.

Interpretation

In Penny's college career, the major theme has been her struggle for a new identity. The movement toward freedom of impulse has been a somewhat incidental benefit of this more-or-less successful and continuing struggle. In the change that has come about, the crucial factor has been, as Penny herself knows, the relationship with Mr. A. It is probable that she will always think of him as a decisive influence in her life. Mr. A.'s crucial role was to make it possible for her to break away from her original peer group; and this breaking away was necessary to her new freedom, because this group had become the major support of her restrictive superego and her authoritarian position.

Only an adult—not a peer or group of peers—and an admired one who represented intellectual values and enlightened conscience could have played this role. No other agency could have stood in effective opposition to the values represented by the early peer group and fully espoused by Penny herself. She needed a figure who was in some part a superego representative but who could at the same time nourish her developing confidence in her own intellectual powers.

That the peer group was primarily a superego representative seems plain enough from the record. We can well believe Penny when she tells us that one of her new friends was the first girl she ever really enjoyed being with. Her close association with her early friends was not a source of enjoyment but a matter of necessity. The group of freshman girls to which Penny belonged, who thought they were, as she says, "really something," were constantly telling themselves in effect that they were "good," "all right," beyond moral reproach, while those whom they excluded were "bad" or "low." Not to belong to the in-group was to belong to the excluded group, into which the girls projected their own "badness." It was for this reason that fear of being rejected drove Penny into depression and religion. Yet she was bound to fear rejection because however tightly she clung to her friends—"depended" on them—she was unconsciously rejecting them in seeking some freedom from the restrictions they represented. She was indeed in a bad spot when Mr. A. came to the rescue.

After the relationship with Mr. A. became firmly established, Penny could make friends with an entirely different group of girls, who now became important as supporters of her new value system and self-conception. And she could be friends with other faculty members, who served her in the same way.

But by no means all college girls have the inclination or the capacity to break away from a peer group such as that Penny belonged to, and by no means all the students in Mr. A.'s class were affected in the way she was.

There was something in Penny already that made her dissatisfied with her situation in her freshman peer group and no doubt something that made her particularly open to the influence of someone like Mr. A. There is much in the life-history material to suggest, and nothing to contradict, the notion that, although the superego we have been concerned with came mainly from an identification with her mother, Penny also got a great deal from her father. Very likely she got enough from him, both from their love relationship and through identification, to suggest to her that rebellion against her mother might be possible as well as highly desirable. This might well be the major source of her drive and fight and of her desire for something beyond that which was allowed by her peer group, and, of course, of her capacity to go along with Mr. A. when powerful women of the faculty were suggesting that she was being foolish. It was probably important, then, that the admired teacher should be a man, and one toward whom she could feel affection and nurturance as well as respect. Be it noted, finally, that there is nothing in the material to suggest that Penny ever sexualized her relationship with Mr. A. or that he, for all his boyishness, ever indicated to the girls that he valued them for anything beside their intellectual and human qualities. Any departure from these restraints by either one of them would, of course, have spoiled the whole drama.

CONCLUSION: THE FREEING OF IMPULSE IN COLLEGE

When we say, on the basis of mass testing, that impulse expression increases during the college years, we are saying quite a lot. But we are also leaving much to obscurity, for we know that two students who obtain the same or similar scores on the IE scale may differ very much both in the quality of their impulse expression and in the broader system of personality within which it occurs.

With hindsight, it appears that this major point might have been more sharply made had we studied a girl like Pat whose IE scale score was closer to that of Penny. This could have been done. As matters stand, there is the possibility that the difference between compulsive acting-out and genuine freedom of impulse is reflected in the height of the IE score; that a subject like Penny who is moving toward genuine freedom could hardly be expected to go above, say, 90, and any score above that would indicate the presence of defensive impulse impression. But we cannot ask of a scale that it supply reliable interpretations of this kind, for there remains the possibility that two subjects could obtain the same high score and yet differ in the same way, and almost as much, as the two we have considered.

One might, of course, obtain quantitative indexes of the differences we are concerned with by using a number of tests and examining the test profiles. We have seen, for example, that the differing F-scale scores of Penny and Pat were quite consistent with what our case studies revealed. But it is too easy to imagine a subject (we have some in our samples, in fact) who acts out in the way that Pat did but obtains an extremely low score on the F scale.

The need is for some new scales or other instruments of measurement. The study of more cases like Pat and like Penny could supply a good basis for the construction of a scale for measuring compulsive impulse expression and a scale for measuring ego-integrated impulse expression. But finer differentiations than these are needed, and quantitative indications of them should be sought. Clinical studies of the kind offered here show how much our existing instruments do not say.

What is required cannot be attained merely through the manipulation of existing items. It is easy to imagine what might happen should the IE scale achieve the visibility enjoyed by the F scale during the decade of the 1950's. Many studies could be directed to its statistical properties, to the further specification of its content, and so on. This, by itself, will not suffice. Somebody must get back to cases, from which all our quantitative blessings flow. And in doing so he must be guided by a theory that formulates the connections between test responses and hypothetical processes nearer the core of the personality.

Meanwhile, the formulation of a theory about the determination of impulse expression need not wait upon test construction, nor can educators afford to await further developments in psychology before giving thought to how they should deal with educational problems of the sort presented by our two cases.

Penny seems to exemplify the processes that most commonly give rise to increases in IE during college. There is a softening of the superego as the student comes under the influence of more enlightened representatives of culture and as he becomes increasingly able, because of the development of his ego, to decide moral questions on the basis of his own knowledge and thought. Not only is more allowed under the new system of values, but the individual can permit himself more gratification as his confidence in his ability to control himself increases.

The case of Penny also shows the enormous importance of academic education in the kind of change we are speaking of. Both Pat and Penny discovered that they could express some of their strongest impulses in the intellectual-cultural sphere, Pat in drama, Penny through imaginative work in social science. In the case of Penny, we can see, not only that understandings gained in courses broadened the conscious ego, but that the relationship with Mr. A. was largely carried forward in the realm of ideas and values. For her, the freeing of impulses was a kind of intellectual adventure story. And here it must be said that Penny's high intelligence was an important factor in determining the course of events; it was important both in what she was able to understand and do and in the kinds of responses she got from faculty members.

It is somewhat discouraging to consider, as we must with Penny's case before us, how difficult it is for some students to change developmentally in college. But at least this case helps us to understand, and to understand with a fresh enthusiasm, the importance of putting student peer groups under strain and of creating conditions that favor the development of relationships between students and faculty.

In the case of Pat, it seems also that an increase in IE score was due in considerable part to participation in a new culture. It seems unlikely that her need to act out her impulses for defensive reasons became increasingly acute as she went through college. It seems rather that she found in the Department of Dramatic Art—in the faculty and students there—support for and reinforcement of a defensive operation that was already in motion. Many of the activities that now serve her defensive purposes are more valuable culturally than some of the patterns she exhibited as a freshman.

We may ask whether the college might have done more for Pat. It seems that, in the matter of skills and knowledge in the area of her specialty, a great deal was accomplished. Yet, one can accept Pat fully as she is and still wish that her college education had been broader. Suppose she does not succeed as an actress. (And in this field, where many are called and few are chosen, it must be considered that her chances are slight.) One would wish that her education had been such that she could work contentedly at various jobs in the world of the theater, perhaps as a promoter and organizer of a community theater. Again, although there is no doubt that Pat will continue to be an interesting and entertaining person, it seems too bad that she does not have more scope. If we imagine her presiding over a salon, as well we might, it is a little distressing to think of her being limited to theater talk. It seems possible that, had a different set of educational objectives been conceived for Pat in the first place, she could have been influenced by a number of men, in several different departments, to somewhat the same extent that she was influenced by Mr. Y.

One may raise a more searching question. Should a college be content to leave the character of a girl like Pat the way it finds it? The most disquieting thing in her case is the high F-scale score and what lies behind it. It is difficult to see how an anti-Semitic girl who depends on social status could get along very well in the world of the theater. More seriously, it is hard to see how Pat can develop further as a person without there being some radical shaking-up of the existing personality structure. In a sense, the drama major was a reasonable course for Pat. Here was a girl who was looking for strong external control; she could hardly be expected to accept such control unless it favored a major purpose of her own; what better arrangement, then, than bringing her under the discipline of a strong director in the theater? We have seen that, within limits, this arrangement worked very well. But it does not appear that the discipline has been carried over to other spheres of life or that Pat's need for strong external controls has been reduced. Must she go through life making sure that she always has a strong hand to rule her, be it a director or a husband?

The problem is a difficult one. We know that authoritarianism in personality can be reduced in college, but it is not clear what can be done with a student who as a freshman is as impulse-ridden as Pat was. Perhaps nothing can be done. And we must respect the opinions of those who think that nothing should be done. Yet it seems that we have no alternative to trying to increase our knowledge of impulse expression and authoritarianism, and personality development in general, so that the colleges and, more important, the student herself will have greater choice in the matter.

2: INBURN

An American Ishmael

Kenneth Keniston

Call me Ishmael. . . . Whenever I find myself growing grim
about the mouth; whenever it is a damp, drizzly November
in my soul; whenever I find myself involuntarily pausing
before coffin warehouses . . . then I account it high time to
get to sea as soon as I can. . . . If they but knew it,
almost all men in their degree, sometime or other,
cherish very nearly the same feelings toward the ocean
with me.

—MELVILLE, *Moby Dick*

Somehow once he got into the water it became not the
Atlantic Ocean or the Mediterranean, but it was just *a*
sea, *the* sea, with nothing on the surface, with no
continents to go back to . . . and the place not being there
from which he set off anymore . . . This is the kind of an
extended moment which he wouldn't mind going on with
forever—which he probably will, just continuing down
into the dark water. . . .

—INBURN, T.A.T. Card 16

Inburn's appearance in no way set him apart from other undergraduates. Tall, with blue eyes and sandy hair, he wore the uniform of his classmates: baggy corduroys, a button-down shirt, horn-rimmed glasses, and a tie more often than not slid down from the collar. He walked with something of a slouch, hands deep in his pockets, his eyes mostly fixed on the pavement as if he were deep in some private thought. From the cafeterias he frequented, one versed in the ways of the college might have surmised that he was of literary bent, and from the fact that he so often ate breakfast in one particular cafeteria at 11:00 A.M. (having overslept the dining hall's more Spartan hours), that he was given neither to regular hours nor to impeccable attendance at lectures. But these qualities in no way distinguished him from a goodly proportion of his fellow sophomores.

Nor did he create an unusual impression on others. The opinion of a woman of fifty who knew him casually can perhaps stand as typical: "I rather liked him. He is thin and pleasant—perhaps not a decisive, strong-willed person, but always agreeable, never obviously depressed, perhaps a little shy, as talkative as most men his age." A psychologist who knew him slightly commented, "He is a nice-looking fellow, with a deep voice that might go over well on the stage. He speaks hesitantly but well, despite pauses and hesitations—more like written prose than ordinary speech." His manner was polite, reserved, and even detached, which implied to some that he was proud and condescending, and to others that he tended to brood. Though he seldom looked directly at the person to whom he was speaking, occasionally, when caught up in a topic, he would gaze deeply and intently into his interlocutor's eyes, suggesting deeper feelings than his outward manner expressed.

On the surface, his background and interests were also altogether unextraordinary. Like many of his classmates, he came from a middle-class family outside of New England, and he had gone to a good high school where he had graduated near the top of his class and been editor of the school paper. Even his outstanding intelligence, however, did not distinguish him from his classmates, also of high talent; and although his grades in his freshman year were slightly uneven, they adequately reflected his ability, and he made dean's list. His father was an executive in a large Detroit corporation; and his mother, for a time a schoolteacher, had early abandoned her career for domesticity. Inburn himself had been undecided for a time as to his major, but had finally settled on English literature as a field in which he could combine his interest in writing and his superior high-school training in literature. Like other students with artistic interests, he had tried his hand at student dramatics and at writing, a career he sometimes thought of following. He was a student who was in good standing with the college authorities, who had caused no one any trouble, and who would not easily be picked out in a crowd.

In the most public sides of Inburn's personality, then, there was little to suggest what was the case: that he was deeply dissatisfied with society, the world, and himself; that he almost completely rejected the institutional forms within which he was living; that he would spend his first reading period for exams in platonic partnership with a call girl whose memoirs he was ostensibly recording for future use; and that, though he passed his exams, he would withdraw from the college at midyear, never to return, heading instead on a motorcycle across the country to live with an "irredeemably dissolute" high-school friend in San Francisco. Despite his conventional surface, indeed because of it, Inburn can stand as a prototypically alienated young man, separated partly by his own volition from the people, institutions, and beliefs which sustain most young men at his age in America; rejecting the forms by which most American men and women live; and condemned, like the Biblical Ishmael by his past and like Melville's Ishmael by his own temper, to live on the outskirts of society. We do not know what has become of Inburn in the years since he volunteered to be studied in a clinical research project, whether his alienation persisted or dissolved with time and benign experience—though he himself implied in one Thematic Apperception Test story that the best resolution of his estrangement would be its incorporation in the role of a writer. In Inburn we see alienation—the rejection of the roles and values and institutions he sees as typical of adult American life—in unusually pure form; and the themes of his life can stand as introduction to and summary of comparable themes in the lives of others like him.

AN ENDLESS AND FEATURELESS COUNTRYSIDE

Like seventy other volunteers for a psychological research project, Inburn took a battery of paper-and-pencil tests, many of which were designed to measure alienated outlooks.[1] He first came to our attention even before the questionnaires were scored, because of his mordant marginal comments on items which he considered stupid or irrelevant. He made among the highest scores on every index we then had of alienation—on distrust, pessimism, resentment, anxiety, egocentricity, the sense of being an outsider, the rejection of conventional values, rejection of happiness as a goal, and a feeling of distance from others. And, had other subsequently developed measures of alienation been available, it is clear he would have scored high on them—on subspection (the desire to look beneath appearances), self-contempt, interpersonal alienation, dislike of conventional social groups, rejection of American culture, and the view of the universe as an unstructured and meaningless chaos. But even more revealing than test scores are some of the individual statements which he marked "strongly agree," often with exclamation points added; taken together, they constitute a kind of credo of disaffiliation: "The idea of trying to adjust to society as now constituted fills me with horror"; "There are sad and depressing times when the whole world strikes the eye as a huge, heartless, impersonal machine, almost devoid of understanding, sympathy, and mercy"; "I sometimes feel that I am the plaything of forces beyond my control"; "I feel strongly how different I am even from some of my closest friends"; "I have very little in common with most of the people I meet"; "I don't think I'll ever find a woman who really understands me"; "I have very little self-confidence"; "I usually try to keep my thoughts to myself"; "I sometimes wish I were a child again."

Soon after, when Inburn was asked to write a statement of his philosophy of life, he was unique among twenty-five students chosen for intensive clinical study in that he wrote an allegory instead of a formal statement:

> A group of men are motoring through an endless and featureless countryside in a tightly closed car, with all the windows rolled up. They reach a city, emerge from their vehicle, stretch their legs, and look around. They have a two-week stay ahead of them; after that they must move on into the wastes on the other side of the town, the same as before they arrived.
>
> "Well," I ask (being one of them), "what shall we do?" To all our surprises, each wants to spend his time differently. . . . "Personally," say I, "I would like to see the sights of this place."
>
> In this rather naïve allegory lies the ideal of my philosophy of life. If human (i.e., *my*) existence is looked on as a short time spent on a physical world with an inscrutable void on either side, it seems that the time can be

[1] The bulk of the research reported here was done at the Annex to the Center for Research in Personality and was partly supported by grant number M–1287 of the National Institute of Mental Health, Dr. Henry A. Murray, project director. I am especially indebted to Dr. Murray for his help and guidance and to Erik H. Erikson and David Riesman for their insight into the close interweaving of personality development and social setting.

most profitably spent in accumulating the most varied, the most valuable, and the most significant set of sense experiences it is possible to take in. . . .

One must not see the same sights over-frequently. What experiences are most valuable to fill this sixty-to-seventy-year interlude are those that bring one into the closest contact with reality, with the ground, the bedrock of sheer existence. This, of course, involves living close to nature, outside of (or rather beneath) the superstructure of tin and shit and kite-paper man has built up to live in.

Rather obviously, I am not practicing what I preach to any extent at all now. I wouldn't be in this room writing this little essay if I were. So far, all I do is insult myself by saying it's a fine idea, in fact, it's the only idea in the universe, but you don't have the guts to put it into practice.

Inburn's statement is as noteworthy for what it excludes as for what it says. Unlike many other students, whose philosophies of life stress the importance of other people, Inburn mentions others only once, and then to state that he is different from them. Also unlike many of his classmates, he explicitly rejects the "superstructure" of society and seeks above all the accumulation of sense experience, defined as that which will bring him into contact with "the bedrock of sheer existence."

Inburn's generally distrustful view of people was amplified when he was asked what harms and benefits he chiefly anticipated from his fellow men. He listed only "hostility, injustice, hypocrisy, slander, abuse." Asked whom he admired, he said: "I never thought about it. Alexander maybe. Hemingway in Paris. Chopin." But asked whom he disliked, he responded with a long catalogue which begins, "Nearly everything, and everyone that's complacently middle-class"; enumerates many specific examples; and concludes, "I hate officious, supercilious, imperious, pompous, stupid, contented, or bigoted persons. I especially dislike opportunists." And asked what his chief satisfactions and ambitions were, he said, "I don't think I'll ever have a main source of satisfaction. Only to live so that I may have the truest picture of the world possible when I die. You mean vaulting ambition? Nobody strives for ideas any more. It's hard enough just to strive." And asked how he would reform the world if he could, he said, "This is an unfair question. I guess I'd like to have us all go back to the womb."

Here, then, is a young man whose every attitude fits an alienated pattern. Full of distrust, he expects only harm from his fellow men; he has few admired figures, but many he dislikes; he sees life as a meaningless interlude whose chief object is the accumulation of varied sense experiences. He rejects society and conventional institutions; though he has no plans for his life, he clearly wants something different from the conventional life which draws most of his classmates, he denies all ambition; and his facetious Utopia is the womb.

MORE THAN A MERE MOTHER-AND-ONLY-CHILD

Inburn's autobiography, written for the research project for which he had volunteered, begins to provide some clues as to the development of his alienation. Like one or two of the more literarily ambitious research subjects, he began his autobiography in the third person:

> He came screaming and red-faced into the world on a December night in 1938, loath to leave his insensible sanctuary. . . . It was in a hospital in St. Louis; his mother was a small, young woman and she never had a child again. His parents were both schoolteachers and poor, after the ravages of the depression. His mother was particularly good-looking when she was young—black hair, a good nose, striking dark eyes, a sensuous lip, and a delicate yet hard, vibrant, vivacious body.

Inburn goes on to describe his mother's Greek immigrant parents, her mother "a simple, exuberant, and cruel woman," and her father, who ran a small restaurant, "a strong man, and strong-willed, tireless, too tireless."

His further description of his mother is extremely detailed. Despite her immigrant parents, "she made herself socially to nearly every family in St. Louis" [*sic*]. "Her petite and much-in-demand bottom was between two worlds. . . . She dropped her restaurant-owner's daughter's bad manners and grossness and made herself, completely, at the cost of great emotional and psychological complexity." She was ambitious; she taught herself to play the piano beautifully (she even gave recitals). "She *would* read poetry (though she never wrote it), she *would* paint, she *would* play tennis on the bank president's private court, and with his son." Despite her parents' lack of sympathy with her educational goals, she worked her way through high school and college, finishing each in three years. Elsewhere, Inburn notes that his mother is at the extreme end of the temperament scale: "volatile, passionate, typically Mediterranean"; and he adds that she "has a delicate constitution and has been warned against severe mental as well as physical strains."

In contrast to his full description of his mother, Inburn has far less to say of his father. His father's family originally came from a farm in the Midwest, and Inburn's grandfather married his own brother's pregnant and cast-off girl friend, became a milkman in St. Louis, and was thereafter dominated by his wife, a "scolding, officious hypochondriac." The father's ancestry was primarily Welsh, with a mixture of German and Irish. Inburn's father showed early signs of intelligence and musical talent and worked his way through high school and college, where he met his future wife. As a child, he seems to have been dominated by his mother, the "scolding, officious hypochondriac," who forced him to work in the evenings for the family landlord, "an idea he has recalled with bitterness at times." Awarded a scholarship to an Eastern college, Inburn's father was unable to accept it because he had to help support his parents —a responsibility which included helping to pay his older half brother's debts. Inburn describes his father now as a "phlegmatic, deliberate, steady-minded Welshman," noting the extreme contrast with his mother. "Father is pretty much of a failure in his own eyes," he comments, adding: "He's done pretty well as far as the world is concerned, though." Elsewhere he calls his father "a pillar in the community," adding parenthetically, "Small pillar. Small community." He describes "a great distance" between himself and his father, noting rather unenthusiastically, "We are friendly, though, except when my Greek side is up and I become disgusted with him and he annoyed at me."

His parents were married immediately after graduating from college, and both worked as high-school teachers, his father occasionally holding two jobs to supplement the family income. Inburn's account continues:

This, then, is the situation (one might say predicament) Inburn was born into. By 1938 his parents had saved enough money to have a house of their own . . . they hired an architect and had the place built just as they wanted. The father is acquiescent and the mother has excellent taste, and it came out beautifully.

The first memories Inburn has are of this house—door knobs, the carpeting, the bright yellow and white kitchen, the apple tree in the back yard, the plum trees in the field beyond. It was in a fairly undeveloped suburban section, staunchly middle class.

He was pretty as a child, a little plump, with his mother's eyes and grace and quite curly blond hair. Mama tells me proudly how people often stopped her on the street and exclaimed about him. The closest friend he had in preschool days was a girl his own age. . . . He had nearly no male companionship until he entered school in the first grade, a year early, and he was somewhat precocious (not alarmingly so). He seems to have been quite well adjusted, pretty well liked by everyone, quite well liked by his teachers.

Although he showed some intelligence, he was not remarkable. He liked his dog, his home, radio programs, soccer ball, brick walls, the janitor at school, trees, mornings, green lawns, walking, playing with toys, having imaginary adventures with the boy across the street in the orchard behind his house.

But as with most children his age, the Second World War profoundly affected Inburn:

When he was five years old, his father went into the war; he was gone for four years. In these four years he and his mother had the most intimate of relationships. They were one. Every thought, every action of one could be anticipated by the other. Somehow it seemed more than a mere mother-and-only-child relationship. We were in complete spiritual and mental and physical harmony with each other. Sometimes she was even shy with me. It was a strange relationship.

This description is as remarkable for the element of fantasy it contains as it is for the undeniable facts it must refer to. Inburn emphasizes the fusion of mother and child, the completeness of their understanding, their total anticipation of each other's thoughts and actions, their oneness. But in fact, such oneness and fusion can seldom occur after the first year of life; thereafter, mother and child assume an increasing separateness which usually eventuates in the child's independence as an adult. That Inburn so describes his relationship with his mother at ages five to nine suggests a strong element of wish, perhaps on the mother's part, but certainly on Inburn's, that all separateness between him and her be obliterated.

The end of the war brought a double dislocation for Inburn: first, his father returned; and, second, immediately thereafter he left teaching and moved with his family to a more lucrative and more bureaucratic position in a Detroit corporation, where he is now, in his son's words, "a kind of minor official." Inburn himself makes little of either of these facts; but without noting the connection, he dates several changes in his behavior from the age of nine or ten. Of his state of mind, he writes, "From about nine or ten on, he got to be very moody, thinking too much or reading the wrong kind of books. The moodiness was always well within himself, though, and he was seldom snappish, perverse, or irritable." Elsewhere, he dates the beginning of intermittent constipation from the same age. And in a supplement to his autobiography, when recounting his sexual development, he writes:

> I was disturbed when I was finally convinced that children came out of women. I didn't want to believe it. It seemed base and carnal at the time. . . . I thought that if people wished for children strongly enough they would just come. I was first enlightened by some slightly older boys [9–10?]; later and more clear-headedly by my parents, though sketchily [14].

After the move to Detroit, Inburn's family continued to travel during summer vacations, which he recalls with pleasure. But he also notes: "But the summers away made it impossible for Inburn to play baseball. In that red-blooded American community baseball was a big thing. I was a little estranged from my fellows because of this."

Expanding on his subsequent relationships with his peers, he says:

> I was accepted, but made people indignant toward me because they felt I was not only superior to them but scornful of them. All but one friendship pretty casual, red-blooded. Few quarrels. It didn't matter that much. Frequent periods of extreme moodiness and solitariness. Disenchantment—estrangement.

In sum, his father's return and the family move to Detroit seems to have been a turning point in Inburn's life, marking the beginning of his moodiness, his constipation, his estrangement, and even coinciding with his disgust at the "base and carnal" nature of birth. But all of this is our surmise, and Inburn himself does not note the coincidence of dates.

When he was fourteen, Inburn first became interested in girls, describing himself as "struck dumb" by a girl "with eyes as blue as his, and deeper, framed in a simple kerchief, staring into his face in an autumn dusk." He continues:

> Not long later sex reared its ugly head. He fell in with some of his male contemporaries. And boys can be dirty. They can be vile. A hundred times we talked about the girls at school, describing with great vigor their proportions, or lack of them. Girls with breasts the size of five-cent ice cream cones. . . .

He reports "excessive masturbation," accompanied by "great clouds of guilt," and characterizes his major current feelings about sex as "anxiety, shame, disgust." Not surprisingly, he has never had intercourse.

No further events of outward importance occurred in Inburn's life until he was a junior in high school, when he met Hal, who played a major role in the development of his outlook:

> Hal was, and is, a cynical young man. Cynical, profound, skeptical, sarcastic, highly intelligent, casual in his manner, yet intense in his questioning. And he always questioned. His cynicism infected me; he became my very good, my best friend, the best and closest I ever had. What were we cynical about? You, for one thing, and ourselves, our teachers, our world— cynical about the very act of existence. Or rather, the fact of existence, for with us it was a passive experience. We let time and values and actions pass over us like a wash, like a coating of wax. We both had been raised as agnostics, but it was a mild sort of agnosticism, an unthought-about agnosticism. First of all we turned everybody's religion upside down and we shouted. We were roundly condemned, but Hal more, since he shouted more, and louder. They went by the board and we began on our contemporaries and on our society. We attacked everything, every person, every institution, with a bitter tooth. Our long secret conversations were rank with contempt. We were full of a magnificent disdain, and we fed it with all the knowledge we could get (and what wouldn't fit we disregarded)— Kafka, D. H. Lawrence, Hume, Rousseau, Voltaire, Shaw, Jung, Freud, Marx. We read voraciously, but not the right things, and not enough.
>
> Hal is gone now. He went to college in Berkeley for a while, but now he is apparently irredeemably dissolute. . . . And he just doesn't give a damn. There was a great rift between us when I went to the college. He thinks that it will ruin me and now calls me a coward for not "finding out some things" on my own.
>
> Maybe he's right. If he means I'm becoming more complacent, I must plead guilty. As far as I can see, we both want knowledge; we want to know about the underpinnings of existence. I'm trying to do it through the institutions of my society, the college, for example. Hal is trying to "find out some things" on his own.

And on this inconclusive note, Inburn ends his autobiography.

In what he tells us about his life, certain themes and facts stand out. First is the marked contrast between his two parents. His mother emerges from his account as "Mediterranean," ambitious, energetic, high-strung, driving, volatile, passionate, and, in her son's eyes, sensual and physically attractive. Even her family is characterized as strong, tireless, simple, exuberant, and cruel. But he suggests that she has paid a high price in "complexity" and in a "delicate" constitution and psychology for her efforts in "making herself." Inburn's father, in contrast, comes from Celtic stock and from a long line of men who were dominated by their women. Recall how his chances for a better education were limited by having to pay his half brother's debts. And consider his move from his first love, teaching, to a more lucrative job, where he now considers himself a failure despite contrary community judgment. Without fully stating it, Inburn clearly implies his father's weakness vis-à-vis his mother's drive ("My father is acquiescent and my mother has excellent taste. . . ."). Further, it is clear that Inburn finds his mother's vivid sensuousness far more interesting than his father's phlegmatic and taciturn nature. All of this makes Inburn's father a man difficult to emulate; and we would anticipate that this fact, coupled with Inburn's unusual past relationship with his mother, would cause him difficulty.

In addition, several events stand out as having crucial importance in Inburn's life. One is his romanticized idyl with his mother during the war. The absence of any child's father for three or four years would be important to his development; but for Inburn, its importance must have been accentuated by his "unique, more than a mere mother-and-only-child relationship" with her. His friendship with Hal, too, was crucial. Until Hal, Inburn's life seems little different on the surface than that of most young men his age, "with his moodiness . . . always well within himself": Hal acted as a catalyst for Inburn's alienation. Inburn's initial unwillingness to accept the fact of birth, his inability to work through his not unusual first reactions to sex, and his current anxious attitudes are also worth underlining. Although many a young man in our society has difficulty in reconciling himself to the "facts of life," it is remarkable at the age of nineteen to list "anxiety, shame, and disgust" as the only three emotions which sex evokes. And finally, Inburn's relations with his peers follow a familiar pattern for an alienated young man. He was not good at the games which mattered in his "red-blooded" community, his fellows felt that he was scornful of them, and he felt "frequent periods of estrangement." Even when he became editor of the school paper, with his friend Hal, the two of them "managed to ruin it in three months."

But so far, we know only as much about Inburn as he himself knows and is willing to tell us. To understand the underlying dynamics of his alienation, we must turn to his stories in the Thematic Apperception Test, for in these he gives us a deeper and less conscious picture of the way he views the world.

THE CAT THAT SWALLOWED THE CANARY

Inburn's image of older women in the T.A.T. adds several new elements to the description of his mother in his autobiography. Confronted with a picture of a young man, a woman, and a girl with books in her hand (Card 2), he is reminded of D. H. Lawrence's book, *"Sons and Mothers"* [*sic*]. The older woman is described as "a rather possessive person," "obviously a strong figure," who feels "not quite like the cat that swallowed the canary but rather supercilious towards the girl and proud of her victories since the girl has . . . gone back to the family." Reminding himself of the play, *The Silver Cord,* he cannot decide whether the girl will be "finally engulfed by the mother at the end" or whether she will escape the mother's clutches. Or on Card 5, which shows an older woman peering around a half-opened door, he describes a woman spying on a boy. He says several times that the woman is "some kind of odd member of the household," that there is an

> . . . odd relationship between her and the boy. . . . There's something between them so they can't get close to each other. I said that there was something between them, but I didn't mean that, I mean there's *no* relationship between them because there's something blocking their getting closer to each other. She suspects on the part of the boy some monstrous and horrible act of some kind . . . something insidious and disgusting. Maybe it's some sexual act with himself, or maybe it's not that at all.

In the end, the boy, who, Inburn tells us, is not doing anything wrong at all, begins "to wonder whether there's something monstrous that *she* commits. . . . The boy would seriously consider looking in on her [in her room] sometime to find out. . . . But he never does . . . nothing comes of it."

Another story (Card 10) again involves a similar bond between a man and a woman.

> The girl . . . is a rather unstable character. . . . She is violently in love with the boy and has more or less thrown herself at him. The boy has been sort of disturbed at this . . . and finally decided to play along . . . it wouldn't hurt—why not? . . . He would be just about to make a proposal that they go to bed with each other. She will undoubtedly agree, and if he can close his eyes just a little more and block out that rather unpleasant nose of hers, he'll be delighted because well, why not? And she'll be delighted because she thinks . . . this particular device will certainly bind him to her more strongly. . . . Afterwards . . . the boy again feels wretched. . . . He feels that it was something that shouldn't have been done . . . for he has no real affection for her other than a kind of— not a man-to-man relationship exactly, but just a kind of friendly, some-

what intellectual relationship. . . . Other than that he has no real desire
for her, although he thinks she is a desirable girl . . . but then maybe he
has known her from too early an age or something, but she's just grown up
with the wrong relationship with him and nothing would ever be successful in that way. . . .

Here the woman is dominant and initiating, seeking with sex to bind the
man to her, while he feels that "maybe he has known her from too early
an age" for there to be anything but a platonic and "intellectual" friendship.

In another story (Card 7), he tells of a man who has committed a
minor transgression and who returns home to face his accusing mother.

It's not important to anyone with any reasonable perspective on the
situation. But both he and his mother have a funny perspective on the situation. Maybe something silly. . . . He will probably continue to do these
things wrong again in the future and his mother will continue to rail at him
until he's fifty years old, I imagine.

And, significantly, in yet another story, when he is trying to imagine
an especially unpleasant treatment for one of his characters, he recalls the
scene in *East of Eden* where one brother takes the other and "pushes him
. . . onto his mother, not in a sexual position but just makes them both
fall to the floor and rub against each other, which is somehow an incredibly vile and loathsome thing to happen. . . ."

In all of these references to women, Inburn intertwines two related
themes: the fear of domination and the fear of sexual closeness. His
heroes are caught in "odd relationships" with their mothers or other
women who dominate and control them, although at the same time the
heroes remain bound because of their "unreasonable perspective on the
situation." Mothers are seen as "possessive" and "not quite like the cat
that swallowed the canary, but. . . ." Parallel with this is the "peculiar"
nature of relationships between men and women, a "strangeness" which
appears related to the ambivalent fear of sexual intimacy. Thus, the
strange woman who spies on the boy suspects him among other things
of some "monstrous" sexual act with himself; but in the end, the boy, instead of proclaiming his innocence or leaving, considers spying on the
older woman as well. Throughout these stories there is "something between" men and women which prevents them from either intimacy or
satisfactory sex, "something" related to their having known each other
"from too early an age," perhaps something like the fear of the "most
incredibly vile and loathsome thing," incest. Unconsciously, then, Inburn
sees himself as bound to a possessive and even predatory mother, unable
to break away from her, and at the same time both tantalized and horrified by the sexual connotations of closeness to her.

THE FATHER, BEING ABSENT . . .

Just as he says less of his father than of his mother in his autobiography, so in his T.A.T. stories Inburn has less to say of older men than of women. Characteristic of all his stories is his reference to the father of the girl with the possessive mother (Card 2), of whom he notes, "The father, being absent, sort of leaves him out of my mind. . . . He was rather inconsequential." And when he does tell stories involving older men, his tales are usually facetious or cynical. Thus, he tells a caustic story about heaven (Card 15) in which it turns out that "Jehovah Himself is an incredibly ugly figure. . . . Regrettably the situation up there has been a little deceptively colored . . . sold a little better than it is by the angelic ad men and the established church." Or again, to a picture of an older man who outstretches his hand over a prone figure (Card 12), he tells of an "evil German-doctor type" who gets boys under his mystical spell and eats them: "He's just an evil fellow through and through." And perhaps closest to his conscious image of potentially helpful older men is a story of a kindly teacher who understands and wants to help the hero (Card 7). The young man

> thinks [the teacher] is a fine person and that there should be more like him. And yet somehow he is repelled by the picture of himself being like this, and he realizes that that's how it must be if he is to go along and follow along, drop in line, follow suit and so forth. . . . [The young man thinks of Marlowe and musical geniuses who died young, or] a man who lives with such vigor and strength and intensity that in twenty-five or thirty years he's burned himself out and drops dead because he hasn't anything else to do. . . . He wonders whether an intenser life like that wouldn't be a better thing than just fobbing along course by course and day by day, the way the venerable and openly respectable [teacher] has done.

Inburn's anger at older males breaks through fully in only one story (Card 18). He starts a facetious account of the president of Harvard College, who on a pretext sneaks away from his wife to buy a pizza pie at a nearby tavern. The president is, however, set upon by a three-armed man who has been installing sewer connections, and "this dreadful three-armed man with a dirty sleeve on each arm of his jacket" rubs against him in that "incredibly vile and loathsome way" which, as we have seen earlier, Inburn associates with a son in sexual position with his mother. When Inburn fully expresses aggression at a paternal figure, he does it in what he makes clear is the most disgusting and degrading way possible. But though this is the most direct instance, Inburn always sees to it that older men, when not omitted from the action, are debased, defiled, or ridiculed. Paternal figures are not what they seem: the doctor is an evil hypnotist; Jehovah has been oversold by the heavenly ad men; the president must sneak pizza pies and is vilely humiliated by the three-armed man from the sewer; and even the venerable teacher, for all of his understanding, turns out to be dull and pedestrian. But most important is Inburn's comment that "the father, being absent, sort of leaves him out of my mind."

EXISTENTIAL PESSIMISM

Many of Inburn's stories imply a kind of pessimistic, existential world view, stressing the futility of endeavor, the intensification of life, the emptiness of love, and the desirable role of detached observer and commentator. In one story (Card 14), the hero, after a long and arduous climb up the inside of a dark tower, at last pushes open the windows:

> He looks out on the surrounding country and somehow he doesn't like the view very much. He doesn't think it's much of an accomplishment after all. He thought he would really get something out of it, but the country just looks farther away from the way it was on the ground. And there's no change in it; there's nothing he can see farther from his vantage point. So I'll just leave him there standing looking out of the window. . . .

The arduous effort has proved futile: the view is merely more distant.

In the story of the kindly teacher, Inburn has wondered whether it would not be better to "burn himself out" in twenty-five or thirty years rather than lead a dull, plodding life. To Card 17, showing a man climbing a rope, he tells a story of a hero who actually does die an early death: he is a circus acrobat in a land where there is

> . . . nothing but side shows and other circuses. [The hero] is in the springtime of life, as many have undoubtedly said, free and free-limbed. He is strong and not only strong but proficient in acrobatics and light, not a clumsy kind of strength but not delicate exactly either. He's refined his talents which are nearly entirely bodily. . . . There is no such thing as intellectualism in this delightful land. He is free from any foreboding thoughts but . . . here he is just before his death. After doing a stupendous trick from which he gets a great roar from the crowd . . . he falls off the rope, not meaning to . . . falls a long way down and kills himself with a smile on his face . . . with no regrets on the way down. . . . Afterwards the crowd . . . does not gasp, is not horrified. . . . There is no great tension. . . . Things just go on as usual. They don't take him away at all. [The crowd envies him] because here is a man in the prime of youth, who is in tune with life, who can get up in the morning and sing and fall asleep at night without a wrinkle on his brow and has done this all his life—he's never known death or old age. And his life has been made more perfect by annihilation. . . . He will never know the infirmities of old age in all their various forms—in the mind, in the darkening sight, and the creaking body. . . . And then the show is over, and people pour out into the little streets and passageways that a carnival has. And then things go on as usual.

Here Inburn extols a purely unreflective and physical existence and returns to his earlier value of dying in the height of life.

Another story stresses the same value in another way. Inburn tells of a pious boy who self-righteously keeps himself apart from the grossness, murderousness, and sensuality of the world (Card 8) :

> But the boy has refined himself away to nothing, kept out of any sort of relations with people . . . and for this reason he has got so far away from everything that he indeed is not living life as much as the people who are murdering. . . . It's better to murder, which is just an act, than to make no acts at all. . . . It seems more desirable right now, if one must choose, to choose the part of those horrid old men in the background cutting up other horrid old men than to be the snotty over-refined, completely ineffectual boy who is, in fact, wasting his life much more than the men in the background are.

The gratuitous act, even if it be murder, is better than no action at all.

Even the most optimistic and forward-looking of Inburn's stories has something of the same "existential" quality. His hero in one story (Card 9) is said to be in some way "different" from his bum-companions:

> Maybe some day he will be a kind of spokesman for this group of people. Maybe he'll write a book about them, or maybe he will try to portray them on the stage, or maybe he'll try to paint them. . . . He's different because he's not only a complete product of his times and his society, and so forth, but he's a man that doesn't come along very often . . . a man who can understand the society that he's in—which is probably the greatest trick in the book—who can look at himself in context and can understand completely what's going on, get it in the right perspective . . . understand why he is there, not in the great metaphysical and religious sense, but why the social forces have put him where he is. . . . At least he has this latent in him, the power to bring this out and put it down for others to understand. . . . And he will write a book . . . it'll be a good book, I imagine. . . . It's not a social criticism, it's not that he'll be making a plea. . . . He's not unhappy that these people don't have the best food in the world, that they have to sleep on the ground like that. It's not a matter of that; it's a judgmentless kind of interpretation and explanation rather than an emotional and sentimental *Uncle Tom's Cabin* business.

Here Inburn doubtless speaks of himself and his own best potential; and this story has an affirmation and hope lacking in all the other nineteen. But even here he rejects "judgment," "social criticism," "making a plea," and any "emotional and sentimental *Uncle Tom's Cabin* business." In other words, morality has no conscious place in his scheme of things.

Consonant with the lack of any inherent meaning or values in life is Inburn's image of love. Long-range intimacy between two people is never mentioned, and the act of sex is empty. In one story (Card 13) the hero is walking down a New York street:

> It is late in the afternoon, and in the afternoon those brownstones take on a particularly remarkably intense russet color. It seems to stand out and

glow, almost. . . . He notices a girl . . . looking out the window on the second floor of one of the brownstones. . . . She happens to look at him, and he glances up at her and, just by chance, their eyes meet naturally. And he stands there a long minute, just looking up, oddly. And she doesn't divert her eyes, and it's a kind of a very long instant that stays in one's mind. . . . There's something about the whole scene that entrances them both. . . . He keeps staring at the window. And in a few moments she appears below, behind the door, which has got a kind of curtain in front of it and an iron grill. And then she opens the door, and after a moment he crosses the street and goes up the steps . . . the polished white steps. She's rather thin and not good looking—drab hair and a very cheap dress. . . . And without a word but "with eyes on the double string," or whatever that quote is from Donne, they go up the stairs to a . . . kind of single room. The shade is pulled down and there's a very warm color on the window shade, even from the inside. . . .

Finally, after all, they fall asleep. And he's awakened when it's dark at night by the window shade flapping, with some wind and some rain coming in, and the cold air wakes him up. It doesn't wake her. Now there's a light in the window shade, too, which is the street light from outside shining in, which is rather bright. . . . He gets up and dresses and doesn't do anything. Leave a note? It would seem a little ludicrous. He puts on his tie and coat and leaves. The hero eventually finds his way into a church, and the story ends.

In this *nouvelle vague* story, Inburn makes the lovers silent, neither is described except in externals; they have no relationship; the man leaves the woman without saying good-bye; and throughout, the narrator is more interested in eyes, lights, architectural details, and colors than in the man and woman.

All of these stories entail the same denial of meaning in life apart from unreflective action, perception, and sensation. At worst, Inburn's heroes are Raskolnikovs who would rather murder than do nothing; intermediately, existential acrobats who die happy at the acme of their flight, strangers who love and depart without speaking, or strivers whose efforts are futile; and at best, mere observers of their world who firmly refuse to judge, influence, or change it. All of this is an elaboration in fantasy of Inburn's earlier more intellectual assertion that as a stranger in a foreign city, his best plan is to "see the sights" and to accumulate "the most varied, the most valuable, and most significant set of sense experiences it is possible to take in."

THE RAGE TO RE-ENTER

Inburn's autobiography begins with a description of him as "screaming and red-faced, loath to leave his insensible sanctuary." Here he states unequivocally what is the major theme of his life and the dominant motif of his T.A.T. stories: his longing to return to that first claustrum of security; his rage and desolation at being expelled; his continual sense thereafter of being a stranger in a foreign city. More than half of Inburn's stories contain some variant on the theme of being inside or outside, beginning with the first card, where he tells of a son of professional musicians who smashes his violin as a "violent rebellion." The father is restrained from "throwing him out in the street" because of "certain ties that he has—certain obligations to the family and the community"; but the boy will thereafter be "an estranged member" of the family, and "he'll probably leave his family at an early age and won't be associated with them any more." In his second story, too, the central conflict is about leaving the girl's home and getting away from the mother who is "not quite like the cat that swallowed the canary, but. . . ."

Having as it were introduced his main theme, in a variation whereby the hero *chooses* rebellion and estrangement, Inburn states it in almost pure form in the third story. Here he tells of a student walking down the street at night on his way home from the library, where he had read a book which disturbed him. He stopped in front of

> . . . an old gray house, one of those turn-of-the-century jobs with a slate roof on it and this phony Greek revival business with all the pillars and the stuff in wood on the porch. He stops on the steps of the house. . . . He noticed one of the windows on either side of the door. The door was in the middle and there was a large window on either side. It was dark inside the little hallway. . . . He stood there looking at the window for ten or fifteen minutes, with this unusual, indescribable ding-batty he has in his hand. . . . It could be any kind of odd piece of iron that he somehow picked up. And he stood there a long time, sort of standing there contemplating smashing the window. And if he could have just smashed it and gone away, throwing the thing through, or just smashed it holding it in his hand, it would have been all right. . . . He would have got whatever it was inside out of him. But he could not force himself to smash the damn thing. He stood there, as I say, for a long time, standing there very "still and stiff" with his arms down at his side and finally walked away, walked down the steps. . . . I remember in Herodotus the story of tying the woman's legs together just when she's beginning to be pregnant and then letting things go on as they did . . . probably the most exquisite torture that could be devised. Maybe this is the same sort of idea that he's got something enormous, monstrous inside of him, but he can't get it out. He could have got it out by smashing the window but he still got it in him. . . .

In contrast to the two previous stories, in which his heroes sought to escape home and mother, here the hero tries to break his way back into a house. Unable to force an opening with the "ding-batty" in his hand, he is left "something enormous, monstrous inside of him," which he associates with a child within his mother's womb. (Recall his facetious remark, "I guess I'd have us all go back to the womb.") Note, too, the detail with which Inburn describes the architecture of the house, emphasizing the central door and the windows, which mirror the hero's preoccupation with looking.

From this story alone we would have grounds for surmising that Inburn's "violent rebellion" and self-imposed estrangement overlays a deeper wish to re-enter his "insensible sanctuary" and that his "estrangement" was not only chosen by him, but first forced upon him by a closed house which he cannot re-enter. In the primitive logic of fantasies and dreams, houses, wombs, maternal warmth, and women's bodies can stand for each other; and the regular symmetry of the face parallels the configurations of the house façade: the windows are for seeing from and into, the door is the mouth of entry. In such equations, to look into a window, to gaze into the eyes, to enter the door of the house, or to re-enter the surrounding warmth of a mother's arms become equivalent. These interpretations are supported in other stories. Through them all runs the same preoccupation with seeing, gazing, and looking—especially with a kind of obsessive standing and staring into the eyes of another or the windows of a house. (Recall his first girl friend, "with eyes as blue as his, and deeper . . . staring into his face in an autumn dusk.") In the previously discussed story of the silent lovers, the descriptions of the façade of the house, of looking into the window and gazing into the girl's eyes, the account of the light that comes in the window—these narratively extraneous elements overpower the ostensibly central theme of the relation of man and woman. And in the end of that story, the hero again stands looking, "much longer than he stood looking at the window," at the church which he finally enters. In this story, it is as if Inburn's seeking could finally be solaced neither by sex nor by looking, but only by entering a church, whose secure walls signify asylum. And even with Inburn's writer-hero the highest form of perception is looking at the world around him and understanding it.

As counterpoint to these stories in which the hero is outside an enclosure looking in, Inburn tells three in which the hero manages to get inside and look out. In one previously mentioned (Card 14), he is inside a

. . . tower that goes very far up with a turret on it. . . . He enters through the door and finds darkness is throughout the place. It's a vertical maze: it goes up instead of spreading out. The tower, incidentally, has no windows except one toward the very top, on the other side of the building from the door he entered by, so that he doesn't know it's there. He goes up and all is in darkness, and he is feeling his way around. Finally, he works his way all through the day and the next night and gets to the top, gets into a final room where there is a casement window, but he can't see it. It's closed, and there's no light coming through. . . . [He] finally comes to the window, which he feels out and finally gets the handle of. . . . He's tired and hungry and exhausted and covered with sweat. With his last bit of force, he pushes open the two windows one with each hand, and the bright light of the early morning streams in on him. . . . The window is facing the east, and he's blinded for a few minutes. . . . The feeling he has on

his skin and on his silk shirt is like climbing up—how many flights it is up
that circular thing?—the Statue of Liberty, and finally looking out her head,
out of one of those windows and usually getting a cold from it. He looks out
on the surrounding country and doesn't like the view very much. He doesn't
think it's much of an accomplishment after all. . . .

Here the identification of the inside of a building and the inside of a
woman's body is explicit, although, at the same time, Inburn seems to
wonder if his obsessive search for a way back in is doomed to failure—
perhaps the view from within is really no better than the view outside.
The scene calls to mind a small child's wonder at his mother's height,
his curiosity about whether what she sees is different from what he sees,
and his fantasy that perhaps he could enter her body and see through
her eyes.

But in two other stories, the view from within is unqualifiedly good.
One story (Card 18) tells of

> . . . a cheerful presentation of Noah's Ark . . . the two little windows,
> sort of homey portholes with curtains. There are two comical little ani-
> mals—in a pair, of course—looking out . . . animals who have got a nice
> berth on the ark and they're enjoying the view. . . . [He wonders why
> there is a smokestack in the picture.] The clouds would be all sorts of fan-
> tastic colors—purple. . . . The water, of course, would be blue and the
> ship would be all sorts of colors. The animals would be brown, I imagine.
> They've been sailing for a long time. And I suppose the most remarkable
> thing is that they just keep sailing. They don't land anywhere. The water
> never recedes; that's the most pleasant part about it.

Inburn's "cheerful presentation" here has "comical little animals" looking out on the never-receding waters in a childhood idyl and happy because there is no landing, no receding waters to break up the happy
communion of son and mother. With its bright colors and "comical"
animals, the story is reminiscent of a childhood fairy tale, covertly expressing the child's wish to sail away forever inside the life-filled ark,
which represents the secure warmth of his mother's surrounding presence.

But perhaps the most remarkable portrayal of a full return to
claustral security, coupled with gazing out, is found in Card 16, in which
Inburn manufactures both picture and story:

> Well, the scene is rather dark, streaked with light. It's under water, very
> warm water, although it's apparently a sea. . . . This missile most re-
> sembles a one-man submarine. It's propelled by a very unbulky kind of
> machinery. It's just very simple, cigar-shaped, I suppose. . . . It's angling
> down toward the bottom right-hand corner of the card. . . . The water is
> uniformly dark . . . since the surface is at this time considerably far above
> the top of the card.
>
> And inside this thing is a face which you can see. In a kind of window in
> front, a man is stretched out. Well, the thing is small. It's only about eight
> feet long, perhaps even shorter than that. He's on a cushion inside, a long

cushion. His hands are at his sides. He's on his stomach, with his chin not resting on anything, looking forward, looking out into the water. And although we can see the thing, it's very dark to him. He can see, oh, perhaps some of those small fish that glow, but that's about all. That's the only thing that lights up, that lights up the scene. As I said, the water is very warm. This is hard to illustrate, but it's that, and heavy. . . . This thing was custom-built for him, fitted for his size and height. And he does have controls. . . . He can go up and down and to the left and to the right, though there's no change in speed.

This is the fulfillment of something this young man has always inanely wanted to do since he was a very little boy. In fact, he pictured himself doing just this when he was perhaps seven or eight or nine or ten years old. . . . The idea occurred to him once when he was in his bedroom stretched out on his bed in this kind of position with his elbows up supporting him, and it was dark and very hot in the room. The room had grown slowly dark—he didn't notice the absence of light from the windows until it was all gone. And then this idea occurred to him, that of slipping through these heavy, silent, liquid seas in a very warm and utterly comfortable state. And he was eating some crackers out of a box. . . . This was a very pleasurable sort of thing.

As a matter of fact, in the picture the young man is . . . eating crackers from a small box and falling down into the ocean. He didn't direct his life toward doing this, but circumstances just sort of permitted it. He remembered his urge and had enough resources, enough leisure time to do this thing. He's probably not going to surface, just go down, down, and down. Somehow once he got into the water, it became not the Atlantic Ocean or the Mediterranean, but it was just *a* sea, *the* sea, with nothing on the surface, with no continents to go back to . . . and the place not being there from which he set off anymore. . . . This is the kind of extended moment which he wouldn't mind going on with forever—which he probably will, just continuing down into the dark water. . . .

If Inburn were consciously searching for an analogy on the intra-uterine condition, on the symbiosis of mother and child, he would be hard pressed to find a better one. Even the age at which this fantasy first occurred to the hero is significant, for it was at "seven or eight or nine or ten" that his father returned to break the oneness of mother and son, and inevitably to awaken a powerful wish for this unity to be restored. And how better restore it than by re-entering that sanctuary from which, as Inburn had recently learned with revulsion, he had been born?

Thus, the central and unifying themes in Inburn's fantasy life center on the rage to re-enter the "insensible" sanctuary he had with his mother. So intense is this wish that it surpasses the desire for a more adult intimacy with her or any other woman, and it is expressed symbolically as a craving to re-enter the body of the woman who bore and nurtured him. That the re-entry and fusion are to be accomplished through the eyes, through looking, through the communion of a gaze, and through an often obstructing window is doubly understandable. The infant first perceives his mother when he gazes into her eyes while nursing; and thereafter, for most people, to "look deeply into someone's eyes" remains a symbol of that communion which anticipates and forever thereafter surpasses all mere speech. But also, for Inburn, the eyes are the organ of the body farthest from that "base and carnal" place from which infants truly emerge; and for a young man who can identify himself with a "man from the sewer" and who feels only "anxiety, shame, and disgust" about sex, communion through the eyes is far less "vile" than that other communion which adult men and women can know and by which men regain at least temporary sanctuary in women. Indeed, the story of the Greek revival house with the hero's "indescribable ding-batty" in his hand, the tale of silent lovers in which the empty act of sex is followed by entering a church, the intrusive smokestack on Noah's ark, and the cigar-shaped submarine suggest that Inburn's sexuality is at times an irrelevant intrusion on his central fantasies about women.

THE OUTSIDER WHO WOULD BE INSIDE

We now have learned enough of the central themes in Inburn's life to enable us to try to reconstruct the origins and current functions of his alienation. In any such reconstruction it is well to keep in mind that the principle of parsimony seldom applies in explaining individual lives; rather, only when we have begun to understand the subtle interweaving of themes, the "overdetermination" of any single act, belief, or fantasy, and the multiple functions that every dream, wish, behavior, and philosophy serves, do we begin to understand something of an individual. Thus, even with the best of intentions, the psychologist must continually oversimplify, and by singling out one set of alienated beliefs and outlooks for special explanation, I here oversimplify Inburn the more.

To begin with, the outward circumstances of Inburn's life provided a setting within which his alienation became more than casually possible. As an only child, he was destined to experience and feel more intensely about his parents than would a child who had siblings or an extended family to dissipate the concentration of his affections and angers. Further, his father's absence for the four crucial years of the war must inevitably have intensified his pre-existing feelings about his mother. And then, too, an American son of a third-generation Greek mother and a father of northern European stock is very likely to note a sharp temperamental contrast between his two parents and their families. But these assured facts only provide a setting for the more central psychological events and fantasies which underlie Inburn's estrangement.

For further explanations, we must assume that Inburn's account of his parents is in many ways correct, at least as it describes their impact on him. His mother, as we have noted, emerges as a possessive, ambitious, driving woman, who, however, once she stopped teaching, devoted herself exclusively to domestic life. And at the same time, Inburn describes her as moody, passionate, highly sensual, and physically attractive. The T.A.T. story in which a woman seeks to bind an unwilling man to her through sex again suggests that Inburn sees his mother as not only possessive, but as emotionally seductive, seeking from her son a kind of emotional fulfillment he could not provide and perhaps unconsciously attempting to use her attractiveness to bind him to her. Thus, even as a small child, Inburn probably felt torn between his dependency on his mother and his enjoyment of their extraordinary closeness, on the one hand, and, on the other, her possessiveness and her unconscious needs that he be more to her than a son.

With a strong and vital husband, a possessive and seductive mother's effects on her son are usually limited; indeed, with such a husband, a woman is less likely in the first place to seek excessive fulfillment in her relationship with her children. But Inburn's father, at least as Inburn perceives him, was neither strong nor vital. "Taciturn," "phlegmatic," and "acquiescent," he had probably been better prepared by his own childhood for the role of the dominated than the dominant. Inburn also suggests that his father was disappointed with his own life, perhaps partly because he "acquiesced" by leaving his original vocation for a better-paying, if less idealistic, job. And, finally, one can only wonder how the father felt about being denied an excellent education, about struggling in the Depression, or about the war which took him away from his family, work, and country for four years. In short, Inburn gives us little ground for believing that his father had the zestful qualities to offset the mother's drive and sensuousness.

Even without Inburn's father's long absence during the war, such parents would have made for a rivalrous family triangle of singular intensity and dubious outcome. More often than we generally acknowledge, husbands must struggle with their children for their wives' affections, especially with only sons, who may draw the full force of excessive maternal devotion. And if the wife should come to find her husband dull or a failure in life, then the outcome is especially difficult. But in Inburn's case, the wish to supplant his father must have been overwhelmingly reinforced by the latter's sudden departure for the war. Few five-year-olds could resist the temptation unconsciously to consider such a four-year absence a token of their own triumph. We know something of the ensuing relationship from Inburn's idyllic account of his "unique" understanding with his mother; and we learn more from his T.A.T. stories in which the central relationships are peculiar intimacies between young men and women, with fathers and older men either absent or somehow debased and scorned out of significant existence.

I have already noted the component of fantasy in Inburn's recollections of this idyl, which he endows with qualities more like those of an infant-mother symbiosis than those of the relationship of a five-year-old child with his mother. In part, this symbiotic relationship must have been real, perhaps encouraged by his mother's increased need of and responsiveness to him in her husband's absence. But some of it was clearly a fantasy, and time alone would have probably sufficed to break the illusion of perfect understanding and oneness. But his father's sudden return exacerbated, underlined, and made more traumatic Inburn's probably dawning awareness that he was less and less his mother's pretty little child and more and more a separate person, alone in crucial ways. It is from the age of nine or ten that he dates a variety of new feelings of moodiness and estrangement, and it is to about the same age that his submarining hero traces his wish to slip forever downward in the deep warm sea. Repeatedly, Inburn, as a college sophomore, expresses or symbolizes this overpowering wish for fusion with the maternal, for a blissful state without consciousness, for an "insensible sanctuary"—the wish, in the last analysis, to be like a tiny infant in his mother's arms, who by gazing into her eyes enters her enveloping protection. What time and his increasing age had not accomplished in destroying the possibility of asylum, his father's return completed.

For most children, such a loss—which is after all universal—can be assimilated without excessive backward yearning because there are active pulls into a future seen as better than what must be abandoned. For a boy, such forces are usually embodied in his father, who by the mere fact of an admired existence implicitly teaches his son that it is worthwhile to grow up to be a man. When there is no such father, when the mother's excessive devotion to her son undermines her mate's relative worth in the son's eyes, or when the father considers himself a failure and thus implicitly denies that the son should become a man like him—then the son's incentives to leave gracefully his ties with his mother are diminished, and physiological growth goes unmatched by psychological readiness.

For Inburn, then, there was an especially great deal to lose and especially little reason to give it up. Once he had been the apple of his mother's eye, fused at least in fantasy to her answering gaze, the child with whom she had been so strangely intimate as to be shy. In his desire to retain his claustral estate, however, he had, without wishing it, lost it and was left instead with a possessive and sensuous mother and no father. Small wonder that his father's return brought moodiness, brooding, and constipation and that when, during the same year, he learned the facts of birth, they seemed "base and carnal" compared with his own developing fantasies of regaining his former sanctuary. Henceforth, Inburn was to consider himself an outcast, dreaming of an Eden from which he perhaps dimly recalled he came, forever comparing his exiled realities of a dominating, seductive mother and a taciturn, psychologically absent father with the cozy cabin in Noah's Ark and the down-slipping submarine in the warm sea.

But so far, his inner feelings of estrangement were "always well within himself," and he was "seldom snappish, perverse, or irritable." In the development of a more overt alienation, two further facts are crucial. The first is Inburn's sexual maturation and its accompanying psychological changes, which he describes in his scornful account of "sex's ugly head" and the "dirtiness" and "vileness" of adolescent boys. Few boys in our culture, however enlightened by their parentage, can pass through adolescence without further reassessing their closeness with their mother; and for many the acute fear of any sexual intimacy with anyone like her continues throughout life. But such fears, normally a part of development in American society, can reach panic proportions in a youth who brings into adolescence an unresolved need to enter a woman not as a man but as a child seeking shelter. When coupled with a prior notion that sex and birth are base and carnal (undoubtedly transmitted in part by parents), deep anxieties about sex can last long into adulthood. And finally, if, as for Inburn, the prospect of becoming a man like one's father is deeply disconcerting and implicitly discouraged by mother and father alike, then the advent of manhood is even more disruptive. Adolescence must have further complicated Inburn's already tortuous relationship with his mother, adding to her possessiveness the new threat of that "most loathesome thing," incest.

In all young men and women the advent of adulthood releases immense new energies and potentials, which in most are greatly involved in establishing new intimacies with the opposite sex. Such new learning is seldom smooth; but when it is severely blocked by unresolved needs and frustrations from the past, it takes only a slight catalyst—or sometimes no catalyst at all—to transform these energies into rage, scorn, and aggression, often symbolically directed against those who have stood in the way of full adulthood. It was Hal, then, who provided the second crucial fact, the catalyst and vehicle for the transformation of Inburn's inward moodiness into an open and scornful alienation. From Hal, or with his help and encouragement, he learned cynicism, disdain, scorn, and contempt for the "superstructure of tin and shit and kite-paper" which represented society to them. Hal became for Inburn a kind of antisocial superego, so much so that Inburn put his discontents with college into Hal's mouth, and when he finally left college, it was not to return to his parents, but to live with Hal and demonstrate that he had not, in fact, become "complacent." Further, with Hal he learned the vocabulary and logic of his instincts, culling from the works of the most alienated writers of the last two alienated centuries the diction of estrangement. The sense of alienation and exile, the rage and frustration which might have found outlet in delinquency in a youth of less intelligence, perceptiveness, and articulateness, in Inburn were aimed at targets sanctioned by usage and made meaningful by their personal symbolism, and thus found expression within a historical tradition. What had been contained was now released, and Inburn became overtly alienated.

Inburn's alienation in word and deed thus serves multiple purposes. Most centrally, it rationalizes his felt condition as an outcast from his first sanctuary: the feeling of exile is generalized, universalized into the human condition, as in his tale of the travelers in the endless and featureless countryside. Furthermore, by condemning the society and the forms of society from which he himself came, Inburn states the partial truth that there is no sanctuary and that he does not wish to return. And by attacking society and all its authoritative concomitants, Inburn indirectly criticizes his father and all he stands for: conventionality, being a "small pillar in a small community," being "complacently middle class," perhaps even being a "failure in his own eyes." Inburn's grievance against his father is a double one: his father disrupted the idyl with his mother, and —probably more important—he was not strong enough to offer anything better than the mother-son intimacy that he disrupted. Inburn has accounts to render, and render them he does in his alienation.

MAJOR THEMES OF THE ALIENATED

In Inburn we see most of the features common to other alienated Ss, but in exacerbated form, writ large, as the dominant, even obsessive concerns of his life. It is rare to find a subject about whom we have said so much when we have said that he is alienated; in many other young men themes of alienation take their place, sometimes a secondary place, alongside unrelated motifs of equal or greater importance. But with Inburn alienation forms the core of his personality; and estrangement, exclusion, disaffection, and the rage to return are the nuclear themes of his life. Thus, in summarizing his main themes, we can at the same time state schematically a number of the leitmotivs of alienation in other young Americans.

Expulsion from Early Oral Paradise

The fantasies of alienated young men abound in idyllic references to earliest childhood or the modes of experience most typical of them. And at the same time stories of starvation, separation from the sources of supply, and the disaster which follows such separation are equally frequent. Unconsciously, the alienated look back to early infancy as the model for all later satisfactions and implicitly find all later relationships wanting insofar as they lack the passivity, claustral security, and effortless gratification of infancy.

Fixation on Childhood Modes of Experience

Paralleling the fantasy of an interrupted infantile idyl is a fixation on childhood modes of perception, apperception, and experience in general. Concretely this involves an effort to cut through conventional schemata of apperception to a mode of experience more direct, immediate, and "whole" than normal adult experience. Alienated subjects find Schachtel's concept of "allocentricity" appealing when familiar with it and seek means of heightening sensation to allow a breakthrough to less categorized awareness of their surroundings.[2]

Pyrrhic Oedipal Victory

Like Inburn, many alienated young men show signs of having partially supplanted their fathers in their mothers' affections. The consequence, however, is usually highly unsatisfactory for the subject, in that he is left with a debased image of his father, a mother whose demands he is incapable of meeting, and an excessive fear of his own aggression (which he believes proved so effective). Since the mother is usually perceived as the more powerful of the parents, these young men tend to identify in part with her and strongly to resist identification with the father.

Discontinuous Parental Images

As a result of this inverse resolution of Oedipal rivalries, most alienated subjects have sharply discontinuous images of parental figures. Women are ambivalently seen either as nurturing, supplying, bountiful providers, who shelter and solace, or else as binding, restrictive, limiting, emasculating controllers, who bar the way to full masculinity. Paternal figures are portrayed either as archaic, pre-Oedipal fathers, destructive and unassailable, or, more often, as weak, debased, defeated, dependent, and passive creatures, with whom the subject resolutely refuses to identify. One of the dangers about relationships with either men or women is that one can have little confidence that they will remain unchanged; hence, alienated subjects often see nurturant women as becoming possessive and controlling or apparently strong men as being basically weak and fraudulent.

Distrust

Given a world in which initial images of the crucial male and fe-

2 Ernest J. Schachtel, *Metamorphosis* (New York: Basic Books, Inc., 1959), Chap. 5.

male figures had to be drastically revised, the alienated subject has an implicitly and usually explicitly distrustful view of the world. All appearances are suspect, and not until he has shown the underlying sham, hypocrisy, deceit, self-interest, egocentricity, and resentment in others does he rest content that he has struck bottom. "Reductionism" and "subspection," coupled with an anxious probing for flaws and underlying chicaneries, characterize his intellectual style.

Existential Pessimism

Usually arrived at spontaneously, but sometimes reinforced by reading, the alienated subject's world view resembles that of the most pessimistic existentialists. The universe is inherently chaotic and unpredictable, as are human relations, which are based on mutual exploitation and appropriation. Men live in a Hobbesian state of nature, restrained from exploitative egocentricity only by their fear of punishment. The future looks gloomy, and the state of the world is itself ample ground for acute anxiety—the lot of all men honest enough to face things as they are. Intimacy is impossible, as men are separated by their self-centeredness and their inability to understand each other. Religion, conventional values, social institutions, culture itself—all are arbitrary games played by the conventional and fearful in order to blind themselves to the deeper absurdity of the world.

Exacerbated Identity Crisis

One way of characterizing the late adolescence of alienated young men is in terms of Erikson's discussion of the pathology of identity crisis.[3] They show many of the symptoms mentioned by Erikson: a diffusion of time and inability to work at assigned tasks; a "rock-bottom" attitude combining the search for a viable foundation for identity with the desire to regress to the states of early childhood; role diffusion; the choice of a negative identity (becoming all that they have been warned not to become) ; the coupling of intense repudiation with an inability to repudiate selectively; ideological "totalism" in the form of a refusal to allow any possible validity to outlooks different from their own; and an all-or-nothing attitude, especially with regard to participation in conventional society. In a highly selected college population, alienation is perhaps the most likely form for an exacerbated identity crisis to take.

Confusions of Sexual Identification

As might be expected from their family background, virtually all

[3] Erik H. Erikson, "Identity and the Life Cycle," *Psychological Issues*, I (1959), No. 1, 122–146.

alienated subjects show signs of confused sexual identification, with the central conflict usually centering on the simultaneous desire for passivity (being done to) and masculine sexuality. Thus, the preferred heterosexual fantasies of alienated subjects tend to have a strong passive component; and some subjects are unusually drawn to homosexuality or to relationships with children which do not require active masculinity.

The Failure of Repression

Alienated subjects do not and often cannot repress unacceptable feelings, fantasies, and impulses. On the contrary, they are keenly aware of their socially unconventional and taboo instincts, and they make it a matter of policy to admit them. Thus on personality tests, as in conversation, they defiantly admit neurotic symptoms; and in interpersonal situations they report more unpleasant feelings than they demonstrate in behavior. Creative ability and a capacity for artistic control enable some subjects to cope with the flood of disturbing feelings; but in most others the flood is threatening, only partly controlled, and it sometimes leads to feelings of unreality, to a sensation of being the plaything of irrational forces and fantasies, and to bizarre ideation and unsublimated primary process thinking. These alienated subjects suggest strongly how much repression, ego restriction, and conventional schematization of experience is necessary in our culture (and perhaps in any) for "normal" functioning. At the same time, however, alienated subjects differ from more selfpunitive neurotics by virtue of their outward projection of blame, by universalizing their own into the human condition, and by sharp rejection of those who see the world in more conventional terms.

Alienation: The Rejection of Conventional Adult Commitments

The unifying characteristic of all alienated subjects is their rejection, more or less complete, of adult values, groups, institutions, and roles as conventionally defined in America. These are students who think of themselves as deliberately choosing a deviant outlook; and although they are usually deeply and openly unhappy, they aver that others would be unhappy, too, if they but saw the same things with the same honesty. This alienation fulfills many simultaneous functions: unconsciously, it is often a description of their own felt condition as outcasts from Eden; it provides an ideology for attacking apparently authoritative ideas, constitutions, and principles which might prove untrustworthy; it reflects a fear of commitment to an adult male role which, as instanced by their own fathers, has often proved inadequate and inconsistent; and, finally, in important respects, it contains major truths, though often overstated, about life in America.

THE ROOTS OF ALIENATION

A young man like Inburn would be of limited interest if he spoke for only a small number of overprivileged and overintellectual young men. But these notes on his sophomore year, I think, illustrate the extreme of a trend which exists in more moderate degree in a great many men and women, young and old. Insofar as this is true, we must search for the roots of alienation not only in the individual case histories and fantasies of alienated lives but in the common social, generational, and ideological backgrounds of these lives. Even a partial delineation of this background would be impossible here, but the mention of a few of the broad historical forces underlying alienation may correct that individualistic bias which occurs if one studies lives in a social and historical vacuum.

Most immediately, Inburn himself notes the impact of the "ravages of the Depression" on his parents' initial poverty and perhaps even on the fact that they had but one child. Further, the Second World War took his father away from the family for four crucial years and thus facilitated the development of that "more than a mere mother-and-only-child relationship" of such vital importance in his life. And lastly, when Inburn's father was lured away from his first love, teaching, by the higher salary scales of Detroit's burgeoning bureaucracies, he followed another national social trend and added to his son's scorn for him as a man who is "a failure in his own eyes." In all these respects, the press of history on Inburn's life was immediate, direct, and shared by countless others.

But behind these concrete impingements of social history are other developments less tangible but no less important. For one, consider the contrast, repeated a million times over, between the Greek restaurant-keepers and the midwestern farmers, who were Inburn's grandparents, and Inburn's own life as a disaffected college student. The world in these three generations has changed so vastly as to be unrecognizable to his grandparents; and, more important to Inburn, it has altered so vastly that even the world in which his parents were formed in the twenties is now of chiefly historical interest to him, lacking value as a signpost for his own life. The upward mobility of his parents is but a part of that collective social mobility which has characterized Americans as a nation, bringing shifts in values, technologies, and patterns of life, the like of which have rarely if ever occurred in so short a time. The effects of such changes on individuals are unsettling, in that they suggest to many youths that there *are* no values, institutions, or ways of life that withstand the tests of time. If such is one's conviction, then perhaps the search for "the most valuable and the most significant set of sense experiences it is possible to take in" is the only quest that is left.

Or consider another characteristic of our changing social scene: the consolidation of the isolated nuclear family, or what the French, with greater historical sense, call *la famille réduite*. Such a family, limited to mother, father, and immediate offspring, produces an extreme intensification of emotional ties, especially between mother and child—usually at the very same time that the wider society insists on more impersonal and unemotional relationships in the sphere of work. This intensity of mother-child ties is further exaggerated by the increasing absence of the father at work, leaving the mother (even without wars) to develop further her central role as the primary educative agent. Thus, an ambitious woman like Inburn's mother, condemned whether by fate or modernity to a small family, often finds it hard *not* to feel frustrated, *not* to rejoice in and magnify her control over her domestic realm, and *not* to try to find in her children the satisfactions that her absent husband might have provided in another era. In sum, the family ambiance that we infer in exaggerated form in Inburn's life is far from unique; and a similar if less extreme constellation sets the stage for a life-long contrast in almost every American between the immediacy, intimacy, and dependency of childhood and the impersonal bureaucracies in which he will spend much of his adult life. To be sure, most still find in adulthood sufficient compensation to cancel the backward pull of indistinct and often romanticized childhood recall; but the tension exists for all.

But perhaps most important, a considerable amount of alienation is fully justified, I think, in America in the 1960's; and, even when not justified, an even greater amount is actively reinforced and supported by our society and our world. Our vocabularies brim over with synonyms for alienation—estrangement, neutralism, noninvolvement, apartheid, apathy, disengagement, withdrawal, anomie, detachment, segregation, indifference—and we lack words for the opposite which remain untainted by sentimentalism. In many cases the facts justify such attitudes, for ours is a society in which commercialism and marketing, whether of personalities or of unnecessary goods, have too often replaced value, worth, and merit. And even more than the facts warrant, we are fascinated by the corrupt, the unethical, and the sordid. The prevailing images of our television screens, our newspapers, and our magazines are either those of commercially exploited sentimentality or of violence, depravity, and suspicion. As Nevitt Sanford writes in *The American College*:

> One of the hardest things about growing up in contemporary America is that at just the time when a young person most needs models of private and public virtue he is likely to become aware of corruption in high places, of organized immorality in some of our major institutions, of the inconsistencies in our economic system and in our sexual mores, and of meanness in people close at hand whom he thought he could admire. . . . He courts a new danger: that he will reject the existing order out of hand, and be-

come totally alienated from the society and value system represented by his parents and his community.[4]

Fortunately, most young Americans still develop a capacity for selective blindness to these aspects of society or respond to them only in some dissociated corner of their psyches—though this blindness or learned incapacity often generalizes to prevent response to the beautiful, the genuine, the moving, and the decent as well. But for those who insist on seeing everything, a large modicum of alienation seems justified.

Consider, too, the international situation, with its two superpowers, each deeply distrustful of the other, each unwilling to compromise lest it appear to expose its own feared weaknesses, each poised to annihilate the other on a few hours' (soon, a few minutes') notice. This is a projection of distrust on so large a scale that had it been anticipated in the fantasies of some undergraduate two decades ago he would surely have been deemed borderline, if not paranoid, by assessing psychologists. The world of Melville's *Confidence Man*, with its motto of "No Trust," has been realized on a scale so vast as to be beyond the capacity of even Melville's colossal (and deeply alienated) imagination. Thus it cannot surprise us that individuals sometimes greet their fellows with distrust or view the world as the arena of anxiety and pessimism, no matter how much we may also understand of the individual roots of this alienation.

In sum, in this superficially quite ordinary sophomore there occurs a confluence of individual and historical forces, some of them unique to Inburn's life, some of them congruent with archetypal themes of outcastness from mother, tribe, and Eden, and some which are the reflections on a selectively predisposed individual of social and historical forces, whose impact we seldom know how to fathom. Henry Murray writes:

> It seems to me that the major determinant of alienation is the nature of Western culture and society. The alienating features of it are first perceived by the variant or underprivileged (with ideals or without ideals), who are hurt by it, and by the overprivileged with ideals. . . . The increase in freedom has gone hand in hand with the increase in alienation.[5]

But for all that Inburn is enmeshed in his own, in his generation's, and in mankind's history—most of all when he seeks to deny the fact—I think it likely that from among the Inburns of the world will be recruited those who may eventually learn to relieve the lesser alienations of the rest of us. For the alienated—though they pay a high price in unhappiness, in distortions of personal growth, and in indiscriminate rejection— more often than most retain and insist on an openness to experience, a detachment, and a critical spirit, which are the positive side of estrangement.

[4] Nevitt Sanford, ed., *The American College* (New York: John Wiley & Sons, 1962), p. 262.
[5] Personal communication.

3: SENSE OF INTERPERSONAL COMPETENCE

Two Case Studies and Some Reflections on Origins

Robert W. White

Every interaction with another person can be said to have an aspect of competence. Acts directed toward another are intended, consciously or unconsciously, to have an effect of some kind, and the extent to which they produce this effect can be taken as the measure of competence. When interactions are casual, when we are merely "passing the time of day," the element of competence may be minimal, although even in such cases we are surprised if we produce no effect at all, not even an acknowledging grunt. When matters of importance are at stake, the aspect of competence is bound to be larger. If we are seeking help or offering it, trying to evoke love or giving it, warding off aggression or expressing it, resisting influence by others or trying to exert influence, the effectiveness of our behavior is a point of vital concern. In extreme cases interpersonal acts may have virtually no purpose beyond the testing or display of competence. This is true when dominance over others has become an autonomous end, when "throwing one's weight around" and taking command of situations is done simply for the joy of being effective —a joy that is undoubtedly all the greater when it counteracts a fear that one is not effective.

In the main, competence is not the most distinctive feature of interpersonal behavior, and its significance is sometimes overlooked. If the transaction involves an important need, our attention is drawn to the gratification or frustration of that need, rather than to the background theme of effectiveness in dealing with people. Yet this background theme is always there, and we should always try to reckon with it. When a child wants to go to the circus but cannot persuade his parents to take him, he suffers a frustration of those urges that draw children to the circus— curiosity, excitement, adventure—and he may also be wounded by the revealed shortcoming of parental love, especially if it signifies that a sibling, taken to the circus the year before, is more warmly loved. But implicit in the whole situation is a setback to his sense of competence in dealing with his parents. He has failed to elicit their sympathetic interest in his heartfelt desires; he has failed to secure their cooperation in satisfying those desires. Along with his more direct frustrations, he has suffered a decrement of confidence in his ability to make himself effective in the human environment.

Competence means capacity, fitness, or ability. The competence of a living organism means its fitness or ability to carry on those transactions with the environment which result in its maintaining itself, growing, and flourishing. In the human case, effectiveness in dealing with the environment is achieved largely through learning. The child's attempts to remove his pains and gratify his needs, and especially his playful explorations and manipulations during the spare time between such crises, build up in him a knowledge of the effects he can have on his surroundings, as well as a knowledge of the effects they can have on him.[1] To describe it neurologically, competence is an achieved state of affairs in the nervous system which makes effective action possible; and it can be approximately measured in some of its aspects by tests of aptitude, intelligence, and achievement. The subjective side of this can be called sense of competence. We know that for various reasons one's sense of competence does not correspond exactly to actual competence as estimated by others, though it is always related to it. Abilities to deal with physical surroundings and to control one's body effectively are matters of no small importance to the child, but the central significance of the human environment confers a corresponding significance on the sense of interpersonal competence.[2]

In clinical work, sense of competence has been widely recognized in negative forms: feelings of helplessness, inhibition of initiative, the inferiority complex. The positive side has perhaps been poisoned for many of us by that hastily conceived dream-figure of perfect mental health who has attained invulnerable self-confidence and serene self-esteem—obviously a conceited fool. But the extreme cases, real or fictional, should not draw attention away from sense of competence at the daily operating level. Our best insight comes from the ordinary phenomenon of confidence, which is an aspect of virtually every act. We can detect it by horse sense; that, at least, is what horses do when inexperienced riders are on their backs. A horse can apparently deduce from the first few physical contacts with the novice that the situation is right for a little

[1] These points are developed in detail in Robert W. White, "Motivation Reconsidered: The Concept of Competence," *Psychological Review,* LXVI (1959), 297–333.

[2] The expression, "interpersonal competence," has been used in a much more inclusive sense than the one intended here by Nelson N. Foote and Leonard S. Cottrell, *Identity and Interpersonal Competence* (Chicago: University of Chicago Press, 1955).

fun along the bridle path or an unscheduled return to the stable. Similarly, though with less whimsical intent, a teacher making the acquaintance of a new class will notice how the children approach each activity. At the crafts table, for instance, she will see behavior ranging from picking things up quickly and using them firmly, through all grades of tentativeness and uncertainty, to hanging back or turning completely away. If the tools had horse sense, they could rate the confidence of the children who picked them up.

We can detect the influence of sense of competence in the judgments we are constantly making, often half-consciously, about what we can and cannot do. We can step across this puddle but not the next one; we can build rough shelves in the playroom but not a finished bookcase for the living room; we would be glad to paint and shift the scenery for the play but not to act or promote the sale of tickets; we undertake with relative equanimity to criticize a fault in a subordinate but suffer no small anxiety when the boss calls a meeting to criticize long-range company policy. How do we know so well what we can and cannot do? Since in the beginning we could not do any of these things, even step across the smallest puddle, it is safe to say that we have learned it all through experience. Past actions, successful and unsuccessful, have taught us the ranges of our effectiveness. Sense of competence is the result of cumulative learning, and it is ever at work influencing the next thrust of behavior.

Although these thoughts may rank as self-evident truths with respect to dealing with the physical environment, the part played in the growth of personality by a sense of interpersonal competence has not been so clearly discerned. We shall examine it here by comparing two lives that afford a certain contrast, although neither can be considered to represent a pathological extreme.

CHATWELL AND MERRITT AS COLLEGE STUDENTS

Our subjects are two college students, twenty years of age, whom we shall call John Chatwell and Harold Merritt.[3] They originally crossed the doorstep of the Harvard Psychological Clinic to serve as paid subjects in psychological experiments, but they were persuaded to expand this role by participating in extensive studies of personality, amounting in the end to more than thirty hours of interviews, tests, and experiments. Evidence will be presented concerning sense of interpersonal competence in each young man as revealed in this voluminous material. Then we shall look for the consequences later in life, for both men were studied a

[3] John Chatwell's case has been published by M. Brewster Smith, Jerome S. Bruner, and Robert W. White in *Opinions and Personality* (New York: John Wiley & Sons, 1956), Chap. 5.

second time several years later, when they had become somewhat settled in their careers.

Our plan will be to consider the evidences of sense of interpersonal competence which lie scattered through the case records. These evidences are to be found in the way the subjects write and speak; in the way they remember and report their histories; in the way they describe and rate themselves at the time of study; in the way they make things happen in the realm of fantasy; and in the way they speak about their plans and prospects.

Styles of Speech

As a start, we can avail ourselves of an independent comparison of the two students based entirely on an objective analysis of samples of their speech. Fillmore H. Sanford, author of the study, after giving in detail the precise measurements used, makes the comparison in the following summaries of speech styles:[4]

> In his verbal behavior Chatwell is colorful, varied, emphatic, direct, active, progressing always in a forward direction. His responses are well coordinated, closely interconnected, more evaluative than definitive, and somewhat enumerative. He covers extensive areas verbally and is disinclined to consider details or precision of reference. His speech is confident, definite, independent. In general he appears to use speech not so much to describe the external world and its relations as to express his own individuality and to impress the auditor.
>
> Merritt's speech is complex, perseverative, thorough, uncoordinated, cautious, static, highly definitive, and stimulus-bound. If we go one step further toward synthesis and generalization, we might conceive of his whole style as defensive and deferent. Most of his verbal behavior seems to reflect a desire to avoid blame or disapproval. He is cautious and indirect, rarely making a simple or bald statement. Once he makes a judgment he explains it and presents all aspects of it, leaving little to the auditor's imagination and little for the auditor to question. His concern for the adequacy of every response results in a re-examination of the response and this, in turn, brings about roughnesses in his discourse. His disinclination to venture out "on his own" makes him feel more comfortable in the stimulus-bound situations.

Speech is the main instrument of social interaction, and we can see at once that our two subjects use it with different degrees of confidence. Chatwell, we gather, expects to be able to impress his hearers and to evoke from them an appreciative and respectful response. Merritt is not so sure of the impression he can make; he speaks as if others were likely to be critical and perhaps belittling, so that it is well to explain, qualify, and defend any assertion he is moved to put forth. Neither young man is

[4] "Speech and Personality: A Comparative Case Study," *Character and Personality*, X (1942), 169–198.

inarticulate, but Chatwell uses the instrument of speech with firmer grasp and stronger strokes.

Recollections of History

During Chatwell's boyhood the family circle, which included the parents and a younger brother and sister, was the scene of much lively discussion and some quarreling. Both parents had scientific and other intellectual interests, and the father particularly enjoyed tossing out controversial problems for debate at the dinner table. Chatwell's mother, when interviewed, was a bit apologetic about the high-strung atmosphere of the home, but her eldest son looked back upon it with considerable satisfaction. He made it clear that the quarrels did not run deep: "I never remember an argument on any really important subject such as our education; it was generally on some never-proven point such as the question of who gained or lost the most in the World War." The picture that emerges is one of underlying secure solidarity, which gave the children a feeling of freedom to express and assert themselves. In matters of serious discipline Chatwell was afraid of his father's anger, but in retrospect he registered no complaints against the regime and recollected that his mother worked more through bribes than through punishments. As an undergraduate he considered himself to be highly self-sufficient; yet he felt certain that in any time of trouble he would receive a sympathetic hearing and unquestioning support at home.

Merritt's account of his childhood was a little more somber. His middle-class parents were much involved in local civic affairs, and he recalled occasions when they would be out for the evening, when his older brother would also go out, leaving him alone and tearful in the house. He complained of "never having the real experience of a close family connection" and reported his envy of friends at whose houses he would find "their parents and brothers and sisters sitting in the front room and talking; this is an experience of which a greater part of my earlier life was deprived." He averred that his parents had never shown much sympathy for his troubles or excitement over his successes. "Everything is taken as a matter of course," he said; "I was never helped or admired." Wistfully he mentioned never having been patted on the back, a deprivation that he rectified in one of his thematic apperceptions, wherein a father embraces the son who has done him honor in a football game. In this atmosphere of niggardly affection and respect he had not found it safe to assert himself strongly or to indulge rebellious wishes. He found no injustices in the regime of discipline, and, when punished, he "resolved not to let the situation happen again." He resented it only when his mother continued to scold long past the point at which his inner surrender had been made.

If we turn to interactions with other children, we might conclude that Merritt had made a quicker start toward competence. Chatwell reported himself to have been a cry-baby at the start of school, whereas Merritt remembered at the age of six "inviting all my young friends to play in the yard with me." These sessions in the yard were marred by fits of temper on the part of the host: "I was stubborn and would get angry if they didn't agree to play my games or go where I wanted to go." Merritt represented his growth as a progress from this selfish assertiveness to an ability to cooperate smoothly with others. By the time he reached junior high school he had many friends and was "well liked by teachers and associates." In senior high school he became president of a political science club, but the organization crumbled through lack of student interest and faculty support. Merritt had clearly not developed into a charismatic leader.

Chatwell's picture of his own social growth was one of overcoming anxiety rather than suppressing anger. Filling out an item about his attitudes, he wrote: "When young, obedient; when older, especially at school, critical, aggressive, belligerent, but often cooperative." With respect to the groups with which he associated, he said: "I was respected, perhaps admired by a few; I certainly wasn't picked on." The earlier tendency to cry was successfully counteracted during the third grade, when a grouchy, rheumatic teacher stimulated rebellious mischief: "A friend and I were kicked out of his class three times a week, but I soon got so that I could go before the principal and be perfectly self-possessed." By the time he entered high school and "had gotten past the shy freshman stage," he was ready to take part in all social activities; he made many friends and was chosen for several offices. It became his "favorite indoor sport" to meet new people, talk with them, and get their point of view.

There was an interesting difference in the way the two young men described their relations with girls. As a sophomore, Chatwell wrote rhapsodically about the girl with whom he was then in love; as a senior, falling in love with the girl he ultimately married, he enlarged upon the relation developing between them without any particular emphasis on its physical aspect. To Merritt the sexual side was much more preoccupying, though surrounded by embarrassment and guilt. Chronologically, Merritt might again be said to have made the quicker start: long before puberty he had been in a fist fight over a girl whom he wanted to kiss, whereas Chatwell at this age viewed girls with contempt. But Merritt's head start did not betoken fast progress. He was slow to attain confidence with girls. He wrote as follows, exhibiting in his writing some of the qualities Sanford noticed in his speech:

I have often been told that I am bashful. While I do not think this is wholly true, I say it is true to a great extent, probably because I am a very poor dancer. It is natural at an informal gathering for some few to start dancing. It is here that I am apt to be shy; for, having little confidence in my dancing ability, I would rather withdraw from the active company and not dance—unless I cannot avoid dancing.

At petting parties Merritt was "not at all too aggressive," leaving the initiative to his partner. When, during the spring of his sophomore year, the petting with one of his girl friends became heavy, he was at first "ashamed" of himself, "but she told me that what we were doing was only very natural." And when he realized that this experience was making him want sexual intercourse, he broke off the relationship: "I felt I would regret it because if I did, I'd be 'hooked'—once we would start, it wouldn't end—I'm sure of that because I know what an attraction that girl had for me."

Perhaps Chatwell could also be considered bashful in his first serious relation, in which he held the girl's hand the first year, kissed her the second, and never did much more. As a college sophomore, however, he had already parted with his virginity, and he presently "stormed the gates" with the girl he loved. Despite his martial phrase, this was very much a matter of mutual desire and consent, and in retrospect, after this girl had been swept away from him by a more aggressive suitor, he realized that he had not "handled her right": he was an "abject slave," whereas "she should have been." So with his next girl he started out differently and "mingled more of the cave man" in his behavior, which made her "a bit more respecting," even to the point of becoming a "yes-woman." Having achieved this, Chatwell found that it was not quite what he wanted, and he did not really fall in love until he found the satisfying give-and-take of a more equal relationship. He was not bothered by a fear of being "hooked." He felt able to "tell anyone to go to hell" if necessary.

Self-Descriptions in the Present

As sophomores, the subjects filled out a long questionnaire devised by Murray, consisting of highly specific items of behavior indicative of various needs.[5] The following four needs, each represented by ten items scattered through the questionnaire, are most relevant to a sense of interpersonal competence.

Dominance: to control one's human environment; to influence or direct the behavior of others.

Aggression: to overcome opposition forcefully; to attack, fight, injure; to belittle, censure, or ridicule maliciously.

[5] Henry A. Murray, *Explorations in Personality* (New York: Oxford University Press, 1938). In Chap. 3, the questions are given in connection with descriptions of each need.

Deference: to admire and support a superior; to praise, emulate, and yield eagerly to the influence of such a person.

Abasement: to submit passively to external force; to surrender; to accept injury, criticism, punishment, and belittlement.

Averaging the self-ratings given on the ten specific items in each case and using a scale of 0 to 5, we find our two subjects describing themselves as follows:

SUBJECT	DOMINANCE	AGGRESSION	DEFERENCE	ABASEMENT
Chatwell	3.8	3.6	2.7	1.2
Merritt	3.1	2.5	3.2	2.2

Merritt thus considers himself a shade more deferent than he is dominant and nearly as abasive as he is aggressive. Chatwell, on the other hand, puts himself decidedly high on both dominance and aggression, near the midpoint on deference, and very low on abasement—a picture of easy interpersonal self-confidence.

The same differences appear rather consistently throughout the interviews, especially in the subjects' allusions to their abilities. Questioned about leading and governing ability, Chatwell pronounced himself a good executive, who knew how to delegate authority, and said, "Responsibility in emergencies is my meat." Merritt could not recall taking an active part in an emergency. He felt that "as far as leading others is concerned, I can hold my own"; mentioned specific instances in which others had turned to him for advice; and replied to a question about his persuasive skill: "I think I can get my way—well, I mean, if my point is correct I can persuade others." With respect to economic ability, Chatwell described some profitable deals with other students and characterized himself as "the sort of fellow who can get it for you wholesale"; whereas Merritt said, "I don't bargain for a price, but take the salesman's word for it" and revealed that his mother still bought his clothes. Chatwell announced that he tended to monopolize conversation, whereas Merritt put it that "I can hold my own in conversation"—but only with men, for with girls he continued to be often bashful, self-conscious, unable to "take off this stiff robe and let myself go."

It is not hard to detect in Chatwell's self-picture a certain bravado, from which underlying anxiety could be inferred. He actually did, however, a great many of the kinds of things he said he did. His zest and versatility made him a treasure to the student employment office, which could use him in response to practically any call. One of his assignments was to arrange a series of radio programs involving information contests between teams of high school pupils. This entailed persuading school principals, overcoming the prejudices of school boards, and selling to everyone the idea that an educational purpose would be served. "This was duck soup for me," said Chatwell.

Fantasies Involving Interpersonal Competence

The Thematic Apperception Test can be said to throw an oblique light on sense of interpersonal competence. Fantasies of successful dominance and aggression may be compensatory and wish-fulfilling, representing how the subject would like to be, rather than how he is. It is important to know about such fantasies, but the test can be used in a slightly different way to reveal the subject's unwitting expectations concerning the probability of having desired effects on other people. For this kind of analysis we are not concerned solely with plots in which dominance, aggression, deference, or abasement constitute the main theme. We look rather for the aspect of competence in every plot in which the hero interacts with other characters. Under what circumstances, with what kinds of people, and to what extent do the principal characters created by the story-teller exert a desired influence over others and secure from them what they need? By scrutinizing the stories systematically along these lines, we may be able to learn something about the true depth and firmness of the sense of interpersonal competence.

In Merritt's case this mode of analysis yields a picture which reinforces and amplifies what we have already learned. Friends presumably of the hero's own age appear three times in his stories. Twice the hero turns to them when in trouble, confident that they will be sympathetic and help him if they can. It is noteworthy that troubled heroes turn to others and do not rely on their own resources. The third occasion finds the friends in the pleasant role of coaxing the hero to loaf and neglect his studies; here the significant clue seems to be that he cannot resist these enticements and thus comes to the brink of scholastic disaster and despair. With older people it appears that if they are appreciative and loving, as does not happen often, the hero is warmly and happily deferential; but if they make demands and impose tasks, he is without power to resist. Thus, in a story in which a sympathetic uncle dissuades a young man from a rash, impulsive act, the hero ends by shaking his uncle's hand and "saying that it is necessary for fiery young men to have a wise and calm uncle who can give good advice." But when it is a question of a boy torn between practicing the violin and going out to play, "he decides he really has no choice in the matter, and he wearily picks up the violin." There is one situation in which this helplessness is particularly marked: if the hero is guilty of irresponsibility and moral violation, nothing can save him. The theme appears four times, and no way is discovered to evade the inexorable march of justice.

Merritt's stories imply a tendency more toward abasement and less toward dominance than we might have supposed from the rest of the material. We can infer that such progress as he has made in "holding his own" with other people represents a counteractive victory over an inner traitor always ready to surrender to personal pressure. The stories lead us also to believe that his considerable sociability reflects a very real dependence on the support of a friendly human environment. This belief is further strengthened when we notice that in his self-ratings he gave two of his rare scores of 5 to the statements, "I become very attached to my friends," and "I like to hang around with a group of congenial people and talk about anything that comes up"; and that he assigned the lowest rating to the thought, "I could cut my moorings—quit my home, my parents, and my friends—without suffering great regrets." But if there is a certain softness in the foundations of his sense of interpersonal competence, there remains the important fact that he has managed to bring about a substantial self-improvement, in which he can take pride. Merritt is by no means extremely "low" in interpersonal competence.

Chatwell's thematic apperceptions illuminate his confidence in a somewhat different way. In the first place, they strongly confirm his high self-ratings on autonomy, which were higher even than the ratings he gave himself on dominance. His heroes tend to settle problems through their own decisions, relying on their intelligence and quickness of wit, rather than on help from others. Indeed they are allowed to seek help only when they are infirm and ill, and even then they resist it as long as possible. Chatwell does not put his heroes in conflict with older people or with authority. The boy with the violin, for instance, is under no pressure to practice; he has found an old instrument in the attic and is making up his own mind what to do with it. There are a few flashes of dominance; but the most remarkable feature of the stories taken as a whole is their avoidance of situations of interpersonal stress and their setting of problems, bordering sometimes on the flippant, that can be solved by individual cleverness. Chatwell met the challenge of the Thematic Apperception Test by taking it not too seriously.

We have already sensed that there might be a streak of bravado in his professedly high social competence. Now we begin to see how he has achieved it and within what limits. From his mother we learned that as a child he was physically timid. Slight of frame, though wiry and boundlessly energetic, he knew anxieties and humiliations in the days when physical prowess was all important. In one of his stories he told us indirectly what happened then. The hero, laboriously playing football with the knowledge that he could never do it well, came to the conclusion that "he didn't like the way the whole sport was organized at college. But instead of merely giving voice to his objections, he suddenly threw himself wholeheartedly into modifying the system. He found that he had just the qualifications for doing this successfully." Chatwell found that he had just the qualifications—high intelligence, quick wit, and an extraordinarily well-furnished memory—to meet challenges fearlessly and to establish competitive dominance when things could be kept in the realm of the verbal, the abstract, and the not-too-deadly-serious. This kind of dominance became his element—his "duck soup."

Impressive as was his achievement in developing a sense of interpersonal competence, it by no means left him without problems. He was aware of a certain lack of content and conviction in himself; it pleased him, yet also worried him, that he could so persuasively take either side in an argument. In considerable degree he went through what we have since learned to call an identity crisis, when he was much concerned that he lived so wholly in the present and could stabilize no enduring interests or plans for the future. He complained that he lost interest in things when there was no more anxiety to overcome, a clear indication that the compensatory function of much of his behavior was getting in the way of intrinsic satisfactions. There was thus a considerable element of struggle, and a certain evasion of the most serious issues, in Chatwell's attempts to influence and dominate his social environment. No one would hesitate to rate him above Merritt on strength of the sense of interpersonal competence, but he was by no means a perfect "high."

Plans and Prospects

As sophomores, Chatwell and Merritt were both asked to write something about their self-estimates and expectations for the future. In the mantle of prophecy, Chatwell wrote as follows:

I like people, and I think they like me. I get along well with people and can generally get them to do what I want—within reasonable limits, of course. I am well enough informed to be able to carry on a decent conversation with people from whom I may learn more, although I might never admit that to them. Unfortunately, perhaps, I think rather well of myself, although I realize my limitations. I know that there is some combination of things that I can do better than anyone else; I also know that there is no one of them that someone else cannot do better than I. I have a better than average mind, but I am also more lazy than the average. I have supreme confidence, if not in my skills, in my ability to figure out a way to get something done eventually.

Merritt's inspection of the crystal ball yielded a more guarded picture.

I think that those whom I know have a favorable attitude toward me. I say this because there are very few people with whom I do not get along. I am treated well in my society—I can see that those of my associates who do not go to college respect me because I do. There are members of my family (whom I have heard speak of me) who say that I ought to be successful because I have a pleasing personality and can get along with people. As for my own estimate of myself, I might say that I do think that if upon graduation the opportunity presents itself, I can make a success of myself. That is, I feel that I have ambition to graduate from one position to another, until, after ten years or so, I think I can be in a fairly "well-off" position. I think that in the right position, that is, one for which I am cut out, I would be a success, because I hold myself to be intelligent, willing to learn, willing to work hard for success, and I think I can hold my own against any equal.

The curiously equivocal ending of the last phrase, possibly a slip, symbolizes beautifully the underlying uncertainty in Merritt's sense of interpersonal competence.

Do our subjects possess the gift of prophecy? Fortunately, we can find out.

CHATWELL AND MERRITT A DECADE LATER

Born when they were, these two young men were destined to go very soon into military service with the prospect of active duty in World War II. Their lives after college will be examined here with respect to three main spheres of activity: career in the service, courtship and marriage, and the finding of a vocation.

Military Service

Merritt's transition to military service was smoothed by the fact that he had taken an officer-training program in college. After brief further training he was ordered to an executive office outside the United States. "I ran into a funny situation," he said; "the commanding officer took an immediate dislike to me. I excuse myself by saying he felt that way, but I used to ask him everything I didn't know, and he didn't like being bothered." If the officer's dislike was immediate, it may have been because Merritt is Jewish, but we notice also an adaptive miscarriage of our subject's deference, with its hint of underlying uncertainty and dependence. His next assignment may have had a punitive element, but it turned out well for Merritt. He was sent to a unit occupying a remote and barren air transport base in Alaska. Although enemy attack was not particularly likely, the base could not be effectively reinforced and the unit was considered expendable. This created anxiety for all, but it contributed to an excellent *esprit de corps*. Conditions were primitive, but the men were "a swell bunch." Merritt came to feel that "adequate food and shelter and good companionship . . . are mighty important." He was able to take with good grace the ribbing that fell to him as the junior officer, including sarcastic remarks about the use to which he was putting his Harvard education.

Merritt's further career in the service involved danger; anxiety, which he was able to control; and responsible duties, which he performed with scrupulous care. Although not a spectacular officer, he was equal to the national emergency and made his contribution.

Chatwell was in line to be drafted after graduation, but, rather than suffer the inevitable delays, he enlisted at once in that branch of the service which he perceived as offering the most likely avenue to officer status. "I found that I adapted to the military life with great ease," he wrote; "in fact, I was enthusiastic about it." Within a week he had applied for officer training; but, long before he was eligible, he found a way to improve his position as an enlisted man. Hearing two lectures on mathematics badly given, he applied for the job of mathematics instructor and soon found himself teaching "without difficulty" classes of five hundred men. This job brought him in contact with officers and speeded his progress to Officer Candidate School, where he found the life "stimulating and healthful," the goals "tangible," and the competition "keen and real, as opposed to the ivory tower that so irked me at college." The training period, with its discipline and his own fired enthusiasm, "produced a systematic, determined, conscientious Chatwell that would mystify the Harvard authorities."

He was made an instructor in the school, was advanced rapidly, and later went overseas as an intelligence officer. On one occasion the unit was obliged to establish its base in a jungle wilderness. "I must say," he wrote, "that one of the most satisfying things I know of is to go into a jungle and set up a reasonable degree of civilization there with your own hands—water, light, sanitation, etc." Such experiences led to a natural re-evaluation of what was important: Chatwell specified "food, independence, warmth, dryness, affection of women, opportunity for productive work, liquor, tobacco—in no particular order." More explicit and detailed than Merritt's list under similar circumstances, it makes no mention of the good companionship which so fortified Merritt at the isolated Alaskan base.

The military careers of our two subjects exhibit strikingly their difference in sense of interpersonal competence. Chatwell started lower in the military hierarchy but ended higher. He was challenged by competition with other men, and he lost no opportunity to advertise his skills and bring himself to the attention of his superiors. His confidence rose and his self-respect became firmer as a consequence of his success; we get less feeling of bravado as we find him constantly "delivering the goods." Merritt was unable to muster such impressive initiative. His first moves were nearly undone by an unwelcome hesitancy and deference. When the atmosphere included good companionship, he was content and functioned well, but he showed no inclination to push his career in any way that would imperil this source of security.

Courtship and Marriage

Like so many of their contemporaries, both young men married during the course of their military service. Chatwell married the girl with whom he had fallen in love in the spring of his senior year, the fourth girl in whom he had had a serious interest. Merritt married the girl who had brought out his sexual interest during the spring of his sophomore year, the only girl to whom he was ever strongly drawn.

As a boy half way through college, fearing intercourse with its implication of being "hooked," Merritt had rather sternly broken off his relation with this girl and substituted less involving friendships. But the girl continued to be fond of him, and her parents, though possibly not his, had hoped that a match would occur. By a course of events which he could not clearly recall at the time of the second study, he drifted back into her company and became strongly aware of her hopes. She was tearfully present when he was seen off to the war, but he left without committing himself. His own decision took place one night at the Alaskan base, when there was strong rumor of enemy action with its inevitable choice between death and capture. In the midst of his anxiety he said to himself, "If I ever get out of here, I'll go back and marry her"—as indeed he did on his next furlough.

This incident calls to mind the sequence so common in the history of Roman Catholicism, in which a person in grave danger implores the help of a saint and vows eternal devotion and great gifts if the help is granted. No such content is available to a young American Jew, but there is something similar in the underlying feeling. It is as if he said, "If I am saved I shall be greatly indebted," and then, looking around for someone to whom debt could appropriately be paid, he discovered that it was to this girl that he had the strongest feeling of obligation. Yet her only actual claim upon him was her *desire* to marry him, a desire which up to then he had resisted. The fact that terror should finally shake his resolution on just this point is eloquent testimony to the force with which other people's expectations worked upon him. To be sure, a strong physical attraction took sides with his feeling of obligation, but it was not this that was strengthened by danger. If his life was spared he must give, and the person who wanted him to give was the girl whose tears he could dry by offering himself in marriage.

Merritt's pattern of courtship reflects a weak sense of interpersonal competence with girls—a continuation of the bashfulness that troubled him in college. He took the first girl who gave him real physical satisfaction; and, overriding his reservations about their ultimate compatibility, he took her more because she wanted him than because he wanted her. He would be lucky if after such a slight search he found an ideal partner. In point of fact, the marriage has worked out, though not as a source of much ecstasy. His wife has had numerous illnesses that have required him to participate rather heavily in the housework, but in an undemonstrative way he likes and is perhaps somewhat dependent on her company, enjoys being a family man, and is quite wrapped up in their young daughter. Apparently the marriage has reached an equilibrium.

Chatwell's final falling in love was the culmination of considerably more experience. As we have seen, he had already gone through the waxing and waning of three love affairs, and he had found his way from a rather abasive to a somewhat more dominant relation. But he by no means sought the competitive dominance that was so dear to him with respect to other men. His girl was lively and intelligent, a proper partner for his conversational talents, but she also provided a welcome sense of peace and security at the end of the day. He described himself as liking busy days but then wanting a place where he could take off his shoes. He was, in his own words, "sunk without firing a shot in about two months," and his only misgiving was that the feeling of security might be influencing him too strongly. His girl seemed to him to be "an ideal combination of intelligence, tenderness, and physical attractiveness." He kept after her, this time with no dying down of interest, for the year that was necessary to persuade her to become his wife; and he was both happy and proud when they were married.

As a married man with two children, Chatwell spoke of his wife as follows:

> I trust her absolutely. There's a feeling of—well, I get intellectual and emotional and all the other kinds of response I want, all at once. We seem to share the same values. . . . We have never gone to bed mad at each other since we were married. She rides me a good bit, but for cause—more than I ride her. I am messy and lazy and it's a cause of dissension. I don't see things to do around the house, and she doesn't like to have to ask me to do them.

He talked freely of disagreements over punishing the children and other common forms of domestic strife, but there was no bitterness or attempt at self-justification. One got the impression of a marriage in which deep devotion could easily absorb the frictions of domesticity.

Finding a Vocation

The occupational histories of Merritt and Chatwell illuminate with unusual clearness the problem of job satisfaction. For both of them, fitting the peg to the hole involved not only the gratifying employment of abilities but also the finding of a congenial pattern of human relations.

At the time of the second studies the positions they occupied seemed to be almost perfect expressions of the strength and pattern of their respective senses of interpersonal competence.

During the interval between graduation and military service Merritt held a job from which he was fired and a second one in which he was successful. The first venture was in a department store, ostensibly in an executive training program. His heart was not in it; after the declaration of war especially, it seemed trivial to be fussing over ladies' garments. He was actually dismissed for an error in handling some merchandise, but he was told that he was in the wrong line of work. His supervisor informed him that he was far too polite and would never get ahead in such an aggressive business. Next, he found work in a government agency, where he was pleased to find university graduates in charge. Realizing the advantage of a fresh start, he developed the trick of speaking on the telephone "in a deep voice, which I didn't have naturally at that time." He began to develop confidence in himself, but the job was interrupted by his call to arms.

After the war he found a position in the New England office of a large financial corporation. At first he felt that he and other veterans had been put in the false position of supervising people who already knew their jobs. Presently a high official came from the central office to look things over.

> The job of working with Mr. Driver was thrown to me, and I took an interest and got to work closely with him. He had the reputation of being the meanest so-and-so, but I found him upright. I never argued with him. A man who opposed him was fired after two months and I was put in the job, being made chief of one of the floors.

The people on that floor had wanted to promote one of their own men, so Merritt was "in a fairly tough spot, but to this day I don't have an enemy over the place." He continued to enjoy the support of Mr. Driver, who liked both his loyalty and his intelligence and who gave him opportunities for special training in new procedures. He could even have gone to the central office at higher pay, if he had not been disinclined to move away from friends and family connections. On the whole he was well satisfied: "I think I've done pretty well for myself. Someone I think is important thinks I'm important, and that has given me a lot of confidence. That, in turn, lets me do a better job."

Merritt has found virtually the perfect way to utilize his interpersonal competence. His unusually strong deference allows him to become the servant of an overbearing, unpopular boss, and his uncertainties are dissolved by his being merely the instrument of company policy. At the same time he manages to melt the antagonism of those below him through fair and considerate behavior fashioned by his need for their friendship. One must admire his skill in thus serving two masters. It is not easy, and he often finds himself under considerable tension. At the annual Christmas party, for instance, he must take a clear stand for company policy that no liquor be served and at the same time not spoil the festivities by noticing violations. But he manages well, and thus he fulfills his own prophecy that "in the right position, that is, one for which I am cut out, I would be a success."

Chatwell emerged from military service with the decision fairly well made that he would become a lawyer. He was presently in a position to choose between a large and a small firm, each of which would employ him as a law clerk while he pursued evening study. He made the choice that Merritt probably would not have made: the small firm, he believed, offered greater chances of advancement through independent achievement. Both then and later the work proved to be another instance of "duck soup." In the law classroom he argued the cases with tremendous zest, holding the floor and sometimes even clashing with the professor. In preparing briefs, he was strongly abetted by his excellent memory, wide range of information, and speed of learning, whatever technical matters the case might involve. The pattern of his enthusiasms, intense but short-lived, was no handicap in a business where each case had to be prepared rapidly but then put aside for an entirely different one. He was delighted with the combination of legal scholarship, new facts to be mastered, and "constant strife and argument to exact care and method from my disorderly soul." His seniors in the office accepted him as one of them and were, as he put it, "patient with me and kind to my ego, both when I failed and when I succeeded." His own summary varies but little from his sophomore prophecy:

> And so you see that I am very, very happy, busy as hell, with independence, a measure of security in a form in which I can accept it, a future with several broad avenues besides the attractive one I'm on, and plenty of problems—interesting problems, and none beyond my abilities.

In their military service, in their marriages, and in their jobs, Merritt and Chatwell exhibit the differences in sense of interpersonal competence that could be observed when they were in college. Although they had stripped away some of the illusions of that time of life, both had made gains in confidence and established self-esteem on a more solid basis. Both have been able to find and then to mold situations that went well with their needs and strengths in human relations.

SOME REFLECTIONS ON ORIGINS

The question of origins is always fundamental in the study of lives. We would like to know, in particular, how it came to pass that Chatwell and Merritt differed so distinctly in social confidence and, in general, what forces and what conditions in a child's life affect the level of his sense of interpersonal competence. Even if we confined ourselves to these two young men, the answer would be complex and somewhat difficult to establish with accuracy in retrospect. But perhaps the large outlines of the problem can be clarified at this point by considering another well-studied level of interpersonal competence—the lowest level.

Interpersonal Incompetence in Schizophrenia

The schizophrenic, we are repeatedly told, withdraws from reality. This phrase has performed miracles in obscuring our understanding of the schizophrenic disorder. For company-hungry Americans it is a wicked thing to withdraw, a sign of secret pride and an evil sense of superiority; and this judgment seems to be verified if the patient entertains grandiose fantasies of his own importance. The implication of the phrase is that the patient has a happy, secret place to which he can retire, a utopia of lovely fantasies which draw him like a magnet when the going gets rough in the responsible adult world. But surely this is the daydream of slightly weary responsible citizens, rather than the experience of schizophrenic patients, whose jumbled world is often full of suffering and pain.

A small change in the formulation may, it seems to me, bring us closer to the psychological truth. The patient, let us say, gives up in his attempts to make himself effective in his human environment. He does so because he has always felt his influence upon it to be small and because even his modest hopes have been shattered by recent disappointments. One aspect of the disorder, in other words, is a chronic weakness in sense of interpersonal competence, which leads under stress to a surrender of effort in actuality and thus to a loss of control over dreamlike ideation. This is not, of course, the whole story of schizophrenia, which may have constitutional and biochemical aspects, as well as peculiarities in the direction and control of impulses; but I believe that it expresses correctly a significant aspect of the disorder. Even in the paradoxical case in which the patient fancies himself to have the power of Napoleon, his sense of actual interpersonal competence is often enough represented by a docile conformity to hospital routines.

It is often said that schizophrenic patients have strong latent dependent needs. To this we must add that they feel remarkably incompetent to obtain satisfaction of their needs. They may, like a borderline case beautifully described by Rickers-Ovsiankina and Riggs,[6] view the human environment as a mysterious puzzle-box to which they have not found the key; they may ask the therapist to tell them what he knows

---

[6] Maria A. Rickers-Ovsiankina and Margaret M. Riggs, "To Be or Not to Be: A Schizophrenic Personality," in *Clinical Studies of Personality,* A. Burton and R. E. Harris, eds. (New York: Harper & Brothers, 1955), Chap. 4.

about the inscrutable business of handling people. They show their low expectations by breaking off the therapeutic relation if there is even a hint of indifference on the part of the therapist. They feel themselves to be at the mercy of what other people do to them, even to the point of entertaining delusions of hostile intent and of humanly inspired influencing machines. They see no way to set these things right.

Why do schizophrenics find the human environment so intractable? Clues are now coming in from the study of disorders very early in childhood. It is characteristic of autistic children that they do not interact with the human environment. Often they look around people rather than at them, and it is extremely difficult to draw them into games such as pat-a-cake or rolling a ball back and forth.[7] Kanner[8] and Ritvo and Provence[9] point out that in some cases this lack of interaction is specific to the human environment; with inanimate objects the child plays in relatively normal fashion. There are two possible reasons for this state of affairs: what Erikson has called a "lack of sending power in the child";[10] and what Kanner, Eisenberg, and others have described as cold, preoccupied, mechanical attitudes in the parents.[11] Whatever may be the relative influence of the two factors, the result is that the child does not experience his own effort as having any effect on the human environment; therefore, it draws his interest no more than furniture, over which he has no influence. If the human environment inspires anxiety, lack of interest may be frozen into an inhibition of interest.

These observations suggest that one of the factors contributing to schizophrenia, with its fragile social confidence, is a bad start in eliciting response from the human environment. And they further suggest the more general formulation that *sense of interpersonal competence develops through effort and its efficacy in human interactions.* This provides us with a clue to the kinds of events that are likely to be important for development.

Developmental Crises of Interpersonal Confidence

Interaction with the human environment is a continuous process, but like any other form of development, it tends to have dramatic moments

[7] Beata Rank, "Adaptation of the Psychoanalytic Technique for the Treatment of Young Children with Atypical Development," *American Journal of Orthopsychiatry,* XIX (1949), 130–139.

[8] Leo Kanner, "Autistic Disturbances of Affective Contact," *The Nervous Child,* II (1943), 217–250.

[9] Samuel Ritvo and Sally Provence, "Form Perception and Imitation in Some Autistic Children," *Psychoanalytic Study of the Child* (New York: International Universities Press, 1953), VIII, 155–161.

[10] Erik H. Erikson, *Childhood and Society* (New York: W. W. Norton, 1950).

[11] Leon Eisenberg, "The Fathers of Autistic Children," *American Journal of Orthopsychiatry,* XXVII (1957), 715–724.

and critical peaks. It is misleading, I believe, to identify these peaks with Freud's stages of psychosexual development; the growth of competence is not captured by these affective crises, however important they may be.[12] I shall not undertake here a systematic sketch of development; let it suffice just to mention some of the situations that are likely to be critical.

One of these is the situation of play with the parents apart from the satisfying of bodily needs. Does the child show initiative, and do the parents respond with pleasure and interest, or do they find it a bit of a bore? Another is the situation created by the child's early steps toward independence, as when he undertakes to feed himself. Is he eager and persistent in these attempts? Do they meet maternal acquiescence, or do they produce irritation at the slow progress and messy spilling? The theme of independence continues through various stages, as manipulation and locomotion permit the child to explore larger and perhaps more dangerous spheres. Another crisis may occur over the expression of will through language. The often observed period of negativism, which we must now interpret interactively as probable negativism on both sides, comes when the child is first capable of issuing verbal commands and offering verbal defiance. How vigorously does he pursue these investigations, and to what extent will his parents think it necessary to "break his will" and assert their own? Then there is the question of justice, which is often sharpest in disputes between siblings. Can the child plead his cause and be heard, or does he feel that nothing is effective, either because of favoritism or because of a blanket injunction against quarreling?

In all these situations the interaction is mainly between child and parents, but new crises occur when the child ventures into play with other children. Is he able to influence the course of interaction, dominate the play, and keep his toys; or does he have to follow unwillingly and lose a few of his possessions? Can he cut an effective figure in competitive activities and thus elicit the respect of his contemporaries? Can he, like Chatwell, become something of a persuasive force and exert a share of leadership in serious pursuits? These issues extend all the way into adolescence, when a further crisis may arise, as Merritt so clearly realized, from the revitalized problem of confidence with the other sex. And of course the problems continue even later, as we have seen by pursuing our two subjects into their late twenties.

In 1938 Murray wrote as the opening words of *Explorations in Personality:* "Man is today's great problem." If "today" is moved forward to 1963 the statement is only the more true. The study of lives must set for itself the goal of understanding development in all its significant as-

---

[12] Robert W. White, "Competence and the Psychosexual Stages of Development," *Nebraska Symposium on Motivation* (Lincoln, Nebraska: University of Nebraska Press, 1960), pp. 97–141.

pects. Merritt and Chatwell have shown us the importance of sense of interpersonal competence, testifying that it was significant in their lives, that it could be richly gratifying and enormously frustrating, and that they were prepared to work hard to make it more satisfactory. And if sense of interpersonal competence develops through effort and its efficacy in human interactions, we shall not fully understand today's great problem without uncovering this theme in the life history.

4: THE HARLEQUIN COMPLEX

David C. McClelland

To modern man, death is the ultimate catastrophe. To philosophers like Bergson, it is the source of man's uniqueness and also of his dismay, because man alone among the animals realizes that he is going to die. He can understand infinity, but must learn to live with the hard fact of his own finiteness. To theologians like Kierkegaard, the acceptance of death and mastery of the anxiety it creates are the beginnings of religion. To psychoanalysts, death represents the castration fear—the old man with the scythe. To the man in the street, at least in twentieth-century America, it is something to avoid thinking about so far as possible, to push under the rug, to deny with phrases like "passed on" or with elaborate rituals symbolic of immortality. At best people manage to face the inevitable end with stoic indifference, as Freud recommended, yet even the stoics confess in moments of honesty, in the words of the medieval hymn, *Timor mortis conturbat me*.

In view of the widespread fear of death, it is surprising to come across a person, usually a woman, who not only does not fear death but actually appears to be looking forward to it with a sense of excitement. The possibility both thrills and attracts her, at the same time that it frightens her. Yet often the thrill seems as strong as the fear, in much the same way that it is for a person who is about to make a ski jump or a very high dive. Such reactions to death do exist, particularly among women, and they are a challenge to the psychologist interested in how people actually react, as opposed to how they are supposed to react according to philosophy, religion, or psychoanalysis.[1]

The positive or at least ambivalent attitude toward death has of

[1] This is one of a series of reports on research in the diagnostic significance of variations in fantasy conducted at Harvard University under a grant to David C. McClelland by the National Institute of Mental Health. I am deeply indebted to Ellen Greenberger, who carried out the empirical research reported and who has discussed many of the ideas in the paper with me over a period of years.

course often been noted by psychiatrists. Bromberg and Schilder in their survey of attitudes toward death report a number of positive meanings that it had for various people,[2] such as "an equivalent for the final sexual union with the ideal mate" and "the final narcissistic perfection which grants eternal and unchallenged importance to the individual."[3] For such people death is like a blank screen on which the life instincts create the images that satisfy them. Thus even negative connotations of death, as in the expectation of eternal punishment in hell fire, serve to gratify urges to punish oneself for misbehavior. However, "fear of death is the fear of loss of something positive," of the life instincts themselves. Therefore, fear of death is more basic or reality-oriented than attraction to death, which involves merely gratifying impulses in fantasy life, not denying such impulses altogether. Nevertheless, we cannot dismiss the attraction to death as of secondary importance, as mere fantasy. It plays an extremely important role in some lives. The role may be different in women from what it is in men. The interpretation given by psycho-analysts may be far too simple and may itself be a product of our century, in which the death instinct has been repressed and fear of death has been considered primary. The whole subject needs careful exploration.

Let us begin with a simple modern tale, which has roots in the history of Western culture going back at least a thousand and perhaps 2,500 years or more. It is told by Agatha Christie, the detective-story writer, under the title *The Mysterious Mr. Quin*.[4] The central character she has created is a certain Mr. Harley Quin, who keeps appearing and disappearing in connection with various deaths or murders, which are unraveled for the reader in the classic manner of detective story fiction. Although Mr. Quin is a recognizable English gentleman, it is not altogether clear at first who he is, because he appears to possess certain magical powers. However, in the last story he finally appears as death himself, a charming yet sometimes invisible and mysterious lover. What finally reveals him is the momentary abandonment of a lovely woman by her husband for a pretty young girl. A famous Russian ballet dancer has settled in England and given up her dancing for her husband who, as he grows older, develops into a middle-aged bourgeois type and characteristically becomes infatuated with a local village girl. The unhappy wife through a series of accidents decides to dance again as Columbine in a locally produced ballet, and her partner, dressed as Harlequin, is none other than the mysterious Mr. Harley Quin. Later in the evening she is found dead at the bottom of a pit at the end of a lane—sometimes called

[2] W. Bromberg and P. Schilder, "Death and Dying," *Psychoanal. Rev.*, XX (1933), 133–185; "The Attitudes of Psychoneurotics towards Death," *Psychoanal. Rev.*, XXIII (1936), 1–28.

[3] *Ibid.*, p. 3.

[4] New York: Dodd Mead, 1930.

Harlequin's Lane or Lover's Lane—but not before at least one person has seen her walking down the lane with her Harlequin lover of the ballet. As she herself had said earlier, "No lover ever satisfies one, for all lovers are mortal. And Harlequin is only a myth, an invisible presence —unless his name is Death." This story will serve to introduce us to the theme of death as a lover, as a mysterious dark figure who comes and takes a woman away to her death. This theme, which, with all its variations, we will call the Harlequin complex, is at least as old as the Greek story of Hades coming up out of hell to take Persephone away to the underworld.

But why associate Harlequin with death? At first glance the notion seems a little far-fetched. Standard reference works describe Harlequin as the lover of Columbine in pantomime or in ballet, who typically wears a multicolored suit and a black mask. In earlier days, in the classic Italian *commedia dell'arte,* he was noted for his acrobatic tricks and practical jokes performed with the aid of his magic wooden bat or slapstick. Certainly he has always been a lover, whether as a comic seducer of the servant girl Columbina, or as her romantic partner in an etherealized love story in ballet, but apparently only his mask suggests mystery or any connection with death. In recent standard reference works, the connection with death is not explicitly mentioned. For example, Niklaus, in reviewing Harlequin's later history on the stage beginning in 1585, says little or nothing about his origin in the underworld, although she is admittedly puzzled and a little shocked at the feral hairy mask that he wore in the late sixteenth and early seventeenth centuries.[5] She decides that he is the descendant of certain Italian, and ultimately Roman, clowns and satyrs and somehow represents "the enigmatic personification of the life force."[6] Yet the connection with death is clear even in the period she reviews. Watteau's famous painting shows a sinister, black-masked Harlequin making love to a somewhat frightened, genteel Columbine.[7] Harlequin pantomimes regularly consisted of "dark" scenes and serio-comic love scenes in which Harlequin pursues Columbine despite obstacles placed in his way by her father or guardian or suitor Pantaloon.[8] In the "dark" scenes Harlequin is definitely connected with such stark underworld figures as Dr. Faustus, Pluto, and sorcerers. For example, in England in 1723 at Lincoln's Inn Fields, John Rich staged *Harlequin Necromancer and Dr. Faustus,* in which the opening scene of the farce deals with the contract Harlequin signs with Pluto, the king of the underworld, for all the "Whores of the Universe" in exchange for a

[5] T. Niklaus, *Harlequin Phoenix* (London: The Bodley Head, 1956). See the reproduction between pp. 16 and 17.

[6] *Ibid.,* p. 24.

[7] *Ibid.,* p. 81.

[8] *Ibid.,* p. 141.

demon's power.[9] The association of death, seduction, and demonic power
is unmistakable in most of these "dark" scenes. The idea occurred even
in the most slapstick Italian *commedia dell'arte*, in which Arlecchino
plays the part of the doltish, acrobatic servant. In one episode, for example, in which he is the "go-between" for two unfortunately separated
lovers, he tells each one that the other has died of a broken heart. As a
result, each of them nearly commits suicide to join his departed love.[10]
Although much disguised by his burlesque comic manner, Harlequin is
still somehow the agent of love and death.

The reason for the "dark" scenes and Harlequin's connection with
death is made obvious in an excellent but little-known book by Driesen,
in which he demonstrates fairly conclusively that "the comic Harlequin
is no other than the old French devil Herlequin."[11] Despite Driesen's
book, later authorities have apparently continued to be misled by the
fact that the first Harlequin play for which we have the manuscript was
given in Paris in 1585 by an Italian troupe from Bergamo. From this
they conclude that Harlequin was of Italian origin, despite the fact that
there was no previous Arlecchino tradition in Italy, although there was
a Herlequin tradition going back at least six hundred years in France.[12]
Furthermore, the evidence is that the French readily identified the supposedly Italian creation as their own well-known demon. Henry IV and
Madame de Sevigné referred to him by his French name, Harlequin,
when he first appeared on the stage in Paris, and not by the Italian version, Arlecchino.[13] Finally, Driesen demonstrates that the word Harlequin
appears in a French manuscript written in Latin in 1514, long before the
Italian players staged their drama in 1585. He argues that the well-

[9] *Ibid.*, p. 153.

[10] See the scripts in R. Leydi and R. M. Leydi, *Marionette e Burattini* (Milan:
Collana del "Gallo Grande," 1958).

[11] O. Driesen, *Der Ursprung des Harlekin* (Berlin: Alex. Duncker, 1904), p. 18.

[12] For example, Andrea Perucci wrote in 1699: "Nascono, delle vallate ber-
gamasche, delle genti semplicissime e ridicole"; and Renato Simoni in 1932: "Dai
monti di Bergamo discese, appunto, Arlecchino, alla piana, e girò per il mondo."
(Quoted in Leydi, *op. cit.*, p. 199.)

It is amazing how often Harlequin's origin is attributed to the valley of Bergamo,
Driesen's careful research and its citation in the Eleventh Edition of the *Encyclo-
paedia Britannica* notwithstanding. Some of Arlecchino's clownish characteristics in
the *commedia dell'arte* did "descend from the Bergamese mountains" to the plains,
but not his name or his essential mythic character. Dante's Alichino (*Inferno*, cantos
21 and 22), a demon to whom the Italian form of the word is sometimes traced,
is the single known instance of the use of a similar name in Italian until early in the
seventeenth century, when the Italian players had borrowed it from French tradition, according to Driesen. Dante of course could have gotten his term from the
Latin form "Allequinus," used by Etienne de Bourbon in France toward the end
of the thirteenth century shortly before Dante wrote the *Divine Comedy*, a hypothesis strengthened by the fact that the name was not subsequently used by other
Italian authors. (Driesen, *op. cit.*, p. 63, pp. 190 ff.)

[13] Driesen, *op. cit.*, p. 15.

known old French demon Herlequin got his name spelled Harlequin in Paris because the local dialect pronounced "Herle" as "Harle." Then the visiting Italian players converted his name to Arlecchino in their language.

Who, then, was Herlequin in medieval French tradition? Actually, he was not initially one person, but a family. The first reference appears in an eleventh-century manuscript written by Ordericus Vitalis, the Norman historian. He tells a dramatic story in which a priest, returning home late at night by moonlight, is suddenly confronted by an army of dead condemned souls wandering restlessly through the night and making a tremendous noise. He sees coffins carried past him on which dwarfs with big heads are seated; a bloody martyr being repeatedly stabbed by a devil; women riding on sidesaddles containing glowing hot nails, so that when they bounce up and down in the storm, they are stabbed and burned for their misdeeds in life; then masses of clerics and soldiers, all suffering and sighing, from the kingdom of the dead. The monk realizes that he is seeing what he has often heard about—the Herlequin family ("Haec sine dubio familia Herlechini est"). The term obviously refers to an army of dead condemned souls.[14]

Later, in a play by Adan de le Hale, written in 1262, Harlequin is represented as a single person, as a king of the spirit world who sends his lusty representative, Croquesots ("fool-biter"), to woo the fairy Morgue, who returns his love despite the protests of her friends.[15] It is at least suggestive that her name, Morgue, which in French refers to an arrogant or set face, was also applied to faces of dead people, and eventually to the place where dead people are put.

Driesen also makes much of the fact that Harlequin's representative in Adan de le Hale's play asks the fairies how they like his hairy face ("Hurepiaus"), from which Driesen concludes that he is wearing a devil's mask. For the term *Hure* was regularly applied to men with heavy beards, to animals, and to devils.[16] This may give us a clue to the origin of the form of the name Harlequin which has come down to us, though it is a clue not mentioned either by Driesen or by the etymological dictionaries. The words "herle" and "harle" also mean hair in Old English; in other words, Harlequin's name may have been derived from the hairy devil's mask he wore. The importance of this demonic mask is further underlined by the fact that in the religious theatre of medieval France, the entrance to hell on the stage was a giant devil's head called *chape de Herlequin,* or Harlequin's cap or hood.[17] Still later the simple black

[14] *Ibid.,* pp. 24 ff.
[15] *Ibid.,* pp. 40 ff.
[16] *Ibid.,* p. 58.
[17] "Die Struwelfratze des Hölleneingangs, das Teufelsgesicht als Wahrzeichen der Höllenbewohner, ist nichts anderes als die vergrösserte Struwelfratze des Herlekin

curtain in the front part of the stage was called *manteau de Harlequin* as it was right up to the twentieth century in the French theatre.

Relevant, also, is the story in verse by the thirteenth-century Norman poet Bourdet of how the sinful old woman Luque, dying, took to her bed and begged "Hellequin" to come get her because she wanted to marry him.[18] She didn't give a damn for her husband, but wanted a big wedding feast on her death bed. Harlequin (Hellequin), delighted, led three thousand devils out of hell with him to the festivities. They found the poor old woman, took her soul up in the air, tried to get her into the church, failed, and so took her to hell. Here Harlequin appears as a comic, lusty devil clearly associated, for women, with death and sexuality.[19]

In the fourteenth century, Harlequin figures were prominent in wild street carnivals and masquerades in France, particularly in the institution of *charivari* (chivaree) which has persisted in somewhat attenuated form right up to the present day. Chivaree involves a rowdy gang that makes a lot of noise and plays practical jokes on the night of a wedding outside the house where the bridal pair are spending their first night together. Nowadays the chivaree tradition is usually reduced to tying some tin cans or ribbons to the "get-away car," accompanying it with horn-blowing, and playing a few tricks on the bridal couple; but originally the revelry was more boisterous, and the chief reveler was often the man in the devil's mask, Harlequin. Again the connection of Harlequin with deviltry and sexuality is clear.

If further evidence is needed, it is provided by the story of the first Harlequin play for which the manuscript still exists. In it Harlequin makes a descent into hell to save "Mother" Cardine, madam of a famous bordello in Paris at the time, who had recently died and who, according to the play, was carried off to hell and married to Cerberus.[20] Harlequin succeeds in getting her out of hell because he charms everyone with his acrobatic tricks and good humor—first Charon into ferrying him across the River Styx and then Pluto, who offers Harlequin a job as his chief hangman or anything else he wants. In a slightly later version of the story, Harlequin charms Pluto's wife Persephone, who promptly makes love to him. He responds, saying in effect, "I'm your boy from now on."[21] Harlequin asks for Cardine as his reward. Pluto, although furious at having to give her up, finally agrees, for a god cannot go back on his

---

Narrenbeisser. . . . Dieser Herlekinkopf führt selbstverständlich die beiden Name, die uns für den Begriff 'Herlekinkopf' vertraut sind: 'Struwelfratze' (*hure*) und 'Herlekinkappe' (*chape de Herlequin*)." (Driesen, *ibid.*, pp. 72–73.)

[18] *Ibid.*, p. 94.
[19] *Ibid.*, pp. 93 ff.
[20] *Ibid.*, pp. 158 ff.
[21] *Ibid.*, p. 258.

word. On his way out with Cardine, Harlequin boasts to Charon that he has tricked Pluto and all the devils under his scepter, that his name is Harlequin, from which "you can see that the devils don't know any more than I do."[22]

His connection with seduction, illicit love, and death was thus firmly established and continued, though with diminishing emphasis, in the "dark" scenes of the harlequinades in subsequent centuries. Driesen's argument is that a group of traveling Italian players, probably Ganassa's troupe, became acquainted with the Harlequin tradition in France and decided to please their French audiences by staging a play in that tradition, but modified it to include considerably more of the clownish tricks from the Italian *zanni* tradition. Ganassa's troupe probably first performed it at the wedding of Margaret de Valois to the king of Navarre in 1572.[23] By this time Harlequin's characteristics were well established: his name, which meant devil to the French audience; his multicolored suit, which was originally a skin with patches sewed on to show he was a devil; his "bestial" hairy mask, which even had small horns to leave no doubt of his devilish connection; his character as an "evil" but lusty lover and seducer; and his extraordinary tricks and acrobatics, which derived in large part from the Italian tradition, though they were consistent with the notion that he was a demon. As Driesen sums it up, "Allerdings ist der Harlekin der Teufel."[24] In every respect Harlequin was the devil.

The idea of death as a lover has not always been represented by the Harlequin image, of course. It is far too universal a theme in human existence to appear always in the identical mythopoetic form. The best known version of the story for the Western world occurs in classical Greek mythology. In the *Homeric Hymn to Demeter,* her daughter Persephone is pictured as playing happily with friends in a meadow, when she suddenly sees a beautiful narcissus in flower, the perfume of which is so overpowering that it shakes the earth, the sky, and the sea. She reaches for it but discovers too late that it is a trap; the earth opens up, and she is grabbed by Hades, prince of the underworld of the dead, and taken away to his kingdom.[25] Demeter searches for and mourns her lost daugh-

---

[22] *Ibid.,* p. 254.

[23] For certainly, by 1574 Ganassa's troupe was presenting Arlecchino in Spain. According to a Spanish historian, Don Casiano Pellicer, writing from documents on file in the Madrid library in 1804: "El mismo año de 1574 habia en Madrid una compañia de Comediantes italianos, cuya cabeza y autor era Alberto Ganassa. Representaban comedias italianas, mimicas por la mayor parte, y bufonescas, de asuntos triviales y populares. Introducian en ellas las personas del Arlequino, del Pantalone, del Dotore" (*ibid.,* p. 229).

[24] *Ibid.,* p. 189.

[25] He is usually described in Greek as πολυδέγμων, translated by Lang as "the host of many guests," which is accurate enough, though the meaning of the phrase doesn't get through to the English reader immediately, partly because he doesn't

ter and finally in anger refuses to rejoin the other gods on Olympus or to allow the earth to bear fruit until she sees her daughter again. Alarmed at the possibility that the race of men may die of hunger, Zeus intercedes with his brother Hades, who allows Persephone to return to her mother, but only for part of the year. Before she leaves, he gives her some pomegranate seed to prevent her from leaving him forever, for whoever eats food in the kingdom of the dead must return. Two facts—one psychological, one historical—about this story are of particular interest to us here.

What is important psychologically is that Persephone appears to be somewhat ambivalent about her deathly lover, the prince of the underworld. She is attracted by something overpoweringly pleasant (the narcissus), but in reaching for it she is undone (abducted to the underworld). Eating the pomegranate also has its double aspect: she eats it apparently willingly at the time but later complains to her mother that Hades made her eat it against her will. Furthermore Hades is pictured not as a cruel rapist but rather as a gay, if crafty, seducer; and Persephone is described as "prudent" or "good." One can hardly avoid the conclusion that she feels some attraction to her dark lover though protesting like the good girl she is that she was seduced. Here, again, the prince of the underworld appears, as he does in the Harlequin myths, both as a figure of terror who takes women away to their deaths and as a gay seducer.

The historical fact is that the *Homeric Hymn to Demeter* also describes the origins of the famous Eleusinian mysteries, which were consecrated to two goddesses, Demeter and her daughter Persephone. Unfortunately, the cult guarded its secrets well, and we know little about them today, despite the fact that they were known to thousands of people who were initiated into the rites annually for nearly two thousand years. What were the Athenians hiding with such zeal that they nearly killed their favorite young hero of the moment, Alcibiades, for mimicking the mysteries too openly at a drunken party? We can never know for certain, but Jane Harrison has made some very shrewd guesses based on analogous, and better known, rituals for women.[26] The *Hymn* itself provides the main theme: deprivation and enhancement. The rape of Persephone deprives a mother of her daughter; most of the story is about Demeter's greatly enhanced need to nurture someone (she even tries to adopt a baby for a while). This theme was also represented (1) in the reference in the *Hymn* to the barrenness of the earth during the winter, followed by its

---

associate Hades with death as directly as a Greek would have. A paraphrase is better in English: "death, who receives so many hospitably." The point is that Hades, or death, neither here nor elsewhere in the *Hymn* appears as the "grim reaper" of modern mythology. See the later discussion of Persephone's ambivalence about her seducer.

[26] *Prolegomena to the Study of Greek Religion* (New York: Meridian, 1955).

greatly increased fertility in the spring (after Persephone returns) ; (2) in the purification rites for participants in the mysteries (self-denial to enhance holiness) ; (3) in the ritual lowering of pigs' flesh into the earth to let it rot before hauling it up again to spread on the fields to increase fertility; (4) in the darkness of the central part of the ceremony punctuated at a critical moment by a great flash of light. To put the theme in slightly different words: the Eleusinian mysteries celebrated the nearly universal ideas that one must deprive oneself to develop a stronger appetite; surrender or go down in order to come up, give of oneself in order to get; die to live—an idea which sums up the unique role of women particularly well. Whether in giving birth to a baby, nursing it, looking after a husband, or participating in the sexual act, a woman can be thought of as yielding or giving or surrendering herself in order to gain satisfaction. The odd thing about the mysteries to our male-dominated culture is that, both in the *Hymn* and, as far as one can tell, in the ritual itself, the male figure is present but rather shadowy. He is, like Hades, simply a means to an end, a projection of a woman's need, the agent who enables her to learn her most fundamental lesson—that she must die or be taken under in order to live fully. The mysteries acted out this theme both literally[27] and symbolically and initially largely for women.[28] Later they were infiltrated or replaced by the male-oriented cults of Dionysius and Orpheus, in which the shadowy male figure became the key actor in the drama.

At any rate, by the time Harlequin appears, it is he who is clearly the central character, not the woman who sees him as a means of learning the central lesson of her life. But why connect him with the Persephone story at all? First, on historical grounds, it is a fact that the Harlequin plays regularly contained scenes involving Hades and Persephone. Someone saw a connection. The hypothesis of historical continuity over a thousand years of folk tradition seems highly improbable, although one fascinating clue to such a tradition exists. Driesen quotes from a letter of William of Auvergne, bishop of Paris (died in 1248), which states that the common people in Spain believe any man under the protection of Ceres, goddess of agriculture, cannot be harmed by the ghostly army of Harlequins.[29] In other words, in Spanish folk tradition Ceres (Demeter) was still able to protect one from the devil, now identified as Harlequins not as Hades or Pluto of the classical Greek myth. Could Harlequin somehow be the historical survival of Hades?

But a psychological explanation of continuity seems more probable.

[27] Cf. J. Humbert, *Homère Hymnes* (Paris: Société d'édition "Les Belles Lettres," 1951), p. 31: "Un autre aspect de ce culte était funéraire et le 'Dieu et la Déesse' en étaient les objets."

[28] Harrison, *op. cit.,* p. 151.

[29] *Op. cit.,* p. 239.

In every generation, and to some extent in every woman, the image of dying to live, or more concretely of death as a lover, recurs. The particular form in which the theme is expressed in song and story will vary, but it obviously will draw on well-known treatments of a similar theme in the past as well as on new experiences. Thus the revival of interest in Greek and Roman mythology in the Renaissance made the ancient tales familiar once again, so that both author and audience could understand and appreciate the Persephone version of the universal theme in a harlequinade. As the author of the *Homeric Hymn to Demeter* so aptly puts it in introducing Hades to the reader, he is πολυώνυμος, "worshipped under many names."

Shakespeare gives him no name at all. Romeo simply says when he enters the tomb where Juliet is lying:

> . . . Ah, dear Juliet
> Why art thou yet so fair? Shall I believe
> That unsubstantial Death is amorous,
> And that the lean, abhorréd monster keeps
> Thee here in dark to be his paramour?

For others death, or Hades, became Dr. Faustus or Mephistopheles. Over and over the theme has been played out in different guises, often without any knowledge on the part of authors or readers that they are recreating an ancient or universal story. Agatha Christie, for instance, created Harlequin[30] as a symbol of both love and death entirely, so far as she knew, out of her own imagination. Here is one mystery that the mistress of detective fiction failed to penetrate! We may well believe her in the literal sense that she did not know of the antiquity of her theme. However, it is not surprising that, as a woman—and one much concerned with death in her writing—and as a product of Western culture exposed to classic mythology and harlequinades in many forms, she recreated the classic drama of Hades and Persephone, which in its universal form we are here calling the Harlequin complex.

Several other cultural images with a strong hold on public feeling can be connected with the Harlequin theme, though less certainly. One of the most fascinating is the bullfight. Certainly the matador looks and acts like Harlequin. He wears a "suit of lights" and a hat that could readily pass for a traditional Harlequin costume.[31] Furthermore, he performs the same kind of acrobatic tricks that Harlequin does, including the final play with his sword or dagger at the end. Finally, and above all, the matador represents death, the inevitable end that awaits even the strongest expression of the life force (the bull).

---

[30] *The Mysterious Mr. Quin, op. cit.*
[31] Cf. Niklaus, *op. cit.*, facing p. 121.

But if the matador is acting out the part of Harlequin or Hades, where is Persephone, and just how does the bull represent the life force? If the interpretation is correct, the matador should be fighting the bull to win a fair lady (Persephone). The modern bullfight retains only one small bit of evidence that it ever had such a meaning—namely the *brindis,* or ceremonial dedication of the bull to an important personage in the audience, made by the matador at the beginning of the *tercio* before he moves in to the kill. Unfortunately for our thesis, the person is usually a man, though on occasion it may be a woman. However, the bullfight in its Spanish form is nearly a thousand years old, and for most of that time, or until 1700–1750, the matador was a member of the gentry who fought a bull on horseback with a lance, to win the favor of a lady, in the tradition of courtly chivalry.[32] For example, D. F. S. de A., evidently a member of the Spanish nobility, in writing a history of the bullfight in 1873 bemoans the fact that men fight bulls "nowadays" for money rather than for the respectful love of a woman, whereas in former times they risked their lives in exchange for the admiring glance of their beloved. He also complains that the women have changed, too. In the 1870's ("nowadays") they are frightened by the slightest movement of the bull's head, whereas earlier they were at the fights, ready, with the bravery and calm proper to heroines, to award the prize or withdraw their favor from their idols.[33] In short, the bullfight traditionally did involve the theme of the struggle of a man for a woman's affection and admiration. What happened was that the idea tended to be obscured when the "lower orders" took over fighting the bull, since now the matador often fought on behalf of his patron, a member of the gentry, whose place he was taking.

If our reasoning is correct and the matador was originally Hades fighting for his love Persephone (the death-as-a-lover theme), whom is he fighting? Traditionally there is only one possible answer: the bull is Demeter, the life force, who represented for the Greeks the source of everything living—both plants and animals. She was earth, the patroness of man in this world of the living, as Hades was the host of man in the underworld of the dead. It is hard to see how a female goddess got turned into a very male bull, but it is known that some kind of bullfight or dance

[32] D. F. S. de A., for example, describes bullfights in former times as follows: ". . . come favorite diversion de la nobleza, senalándose en la liza de los toros por su valentia, distreza y agilidad, muchisimos caballeros que eran los que cautivaban el corazon de las damas más principales." *Las Corridas de Toros* (Madrid: Imprenta y Litografía de N. Gonzalez, 1873), p. 55.

[33] "En el dia las damas de alto coturno y de bajo escarpin se asustan del movimento del testud de un toro; entónces presenciaban, con el valor y la calma proprios de heroinas, aquellos rudos combates del hombre con el hombre ó con las fieras, dispuestas siempre á dar el premio ó retirar su cariño al ídolo de sus esperanzas, segun su noble ó menguado proceder" (*ibid.,* p. 47).

was connected with the worship of Demeter-Persephone at Eleusis[34] and also that in Spanish folk dances, at least as they have survived in Mexico, the woman playfully assumes the part of the bull in running at her romantic partner's kerchief.[35] We must be satisfied for the moment with the psychological parallels: the bullfight certainly dramatizes the struggle of death (the matador) with life (the bull in all his power and strength) for the love of a lady. What is extraordinary in cross-cultural perspective is the arrogance of the Spaniard in identifying with death, the killer and destroyer of the strongest life urge; but as Paz puts it in speaking for Mexican culture, "Death is present in our fiestas, our games, our loves and our thoughts. To die and to kill are ideas that rarely leave us. We are seduced by death." Life is *Muerte sin fin*—"death without end."[36]

More recently Harlequin has appeared in the United States as a seducer of women in the once popular image of the hypnotist Svengali or, more importantly today, as the dark, mysterious foreign psychoanalyst. As Bakan points out, Freud more or less explicitly, though only half seriously, allied himself with the devil, with the dark, irrational forces in man's nature, with the underworld of the psyche.[37] Furthermore, he and other psychoanalysts played out the Harlequin image in two other important particulars. They carried out their treatment with their patients, in the beginning usually women, stretched out on a couch as if ready for sexual intercourse and also as if dead on a bier; and the treatment involved a specifically sexual relationship between the woman and her "hidden" male analyst (transference). While the death and seduction aspects of psychoanalytic treatment were muted and treated only symbolically, much of the force of the popular image of psychoanalysts as dark foreign "devils," and perhaps even of the treatment itself, may have come from its re-creation of the eternal Harlequin theme, of a woman being sexually seduced by death.

One final example, this time from Hollywood. The Western film is to American culture what the bullfight was to Spanish culture—a mirror of some of its profoundest impulses. Hollywood has recently (1961) put Harlequin in cowboy dress and dramatized the age-old theme, with suitably Freudian overtones, in a movie called *The Last Sunset*. The key figure is a cowboy, O'Malley, a gay seducer with a demonic temper. The Harlequin image is underlined by a number of facts. He dresses in black; often wears a mask (over the lower half of his face, in true cowboy style); carries a derringer, which, instead of a slapstick, is his magic

[34] Harrison, *op. cit.*, p. 147.

[35] Cf., for example, "El Torito," part of the "Fiesta Veracruzana" in the repertoire of the Ballet Folklorico of Mexico in 1962.

[36] O. Paz, "The Eye of Mexico," *Evergreen Review*, II (1959), 22–37.

[37] D. Bakan, *Sigmund Freud and the Jewish Mystical Tradition* (Princeton, New Jersey: Van Nostrand, 1958), pp. 187 ff.

weapon; and generally looks and acts Mephistophelian. He recites poetry and handles animals in a way which makes his association with the spirit world clear. He is a seducer of women—in fact he announces to the heroine's husband that he intends to seduce her; he is a charming yet fearful figure, capable both of great tenderness and of violent rages in which he kills; he particularly attracts young girls searching for the ideal "dark" lover, in this case fatally—a young girl whom he discovers too late is his own daughter. So in the end he can safely go on being the "demon" lover only by dying and returning to the spirit world, from which he came.[38]

He is, then, doubly associated with death, as a killer himself and as someone whose death is the climax of the movie—a death that ennobles and purifies his love for his daughter and her mother, since he deliberately chooses to die, or to "live on" in the hearts of the women he loves as a spirit lover—in other words, as Harlequin. It is a mark of the influence of psychoanalytic thinking on art in our day that Harlequin—the illicit, good-bad lover—is here clearly identified as the father.

But it is time to move out of the world of myth and culture history and into the world of modern empirical science. What our explorations have demonstrated is that the notion of death as both attractive and repellent, as a lusty but evil seducer of women, is by no means of recent origin, at least in the West. It is a human experience important enough to be well represented in myth and story, most commonly in the form which we have called the Harlequin complex. But if it is a common experience, then women who are dying should have two opposite but related fantasies—negative ones like the "dark" scenes in the harlequinades, representing hell, horror, and punishment for being bad, and more positive ones like the scenes in a tale of seduction and illicit love in which Harlequin is chasing Columbine. Such an hypothesis is specific enough to be checked by the methods of modern empirical psychological science. Greenberger put it to the test very simply by collecting fantasies from women who were dying of cancer and comparing them with those of similar women hospitalized for minor illnesses.[39] Since the findings of the first study were promising, she cross-checked them on another group of severely ill women to make certain the results were not due to cancer as such, but to the imminence of death.

Her procedure in all cases was to arrange through the hospital authorities to give some "tests" to women who were in bed in hospitals for various reasons. They were middle-aged (average age around forty-

---

[38] For a more sophisticated treatment of the same theme in the art-film form, see *Last Year at Marienbad*.

[39] E. S. Greenberger, "Fantasies of Women Confronting Death: A Study of Critically Ill Patients" (unpublished Ph.D. thesis, Radcliffe College, 1961).

five), largely lower class (since these were public hospitals), more often Catholic than Protestant, and had been in the hospital about a week on the average. Every attempt was made to maximize the differences between two groups of women in each of the two studies on the extent to which they were under sentence of death, so to speak, and to minimize the differences between them on everything else (age, religion, social class, length of stay in the hospital, etc.). That is, the cancer patients knew they had cancer, which is generally accepted as a fatal disease, and half of them were tested just before an operation. On the other hand, the control patients were hospitalized largely for minor surgical operations and were all tested post-operatively. In the second study it was difficult to find other diseases which are accepted as so fatal as cancer; but the severely ill women (most of them with critical heart conditions) certainly must have been more aware at some level of the imminent possibility of death than their matched controls, who were in the hospital for minor illnesses.

The test of major interest here was a version of the Thematic Apperception Test. Although most of the women protested that they were not very good at telling stories, they were all able to do so after some encouragement, and normally the critically ill women in particular were only too glad for some form of pleasant social interaction. The stories they told were quite different in the two key respects in which we are interested. The women for whom death was a real possibility thought *almost twice as often* about punishment and illicit sex as the women who were about to go home from the hospital after a minor illness. Interestingly enough, the critically ill women did not repress thoughts of death: they spoke of it at least as often and possibly more often than women who were not so sick. Though Americans may deny the reality of death in public, these women at least did not (or were not able to) force it from their thinking.

But what were the stories like that were coded as containing themes of punishment or illicit sex? Obviously these women had a fairly low level of education and could not produce full-blown harlequinades on the spot, but in their own words they expressed the same ideas clearly enough. For example, one said: "Her husband could have come home on a drunk, beat her, threw her on the bed. . . . She had a boyfriend. . . . Her husband didn't care for that." The fact that someone is beaten for what she has done is scored for punishment; the further fact that a married woman has a boyfriend is scored for illicit sex. How reminiscent of the sinful old witch Luque who on her death bed didn't give a damn for her husband but called for Harlequin! Other types of illicit sex included unwanted pregnancy, seduction or abduction, "affairs" out of wedlock, adultery, etc. Here is an almost perfect statement of the rape of Persephone as told by a dying woman in the twentieth century, who had almost certainly not read the story as it was first recorded 2,500 or more years ago: "That man is there to take her away on his horse, and she doesn't want to go. That's her mother. She doesn't want her to go."

Who is the man who wants to take her away? From the orthodox psychoanalytic point of view he is obviously the incestuous love object, i.e., the father—the unlawful sexual partner.[40] Perhaps some slight support for such an inference may be drawn from the fact that in both studies the number of references to illicit sexual activity made by the critically ill women was greater for those who had no current sexual partner (because they were single, widowed, or divorced) than for those who had a husband. In other words, those who were dying who had husbands may have had less reason to refer back to the original love object—the father—since he had been replaced by another. But this evidence is at best quite indirect and open to other interpretations. So Greenberger tried another method of tracking down the identity of the illicit lover. She reasoned that, although the women would be unlikely to label him as a father or fatherlike figure, perhaps their longing for intimacy with the father would show up in more generalized references to reunions with him or even with the mother. The expectation was not borne out. The average number of references to reunion with parents was not significantly higher among the critically ill women than among other similar women who were not so sick.

There is little empirical support here for the psychoanalytic hypothesis that the illicit love partner is the father with whom reunion is sought. Perhaps the test of the hypothesis is not adequate, but it is difficult to think of one that would be better. In a sense, psychoanalysis does not need further evidence—the fact that a woman under such conditions thinks about an illicit sexual relationship with a man is enough; the man ought to be the father, from the theoretical point of view. But it is certainly more in line with scientific caution to regard his identity as unproved. So let us stick closer to the empirical findings and refer to him as Harlequin, the unknown seducer of whom women who are about to die dream more often than women who are in a hospital for a minor illness.

But a sceptic might interrupt at this point and ask whether we are not being too romantic and reading too much into a simple association

---

[40] Freud touches on many of the themes related to the Harlequin complex in two papers, but as always he treats them from the male standpoint, which prevents him from reaching a profound understanding of the nature of death as it appears to women. The meaning of death to men is quite another topic, deserving separate analysis and research. Cf. "The Theme of the Three Caskets" and "A Neurosis of Demoniacal Possession in the Seventeenth Century," *Collected Papers* (London: Hogarth Press, 1949), IV, 244–256 and 436–472.

between death and love, which might characterize men as well as women and which might mean no more than that a human being about to die is likely to think of the pleasures of the flesh, of which death is about to deprive him or her. Such an explanation is appealing in its simplicity, but unfortunately it is not well supported by some other facts. Greenberger tried to check directly to see if there was an increase in narcissism (self-indulgence, gazing at one's image in a mirror present in one of the pictures, etc.) in women who were about to die, but could find no evidence for it. The increase she found was specific to sexual activity—illicit sexual activity at that—and furthermore it was by no means described as pleasurable most of the time.

That still leaves the question open of what men might feel under similar circumstances. Might they not see death as an illicit sexual attraction for a woman—the mother? Unfortunately, Greenberger's study has not yet been carried out with men, but there is both cultural and empirical evidence that death has a different meaning for them. Although it is true that the image exists in myth and story of "la belle dame sans merci" who is waiting to take men away at their death, she is hardly a seductive or thrilling figure the way Harlequin is for women. In fact she fits rather well with those images of death as a castrating figure which are in such common use in our male-oriented culture—e.g., the old man with the scythe.

A rather simple direct test of the hypothesis that men and women view death differently was carried out by asking random samples of forty male and thirty-eight female college students to rank order the following metaphors in terms of their appropriateness for describing death: An understanding doctor, a gay seducer, a grinning butcher, a last adventure, a threatening father, a misty abyss, the end of a song. No significant differences appeared in the rankings by men and by women except for one metaphor—namely, "a gay seducer," the Harlequin image. It was not particularly popular with either sex, but significantly more women (66 per cent) than men (40 per cent) ranked it in the upper half of the distribution of ranks ($x^2 = 5.15$, p $<$ .05). Even consciously, women can see the possibility of death as a lover more easily than men can.[41] The one other point of interest in the results concerned the metaphor which was preferred more by men—namely, "a grinning butcher." Although there was no over-all significant difference in the preferences for it be-

[41] Unfortunately the interpretation is not so straightforward as one could wish, because, if the term "seducer" is considered male, no metaphor in the list is clearly female. Thus the men may not really have been given a chance to express a preference for a metaphor picturing death as an illicit female lover, e.g. as "a dangerous enchantress." This possibility does not completely undermine the interpretation of the finding given in the text because the term "seducer," like "lover," is somewhat ambiguous as to gender, but certainly one would wish for further evidence on the point.

tween the sexes, 7 out of 40 men (18 per cent) put it in first place as most appropriate, compared with only 1 out of 38 women (3 per cent). In short, though the data are not extensive or by themselves enough to close the issue, they do lend support to the hypothesis that the association discovered by Greenberger between death and illicit sexuality may be considered more characteristic of women than men. The sceptic's doubts cannot be put wholly to rest, but perhaps his alternative simpler explanation seems sufficiently questionable to permit us to follow the Harlequin theme to its conclusion.

To return to the stories told by critically ill women in Greenberger's study, what is the meaning of the increased number of references to punishment? Are the punishment and guilt related to illicit sexual activity? Sometimes, but not always. For example, in one of the stories quoted above, the husband comes home and beats his wife for having a boyfriend. Here the woman is directly punished for her illicit sexual activities. But actually the scoring categories are discrete. That is, references to guilt and punishment may have nothing to do with sex at all, e.g., "He's done something wrong and is being chastised," or "He killed her and he looks regretful." All that one can legitimately conclude is that impending death increases the frequency with which women think about guilt and punishment, not over any particular type of wrongdoing, but over wrongdoing in general. In the more vivid imagery of the Middle Ages, they think more about hell, about the place or condition that symbolizes sin and punishment. Oddly enough, the Harlequin stories are similarly vague about who gets punished for what. The "dark" scenes take place in hell—there are plenty of demons about and references to condemned souls—but it is not always clear that it is the sins of the women, like Luque or "Mother" Cardine, which cause them to be taken there or to be punished. The background is hell, the world of punishment, but as in these stories, the punishment does not always fall on the guilty lover, on the woman who may have betrayed her husband for Harlequin or who may have been a prostitute in real life. It is as if the punishment and guilt have been displaced. The themes are there all right—one cannot talk about devils and hell without suggesting punishment and guilt —but they are not openly and directly described as consequences of illicit sexual activities.

On the other hand, the very fact that the sexual activity is illicit suggests that something is wrong that might imply guilt or punishment. In a sense, all references to illicit sex might also have been scored under punishment by inference, but it seemed safer to stick to what the women actually said in their stories and to score for punishment only when they mentioned it. The point can be made clearer by an illustration. Here is a part of a story told by a woman dying of cancer:

[Picture of couple embracing] I first thought it looks like he is enticing her, if he is a "he," but I don't like the theme of enticement. He is imparting some kind of message—a very special message. It has such an ethereal quality. He's telling, assuring her that something is all right, but I'll be damned if I know what. What could it be? It looks like a romantic scene, but I'm trying to steer away from a romantic scene. This is a tough one. There is a third person concerned. I think maybe I will get back to romance. The third person concerned is an illegitimate child that belongs to them. It was put in a home and lost to them for years and finally they traced it, and it means a lot to them.

This is a pure case of what we mean by the Harlequin theme—the mysterious enticing stranger whose embrace represents illegitimate sexual union. With his special message of an ethereal quality, it is not hard to imagine that he is somehow connected with the death that is approaching this woman. But note that there is no guilt or punishment directly connected with the illegitimate child. Society might regard such a child as a "punishment," but for this woman the child is actually a reward—"it means a lot to them." But the same woman fills her other stories with guilt and punishment. For example, in the story just prior to the one already quoted, she says:

[Man and half-naked woman on bed] Oh, your people are sad! I am not going to say he murdered her. He tried to, but he didn't. He's perfectly scared realizing he came darn near it. Mmm. We'll have a very common, ordinary story. He thinks she has someone she likes better. Just the same old jealous fancy. He finds out later he was all wrong. He feels like shooting himself, but he doesn't.

Again the Harlequin theme. She might have betrayed him. But now both punishment and guilt are mentioned. He tries to murder her and then feels like shooting himself. But even here the retribution is not wholly appropriate: she didn't actually betray him and he feels guilty, not she. So, just as in the harlequinades, the stories of critically ill women more frequently center in two themes—one involving punishment and guilt and the other, illicit sexual pursuits. The two themes are not explicitly connected—in the sense that the punishment and guilt are for illicit sexual activities—although, of course, it would not take much subtlety to infer that they are in fact implicitly connected. But there is no reason to be subtle. Let us remain with the simple factual conclusion that imminent death in women gives rise to associations of punishment and illicit sexual activities.

Having established such an empirical relationship, we can now turn it around and ask the diagnostic question. Does it follow that women whose fantasies are filled with references to punishment, guilt, and illicit sexual relationships are concerned about death? Such an inference is, of course, not logically permissible, but psychologically it may make good sense. In a number of other instances it has been found that, having established that a given state of the organism gives rise to characteristic fantasies, one can then make use of those fantasies to infer the state of the organism which normally gives rise to them. Since hungry subjects produce more fantasies about food shortages and means of getting food, one can infer how hungry a person is from how often he writes about such things.[42] Or, even more usefully, it has been found that experimental achievement pressure increases the number of story themes dealing with doing something well, so that the number of such themes appearing in the record of someone not under immediate achievement pressure can be considered diagnostic of his concern for achievement.[43] Thus there is ample precedent for suggesting that the Harlequin complex—a concern with punishment and illicit sexuality in women—might be diagnostic of the state of the organism that produced it—namely, concern with impending death. But how can such an inference be checked empirically?

Again a return to the late Middle Ages, when Harlequin was very popular, may be of help. It was also a time when the fear of witches was widespread. Zilboorg's *History of Medical Psychology* gives a graphic account of the persecution of witches in Western Europe.[44] It was a persecution that reached its height in the sixteenth century under the influence of the "witches' hammer," the *Malleus Maleficarum,* a treatise on witchcraft prepared by two priests to help people identify and punish witches. The characteristics of a witch were as follows: she was dangerous and could injure or even cause the death of another person with her magical powers; she was a sinner who had renounced God and was in league with the devil and his cohorts, with whom she had sexual relations; and, finally, she could not be cured but had to be killed to get the devil out of her. The point of interest to us here is that there was ample opportunity for the association of the three ideas with which we are concerned— namely, punishment, illicit sexuality, and death. The witches who were caught confessed (1) that they were concerned with punishment, that is, with punishing others for real or alleged mistreatment of them and with their own punishment in hell for misbehavior; and (2) that they had sexual relations with devils. They were also obviously concerned about death in at least two important senses: they had "died" psychically when they left the world of reality, the Christian world, and joined up with the underworld of demons; and since burnings and hangings for

[42] J. W. Atkinson and D. C. McClelland, "The Projective Expression of Needs: II. The Effect of Different Intensities of the Hunger Drive on Thematic Apperception," *J. Exp. Psychol.,* XXXIX (1948), 643–658.

[43] D. C. McClelland, J. W. Atkinson, R. A. Clark, and E. L. Lowell, *The Achievement Motive* (New York: Appleton-Century, 1953).

[44] G. Zilboorg, *A History of Medical Psychology* (New York: Norton, 1941), pp. 144 ff.

witchcraft were common and well publicized, they must have had a realistic basis for expecting their actual physical death. In fact, one can even argue that the confessions themselves, filled as they are with tortured versions of the Harlequin complex, are the fantasies of women confronted with imminent death, since they knew that death was the most probable outcome of the proceedings against them.

But Zilboorg adds a further and highly significant fact. Many of these women were certainly mentally ill, suffering from what psychiatrists would today call schizophrenia. In fact, if a woman began behaving in a peculiar way, showing the lack of touch with reality that schizophrenics usually show, she was very likely to be identified as a witch. But why? What gave people the idea that these peculiar women were witches in league with the devil? Probably there were many reasons, but one of them may well have been the content of the incoherent talk of such women. Both then and now, it contains a high frequency of references to illicit sexuality and to crimes and eternal damnation. Since these are the key elements in the Harlequin complex, might we infer, using the logic suggested above, that schizophrenic women have a heightened concern with death? The hypothesis is an exciting one, though at first glance it may seem like a rather far-fetched and certainly overly simple explanation of the complex symptomatology of schizophrenia. What arguments can be produced in its favor?

First of all, in the sixteenth century, before the medical conception of mental illness was developed, men obviously thought that schizophrenic women (i.e., witches) were dead spiritually and should be put to death physically. They had died to the world of everyday reality, to the world of Christianity, and had gone off with spirits and demons in another world (like Luque in Bourdet's poem). In a certain very literal sense, their diagnosis was correct because schizophrenics behave as if they have left this life. The later medical conception of schizophrenia as an illness, much like a physical disease, tended to discount the talk and behavior of schizophrenics as "mere ravings" of no use in diagnosing what was wrong. That is, the mind was simply regarded as disordered, much as the stomach might be disordered, and the peculiar speech and behavior, like a stomach-ache, just showed the doctors that something was wrong without telling him exactly what it was. But if we go back to the premedical diagnosis, it may provide a clue as to what is wrong. Perhaps schizophrenic women are dead psychically, though their bodies go on living. Perhaps Harlequin has come and taken their souls to hell, so that they are dead to this world, as medieval opinion had it.

In the second place, the by now well-studied withdrawal reaction of schizophrenics supports the notion that they are acting as if they are dead to the social world, the normal world of human intercourse. In a recent review of empirical research studies on schizophrenia, Maher concludes "that schizophrenics appear consistently inferior—compared with normals—on tasks in which the stimuli are representative of human social interactions; where the stimulus material is of a nonpersonal kind, this inferiority is less consistent."[45] In other words, they react normally to simple tests of sensory acuity or conditioning, but as the experiment itself requires more and more social interaction or contains stimuli signifying human or interpersonal situations, the patient performs less and less well than a normal subject. He is socially withdrawn, or dead to the human world.

Finally, to return to the fantasies of schizophrenic women, they often do contain the increased number of references to illicit sexuality and punishment which, if our whole line of reasoning is correct, should be diagnostic of a concern with death. In other words, they not only behave as if they were dead, they have the fantasies they should be having if they were dying. Unfortunately, the definitive study has not as yet been carried out which would demonstrate that the fantasies of schizophrenic women in fact contain more signs of the Harlequin complex than fantasies produced by control subjects. So we must be satisfied for the time being with evidence from clinical investigations. Let us look at an actual case, selected to tell the Harlequin story in some detail, but by no means atypical among female schizophrenics.

French and Kasanin have summarized the case of a young female schizophrenic which is particularly useful for our purpose because she recovered and was able to give a fairly full account of her experiences.[46] Most schizophrenics remain socially dead and are relatively uneducated anyway, so that they cannot tell us very well what goes on.[47] Only those who return to social living bring back the strange tales of what they experienced. The young woman in question was twenty-four, a nurse, the youngest of eight children of Italian parents who had been originally Catholic but were converted to Protestantism. She had a fairly normal childhood, "was well adjusted in school, was quite a leader and loved to play and take care of little children. She was a hard worker, had an excellent scholastic record and graduated from high school at eighteen." After this, she went on to become a very successful nurse. However, she was "brought up in a very rigid family discipline . . . the patient was never allowed to go out with boys until she was twenty-two. Even then

[45] B. Maher, *Psychopathology* (New York: McGraw-Hill, in press).

[46] T. M. French and J. Kasanin, "A Psychodynamic Study of the Recovery of Two Schizophrenic Cases," first published in 1941; reprinted in S. S. Tomkins, ed., *Contemporary Psychopathology: A Sourcebook* (Cambridge, Massachusetts: Harvard University Press, 1953), pp. 355–370.

[47] Cf. A. B. Hollingshead and F. C. Redlich, "Social Stratification and Psychiatric Disorders," *Amer. Sociol. Rev.*, XVIII (1953), 163–169.

she had to be in by ten o'clock, and the mother interviewed every man she met. The patient was given a choice of a career or marriage. Inasmuch as she was interested in a career, the parents insisted that she have nothing to do with men."[48]

Her real difficulties began "with an intimacy with her brother's friend, Tracy, who made urgent sexual advances to her. As she later confessed, she had refused intercourse with him only because she was menstruating, but had yielded to tongue kissing and probably to fellatio, which was very disgusting to her. Then she developed cankers in her mouth, became disgusted by everything she ate, and was sure she had syphilis." From then on, she was more and more disturbed, confused, unable to make decisions, depressed, suicidal, and paranoid. "She said that the police had tried to flirt with her and that she had been shut in a room with a policeman so that she would be compromised. When they tried to give her a sedative, she said they were giving her poison. . . . She called on God and announced that she was a sinner. She also mentioned the name of her brother's friend and said that she had been intimate with him."[49] She grew steadily worse and was diagnosed a catatonic schizophrenic in a stuporous state with little chance of quick recovery.

"On admission to the State Hospital, the patient was mute and untidy. She grimaced, gesticulated, and mumbled to herself unintelligibly. At times she was overtalkative. For a long time she wandered about the ward, dirty, unresponsive, with a vacant, dull expression." In other words, she presented the classic picture of the schizophrenic withdrawal reaction, and she would undoubtedly have been classified as a witch in the sixteenth century, particularly if it had been clear to others what was going on in her mind at the time. For in a retrospective account, she recalled:

> I went through what I thought was positive hell. I believed myself to have been dead many years. I thought I had been so wicked on earth that I was not allowed to live on it any more and that only the good people were allowed to enjoy its luxuries . . . to be really dead was my only craving . . . if only I could have ended everything for myself.[50]

Her experiences in hell were agonizing. She imagined that the doctors or visitors hated her, that she was kidnapped and taken to Italy, transformed into a snake, condemned by all for her sins. She even found the equivalent of Pluto: "I thought when my case was read that I was at a trial. I thought the superintendent of the hospital was a judge and that the people could not get out of the hospital. They were being suffocated. The world had stopped."[51]

[48] *Op. cit.*, p. 356.
[49] *Ibid.*, p. 357.
[50] *Ibid.*, p. 358.
[51] *Ibid.*, p. 360.

She also realized that though she was dead, people were trying to get in touch with her. "I heard my friends' and relatives' voices. They all wanted me to return home. I could hear them pleading with me. . . . I wanted to talk to [a nurse], but, as I believed myself to have been dead, I couldn't bring myself to do so . . . when my father came, I did not want him near me . . . because I had been dead. . . . The hydro was like a morgue to me. I felt they were reviving people who were dead."[52]

Eventually people did get through to her. She rediscovered her identity, proving to her own satisfaction by certain scars on her body that she was really herself and not dead. However, her main improvement seemed to revolve around working through her sexual relationship with Tracy, which she went over and over in her mind endlessly. "Tracy always got awfully excited when he loved me. . . . I think he was in love with me. I think he liked me a lot, but he has other girls. He never talked seriously of marriage. He told me I was the woman, but I don't think he meant it . . . he did many other things which were repulsive to me."[53] Clearly he was the evil seducer who had betrayed her into an illicit sexual relationship. The sexual desire he aroused in her apparently led her to fantasy that she was transformed into a snake. "The hairs of my head were each one changing separately into a snake. I, myself, was going to be a huge one. These thoughts sent shivers through me. It was horror again."[54] Her illicit impulses horrified her. She was being devoured by her sexuality, symbolized by the snake. Yet she further imagined that the snake needed to be fed on a proper diet, and this came to symbolize her own cure. She eventually recovered from the attraction and guilt in her relationship to Tracy, and satisfied her sexual desires by falling in love and marrying another man: the snake (her sexuality) was fed on a proper diet.

What is so interesting about this case history is that it reads like a retelling in the dramatic language of schizophrenia of the classic Harlequin story. A demon lover seduces a woman into an illicit sexual relationship. He represents death, and she goes to hell, the world of eternal damnation and punishment for sin. Thus it is that "Mother" Cardine, queen of the prostitutes, of illicit sexuality, goes to hell and is condemned to live with Cerberus, the monstrous lover. But the story sometimes has a happy ending. Another lover comes and rescues her. He is Harlequin, too, in the sense that he is familiar with the underworld of wrongful sexuality, but he also belongs to the world of the living. He is clever and funny and doesn't take such a serious view of this world. We may assume that he and Columbine or Cardine live happily ever after, just as our schizophrenic patient does with the new-found and less horrify-

---

[52] *Ibid.*, p. 359.
[53] *Ibid.*, p. 359.
[54] *Ibid.*, p. 358.

ing lover who becomes her husband. Not always does the half-bad, half-good lover come to rescue the woman from real death or from the living death of schizophrenia. In a sense he cannot come at all to women who are dying of cancer, particularly those who do not have living husbands to replace the dark mysterious figure who is taking them away forever. Yet, in a sense, the deathly lover is better than none at all. He apparently provides some of the thrill that women feel at the approach of death—a thrill which in normal women is compounded out of illicit attraction and fear of the consequences.

Among schizophrenic women, the thrill has passed over into the experience itself, into a kind of living death. The attractive force is too strong, and at the same time too sinful and horrifying to be coped with in any of the normal ways. The patient dies to the human world and gives herself up completely to the grip of the Harlequin complex. Like the schizophrenic patient just discussed, she is out of this world, in hell, where a cosmic battle goes on between her overpowering love for her seducer and her feelings of being sinful, guilty, and in need of punishment. Or to rephrase the struggle in terms of the drama of the Eleusinian mysteries she has "gone down," but is unable to "come up" for a variety of possible reasons. Yielding has become a fearful thing, not the prelude to a fuller life; that is, the demon lover is in a sense the projection of her need to yield in order to fulfill herself. So he exerts a powerful attractive force. Yet at the same time he appears dangerous, because he represents a sexuality that may be considered wrong or, more seriously, a surrender of consciousness or the self—a surrender which may appear to threaten the central core of her being. In normal women the conflict is fairly readily resolved; they fall in love and learn more or less successfully how to fulfill themselves by only seeming to die in order to nurture and create—less rather than more successfully in twentieth century America, where women too often try to pattern their lives after the male model, which is quite different.

In schizophrenic women the conflict is too great; they are stopped in learning the lesson. Perhaps a better understanding of their dilemma can help resolve it. A Swiss existentialist psychiatrist, Medard Boss, has described a case in which a female schizophrenic found her way out of the grip of the Harlequin complex essentially because the therapist helped her through a rebirth process, so that she could "come up" again out of the pit.[55] A gifted artist, she supplied him with vivid drawings of the "personages" in the Harlequin drama (though he did not so identify them)—namely, the dark Mephistophelian seducer (Hades) and the disapproving elderly woman (Demeter). She began to recover when she played the role of a baby herself and, what was more important, began

[55] In a lecture given at Harvard University in the spring of 1962.

to draw pictures of beautiful, happy babies: symbols both of her own rebirth and of her revived capacity to nurture (she had been a highly intellectual, modern career woman).

So the thrill that many normal women feel at the possibility of death turns out to be a clue to a more profound understanding of feminine psychology. For death represents the demon lover—the symbol of a woman's own life urge, which is expressed paradoxically in the thought of yielding or dying. He appears in many guises. We have called him Harlequin, which was his name in the Western world for a millennium. But whatever he is called, he has seduced many Columbines, both on the stage and in real life; he comes to comfort middle-aged women who tire of their husbands and to thrill older women nearing the death that separates them from mortal lovers; and he has trapped many a wretched woman into a terrifying death while she is yet alive, a state which modern science has labeled schizophrenia.

PROCEDURES AND VARIABLES FOR STUDYING PERSONALITY
Part II

Murray's conception of personality has required the development of new strategies of investigation. If we are to learn about our subjects' significant thoughts, feelings, and conceptions of themselves, it is necessary to create conditions that will encourage affective involvement and willing self-disclosure. Situations devised to elicit circumscribed, impersonal responses cannot shed much light on what people consider important about themselves. An atmosphere must prevail in which the subject finds the psychologist interested in him as a person, respectful of his virtues, and sympathetic to his troubles. The highly motivated situation of psychotherapy cannot be reproduced in the study of well people, but, especially with young people, the investigator can often avail himself of a keen desire for better self-understanding and at least an unconscious wish for help in achieving it.

Murray's most telling contribution to method is that of using the same subjects for the whole program of a research group. Dropping in frequently at the research center, the subjects quite naturally become friendly with the investigators, and the investigators with the subjects. This plan has the advantage of exposing the subjects to different workers who bring out different aspects of personality, and it permits the research staff, meeting as a diagnostic council, to pool its findings and arrive at its conclusions jointly. But Murray has also been much occupied with creating concrete situations of an emotionally involving character. Several of these are described in *Explorations in Personality,* and several even more dramatic ones, devised in a time of national emergency, are reported in *Assessment of Men.* He has devoted particular attention, moreover, to imaginative productions as a means of inferring the vital secret wishes and unconscious fantasies which subjects are not able to communicate directly. The Thematic Apperception Test is merely the best known of many procedures leading to this end.

The first three chapters in this section are direct offshoots of these ideas. Nielsen describes a procedure in which a subject is first involved in a serious argument on values with another student and is then confronted with a sound film of the entire scene. The experience of witnessing one's behavior as if through the eyes of an observer tends to disconcert his self-image and produces many kinds of response, several of which are described by Nielsen. Bellak uses analytic methods derived from the Thematic Apperception Test to study selected short stories by Somerset Maugham. He detects in this way a rather unexpected recurrence of themes in stories having widely different plots and settings. The research reported in the chapter by Davids makes use of the "Azzageddi Test," named for a character in Melville's *Mardi and a Voyage Thither* who attributes his confused speech to a devil of that name. The test material consists of spoken passages representing certain needs and values, with interpolated statements standing for quite different needs and values. Davids uses it here for a study of tolerance of ambiguity. Both Bellak and Davids offer reflections on creativity which deserve comparison with the chapters in the third section of this book.

Murray has devoted a good deal of thought to the variables of personality. The necessity for careful, discriminating descriptions of entities and processes was first driven home to him during medical training and practice. One of the chief contributions of *Explorations in Personality* was the development of a systematic taxonomy of the dynamic processes called needs. The growth of such a system requires a persistence and intensity of observation that has often been shunned by psychologists hastening to make their research neat, clean, and small. Although the task never ends, it is not one which the serious student of personality can afford to leave aside.

The last two chapters in this section undertake new steps in taxonomy. Kroeber starts from the ten defense mechanisms recognized in psychoanalytic theory, but he frees these mechanisms from their exclusive connection with pathology. He treats them instead as the less rational manifestations of general coping processes which, under ordinary circumstances, are of great value in adaptation. Shneidman draws on his long experience in the study and prevention of suicide to develop a detailed taxonomy of orientations toward death. He illustrates the procedures used in analyzing real cases by applying them to a famous literary example, the death of Captain Ahab as he pursues the white whale Moby Dick.

5: THE METHOD OF SELF-CONFRONTATION

Gerhard S. Nielsen

In certain cultures, to be photographed is taboo. In our own snapshot culture, we should be accustomed to exhibiting a camera personality; and yet people sometimes become painfully self-conscious when a camera is focused on them, and they are personally involved when going through a collection of vacation prints.

The method of self-confrontation makes use of these camera phenomena: the intense, sometimes painful self-awareness when pictures are being taken, and the involved self-awareness when they are shown to the person later on. In our case, we worked with subjects who were photographed with a sound-motion camera and later saw the film (the self-confrontation). It turned out that the self-confrontation was a valuable method for obtaining information about the person's thoughts and feelings at the time the film was taken—information that could be synchronized with behavior visible on the screen. Moreover, the confrontation created a unique responsiveness in the subjects in regard to their self-image, a willingness to give associations about it, and a particular interest in understanding themselves.

The experiments were carried out at Harvard University as part of an elaborate exploration of dyadic interactions under the direction of Henry A. Murray. A number of subjects met with another person (the alter) in a dyad for the purpose of discussing and defending their personal philosophy of life. These dyads were recorded as sound movies, and each subject, who knew that he had been filmed, was shown his movie in a film interview (the self-confrontation).[1] Thirty-two subjects participated in the playback interviews.

[1] The studies reported in this chapter were made possible by grants from the United States Public Health Service; the Laboratory of Social Relations, Harvard University; and the University of Copenhagen. A detailed account of the studies is being published elsewhere. Cf. G. S. Nielsen, *Studies in Self-Confrontation* (Copenhagen: Munksgaard, in press).

We succeeded in arranging a series of lively discussions heavily loaded with emotions and tensions. The subjects did not know that the alter was instructed to begin rather "easy" and then to increase his attacks on the subject's philosophy and make his criticisms increasingly severe, just as they did not know that he was a stooge and was paid for making them withdraw or qualify their statements. Toward the end of the dyads, then, the two persons were usually engaged in a heavy discussion back and forth.

In one case we almost feared that the verbal arguments would turn into a fist fight. In some cases there was mutual affiliation on the surface and bitter anger underneath, as revealed later in the self-confrontation interviews. In still other cases a good deal of forceful emotion was manifested, although the subjects did not realize this during the discussion and denied it immediately afterwards in a post-dyadic interview. Later, however, during the playback of the movie, when they were confronted with reality, they realized how they had actually behaved. There were cases in which the subjects reported feelings not clearly shown in the movies: either the subjects were able to control these feelings, or the feelings had not become overt in the manner in which we were set to look for them. There were cases in which a subject did not fully realize what had taken place until a year and a half later when he came back for a reconfrontation with the film.

THE SELF-CONFRONTATION

The movies, then, represented a series of highly interesting interpersonal situations in which strong emotions were manifested. The thirty-two movies were later shown to the subjects themselves; within a week or ten days each of them came back to see his own movie. This was called the playback session, the film interview, or the self-confrontation.

Fundamentally, the method is based upon the assumption that a person is able to report a number of subjective experiences which occurred in an earlier situation if he is given the opportunity to relive the event. When confronted with the original situation, he is stimulated to recall subjective experiences which might not be reported by the classical retrospective or thinking-aloud methods, such as Claparède's *reflexion parlée*[2] and Karl Duncker's application of thinking aloud in the study of problem solving.[3]

The method of self-confrontation which was applied in the present studies involved a technique somewhat similar to the one used by E. L.

---

[2] E. Claparède, "La Genése de l'hypothése," *Arch. Psychol.*, XXIV (1934), 1–154.

[3] Karl Duncker, *Zur Psychologie des produktiven Denkens* (Berlin: Springer, 1935), p. 142.

Gaier, applying Benjamin S. Bloom's method of stimulated recall, in a study of selected personality variables and classroom learning.[4] Gaier obtained sound recordings of the classroom discussions and played the recordings back to each subject. At specific preselected points in the discussion, called critical points, the recording was stopped and the subject asked to recall and report the thoughts he experienced in the situation at this particular moment.

The present experiments went one step further, by showing the subjects sound-movie recordings of themselves in an earlier experimental situation and employing the film as a way of stimulating the subjects' recall of the original event. The involved self-confrontation of the playback experiments differed from the uninvolved self-confrontations which may occur in everyday life—e.g. when a person looks in a mirror to comb his hair—the difference being due to several important factors (mentioned below though not necessarily in order of priority).

First of all, the subjects were *set* to look at themselves in the playback experiment even before they arrived; they knew that they had been filmed and that they were going to look at their own movie.

Second, the presence of the experimenter in the self-confrontation interview no doubt made the subjects respond more intensely than they might have done had they been alone with the self-image. The subject was not only dealing with his own image and responding to it but also reacting to the presence of the other person and to expectations of what this other person might be thinking.

Third, the subjects looked at a movie of themselves in which they showed a good deal of emotion, in which a large proportion of their personality had been involved at the moment when it was made. Thus one could expect that a good part of the personality would be involved in seeing the movie.

The fourth factor was the involvement in the dyad, an involvement still existing at the time the movie was shown a week after it had been taken. The experience had not yet faded from or weakened in their memory, and the subjects were involved in the playback with a good deal of their personality; indeed, the movie intensified the emotional reactions easily because they still endured. When a year and a half later the subjects viewed the film again, most of them were able to detach themselves and did not get back the same feelings, although they remembered very well what it had been like then.

Moreover, the subjects saw themselves in a movie, a sound movie, which gave them an opportunity to see themselves from the outside, as others might see them or as they themselves saw others.

The final factor which made the self-confrontation of our experi-

[4] E. L. Gaier, "Selected Personality Variables and the Learning Process," *Psychol. Monogr.*, LXVI (1952), No. 349, 1–25.

ments a more intense affair than any of the self-perceptions that occur as a daily routine arises from the fact that the film self-confrontation contained most of, if not all, the important ways in which a person can be confronted with himself in everyday life. The subject saw his own body, followed his way of moving around, listened to his voice, and evaluated what he was trying to convey; he saw himself in a nervous state, displaying a lot of emotionality, and in a failure situation that he might normally try not to recognize fully; the subject saw himself reflected in the alter's attitude towards him, a situation that reminds us of the self-confrontation that takes place through other people's responses or through an analyst's interpretation to his patient.

One of the subjects, Illsley, is a good example of the involvement in the self-confrontation. The following is the beginning of the transcribed tape-recording of the interview which followed Illsley's first viewing of the film:

> *Illsley:* Oh, brother, I don't want to see this; it was terrible. Oh God! I just kept stuttering, I never said anything; I just stuttered. Oh, It was horrible. [Laughing] I sure am embarrassed. My God! I thought it was horrible [laughing]. I know I'll never go to Hollywood now. [Laughing] Oh, God. I get—you can hear my accent. I just think it was horrible. I mean, I just was tied in knots; all I could do was stutter. [Laughs] It didn't seem this bad to me then, but it seems horrible now. Terrible. I don't want to talk about it. [Laughing] Too embarrassing to talk about it. That's about all I can say. I kept fidgeting with my tie. You can see I bit my fingernail. I rubbed my nose. I grabbed hold of the chair almost three or four times. [Laughs] It's just amusing, that's all. It's embarrassing; it's amusing, that's all. It's so embarrassing. I'm mad at all of you to make such a spectacle of myself. I don't want to continue with these tests any more. I don't know what else to say. He looked awfully cool and collected; I was confused. I must have been terribly confused. I kept stuttering. . . .

Illsley continued for half an hour, talking and laughing, before the film interview really began.

Other subjects were pleased with the outcome, and still others were as dissatisfied as Illsley, as illustrated by the opening remarks transcribed from the tape-recorded film interviews:

> *Ivery:* Well, my first impression was that I was very satisfied with the way it came off. I thought that it was done in quite a relaxed manner. It didn't seem quite as incoherent when I saw the film, as I thought when I left the experimental room where it was taken. I was pretty much pleased with it, with the performance.

> *Island:* I looked about the way I would expect I would look, I guess. I think I seemed to be fairly much at ease, and I felt so certainly during the film. Of course, it's always interesting to see yourself more as others see you on a movie, and I guess I seemed to make a fairly decent impression.

I'm not too pleased with my appearance. I'm not particularly pleased with it, but it could be a lot worse. I know a lot of people that I think I would hate to look like.

Lambic: Interesting, disturbing, in a way, never having seen myself on film before. I didn't like it much. Being, I guess, very egoistical, you're not used to the way you look, sort of objectively. . . . I was sort of uncomfortable. I was surprised to see that I seemed to be such a terribly nervous person: hopping around. And he seemed, even more than at the time, very sort of cool, collected, composed. It's like seeing yourself in the mirror every day and then all of a sudden seeing yourself at a distance: what's the coloring of your own eyes, the way a camera sees you, which projects you quite objectively. I wasn't unsatisfied, seeing myself, but uncomfortable, never having seen myself before. You look quite different. I'd say, for instance, the nervousness, hopping around. I'd never, except once when I'd done a self-portrait of myself using mirrors, for art school, really seen myself—for instance my head—in any proportion as a whole. You only see it from one point of view at one time, where here you can see it all over. You can never really see your head as someone standing off can see it, let's say in the back.

Teenius: I wish I'd known where the camera was; I'd let you see more of my face. I think those were about the main impressions I had. I was fascinated by the whole thing. I suppose an ape who sees his picture on a movie screen is fascinated too; that's about the level of fascination it was, I think. [Generally, however, Teenius was critical about his performance.]

Gildon: I sort of enjoyed watching it. It's the first time I've ever seen myself, and one of the few times, really, I've ever heard myself talk. And it's always kind of alarming. I know that somebody said, somewhere, that you'd never recognize yourself if you met yourself on the street. This is probably true. It's kind of interesting to see what you look like, as the camera sees you if not as other people see you. But it was pretty enjoyable. I think I probably usually, not talk a little more than that, but defend myself a little better. I was in a kind of, not exactly distracted state, but kind of—my mind seemed to be somewhere else at the beginning anyway, and I wasn't particularly interested in what he was asking me. But it was kind of enjoyable to watch, and I enjoyed doing it. As I say, I don't think I'm usually so inarticulate as that; as far as appearance on the film, he seemed more at ease. I don't think I'm usually that bad. I have a lot of nervous twitches and quirks and scratchings and eyebrow raisings that don't seem to have much bearing on what I'm saying, really. I'm also surprised that my voice is so low. It sounds higher than that, when I'm speaking.

Newbrush: I dislike it—in fact, well, for a number of things. One is that my coat, my jacket sleeves, came up to about here, at points, and you can't tell whether I was wearing a short-sleeved shirt or a long-sleeved shirt. At one point you can, because you can see the shirt sleeve. But the coat looked small. I *looked* a whole lot taller than I think I am. I did look too tall! My hands looked very large—not long, because they are long, but just large. I don't know, I didn't like my appearance in it at all. Did you also think I looked taller in the film? Or did I look that tall? [Although Newbrush was critical about his physical appearance in the movie, he was more positive in his evaluation of the arguments.]

Generally, the subjects were, first of all, interested in the movements they made—fidgeting nervously, changing position, rubbing the face, etc. Although under normal conditions we are seldom aware of the many body movements we make, on the film they become very obvious. This fact provided an opportunity to discuss with the subjects some of the meanings a movement could have in terms of its function in the dyad. Some movements initiated long series of associations and past memories which, again, were a result of the confrontation with the self-image. The mere experience of being confronted with the self in an involved and intense way set off a willingness to respond to and associate to the movements, just as the experience of hearing oneself on a tape recorder for the first time has an extraordinary effect and may elicit strong reactions or just as confrontation with a photograph of part of oneself may provoke specific reactions, even if the subject is not fully aware he is judging himself.[5]

Quite apart from the evaluation they gave their performance in the discussion, some subjects did not like to become involved in the intense self-awareness set off by the playback. They indicated that a person could become too preoccupied with himself, that this would not be healthy for him and eventually would become very inconvenient for those who dealt with him. Others loved to spend hours on the movie. They attributed a high value to the admonition "Know Thyself" and seemed to hold the belief that a person may understand other people much better if he has a true insight into himself. These subjects also adhered to the theory that self-insight may cure a man from neurosis or help him solve some of his personal problems.

Certainly the subjects were influenced by the myth that a man may change—for better or for worse—if and when he looks deeply into his own mind. Some of the subjects were curious as to the nature of their inner selves; others were frightened by intense self-awareness and found it quite painful. The confrontation with the self-image left none of them neutral or untouched.

Usually the film brought the subject back to the *status nascendi* of the phenomenon; and perhaps an application of a video-tape recorder (e.g. the Ampex recorder of television), which makes an *immediate* playback possible, might have brought us even closer to the original event. And yet this is not to say that the confrontation method finally solves the intricate problem of getting information about inner subjective processes simultaneously with recordings of manifest behavior. The method (making use of re-experience or what might be called "respec-

[5] W. Wolf, *The Expression of Personality* (New York: Harper & Brothers, 1943).

tion") still only approximates what "really" went on, as do introspection and retrospection. Some subjects were not able to recall certain experiences until a year and a half later; and, although one may question the veracity of a statement which is presented so long after an episode, the point remains that certain experiences need distance to be reported. There are times when one has to be at a certain distance from an event in order to remember what went on.

RECONFRONTATION WITH THE DYAD
A YEAR AND A HALF LATER

Even though the reconfrontation took place a year and a half later, it was able to induce many of the original feelings in the subjects. "Seeing the movie again was like rereading old themes: reminders of a bit of one's past which one would be perfectly content to forget," remarked Crowder. "Viewing the movie again was very painful, even after so long a time," was Illsley's first comment. And yet, most subjects were able to take a detached view of the film as they had not been able to do in the playback a week after the film was taken.

Daibricks: I find that I can sit and watch this session more comfortably now than before. . . .

Ivery: Generally, the film seemed interesting—seeing and hearing the full experiment—although I was surprised at my seeming lack of contact with it today. It would seem as though I were viewing the film of two other people—a film I had lived with for more than a year.

Lambic: I feel a great distance from the two people—greater objectivity and less identification with the character in the film who was myself. If anything I feel as if I am observing a close friend, or a younger brother. I feel marked sympathy for this younger self but less involvement.

Even if a subject did become involved he was now able to handle the situation in a humorous way.

Reconfrontation with the Alter: He Was Not an Ogre After All

It was quite clear that the subjects now tended to judge the alter more as an individual person than they had during the immediate confrontation a week after the film was taken, when they had been more likely to treat him as a type and not really see him as a unique human being.

Candle: From looking at the movie this time, I learned more about the other person than during the conversation. He *is* a person, a man in a conversation trying to talk, trying to listen. He pretty much enjoyed the conversation, or, at least, he was tolerant.

Daibricks: Now that I can take my fascinated and horrified eyes off myself, I can see more validity and "meat" in his argument than I have seen before—that's the same as saying I am not so hostile to anything he says. I can sit now and watch this through and not wish so much to see myself, so I can pay more attention to what he is doing and saying and also I can look at myself more dispassionately.

Illsley: I saw that the other person was bored, and I really cannot blame him. At this viewing I found him neither harsh nor slow-witted. Indeed he seemed congenial and intelligent.

Ivery: I notice, with a degree of satisfaction, that my opponent was not as composed as I had previously imagined. He, too, seemed to have a little difficulty in explaining his stand on his philosophy. However, I did notice his general composure and was impressed by his fluency [in talking about Ivery's philosophy].

Teenius: The dispassionate attitude I adopted toward the other person on the screen, in many ways such a different person, allowed me for the first time, to judge him as another person, rather than myself.

Norges: My general reaction at seeing the film again is concerned with a much more favorable attitude towards the other person. I can readily see now how he handled his part in taking the initiative in the conversation and in proceeding more or less to attempt to cross-examine the other person, in this case myself.[6] I now see certain aspects of his character which I did not notice in the heat of the conversation. I should say that he appears to me now much more congenial than earlier. He seemed more polite than I had thought, much more communicative than I thought at the time. He said more than I thought at the moment, not quantitatively, but qualitatively. He was very good in his analysis of my points.

If the subjects became reinvolved in the dyad, they were less able to judge the alter as an individual and looked at him as representing a type:

Plinmouth: My feelings toward the other participant—can't even remember his name—are, if anything, less charitable than they were. Whether this change is due to some shift in my outlook or to a sudden whim of the present moment—a whim which comes closest to making my blood rise—I don't know. I suspect it is more or less the latter than the former, although my position on many things has shifted gently indeed. I would not now, for instance, be so damned naïve as to let a lawyer (whom as a general class I dislike anyway) twiddle me around his finger.

Generalizing from everyday judgments of other people, I am inclined to say that a man who is emotionally involved in a hostile dyad with another person is likely to judge him (during the meeting and immediately after) less as an individual and more as representing a type or representing a generality of one kind or another. When we are under the influence of strong hostile emotions directed at another person, it is

---

[6] Notice the slight shift in identification.

difficult for us to see what *he* feels, what *he* thinks, how *he* is at the moment. We tend to summarize our view of him in a few and very general impressions, and it may not be until later on that we are able to see through the fog of our own feelings and involvements. It may take some time after a quarrel before we can judge an opponent as a human being with *his* own needs and feelings, with *his* specific interests.

Indeed, the possibility of such evaluative processes poses new and intricate problems with regard to international—face-to-face or voice-to-voice—hostile dyads, which are becoming increasingly frequent because of faster international telecommunication. Thus Telstar may not only bring us closer together in the sphere of entertainment but may present a new problem to be studied and solved: that of immediate response versus delayed thinking. A direct telephone line between President Kennedy and Premier Khrushchev has been suggested, but it may not necessarily be such a good idea when hostility is high. In that case, paradoxically speaking, we should not say, "Let's get together," but, "Let's get away from each other and solve the problem."

Reconfrontation with Self

If we tend to see another person as a type in the moment when we are engaged in a stressful, hostile interaction with him and then later as an individual when we look back or are reconfronted with the scene of passion, then one might say that the judgment of the self follows an opposite trend: when we judge ourselves as we are now, we tend to see ourselves as individuals and unique human beings, and when we look back in time and judge ourselves as we used to be, we see ourselves as types, representing a specific developmental stage. Thus, the subjects described themselves as having been very young or immature at the time when the movie was taken and used this as an excuse or explanation for their performance. In addition they found that they had changed since then. Most of them thought they were now able to put up a better show.

The most interesting result from their re-evaluation of self, however, was the discovery of counterevaluation. Subjects who evaluated themselves negatively in the first playback session tended to evaluate themselves positively in the reconfrontation interview, and vice versa. This circumstance showed that the subjects' evaluations must be regarded as processes rather than as static phenomena and that the subject left the early session with an evaluation of the dyad (positive or negative) that was amplified and elaborated in the ensuing period of time. When he returned for the reconfrontation a year and a half later, he was predisposed in a positive or negative direction. Because of the distance in time, however, he was now able to view the film in the proper perspective and to allow for realistic perception; he therefore tended to apperceive the performance as being better than he had expected it to be, or vice versa. An assimilation of predisposed evaluations and realistic perceptions took place in the reconfrontation.

ASSOCIATIONS AND MEMORIES INITIATED
BY THE CONFRONTATION

Over and above the situational meaning, long series of associations and memories of the past were initiated by the confrontation with the self-image. This was especially the case in regard to idiosyncratic movements, which gave an impression of presenting—in a split second and compressed into a microunit of behavior—a key to important aspects of the subject's personality. A study of the associations to these movements was very valuable for the analysis of the individual personality. Thus, subjects reported interesting stories behind particular, idiosyncratic gestures, tics, motor habits, postures, and ways of sitting; and it was decided to concentrate part of the playback interview on such questions. Here the emphasis was on how much knowledge essential to the understanding of a personality could be gained by recording the associations and memories that were initiated when a subject was confronted with his own particular behavior. The term *particularity* is used to cover any way in which the subject behaved unusually and uniquely, as defined within the given sample of subjects.

The Case of Candle

Most subjects were willing and capable in reporting their original feelings and thoughts, a characteristic that was not at all present, however, in the case of Candle. He moved quite a bit on the outward, behavioral level but claimed not to have experienced feelings and thoughts during the entire dyad.

This assertion must not be interpreted as a conscious denial or lying; rather one must assume that he dissociated himself completely from the ongoing reality of the dyad. This assumption makes a record of his particularity worth while: it was an outstanding example of the proposition that unconscious dispositions may express themselves in outward, muscular behavior. Candle was a case of a particularity that reflected a disposition toward dissociation, which generalized in several areas of his personality.

One of his particularities consisted of holding his right hand in the air, like a policeman saying "stop" at a traffic intersection. He kept his hand in this position for great lengths of the movie, sometimes moving it slightly sideways as if to avert something, but mostly keeping it rigid in the air.

At various points, he held his hand in front of his mouth, sometimes patting his mouth like a bored nobleman at the court of Louis XIV. Sometimes he covered his mouth, touching it with the back of his hand and thus pointing toward the spectator with the palm of his hand.

He looked away for 92 per cent of the time of the dyad. During the discussion he spent a great deal of the time looking into a mirror on the wall.[7]

He was unable to report having had any subjective experiences during the discussion. He was the only subject who was not moved by the confrontation with the movie, that is the movie did not stimulate his recall. When asked to do a recording of fluctuations in felt anger toward the alter—a recording that was made concurrently with the showing of movie—he kept his pencil mark at the bottom of the scale all through the recording. (He had been asked to move the pencil up every time he had experienced any increase of feeling angry with the alter and move the pencil down at any decrease of felt anger.) On the other hand, when he was subsequently asked to record the degree to which he showed anger toward the alter, he kept the pencil toward the top of the scale almost through the entire film. Thus, the discrepancy between felt and manifest anger was extreme in his case, a symptom of dissociated or repressed emotionality. It is ironical that he listed "to have experience" and "to get experience" as the primary ideals of his personal philosophy.

He was reported to have gone through a psychotic breakdown and psychiatric treatment. He came back to school, shifting from science to art, shifted again, and finally left college. We can trace the outset of this development already in the records and his associations to his particular "stop" gesture, as illustrated by the following excerpts from the protocol.

Candle: I get sort of an odd feeling looking at myself. Sort of an inner dislike. I didn't know why. [Pause] I definitely sensed somewhere in my mind, I didn't particularly like looking at it.
Experimenter: Could you specify that more?
Candle: No, no—I mean, it's not conscious. I mean, it's not completely— I can't—I mean, there's no reason why—consciously why I dislike looking. But there's just this sort of feeling inside that I just don't like it, somewhere. And, at the moment, I don't know why. I think it's due to a parental chain. My mother—I have a little bit of a dislike of talking about myself. I mean, I—just now when I said the words, immediately the feeling grew stronger. Sort of a subconscious embarrassing . . . embarrassment. And I think I had that feeling looking at it, and I think I had that feeling afterwards. All the interviews and such and such. Could be the same thing. I don't know. This is what just comes to mind. I get embarrassed easily. I get embarrassed easily by other people doing things. And this is due to my mother's training. I mean, immediately, I suppose you think, well, I was subconsciously embarrassed during this thing. I'm not sure why. [Pause]

[7] Cf. the special study of visual alienation from interaction in Nielsen, *op. cit.*

Mmm. I'm not sure at all why. If I was. . . . [Pause] I had a great deal of trouble having *any* idea what I was thinking during the meeting, when I went through the interview right after the discussion, and—I still do.[8] I suppose you're going to show the film again and ask me to tell you what I was like. If I would hit myself now, I would say I was thinking unpleasant thoughts: I was in pain. That I know—then I could say for certain that I was thinking. But I *can't* say for certain what I was thinking in the movie. And I don't think looking at it helps. I'm sure looking at it doesn't help. I may have been embarrassed during it, but I can't go back, remember what I was thinking, and say, "Oh, yes, I was embarrassed," because I don't know what I was thinking.

Candle [later]: I wouldn't go out of my way to see this picture. I've been taught not to talk about myself; and I have a little bit of revulsion at looking at this. [Laughs] I dislike it—something nasty—revulsion—revolting.

Experimenter: Something nasty. You did the movement with your hand when you said that word. What do you mean?

Candle: Well, the general idea of the movement was pointing down there on the floor—that is, that there was something down there—something ugly. And it would be revolting. I would dislike it. Ugh! Nausea—not necessarily—just association. There was probably some amount of revulsion, due to early training probably.

Experimenter [later]: Do you have some more remarks about the film?

Candle: Well, let me see. . . . [Pause] Mmmmmm. I was looking at my face. It's one of those things that I don't get much chance to see. And just out of curiosity—I don't [laughs] get much chance to see myself. All the world I can go see, but me—no. [Sighs] . . . I used to think my ears stick out. I guess not. If—if there were something else in the world which was—which was constantly kept from me, I would be curious to see it.

We later went through the movie once again. It was stopped at various critical points, and Candle was asked to comment on it.

Candle: What was I thinking of? During the film, I wasn't listening very closely to the dialogue. Let's see. I don't know. I have very little association in my mind—I mean really, very little—none at all with myself while I was doing the movement, except externally. That is, the movements are familiar to me. When I did something like this [demonstrates the "stop" gesture], I sort of automatically did the same thing while I was watching it. Also, I put my hand to my mouth, sort of like this [demonstrates] in the film. And I guess you didn't see it, but just sort of automatically I did the same thing while I was watching. And as soon as I did it, I thought, "Well, this is the same thing as I'm doing there." Automatic reaction. But there is— I mean, it's—there is quite a bit of feeling as if I was watching someone else. I know it's me, but there is little mental or—there's no mental association with the person there. So I don't know what I was thinking.

[A little later: the film was stopped again.] I was trying to think what I was thinking. And I think I found out. And you won't believe it because I *know* I wasn't thinking anything. I never do when I talk. Now if I think

---

[8] The interview to which he refers was carried out by a different experimenter. It took place immediately after the dyad and prior to the film confrontation.

over just what I've been saying in the last couple of minutes, I haven't been thinking anything. The words just seem to come out. And if I try to think what motivation or what thought there was behind them, there wasn't any. And if I consciously think about it, it feels sort of odd. And the same thing was happening when I was talking there. I'm sure I wasn't thinking anything.

Experimenter: Did you see me nod my head a while ago?

Candle: Yes. Well, I was receptive—that is, I was looking, thinking, smiling—I was happy, obviously, when I was smiling. I mean, I smiled— I'm happy. But it feels to me like—as if there was this, say, a black box, and all the sense data were going into it. And words and actions were coming out of it. But I don't have the slightest idea what's happening inside. And I—I mean it really feels as if I wasn't thinking anything. [Pause] Which, of course—which I know isn't true. I mean, I have to think something, but I don't know if I do. I must have forgotten about it, but I forget about it the *moment* I start talking. That is, I say a word—all right, now, I said the word "word." I forgot about it the second or the milli-second that I started to pronounce "rd." So I don't know what I—I don't know what I'm thinking.

Experimenter [later in the film]: You were laughing here.

Candle: Yeah. I'm looking; I see myself smiling, acting. I see that I am hesitant. All right, so I say that I, in my mind, am hesitant. The only reason I say that is because I see myself being hesitant. I see myself expostulating, that is, talking like this at this moment. But—and I—all right, I can tell you that—oh, I turn and look at him. I saw him. This was in my mind. Well, I'm looking at the window, and my mind at the moment is looking at the window in this room. [Laughs] But this isn't significant. I mean, I keep—I close my eyes, when I'm not looking at anything. I open my eyes, and I am looking at anything. That's in my mind. But this doesn't have much to do with anything. I don't remember a thing. That is, that the only—all right, I looked at him. I know that I looked at him because I turned and looked. I had my eyes opened, so I must have been looking at him.

Experimenter: But do you remember it?

Candle: No, I don't remember a thing. The point is, I can't remember anything from a couple of seconds ago. I can remember the sense perception of myself. But the mental part is a complete blank.

Experimenter: Have you really forgotten what we have talked about?

Candle: No, because that's part of sense perception. We've been talking about hand movements.

Experimenter: Your associations to the hand movements, they were not perception. Have you forgotten them?

Candle: They aren't, no. But they were talking. And what came before the talking, I don't know. The feeling of revulsion or embarrassment, that was a feeling. But it wasn't in my mind. I mean, I felt it down here. I felt it just sort of down in my chest or something like that. And it seems to me—this is awful when I start doing it, and I've done it before. I mean, that is, trying to think what I think about what I'm saying. But I know perfectly well that I must—I can deduce that I must be thinking something. But I forget immediately. I can't remember what happened in my mind. [Pause] Honestly.

Experimenter: Were you happy when you were told that you were accepted at Harvard?

Candle: Yes. My mother brought the wire. And I can remember the day. I can remember experiencing it. In fact, I can almost describe the whole action. *But* there's something missing. I mean, I know that I was happy. I said things to indicate that I was happy. I remember—I actually remember feeling happy. But there's something missing. There's some part of it, with respect to me, that I know—maybe I know from just deducing it—but it seems to me that it's there. But I can't remember it. There's something missing in the same way that what I've said in the last few minutes—there's something missing. There's still that great big, monstrous thing that's missing. This may not make sense to you. It seems to me that I may remember it. But as soon as I think about it, it goes away. This may not make sense to you. I can think of things in my mind, I can do problems in my head solving equations in my head. But it's not the same thing. There's still something missing. I still don't know why I say things. [Laughs]

Experimenter [later, when the film was stopped at a new critical point]: You are right here talking about when you do something you tend to do it for the sake of doing it and not for a goal—not necessarily for a goal.

Candle: And I was obviously feeling something. I looked happy. I went forward, which meant I must have had some emotion. And some of it—some of it, I think—is coming back to me. But—still I couldn't. . . . [Sighs] This— I don't know, this is—only in the last year has this come up. In fact—I mean, nothing's changed, but only in the last year has the consideration that I can't remember it—things that I say—come up. And it's been coming up more and more frequently. I mean, it's really the last couple of weeks. I'm merely thinking now—maybe I'm *afraid* to say what I'm thinking. [Pause—sigh.] In fact, I'm sure I am. I'm quite sure I am, but I don't know why. [Pause] Maybe I. . . . [Sigh] My mind plays strange tricks—except [sigh] that this is—this is very hard. I don't know. What was I thinking about? It could be that I am telling myself that I don't know what I was thinking when I actually do. This doesn't—I don't know whether this makes sense or not. But I think I'm afraid of something. In fact I'm sure—I'm sure I'm afraid of something. Right now—and there's a lot of confusion in my mind when I start thinking—being, trying to be, very objective, that is, removing some part of my mind and looking at myself. Confusion results. I'm not sure. . . . [Pause] Because I say something. I think about it. I tell you I'm thinking about—I just said something. I start thinking about that—just start piling up. At the moment, I wish you'd say something I could talk about. [Laughs]

Experimenter: You remember this hand gesture which could mean "stop."

Candle: Yes.

Experimenter: Or a barrier.

Candle: I don't think it does now. That association only came because of the placement of the camera.

Experimenter: Okay. We'll drop the barrier point. But how about the "stop"? Not saying "stop" to others.

Candle: To the camera, possibly? This could only be deduced. I've no reason for thinking it.

Experimenter: Further on in the film you actually hold your hand in the "stop" position quite a long time.

Candle: Yeah. I remember that.

Experimenter: Did you say "stop" to yourself?

Candle: It could be. It's possible. I mean, I would not deny it. I don't know. Mmm. There's something about this remembering business. At the moment I feel that I would like to talk about the hand movements. And I know perfectly well that I don't want to talk about this remembering business. [Pause] Silly. I wish you would say a couple of magic words, and I would understand the whole thing. I know perfectly well that this is important. I know perfectly well that I don't want to talk about it, but this is one part of my mind. The other part of my mind says there is the problem of finding out about it. And some other part of my mind is, at the moment, feeling very—sort of odd about the whole thing. [Pause] I don't know. [Pause] I just. . . . [Pause]

It took him a year and a half to realize more fully what had gone on in the dyad: "I actually was quite nervous although I wouldn't admit it to myself right afterwards. Besides moving my hands around, I fidgeted and assumed positions which made it look as though I wanted to leave. My hand movements: possibly they expressed my immaturity."

It was interesting to observe that he was the subject who increased the most on looking at self when he saw the movie a second time a year and a half later. Recording of the subjects' looking at self (self-attention) during the viewing of the movie was done without the subjects' knowledge, as part of a study of narcissism.[9] Thus Candle went from the lower third to the top of the rank on self-attention. Something had changed in him; he was a different person after psychiatric treatment.

Candle's concluding comment showed that even to himself it seemed as if he had changed and come through a difficult period now better prepared to receive and understand. "As a whole, the movie interested me because it is a record of my past. I have developed beyond this past, but I want to understand it. I vaguely wish my fiancée could see the film. But really. I think that I may have learned enough from seeing the film this time to make up for what I did not, then."

SELF-CONFRONTATION IN THERAPY

Confronting a patient with himself occurs, of course, in all kinds of psychotherapy. The self-confrontation which is involved in the present experiments, however, deals with a person's confrontation with a movie of himself and thus involves self-perception in a more direct way. One might expect that the method could be of some value in therapy, and in this connection it is interesting to note that an experiment on showing psychotic patients photographs of themselves produced strong reactions among the patients and even seemed to have some effect on their treatment.

[9] Cf. Nielsen, *op. cit.*

The experiment was carried out at Boston State Hospital, about the same time the dyad project took place, by Floyd S. Cornelison and Jean Arsenian; and was published as a study of the response of psychotic patients to photographic self-image experience.[10] Initial work, in which patients were shown photographs of themselves, indicated that some of them responded in an unusual manner. They seemed to pay greater attention to the self-image photographs than they ordinarily gave to objects outside themselves. One chronically disturbed man, who was unconcerned when motion pictures were made of him, later displayed extreme anxiety when he saw those pictures. A woman, photographed when she was deluded and incoherent, became noticeably less disorganized within a few days after she saw still photographs taken of her during the acute state.

The basic procedure of the study consisted of the following steps: (1) A photograph was taken of the subject; (2) the photograph was shown to the subject; (3) the experience was discussed with the subject; and (4) the subject's response to seeing the photographic self-image was observed. The still photographs were taken with the Polaroid Land Camera, which provides for development of the final picture, ready for viewing, in approximately one minute. The picture-taking procedure was explained to each patient during the first session, and only four patients made any objections. "Occasionally, in later sessions, complaints were expressed, but the patients usually were co-operative. Snapping the picture produced little change in on-going behavior; some patients focused upon the camera and some did not. One unusual reaction was that of a somber male subject. Each time his picture was taken, he posed with a broad smile; after the shutter clicked, he quickly resumed his downcast demeanor."[11]

The reaction of the normal dyad-subject to seeing himself followed pretty much the same pattern as the psychotic patient's response to seeing himself. The first and immediate response could be extremely emotional, sometimes shocked, but became increasingly matter-of-fact as the experience was repeated.

In our experiments there were no objective measurements of personality change due to the self-confrontation. All subjects had changed somewhat when they came back eighteen months later to view the film once more. They had changed because of age and continuous education; possibly also the whole experience of being a subject in psychological research for a length of time had influenced them. Some of them volunteered the information that they had changed because of what they

[10] "A Study of Psychotic Patients' Reaction to Photographic Self-Image Experience," *Psychiat. Quart.*, XXXIV (1960), 1–8.
[11] *Ibid.*, p. 3.

saw in the movie; e.g. they had tried to get rid of some of the motor mannerisms. Some subjects became curious about their own personalities when seeing the movie again and observing it more carefully and objectively. They wanted to understand why they had behaved the way they did. Others found a ready excuse for their own behavior in the strangeness of the experiment and their immaturity at the time of the filming, and they wanted to forget.

> *Plinmouth:* I'll be damned if I didn't string out the most ridiculous bunch of crap for a defense of my philosophy. But I'll be damned if I'm going to lose any sleep over this whole thing. It's over with and there's nothing I can do about it except file it away under past experience. . . .

What would it be like to see the film twenty years later? It may be that a subject would respond with a classical comment, "What a sad change!" thinking of himself now as being old and seeing himself then as young, striving, hopeful. But a smile, no doubt, would be the first reaction, "Did I *really* look so young?" Perhaps one subject would understand his present position better; perhaps another would not fully understand his young adulthood until he was old enough to see it in the proper perspective. Children ought to be given a sound-film of their parents as young and foolish, and parents ought to be reconfronted with the past. Perhaps it would contribute to the mutual understanding of the dyad between generations.

6: SOMERSET MAUGHAM

A Thematic Analysis of Ten Short Stories

Leopold Bellak

I owe many hours of diverse pleasure to Somerset Maugham. His deft portrayals of the human condition are a delight both in content and in form. If I now attempt a psychological analysis of some of these stories in the hope of a glimpse of the man who wrote them, I do so in a spirit much like his—one of curiosity and compassion, animated by a desire to understand the complexity of human lives. Regrettably, there will be no similarity in our styles.

The use of artistic productions as a basis for inferences about the creator is not new. Freud's study of Leonardo da Vinci,[1] of Dostoevski,[2] and of Jensen's "Gradiva,"[3] and especially his discussion of the relationship of daydreaming to the work of the poet[4] laid a foundation upon which has risen a host of such studies by other psychoanalysts.[5] Nor is this so far-fetched an exercise as it might seem. It is the task of science after all to provide hypotheses which permit the ordering of different observable facts into lawful relationships. Freud gave us the continuum not only between the child and the adult, between the waking thought and the dream, between the normal and the pathological, and between the visible and the unseen, but also between the man and his work, especially his creative work. He was aware, however, of the complexity of the creative process and himself suggested that there was more than a one-to-one relationship, that his view might "prove itself too schematic, but

[1] S. Freud, *Gesammelte Werke*, VIII (London: Imago Publishing Co., Ltd., 1943), 129–211.

[2] *Ibid.*, XIV (1948), 399–418.

[3] S. Freud, *Delusion and Dreams in Jensen's "Gradiva"* (London: Allen and Unwin, 1921).

[4] S. Freud, "The Relation of the Poet to Day-dreaming," *Collected Papers*, IV (London: Hogarth Press, 1953), 173–183.

[5] E. Hitschmann, *Great Men* (New York: International Universities Press, 1956); Phyllis Greenacre, *Swift and Carroll:* "A Psychoanalytic Study of Two Lives" (New York: International Universities Press, 1955).

that possibly it may contain a first means of approach to the true state of affairs."[6]

In his study of poets, Freud pointed out the effects of subjective experience on later perception. But he went beyond that. He suggested the possibility that a certain "bent"—a selective cognitive set—would lead to subjectively meaningful choices of theme.

Pathographies of a psychoanalytic nature, although often persuasive clinically, nonetheless have troubled those concerned with the rigors of methodology. A suspicion of *post hoc, ergo propter hoc* reasoning has not been easily dispelled. It is understandable that Freud and his immediate followers thought in terms of the rather rigid determinism that was common at the turn of the century and largely along lines of motivation and drive expression in creative products. But current conceptual thinking revolves around the degrees of probability with which one fact may be predictably related to another. Ego psychology, itself a product of Freud's thinking, addresses itself to the adaptive, as well as the dynamic, genetic, economic, and structural aspects of all functioning. And of course it also takes into account as determinants of behavior the social setting in its broader cultural sense, the familial situation, the biological factors, and the physical environment.

This increased awareness of the complexity of behavioral determinants makes the task more difficult, but at the same time more gratifying. The problems one confronts in making inferences about Maugham as an individual from a study of his works are not so different from the contemporary problems of clinical psychoanalysis or the problems of psychological testing; the psychological analysis of purposeful literary production and the "story-making" involved in the Thematic Apperception Test, especially, share, in good measure, certain fundamental theories and techniques.

The interpretation of the stories told on the Thematic Apperception Test (T.A.T.),[7] has been influenced by increasing complexity of theory over the years. Originally it focused primarily on the motivational aspects of need and the perception of environmental stimuli (called "press" by H. A. Murray). Ego-psychological thinking has extended the usefulness of the test by including interpretation of the defenses[8] and of apperception, which involves adaptive and expressive features.[9] An il-

---

[6] S. Freud, "The Relation of the Poet to Day-dreaming," *op. cit.*

[7] Christiana D. Morgan and H. A. Murray, "A Method for Investigating Fantasy; The Thematic Apperception Test," *Arch. Neurol. Psychiat.*, XXXIV (1935), 289–306.

[8] L. Bellak, "The Concept of Projection: An Experimental Investigation and Study of the Concept," *Psychiatry*, VII (1944), 353–370; "Thematic Apperception: Failures and the Defenses," *N. Y. Acad. Sciences*, Ser. II, Vol. XII (1950), 122–126.

[9] *Idem,* "A Study of Limitations and 'Failures': Toward an Ego Psychology of

luminating study by Holt[10] brought the cognitive approach to bear on the T.A.T., although the study revolved rather too extensively on the differences between T.A.T. stories and fantasy, overshadowing the features in common.

The main point is simply this: literary product, T.A.T. story, fantasy, and other acts are all products of the person involved and as such must have a significant relationship to that personality. The only relevant question is one which centers on the problem of the complexity of that relationship and our ability to understand it. For many years, both as a psychoanalyst and a testing psychologist, I have been impressed by the continuity of the relationship between test products, artistic production, and the clinical data emerging in the psychoanalytic treatment of artists as patients.

The question of the validity of the interpretation of test product or literary product, allowing for a complex interplay of many variables, seems to me to be primarily one of the logical and procedural tightness of the progression from observable fact to inference. This present attempt will be limited to one level of inference—from the story to the personality of the story-teller. It would be tempting to make a second order of inference—from the story to the genesis of the personality. The distinction between these two levels of inference is often not stated with sufficient clarity. A good deal of success can probably be achieved at the second level, but it involves another methodological step, which we must forego here.

The procedure I have found most helpful for the interpretation of the T.A.T. is the use of a check form which provides a concrete frame of reference.[11] I shall attempt to use this same technique for the analysis of ten short stories by Somerset Maugham.

The initial step of this analysis concerns itself with determining the

---

Projective Techniques," *J. of Projective Techniques,* XVIII (1954), 279–293; *The TAT and CAT in Clinical Use* (New York: Grune and Stratton, 1954).

[10] Robert Holt, "The Nature of TAT Stories as Cognitive Products: A Psychoanalytic Approach," in Jerome Kagan, ed., *Contemporary Issues in Thematic Apperceptive Methods* (Springfield, Illinois: Charles C Thomas, 1961).

[11] *Bellak TAT and CAT Blank* (C.P.S. Inc., P. O. Box No. 83, Larchmont, New York). On this blank, entries are made for each story with respect to the following points: (1) main theme; (2) main hero; (3) main needs of the hero; (4) conception of the world; (5) relationship to others, such as parent figures, contemporaries, or younger characters; (6) significant conflicts; (7) nature of anxieties; (8) main defenses against conflicts and fears; (9) severity of superego; and (10) integration of the ego. The "Summary" and "Final Report" given later in this chapter are printed just as they would be entered on the blank. In the full worksheet form, the summary can be written with all the entries on individual stories in full view; the final report, in turn, can be written with the summary page folded out for inspection. These features serve to maintain a close relationship between concrete data and inferences.

theme of a story on three levels. On the descriptive level one attempts simply to restate the gist of the story. On the interpretive level this statement is reduced in such a way as to eliminate particulars and establish the general psychological relationships that obtain in the story, rather in the old tradition of the tale with a moral. The well-known can serve as an example: the story of the boy who cried wolf reduces itself to the statement that if you cry for help when you don't need it, you will not be believed when you really do need it. On the diagnostic level one begins to make clinical inferences, which involve a further translation of the theme into clinical concepts such as basic need, apperception, conflict, anxiety, defense, superego, and ego integration. In the wolf story one would notice that the superego is active and that anxiety is connected with dependence-inspired departures from the truth. The T.A.T. form starts with the main theme stated at the diagnostic level, and its categories further aid one in capturing systematically other dynamic features. In our example we can note that a wolf is introduced and that the consequence of lying is being killed and eaten. We can make inferences as to certain ideas of death, certain ways of dying (the fear of being devoured). The inevitability of the punishment and its rather unreasonable severity in relation to the nature of the crime would suggest a strict and primitive conscience.

The more samples of observed behavior of one person one has to draw upon, the greater the likelihood of making meaningful inferences. In T.A.T. diagnosis a good many stories are used in order to detect the common denominators. In this literary analysis I want to follow the same procedure and analyze, albeit briefly and sketchily, ten of Maugham's stories. Maugham offers an abundance of riches. Volume I of the complete short stories contains thirty stories; Volume II, sixty-one.[12] Incidentally, Maugham's stories would delight any T.A.T. psychologist by their degree of structure and the clear statement of theme. In his preface the author tells us that the first of the stories of the first volume was written in 1919 and the last in 1931, and that they were written in the sequence in which they appear. In the preface to the second volume he simply says that these stories are the rest of the lot. They are much shorter than those of Volume I and apparently cover more time and traveled space.

It would be tremendously time-consuming to do even a most condensed analysis of ninety-one stories. Therefore, some sampling and selecting had to be done. I used a rather crude method of randomizing, and in Volume One picked stories by their numerical characteristics— 1, 2, 11, 12, 21, 22. With the second volume, I asked my eight-year-old

[12] Somerset Maugham, *Complete Short Stories* (2 vols.; New York: Doubleday Co., 1953).

daughter to make a pencil mark at the margin of four different stories in the table of contents. I think that even the very statistically minded, if they knew Maugham, would not object to this simple procedure of selection. I think it will become quite clear that the themes and characteristics which become manifest in the selected stories have a great similarity to most of the rest of Maugham's writings, including his major work, *Of Human Bondage,* which is considered to be in large part autobiographical.

ANALYSIS OF THE STORIES

The first story in the volume, luckily enough, is "Rain"—luckily, because it is particularly widely known, as a movie as well as the original short story.

"Rain"

Descriptive theme. A zealous missionary, driven by great religious fervor, has always resisted the ordinary feelings of compassion, sex, and fear in his desire to rise above them for the sake of a stern religious morality. When he meets Sadie Thompson, a prostitute, he feels compelled to interfere with her activities in his efforts to save her soul (at the cost of great misery and actual danger to her). However, he finds himself increasingly attracted to her (note his dream of breastlike mountains, his remaining with her later and later into the night) and ultimately makes a sexual advance. He kills himself in consequence.

Interpretive theme. If emotions are very strong, especially sexual ones, and one tries to control them while in intense contact with a woman, control may be destroyed as well as oneself.

Diagnostic level. Presence of strong drives, aggressive and sexual. Attempted defenses are denial, repression, rationalization, withdrawal, and reaction formation. Adaptively tries to deal with his conflict by becoming a missionary. Fears loss of control over drives, especially sexual one. Fears destruction by women. Concern about self-destruction; suicidal ideas are present.

These bald statements leave out many subtleties of the story. Let me plead again the need for economy. However, even though briefly, I must point out a few of the other features. The theme of the missionary is not the only one. He is not the only hero; Sadie Thompson is another.

Descriptive theme. A prostitute is reduced to a fearful clinging wreck by a zealous missionary bent on saving her soul, but she rises contemptuously when his moral principles collapse and ordinary lust shows through.

Interpretive theme. If a lustful woman meets a zealously moral man, she is reduced to weakness, but she recovers her strength if the man appears prey to lust.

Diagnostic level. Woman is seen as lustful, seductive. Moral man is seen as strong. Man unable to control his desires is seen as contemptible by women. Control is very important; its loss is contemptible.

Another subtheme is concerned with Dr. Macphail. One must consider him another identification figure for the author (of course, Maugham projects some of his own sentiments on all the figures). Let me simply remark that the doctor appears compassionate, but tries to remain uninvolved to avoid the discomfiture of too much emotion. He tries to accept with passivity the missionary, his own wife, and the world around him but finds himself uneasy. He engages in action in a desultory way (and with a good deal of conflict) only when he feels he can no longer avoid doing so.

The minor women characters in the story appear as controlling, either by their aggressive attitudes or by their moralistic ones. In fact, the most repetitive concern seems to be with emotions that could overcome one, especially with regard to women who tend to control.

Let me anticipate some broader inferences here by pointing out that the waitress, Mildred, in *Of Human Bondage* is not too different from Sadie Thompson in her effect on the protagonist. Nor is the principal character, Philip, himself a doctor, too different from Dr. Macphail. It is common knowledge that Maugham was a medical school graduate.

"The Fall of Edward Barnard"

In a general sense, one might describe this story as a not so gentle mockery of American culture, especially as seen through the bourgeois pretensions of wealthy women and their effect on men.

Descriptive theme. Edward Barnard is a traditional and upstanding young Chicagoan. Just as soon as he saves enough money from his work in Tahiti, he plans to return home and marry the beautiful, cultured, controlling, and ambitious Isabel. However, he comes to enjoy the easy and simple life of the islands, particularly the companionship of a half-caste girl. Unlike Isabel, she puts him at his ease.

Bateman Hunter, in love with Isabel, but friend to Edward also, is vaguely puzzled and distressed by Edward's change. He tries to persuade Edward to return home. When Edward renounces Isabel, Hunter himself returns to marry her. Isabel's dreams, as she embraces Hunter, are of business success, tea dances, and the look of distinction and solidity which horn-rimmed glasses will give her new fiancé.

Interpretive theme. If one is caught in the demands of petty bourgeois culture, as represented by controlling, ambitious women, one may find life much happier in an undemanding culture (which permits more passivity) and with simpler women (who are no threat and do not make one feel inferior). A selfless male friend helps out reliably.

Diagnostic level. An unease about cultural demands. Sees women of society as subtly controlling, demanding, ambitious. Sophisticated women of this kind produce feelings of unease, inferiority. Attempts solution of anxiety and conflict by withdrawal (geographic and psychological) and by turning to more primitive women and less demanding societies. Uses rationalization, emotional isolation, and withdrawal as defense. A male friend is seen as selfless and dependable. Since we know something of the author's actual life history, we can add that his travels to primitive countries were adaptive ways of dealing with his problems. Writing was another way of dealing with his conflicts. He described writing *Of Human Bondage* as a cathartic experience. His friendships with men were often lifelong, his heterosexual relations apparently either transitory or distant and tempestuous.[13]

"The Yellow Streak"

Descriptive theme. Izzart, the handsome, English-educated son of a white father and half-caste mother, is constantly unnerved by the thought that someone will discover his mixed parentage. During a mission with Campion, a visitor to the Malayan jungle, the men are involved in a boating accident. Izzart is so intent on saving his own life that he ignores Campion's pleas for help. Miraculously, both men survive. Campion is publicly silent about Izzart's part in the near catastrophe, but, triggered by Izzart's fear and guilt, makes it privately plain to him that he attributes his cowardice to the "yellow streak"—the tainted blood.

Interpretive theme. If a man is tainted by a (racially) inferior woman (mother), he fears his inferiority (the yellow streak) will emerge to his shame and peril. His fear that others will recognize this inferiority constantly haunts him.

Diagnostic level. Feels inferior. Projects his feelings of inferiority on others. Inferiority is blamed on a woman, specifically his mother. Woman is seen as something inferior as well as a source of embarrassment and shame. The main concern is one of controlling emotion, particularly fear.

"P & O"

Descriptive theme. Mrs. Hamlyn is returning alone to England from the tropics after twenty years of happy marriage. Her husband has fallen helplessly in love with another woman. She and her husband both view the intrusion of this new love as one would an illness—it is uncontrollable and one must bow before it. On shipboard she meets the vital and forward-looking Mr. Gallagher, a retired planter, who is going home

[13] *Idem,* "Looking Back," *Show,* II, Nos. 6–8 (1962).

to begin a new life. Mr. Gallagher has left behind his native wife, after making what he considered generous financial provision for her. His wife, however, became incensed and cast a spell upon him. When Mr. Gallagher sickens and dies on board, to the consternation of the ship's doctor, apparently as a result of this spell, Mrs. Hamlyn's own anger evaporates, and she feels great compassion for the love that, like an unrestrainable force (a spell), befell her husband.

Interpretive theme. If love befalls one, it is like a sickness against which one is defenseless. If one fights a (native) woman's love, she will kill one. It is best to bow to uncontrollable emotions.

Diagnostic level. Fear of emotion, particularly of heterosexual love. Fear of being overwhelmed by love (for woman). Fear of being killed by hate of woman. Defense used is emotional isolation and sublimation into compassion.

This story also involves the complexities of the caste system in British society, observations on emotional callousness, and the selfless relationship between simple men. Once again, a doctor (the ship's doctor—a sympathetic character) is cast into a hopeless conflict between passivity and activity.

"Mr. Harrington's Washing"

Descriptive theme. Mr. Harrington is the prototype of the proper Philadelphian. He has a strong set of morals and principles of behavior, which he takes with him into the upheaval of revolutionary Russia. There he comes in contact with Alexandra, "a mad Russian," who has had a powerful effect on all sorts of men and whom he significantly nicknames "Delilah." Mediocre, resolute, stubborn, but rigidly sticking to his principles throughout, Harrington insists on getting his laundry before departing the unsafe Petrograd. Alexandra, who loyally accompanies him on this last mission, is attracted by a street crowd. Harrington, trailing behind her, is attacked and killed.

Interpretive theme. If one has a strong set of moral and behavioral patterns, one is helped through many difficult situations. But one may also be led into absurdity. If one gets tangled up with a woman, she is likely to cause one's misfortune and death even though her intentions are the best.

Diagnostic level. Conflict between conventional and less rigid behavior. Gentle mockery of bourgeois mind in unresolved conflict. Woman is seen as powerful and dangerous. Even when she means to be loyal and protective, she may be fatal.

The biographical background to this story, as that of several other stories, is related in Maugham's recent article.[14]

[14] *Loc. cit.*

"Footprints in the Jungle"

Descriptive theme. Bronson, a plantation man, takes Cartwright, temporarily down on his luck, into his home in order to lend him a helping hand. In time, Cartwright and Mrs. Bronson have a love affair "swayed by turbulent passion." Although all three are basically decent people, Mrs. Bronson encourages her lover to kill her husband rather than risk discovery. The police chief learns of the crime, but there is insufficient evidence to bring the case to court. The new couple live on happily, since remorse for a crime does not seem to sit heavily if one can be absolutely sure one will not be found out.

Interpretive theme. If a woman comes between two men, she causes trouble and death. Sexual passion may be the motive for murder even though the people involved were, and remain, perfectly decent people. They may not even suffer remorse.

Diagnostic level. Sees women as causing trouble to men, as separating them, and as being fatal to them. There is the suggestion of an Oedipal problem: one man must be killed for the other to get his woman. Passion is seen as overpowering, threatening to transcend control, specifically control of aggression. An unintegrated superego condones murderous aggression as an uncontrollable force.

"A Friend in Need"

Descriptive theme. A seemingly pleasant, kind, middle-class sort of man is approached by an irresponsible, happy-go-lucky acquaintance who is in desperate need of a job. The former casually sends him to his death by proposing to him a dangerous swimming feat as the price for a job —a job which in fact he doesn't have to offer at all.

Interpretive theme. If one is happy-go-lucky, one may be prey to the most incongruous hostilities of one's fellow man. This is probably due to disapproval and envy of an easy way of life and implied success with women.

Diagnostic level. Fear of and desire for drifting, passivity. Sees people as incongruously and often casually cruel. This ascription of cruelty may be associated with concern over their envy and disapproval of easy-going ways and of success with women. The latter are felt as dangerous. There is fear of helplessness, guilt over sexual desires, and passivity, and a great deal of cruelty is projected on others.

"A Romantic Young Lady"

Descriptive theme. The beautiful daughter of a duchess falls in love with a poor young man who returns her affection. Her mother disapproves and begs for help from a countess who employs him as mule-driver to her valuable and showy team. When the young man is made to choose between his beloved and his glamorous job, he chooses the latter.

Interpretive theme. If a man has to choose between a woman and an esteemed job (with animals), he rather callously chooses the job.

Diagnostic level. A sarcastic, low esteem is expressed for women. "There is not a pair of mules in the whole of Spain to come up to ours . . . one can get a wife any day of the week, but a place like this is found only once in a lifetime. I should be a fool to throw it up for a woman."[15] So says the young man.

A subtheme is also concerned with the fact that the duchess and countess, though rivals previously, get together in this adversity. The beautiful young woman is met many years later, settled down comfortably as the stout, flaunting widow of a diplomat.

"The Kite"

Descriptive theme. A young boy, in joint venture with his parents, learns to love flying kites. As he grows older, this becomes the guiding passion of his and their lives. He meets a girl of whom his mother disapproves and, against her wishes, marries. His marriage is unhappy, his wife interferes with his kite-flying, and in anger he leaves her and returns to his parents. In retribution, his wife smashes his best kite. He retaliates angrily by choosing prison to the alternative of paying her support.

Interpretive theme. If a young man who has lived happily with his parents gets involved with a woman of whom they disapprove, the new woman may make him unhappy, interfere with his freedom, destroy the things he loves. Feels tremendous anger toward her.

> You see, I don't know a thing about flying a kite. Perhaps it gives him a sense of power as he watches it soaring towards the clouds and of mastery over the elements as he seems to bend the winds of heaven to his will. It may be that in some queer way he identifies himself with the kite flying so free and so high above him, and it's as if it were an escape from the monotony of life. It may be that in some dim, confused way it represents an ideal of freedom and adventure. And you know, when a man once gets bitten with the virus of the ideal not all the King's doctors and not all the King's surgeons can rid him of it.[16]

This is what the narrator comments on the events he relates in the story.

Diagnostic level. Tends to see life with parents as peaceful in infantile (sexually?) gratifying way. Woman is seen as making one unhappy, controlling one's life, interfering with infantile phallic pleasures and with man's freedom. Woman is seen as undermining his power. Conflict between monotony and adventurous, whimsical diversion. Woman

---

[15] *Complete Short Stories, op. cit.,* II, 321.
[16] *Ibid.,* p. 647.

is seen as plainly castrating, evil, controlling, interfering with narcissistic (sexual?) pleasures.

"The Happy Couple"

Descriptive theme. An apparently insignificant couple, in love with each other and warmly devoted to their baby, are found to have been the onetime doctor and female companion to an old lady they killed. Her inheritance enabled them to be married. At their trial, the jury found them not guilty despite overwhelming evidence, supposedly because of the fact that they had not had sexual intercourse during their long premarital relationship. The woman had been willing to commit murder to marry the man she loved, but not to have an illicit love affair.

Interpretive theme. People are not what they seem. They may appear to be very decent people and yet commit murder. If people control their sexual desire, anything may be forgiven them. People are very strange. Sometimes one person must be disposed of for others to find happiness.

Diagnostic level. Suspicious of people, of their deceptive appearances, of their complex natures which may conceal murderous aggression. The problem is of reconciling aggression and conscience. Unintegrated superego. Sex appears more prohibitive than aggression. Oedipal problem. Sees people as odd.

It is interesting to compare this story with "Footprints in the Jungle." In both instances one meets a quiet, pleasant, unobtrusive middle-aged couple who have committed murder in order to live with one another. In both stories, the murderers escape punishment for their crimes and live happily (though somewhat furtively) ever after. Once again, in "The Happy Couple," a doctor is the protagonist and is under the sway of love for a woman.

SUMMARY

Unconscious Structure and Drives (1–3)[17]

The subject seems to have a continual struggle with aggressive and sexual drives. He feels strongly that their control is vital. Death follows loss of control. The character structure that has resulted from his attempts to deal with these problems is one of emotional isolation and detachment. He is an onlooker, peering in from the outside with considerable puzzlement and much suspicion of the barely repressed drives that lurk beneath the surface of his fellow men. And yet he is not without compassion. There seems to be a conflict between active participation in the demands of the world, especially those of bourgeois culture,

[17] Numbered headings correspond to those of the T.A.T. blank. Cf. n. 11, *supra.*

and the giving in to passive desires, to the call of simpler living under more primitive circumstances. From the attempted resolution of this conflict arises the beachcomber, the wanderer, albeit in this case a highly sophisticated one. The self-image that results seems that of a mildly ineffective person who feels rather like a leaf in the wind and is not at all aware of his own strong emotions, especially of cruelty toward women.

Conception of the World (4)

Puzzling, demanding, to be faced with wary eyes, full of surprises and overwhelming situations.

Relationship to Others (5)

Urbane, mildly compassionate, warily expectant, but uninvolved manifestly; latent, strongly aggressive, hostile feelings toward women, projected onto them. Sometimes there is aggression toward men, though often men are seen as dependable if not affected by women.

Significant Conflicts (6)

Control versus lack of control of aggression and sex. Conflict between activity and passivity, between conformity and nonconformity, between identification as a man and as a woman.

Nature of Anxieties (7)

To be dominated, constrained, controlled, especially by women. To kill or be killed in triangular conflicts. To be embarrassed. To lose control of aggressive or sexual drives.

Main Defenses (8)

Reaction formation, emotional isolation, repression, and withdrawal from object relations. Extensive projection of aggression and sexual desires. Very superficial object relations.

Superego Structure (9)

An unintegrated superego; it is usually quite harsh, but occasionally, with a touch of cynicism or detachment, aggressive transgressions seem permissible, possibly more so than sexual ones.

Integration and Strength of Ego (10)

The well-constructed stories show an ego strong enough to attain some closure and to maintain control. However, control is attained at the cost of considerable emotional isolation, of constriction and stereotyping of experiences, and of tangential relations to people. The self-image is one of a good deal of ineffectualness, but identification with the role of an urbane, controlled Englishman serves adaptively to maintain adequate functioning, which is enhanced by a very high intelligence and vast experience with the world.

FINAL REPORT

The author seems to have a continuous struggle with aggressive and sexual drives, feeling strongly that their control is literally vital, as seen in the stories "Rain," "The Happy Couple," "Footprints in the Jungle."

The character structure which has resulted from his attempts to deal with these problems is one of some emotional isolation and detachment, an onlooker looking from the outside in, not without compassion, with considerable puzzlement and a good deal of suspicion of the barely repressed drives that might lurk under the surface in his fellow man, as seen through the eyes of Dr. Macphail in "Rain," the narrator in "Mr. Harrington's Washing," and in the plot of "A Friend in Need."

There seems to be a conflict between active participation in the demands of the world, especially of the bourgeois culture, and the giving in to passive desires, generally, and the call of simpler living under more primitive circumstances, specifically, as in "The Fall of Edward Barnard" and "A Friend in Need."

The self-image that results seems that of a mildly ineffective person who feels somewhat like a pebble pushed about by the tides, e.g., "The Fall of Edward Barnard" and Macphail in "Rain."

Women are seen as domineering and demanding, such as Isabel in "The Fall of Edward Barnard," the women in "Rain," the wife in "The Kite"; or as leading to disaster—Sadie Thompson, "Delilah" in "Mr. Harrington's Washing." Women are also often seen as causing a feeling of inadequacy either as Edward Barnard in relation to Isabel or as in the case of Izzart's mother in "The Yellow Streak." Apparently, the author uses his defenses so extensively that he is not aware of his own strong aggressive drives, projected especially on women.

The constant conflict between activity and passivity, conformity and nonconformity, male and female identification can be seen all throughout the stories, with a fear of failure, of embarrassment and shame, a feeling of inadequacy constantly threatening to emerge.

When one is aware of some of the writer's life history, it becomes apparent that his defenses indeed necessitated a certain amount of constriction of his life to a rather restless, tangential relationship to people, traveling a good deal, almost by design an onlooker who participates only vicariously via his notebook in stories which, as seen in the sample examined, center on a relatively narrow range of themes. He was obviously able to function, nevertheless, by conforming with a character quite acceptable within the setting of the upper-crust Anglo-Saxon society—urbane, polished, knowledgeable, and, above all, not causing any difficulties by uncontrolled emotions. He was very sensitive and shy beneath this stiff-upper-lip front, and yet he was often involved in bloodcurdling and sometimes cold-blooded cruelties, as in his work as an intelligence agent. His own account of his married life suggests something less than affectionate warmth.

One wonders if the attempt to control all emotion might be related to the fact that some critics have spoken of Maugham as a great craftsman, rather than a great artist, feeling apparently that his stories lacked depth and were too neatly packaged. Could this same problem, especially in relation to women, also be related to his marital difficulties and to the fact that he wandered the earth so restlessly and aloof?

DISCUSSION

One may legitimately ask what bearing the procedure here followed might have on the broader problems of the analysis of literature and what light it might throw on the processes of creativity.

Creativity is a complex process. Let me summarize from a previous publication:[18] The creative process involves the ability to oscillate between normal and decreased cognitive acuity and is accompanied by a topographical and sometimes a temporal regression. What Hartmann[19] has described as a self-exclusion of the ego and Kris[20] as a regression in the service of the ego I should like to reformulate as a brief, oscillating, relative reduction of certain adaptive functions of the ego in the service of (i.e., for the facilitation of) other, specifically the "synthetic," ego functions. What takes place is that the cognitive, selective, and adaptive functions are decreased. This weakens the sharply defined boundaries of figure and ground, of logical, temporal, spatial, and other relations and permits them to reorder themselves into new configurations with new boundaries which later come under the scrutiny of the again sharply functioning adaptive forces.

In describing regression in the service of the ego, we make specific use of Gestalt concepts and psychoanalytic hypotheses. The conception of boundaries is not alien to psychoanalysis. Freud, Federn, and Schilder used it in various ways in relation to the self concept. The concepts of figures and ground, of their reversibility, of the degrees of clear definition of their relationship and their boundaries, of the emergence of new

[18] L. Bellak, "Creativity: Some Random Notes to a Systematic Consideration," *J. Projective Techniques,* XXII (1958), 363–386.

[19] H. Hartmann, "Comments on the Psychoanalytic Theory of the Ego," *Psychoanalytic Study of the Child,* V (New York: International Universities Press, 1950), 74–95.

[20] E. Kris, *Psychoanalytic Explorations in Art* (New York: International Universities Press, 1952).

wholes—all seem to be exceptionally useful for the understanding of the creative process.

The scope of creativity varies from creative person to creative person. There are a few outstanding personalities throughout history whose creative ability covered a very broad range of activities: Leonardo da Vinci was probably the most outstanding; Goethe was a painter and respected anatomist and naturalist, as well as a versatile writer; the Humboldts were another example of the breadth of creativity. One might postulate a general factor of creativity much as Spearman hypothesized a G-factor for intelligence, aside from specific factors for either creativity or intelligence. But usually an individual is creative in a fairly circumscribed field.

In the case of writers, there are undoubtedly those, even of great stature and productivity, who have only one story to tell. There are others who cover a broad spectrum of content and form. The external features and the geographical settings of Maugham's stories vary a great deal. If one compares him, for instance, with Tennessee Williams, it is obvious that he is not constricted with regard to milieu. Williams almost always chooses the setting of the American South. Yet I believe that Maugham shares with Williams the constrictions of essential subject matter. Whether the adventures are in Malaya or India, Chicago or Petrograd, the theme and its treatment stays fairly constant. Control of the emotions, the difficulties people get themselves into if they do not control them, and especially the dangers to men in their feelings for women are the leitmotivs that govern his work. A certain aloof compassion goes hand-in-hand with urbanity. Stylistically one always notes a form of prompt dispatch in the tightly organized plots. There is constriction here, a measure of stereotype, within the creative personality. We know something clinically about stereotypic thinking and feeling. The early psychoanalytic conception was one of fixation by overwhelming or repetitive experiences at certain genetic levels. I have found it more useful to think both psychoanalytically and in terms of Gestalt psychology: certain apperceptions, a complex Gestalt of past perceptions and adaptive and defensive features, seem to affect all contemporary apperception. This is more apparent in some people than in others.

In coarse clinical terms, the paranoid personality perceives a broad band of experiences in terms of suspiciousness, fear, and defensive aggression. The authoritarian personality[21] and the closed mind which Rokeach describes[22] have rigidly defined frames of reference within which all experience is organized. Freud, in his paper on the poet, men-

---

[21] T. W. Adorno, E. Frenkel-Brunswik, D. Levinson, and R. N. Sanford, *The Authoritarian Personality* (New York: Harper & Brothers, 1950).

[22] Milton Rokeach, *The Open and Closed Mind* (New York: Basic Books, 1960).

tioned perceptual selectivity with regard to the causal relationship between a writer's productions and his personality. In the case of Maugham, it seems that his stories are the result of such a selective viewing of life. They are the product of the forms of adaptation and defenses with which he tried to deal with his own life and his own emotional problems.

We have some clues as to what these emotional problems might be. There are some suggestive relations among his feelings for women, the loss of his mother at an early age, his aggression and his stammer, his personal shyness, his marital difficulties, and his restless wanderings. However, these conjectures with regard to causal interrelations to the early life history are not of central concern to us and could not progress beyond the usual state of loose guesses on the basis of limited material. I think we are on safer ground if we limit ourselves to inferences covering the relationship between literary production and the personality of the author.

However, it is always interesting to speculate: what if Maugham had been psychoanalyzed? Or, if he was, which I do not know, could he have been more successfully analyzed? How might analysis have affected his stature in literature?

Psychoanalysis is far from a panacea. It certainly cannot make creative a person who does not have creative potential. It can, and often does, improve the ability to translate potentiality into actual creativeness. The great similarity between the process of free association and creative writing has been remarked upon frequently.[23] In the course of this process, changes go on which increase the freedom of access to one's unconscious. Whatever the limitations of the psychoanalytic process may be, it is usually superbly effective in dealing with the perceptual constriction which is the result of traumatic experience and with the defenses and character changes reactive to it. I would not hesitate to say that a successful analysis of Somerset Maugham would almost certainly have further improved his stature by increasing his emotional range and permitting a greater variability in essential themes and style. Almost certainly a successful analysis would have counteracted those features in his writing which some critics have claimed make him a superb craftsman rather than a great artist. I think the critics have overstated it, but what they say holds a kernel of truth.

One can further speculate: in what way can the kind of story analysis we have done here contribute to the understanding and critical analysis of literature? The systematic frame of reference for analysis of literary products may be generally useful for any author's work. The

---

[23] L. Bellak, "Free Association: Conceptual and Clinical Aspects," *International J. Psycho-Analysis,* XLII (1961), 9–20.

range and depth of a literary piece are often at the center of critical appraisal, and a T.A.T. type of analysis may well give a more reliable account than the customary free-style appraisal. Perhaps one of the reasons for widely differing critiques may be, at least in part, the lack of any base line of comparison.

The type of psychological analysis presented here may well throw some interesting light on the relationship between an author's personality and his work. I do not know that such enlightenment would add anything to the values of literature, but it might add some interesting facets to the story of man and his behavior.

On the other hand, I suspect that many an author might profit from an analysis of his work similar to that presented here. Certainly this should not be while the work is in progress; the increased awareness might interfere with the creative process. Maybe such an analysis might be useful after the first draft of a story or book has been written and the major, almost automatic, act of creativity is over. With somewhat more certainty I feel that this type of psychological analysis would be salutary after a man has produced for a good many years and either comes to a standstill or feels it would be worthwhile to check his bearings. An increase in reality-testing, in cognitive acuity concerning one's own production might be of service to a writer who feels blocked at such an important turning point in his career.

7: PSYCHODYNAMIC AND SOCIOCULTURAL FACTORS RELATED TO INTOLERANCE OF AMBIGUITY

Anthony Davids

As a result of findings reported by several investigators who have worked with the theory of authoritarian personality, the concept of "intolerance of ambiguity" has come to have many negative connotations.[1] Ambiguity tolerance has been said to characterize people who are well adjusted, unprejudiced, and not authoritarian. Conversely, intolerance of ambiguity is said to characterize the maladjusted authoritarian individual. Although some experimenters report that authoritarian personalities are intolerant of ambiguity,[2] attempts by several independent investigators have failed to find the predicted relationship.[3] That is, in several researches, subjects who are high on authoritarianism were *not* found to be high on "rigidity" or "intolerance of ambiguity."[4]

[1] T. W. Adorno, Else Frenkel-Brunswik, D. J. Levinson, and R. N. Sanford, *The Authoritarian Personality* (New York: Harper & Brothers, 1950).

[2] Else Frenkel-Brunswik, "Tolerance toward Ambiguity as a Personality Variable," *Amer. Psychologist*, III (1948), 268; *idem*, "Intolerance of Ambiguity as an Emotional and Perceptual Personality Variable," *J. Personality*, XVIII (1949), 108–143; *idem*, "Personality Theory and Perception," in R. R. Blake and G. V. Ramsey, eds., *Perception*, "An Approach to Personality" (New York: Ronald Press Co., 1951), pp. 356–419; M. Rokeach, "Generalized Mental Rigidity as a Factor in Ethnocentrism," *J. Abnorm. Soc. Psychol.*, XLIII (1948), 259–279.

[3] Dee G. Applezweig, "Some Determinants of Behavioral Rigidity," *J. Abnorm. Soc. Psychol.*, XLIX (1954), 224–228; A. Davids, "Some Personality and Intellectual Correlates of Intolerance of Ambiguity," *J. Abnorm Soc. Psychol.*, LI (1955), 415–420; *idem*, "The Influence of Ego-Involvement on Relations between Authoritarianism and Intolerance of Ambiguity," *J. Consult. Psychol.*, XX (1956), 179–184; *idem* and C. W. Eriksen, "Some Social and Cultural Factors Determining Relations between Authoritarianism and Measures of Neuroticism," *J. Consult. Psychol.*, XXI (1957), 155–159; C. W. Eriksen and D. Eisenstein, "Personality Rigidity and the Rorschach," *J. Personality*, XXI (1953), 386–391; Elizabeth G. French, "Interrelations among Some Measures of Rigidity under Stress and Non-Stress Conditions," *J. Abnorm. Soc. Psychol.*, LI (1955), 114–118; E. E. Jones, "Authoritarianism as a Determinant of First-Impression Formation," *J. Personality*, XXIII (1954), 107–127.

[4] Since measures of authoritarianism and ethnocentrism have been shown to correlate .77 (Adorno *et al., op. cit.*), the concepts are frequently used inter-

The purpose of the present paper is to inquire further into this controversial matter. The approach here will be somewhat different from that used previously. Since on several occasions we, and others, have found no relation between authoritarianism and ambiguity intolerance, we will attempt to answer the question, "Who likes ambiguity?"

Using both an indirect and a direct measure of tolerance of ambiguous spoken communications, we have previously found in three independent studies that neither measure relates to authoritarianism.[5] In these and related investigations, we asked subjects to rate ambiguous auditory passages on degree of perceived ambiguity and to rate the degree of liking (satisfaction) they personally experienced in attempting to cope with the demands of the task. Dividing the various groups of subjects into those who liked or disliked the auditory projective test, and those who found it ambiguous or unambiguous, we performed chi-square tests of association between each of the two dichotomies and categories of high and low authoritarianism based on responses to the F-scale.[6] In no case, as I have said, did we find a significant association between authoritarianism and either the rating of ambiguous versus unambiguous or the rating of liking versus disliking. The findings in each of the three studies served to refute predictions derived from theory regarding authoritarian personality and from previous empirical findings. In none of these studies, however, did we relate the two sets of ratings derived from reactions to the auditory test; that is, we did not assess the association between the ambiguous-unambiguous rating and the like-dislike rating.

A primary purpose of the present paper, therefore, is to report the degree of association between these two sets of ratings given by several different experimental groups, studied in the varied settings of a university, a naval base, and a mental hospital. Moreover, the empirical findings from these studies will be discussed in relation to theoretical notions about normal personality, creativity, and psychopathology.

METHOD

The Auditory Projective Technique (Azzageddi Test)[7]

This original auditory projective test was developed by Davids and

---

changeably. Also, the concepts of rigidity and intolerance of ambiguity have been used interchangeably (Frenkel-Brunswik, "Intolerance of Ambiguity . . . ," *op. cit.*), and both have been applied to high authoritarians. In the present report we will not attempt to differentiate between these concepts.

[5] A. Davids, "Some Personality and Intellectual Correlates of Intolerance of Ambiguity," *op. cit.; idem,* "The Influence of Ego-Involvement on Relations between Authoritarianism and Measures of Neuroticism," *op. cit.; idem* and Eriksen, *op. cit.*

[6] Adorno *et al., op. cit.*

[7] This rather unusual title assigned to the auditory projective technique was

Murray, who published a description and preliminary appraisal of the instrument's research utility.[8] The technique is designed to measure eight dispositions or traits that are believed to be important components of personality structure: optimism, trust, sociocentricity, pessimism, distrust, egocentricity, anxiety, and resentment. For each disposition, eight sentences and six short phrases were written in accordance with a special design. Four of the statements represent apperceptions and four represent exhortations; some are expressed in plain, everyday language and some in figurative, immoderate, extravagant language. The stimulus material for the auditory test consists of a series of eight spoken passages that were constructed by intermingling these several kinds of sentences and phrases expressive of the different personality dispositions. Thus, each of the passages focuses on one of the eight dispositions, but also contains phrases and sentences selected as representative of the other dispositions. More specifically, each passage consists of four statements symbolic of a single disposition, four statements each associated with a different disposition, and six isolated words or short phrases each associated with a different disposition.

Two of the eight passages that constitute this experimental test are given below by way of example. The first passage contains four interrelated statements designed to portray mainly an optimistic disposition of elation, confidence, and happiness. However, the passage also contains isolated statements designed to represent the dispositions of trust, distrust, sociocentricity, and egocentricity. Furthermore, distributed throughout the passage are isolated phrases associated with several of the different personality dispositions.

> Beware of sly men, laden with malice, breeders of dirty lies, and smearers of character. (Boiling with rage.) Opportunities for happiness are unlimited. (Disbelieve.) It is not what we take up for ourselves, but what we give up for others that truly makes us rich. (Trustworthy men.) Have confidence in yourself and in your future. Life is a great goblet of glorious possibilities, brimming over with enough delight to make us giddy. (Equality for all.) Never lose faith in your fellow men. (Desire for power.) Let neither sorrow nor disappointment bend you down to earth. (Peril upon peril.) People love themselves above all others.

The second passage contains four interrelated statements designed

---

suggested by one of Herman Melville's works, *Mardi and a Voyage Thither* (London: Constable, 1922), in which a character who frequently becomes confused and incoherent in his speech says, whenever this happens, that a devil in him, named Azzageddi, is talking.

[8] A. Davids and H. A. Murray, "Preliminary Appraisal of an Auditoriy Projective Technique for Studying Personality and Cognition," *Amer. J. Orthopsychiat.*, XXV (1955), 543–554.

to portray mainly a distrustful disposition of suspicion and dread. In addition to this main theme, this passage also contains isolated statements and phrases designed to represent the personality dispositions of anxiety, resentment, optimism, pessimism, sociocentricity, and egocentricity.

> Defiance is the only honorable response to the tyrannies, accusations, and hypocrisies of this evil world. (All together.) People are envious of each other. (Overthrow them.) Inscrutable forces are hurtling us towards a fiery furnace of total obliteration. (Sickness and death.) Be suspicious of every man. Some people are nests of ill will, as dangerous as hornets, rattlesnakes, and vipers. (Success is certain.) Let no man say there is nothing to fear. (Heartsick man.) Never trust the honeyed words of snakes who sidle up to you with insinuating familiarity. (Your own good.) There is much cause for joy in this world.

After all eight paragraphs had been constructed, they were electrically recorded on high-fidelity tape. Each of the spoken passages, which are of approximately one-minute duration, is followed by a three-minute interval of silence. The end product of this procedure is a series of eight electrically recorded, spoken passages which are incoherent and ambiguous insofar as they contain inconsistent, contradictory, and irreconcilable ideas.

Subjects are provided with response sheets and told that this is a test of ability to understand what a person is trying to say and what he really means when his thoughts are somewhat confused. The instructions indicate that the test is designed to measure one's ability to grasp the meaning in a difficult passage of speech and to make sense out of apparent nonsense. The subjects are told that following each one-minute passage on the record, they will have three minutes in which to recall all the ideas they can from the passage and to indicate what they believe is the major idea the speaker was trying to convey in the passage.

When the examiner feels that the subjects understand the procedure, the tape recorder is turned on, with the volume control set well above minimum threshold for normal auditory perception. It is not intended to introduce ambiguity by means of inaudibility, but rather by conflict and irreconcilability of ideas. Thus, the speaker had recorded the passages in a clear voice at a normal speaking rate, and the tape is played at normal speed on a standard recorder designed to provide high fidelity. That the goal of audibility was achieved is indicated by the fact that not a single subject has complained of being unable to hear the material clearly, whereas many have reported that they were troubled by the confusion, contradiction, and ambiguity in the content of the passages.

Following completion of the test, the subjects are provided with two rating scales—one for ambiguity and one for personal feeling—on which to indicate their personal reactions to the auditory test. The instructions for the ambiguity rating are as follows: "Now that the test is finished, we would like to know how confused, vague, or unclear the passages seemed to you. In the past, some people have said that these passages were absolutely too mixed-up and unclear to make any sense, while others have said that they were perfectly clear and make good sense. Please mark a cross on the line showing how incoherent (unclear) or coherent (clear) the passages seemed to you." The ratings are made along a six-point scale running from extremely unclear, or incoherent, to extremely clear, or coherent. The ratings can be dichotomized into those indicating a perception of either ambiguity or clarity.

The instructions for rating personal feeling about the test are as follows: "While you were listening to the passages and writing your responses, you probably felt either satisfied or dissatisfied with the test and your ability to do what was asked of you. We know there are big differences in the way different people feel about taking a test such as this, and we are trying to find out whether most people like or dislike it. Please mark a cross on the line showing the degree of dissatisfaction (disliking) or satisfaction (liking) you personally felt while taking this test." The ratings are made along 6-point scales running from extreme disliking to extreme liking and can be dichotomized into the categories of feeling some degree of either liking or disliking for the task.

Subjects and Research Settings

This experimental auditory projective test has been administered to groups of Harvard undergraduates, officers and enlisted men at the New London Submarine Base, and patients at the Boston State Hospital. The experimental settings and the nature of the samples were as follows.

University students. There were three samples of Harvard undergraduates. The first consisted of twenty students who were studied intensively, for two to three years, by a team of investigators working with Murray at the Harvard Psychological Clinic. These undergraduates had volunteered for this long-range program of personality assessment during their sophomore year, and they constituted one of the experimental groups that participated in Murray's unique programs of research on personality and imaginal processes.[9] The auditory projective test was administered to these twenty students in the course of an intensive as-

[9] This research program was facilitated by research grants to Henry A. Murray from the Rockefeller Foundation and from the National Institute of Mental Health.

sessment program, in which they were administered an exhaustive battery of direct, indirect, and projective instruments. The second group of Harvard undergraduates consisted of twenty-two students who volunteered to take a battery of psychological tests in the hope of being selected as research assistants. They were taking a course in personality at the time they volunteered, and many of them were majoring in social relations. The third group of students were obtained from the Harvard student employment office. None of them had taken any psychology or social relations courses, and they had not volunteered to take psychological tests. They were seeking employment, and the auditory projective test was administered as part of a battery of tests designed to aid in selecting students to work as research assistants.

Psychological similarities and differences among the students in these three samples have been described in previous reports.[10] On the findings to be considered in the present paper, however, there were no significant differences between the results obtained in these three samples. For present purposes, therefore, they have been combined to form a group of sixty-five Harvard undergraduates. All of these men were sophomores or juniors, between the ages of nineteen to twenty-one years, with intelligence in the superior to very superior range.

Navy personnel. The auditory test was administered to two samples of Navy men at the New London Submarine Base.[11] One group consisted of forty-eight enlisted men and the other of thirty-seven officers, all of whom were undergoing training at the submarine school and represented selected samples of Navy personnel. They had volunteered for this branch of the service and had been screened for intellectual and personality attributes. The enlisted men were of above average intelligence and were mainly high school graduates; the officers were all college graduates and had demonstrated superior intellectual ability. The majority of men in both samples were in their early twenties. Although these two samples would undoubtedly differ on many psychological variables, they showed no significant differences in regard to the factors that were investigated in the present study. They have been combined,

[10] A. Davids, "Comparison of Three Methods of Personality Assessment: Direct, Indirect, and Projective," *J. Personality*, XXIII (1955), 423–440; *idem* and H. Pildner, "Comparison of Direct and Projective Methods of Personality Assessment under Different Conditions of Motivation," *Psychol. Monogr.*, LXXII (1958), No. 11 (Whole No. 464).

[11] The staff of the Medical Research Laboratory at the New London Submarine Base provided facilities and co-operated in the gathering of the data used in this study. This experiment, however, was in no way sponsored by, or officially affiliated with, the naval service. The opinions, assertions, or conclusions contained in this report are those of the author and are not to be construed as reflecting the views or having the indorsement of the Navy Department.

therefore, to form a group of eighty-five young, bright, healthy males who were undergoing specialized training in the naval service. The auditory test was included in a battery of assessment procedures that was administered routinely to all entering classes at the submarine school.

Mental patients. The auditory test was administered to a sample of twenty-one male patients and a sample of twenty-two female patients institutionalized at the Boston State Hospital. The mean age for this group of patients was forty-three years. All were classified as psychotic, representing various types of schizophrenia. Most of them had been hospitalized for several years, but all met the requirement of being able to understand and comply with the test instructions. These patients were tested individually and although some were hostile in manner and bizarre in behavior, each of them sat through the entire recording, gave some responses to the memory portion of the testing, and stated their personal reactions to the procedure. There were some differences between the reactions of the men and women, which will be described below, but the general findings in these two groups were similar, and they were combined to form one psychotic group for purposes of statistical comparison with the normal subjects in the other samples.

RESULTS

The findings presented in Table 1 reveal pronounced differences among the three groups of subjects. First, let us consider the degree of perceived ambiguity in the auditory stimulus material. Less than half of the Navy men (44.7 per cent) rated the material as coherent, and this reaction was the same for both enlisted men and officers. The evaluations in each of the three subgroups of university students were also very similar and, for the overall group of sixty-five students, 49.2 per cent rated the auditory passages as coherent. The difference between proportions in the Navy group and university group is not statistically significant. In comparing the ratings by the male and female patients, it was found that 91 per cent of the women reported that the spoken passages were clear and coherent. The corresponding proportion in the sample of males was 76 per cent. For the combined group of patients, as shown in Table 1, 83.7 per cent rated the stimulus material as coherent. This proportion is much greater ($P = .001$) than that obtained from either group of normal subjects. These findings indicate that the psychotic patients perceived little ambiguity in spoken communications which were designed rationally to contain considerable ambiguity and which were rated by over 50 per cent of the normal subjects as ambiguous and unclear.

TABLE 1

Comparison of Reactions to the Auditory Projective Test

Ratings

Percentage

Group	Coherent	Like	Coherent and like	Incoherent and dislike
Navy	44.7	31.7	25.8	49.4
University	49.2	63.0	38.4	26.1
Psychotic	83.7	88.3	76.7	5.0

It is clear that, in the present samples, the mentally disturbed individuals tended to perceive less ambiguity than did normal people when presented with verbal communications containing conflict, inconsistency, and contradiction. Now let us consider their personal reactions to having to cope with such communications. The reactions of the Navy enlisted men and officers were very similar, with the group of enlisted men containing the smallest proportion (29 per cent) of subjects who liked the test. For the combined group of Navy men, as shown in Table 1, the proportion indicating a favorable reaction to this task was only 31.7 per cent. The three subsamples of university students showed some differences in their ratings of satisfaction, with 77 per cent of those who hoped to obtain work as a result of the psychological assessment rating the test as enjoyable, and 50 per cent of the intensively studied research subjects indicating that they liked the auditory test. For the combined group of sixty-five students, 63 per cent avowed that they liked taking the test. Comparison of the proportions in the Navy group and the university group reveals a difference of more than 30 per cent, which is highly significant (P = .001) and provides definite evidence that these normal individuals studied in different settings differed markedly in their liking of auditory ambiguity.

The male and female patients were very similar in their avowal of personal feelings about the auditory test, with thirty-eight of the total group of forty-three patients stating that they liked it. This proportion of 88.3 per cent is significantly greater than the proportion in the normal sample of students (P = .003) and the normal sample of Navy men (P = .001). It seems, therefore, that the mentally disturbed people in this study were more tolerant of ambiguity and, indeed, that they actually liked ambiguity in interpersonal communications.

Having looked at the ratings of ambiguity and of liking, let us compare the proportions of subjects in the different groups who both rated the test as coherent and indicated that they liked it. As shown in Table 1, only 25.8 per cent of the Navy men were in this category, whereas 76.7 per cent of the psychotic patients said that the test was coherent and that they liked it. There is no statistically significant difference between the proportion of Navy men and proportion of university students (38.4 per cent) in this category, but the difference between each of these two normal groups and the group of patients is highly significant ($P = .001$).

An alternate way to look at these findings is to consider the proportions indicating the ratings of incoherent and dislike. As shown in Table 1, 49.4 per cent of the Navy men and 26.1 per cent of the university students were in this category. The difference between these two proportions, which is statistically significant ($P = .005$), shows vividly that, as a group, the Navy men tended to dislike ambiguity. Only two of the forty-three psychotic patients gave ratings indicating that they felt the material was incoherent and that they did not like it. This proportion of 5 per cent is significantly lower than that in either of the normal groups ($P = .006$ and $P = .001$).

The findings presented in Tables 2 and 3 show that in both groups of normal subjects there was significant association between rating the test as coherent and rating it as liked. Although the highest degree of association (chi square corrected for continuity) between these two ratings was in the group of Navy subjects, the university students also tended to like clarity and dislike ambiguity. As shown in Table 4, the vast majority of psychotic patients fell into the category of both perceiving the test material as coherent and liking it. There were so few cases in the other cells of the two-by-two table that a chi-square analysis could not be performed.

TABLE 2

REACTIONS OF 65 UNIVERSITY STUDENTS TO THE
AUDITORY PROJECTIVE TEST

		Satisfaction	
		Like	Dislike
Ambiguity	Coherent	25	7
	Incoherent	16	17

$$x^2_1 = 4.93; \ P = .026$$

TABLE 3

REACTIONS OF 85 NAVY MEN TO THE
AUDITORY PROJECTIVE TEST

		Satisfaction	
		Like	Dislike
Ambiguity	Coherent	21	17
	Incoherent	6	41

$$x^2_1 = 19.83; \ P = .001$$

TABLE 4

REACTIONS OF 43 PSYCHOTIC PATIENTS TO
THE AUDITORY PROJECTIVE TEST

		Satisfaction	
		Like	Dislike
Ambiguity	Coherent	33	3
	Incoherent	5	2

These findings, then, indicate that the institutionalized psychotics did not perceive ambiguity where normal individuals tend to perceive it and that they seem to like ambiguity in spoken communications. In both the normal groups, auditory ambiguity tended to be disliked and clarity liked. The group that was the least tolerant of ambiguity was the one composed of the Navy men.

DISCUSSION

One obvious conclusion to be drawn from the present studies is that ambiguity tolerance is not necessarily a sign of healthy emotional adjustment. In studying relations between adequacy of personality functioning and level of tolerance of ambiguity, it is imperative to give serious consideration to the sociocultural setting in which the observations are made.

It seems apparent that in the subculture of a Navy base no great premium is placed on the tolerance of ambiguity. In fact, it is probably not a personally or socially desirable characteristic in such a setting to be tolerant of ambiguity. Orderly, competent, effective functioning in that social system requires clarity and consistency, and there is little room for tolerance of ambiguity either in ideas or in interpersonal relations. In order to function effectively in the submarine service there would seem to be a need for as little ambiguity as possible, especially in verbal communications.

In this regard, it should be emphasized that the members of this subculture are not necessarily prejudiced, ethnocentric, or emotionally maladjusted. In fact, previous research findings have indicated that the Navy personnel were much *less* anxious, alienated, and neurotic than were many of the subjects in the group of college undergraduates.[12]

In the college setting, on the other hand, students undoubtedly listen to and are accustomed to dealing with controversy, conflict, and contradiction of ideas. In such a social setting, it is probably a desirable and rewarded personality characteristic to be tolerant of ambiguity. Moreover, in general, ambiguity does not seem to be particularly disrupting in the usual college setting. Rather, ambiguity of ideas and lack of certainty may well be necessary ingredients for maintenance of an intellectually stimulating atmosphere.

In the present researches we found that the severely disturbed people, who were patients in a mental hospital, were the most tolerant of ambiguity and seemed to be little troubled by the conflict, confusion and contradiction inherent in the auditory passages. Many of them, in the course of the testing, said how much they liked what they heard on the recording. One patient asked if it was the Pope who was speaking. Another wondered if the speaker was Sigmund Freud. Several liked the content and ideas voiced by the speaker, and many said that he was giving good advice. In fact, one male patient said that if someone had spoken to him like this and had told him these things when he was younger, he would not now be in a mental hospital.

In this regard the present empirical findings are in keeping with theoretical concepts presented by Bateson and his collaborators.[13] These investigators, who have been conducting a research project on communications in schizophrenia, believe that one important etiological factor in the development of schizophrenia is disturbed interpersonal communication in parent-child relationships. Weakland, one of the members of the research team, has reported on the "double-bind" hypothesis of schizophrenia.[14] The "double-bind" situation is defined as one in which an individual is involved in an intense interpersonal relationship in which he feels it important to discriminate accurately what sort of message is being communicated so as to respond appropriately; yet he is caught in a situation in which the other person expresses two orders

[12] Davids and Eriksen, *op. cit.*
[13] G. Bateson, D. D. Jackson, J. Haley, and J. H. Weakland, "Towards a Theory of Schizophrenia," *Behav. Sci.,* I (1956), 251–264.
[14] J. H. Weakland, "The 'Double-Bind' Hypothesis of Schizophenia and Three-Party Interaction," in D. D. Jackson, ed., *The Etiology of Schizophrenia* (New York: Basic Books, 1960), pp. 373–388.

of message simultaneously and one of them contradicts the other. The situation is depicted as "that of one person giving another two related but contradictory or incongruent messages, presenting conflicting injunctions of importance, while also acting to forestall escape and to inhibit notice and comment on the inconsistency by the 'victim.' "[15] Weakland goes on to say that although in the very early parent-child relationship this one-way picture of "binder" and "victim" is probably correct, the "victim" soon learns similar or reciprocal patterns of communication, such as giving incongruent messages of his own, or responding to all communications he receives as if they were incongruent and binding. It is felt by these investigators that such a situation leads to the maintenance of the over-all patterns of communication interaction found in families of schizophrenics and that this fact makes it extremely difficult to conduct successful psychotherapy with such patients.

In support of their theory, Weakland and Fry reported on letters written to schizophrenic patients by their mothers.[16] These letters were found to exhibit evasive and highly influential patterns of incongruent communication and fit very neatly with the theory about the double-bind and the importance of incongruent communication in the development of schizophrenia. Weakland and Fry describe the following hypothesized situation: "At the formal level of message structure, the double-bind is seen as a situation (1) in which a person is faced with contradictory messages, (2) which are not readily visible as such because of concealment or denial, or because the messages are on different levels, and (3) in which he can neither escape, nor notice and effectively comment on the contradictions."[17] The empirical evidence led them to report:

> Our detailed examination of these letters has disclosed that almost no statement is ever allowed to stand, clearly and unambiguously. Rather, another message disqualifying it, in any of a variety of ways, occurs. Further, this alteration, and the difference between the messages, is not itself made clear or explicit, as it would be by such messages as "I changed my mind on that" or a statement of different context. Instead, the differing statement is given as if it were a continuation along the same line, so that each is cast in question by the other, while the incongruence between them is ignored and obscured. In terms of formal patterns of communication, this amounts to the existence of a pervasive pattern of concealed incongruence between closely related messages.[18]

It seems, then, that the auditory stimulus material used in our projective test bears considerable similarity to the type of message that frequently transpires between parents and their schizophrenic offspring.

[15] *Ibid.*, p. 375.
[16] J. H. Weakland and W. F. Fry, "Letters of Mothers of Schizophrenics," *Amer. J. Orthopsychiat.*, XXXII (1962), 604–623.
[17] *Ibid.*, p. 607.
[18] *Ibid.*, p. 622.

If so, this may well account for the fact that the schizophrenic subjects in the present research tended to perceive little ambiguity in the messages and also reported that they enjoyed hearing them. The finding that they avowed liking the passages may be attributable to the fact that the parents of schizophrenics prohibit their children's expression of confusion or misunderstanding in regard to the contradictory messages. Weakland reported that concealment, denial, and inhibition were used on the part of the parental figures over and above the basic contradictory component of the messages.[19] Because of these defensive mechanisms employed by the parents, the children were never able to understand the reasons for or the nature of the interpersonal ambiguity and therefore were unable ever to cope with it. Weakland and Fry say, in this connection, "It seems reasonable to expect paralysis or frantic activity, plus general confusion or suspicion, in response to such a pervasive and general pattern of concealed strong but incompatible influence."[20]

In considering the formation of doubt and suspicion as basic personality components, most current theories of child development emphasize the negative influence of inconsistent mothering. Erikson's theory of psychosexual development pays great attention to this factor and emphasizes the importance of relations between experiences during the oral stage of development and adequacy of the child's resolution of the nuclear conflict of "basic trust versus basic mistrust."[21] According to Erikson, if the child does not receive sufficient food along with warmth, comfort, love, and consistency during the oral stage of psychosexual development, he will not develop a basic trust in his personality structure. Rather, he will develop lasting traits of suspicion, doubt, and basic mistrust—personality attributes that will pervade and color the person's interpersonal relations in adult life.

It is noteworthy that empirical findings from the present research fit neatly with Erikson's theoretical discussion of the infantile conflict between trust and mistrust and the role of this conflict situation in the development of psychoses. Thus Erikson states:

> In psychopathology the absence of basic trust can best be studied in infantile schizophrenia, while weakness of such trust is apparent in adult personalities of schizoid and depressive character. The re-establishment of a state of trust is found to be the basic requirement for therapy in these cases. For no matter what conditions may have caused a psychotic break, the bizarreness and withdrawal in the behavior of many very sick individuals hides [*sic*] an attempt to reconquer social mutuality by a testing of the borderlines between senses and physical reality, between words and social meanings.[22]

We have not been concerned here with the content of the subjects'

[19] Weakland, *op. cit.*, p. 377.
[20] Weakland and Fry, *op. cit.*, p. 622.
[21] E. H. Erikson, *Childhood and Society* (New York: W. W. Norton, 1950).
[22] *Ibid.*, pp. 220–221.

selective auditory memories. In the present context, however, it should be reported that the psychotic patients tended to focus on the distrustful material. Actually 12.5 per cent of the content of the test is designed to relate to the personality disposition of distrust or suspicion; yet almost 30 per cent of the selective auditory memories reported by the psychotic patients were related to the characteristic of distrust. In other words, in listening to the records, the psychotic patients tended to focus upon, select, and accentuate the distrustful ideas that were being voiced by the speaker in the context of conflicting auditory messages. Unpublished findings from studies we have conducted with institutionalized emotionally disturbed children have also revealed that, in response to a children's form of this auditory test, schizophrenic children tend to report mainly distrustful content. It seems, then, that utilization of this auditory projective test in future studies of emotionally disturbed children and adults may well uncover further objective evidence that will help to validate hypotheses derived from theories of psychopathology.

Let us now consider the phenomena of cognitive complexity, creativity, and psychopathology. Barron has discussed complexity-simplicity as a personality dimension.[23] Using the Welsh figure preference test, which presents subjects with a set of abstract line-drawings ranging from simple and symmetrical figures to complex and asymmetrical ones, Barron reported finding two factors: one labeled "acceptance-rejection," according to whether the subjects liked or disliked the figures, and the other labeled "complexity-simplicity." Barron noted that Eysenck had identified similar factors for a number of stimulus classes, including colors, odors, paintings, polygons, and poetry.[24] At one pole there is preference for simple polygons, strong obvious odors, poems with obvious rhymes, and simple highly unified pictures. At the other pole there is personal preference for complex polygons, subtle odors, poems with variable and loose rhyming schemes, and complex diversified pictures.

In an attempt to validate the figure preference test, Barron and Welsh administered it to groups of artists and found that they liked figures that were highly complex, asymmetrical, restless, and moving in their effect.[25] By comparison, however, they found that most people tended to prefer the simple, symmetrical figures—those that were predictable and followed some easily perceived principle.

Barron proceeded then to the study of relations between figure preferences, preferences in paintings, and self-descriptions of personality

[23] F. Barron, "Complexity-Simplicity as a Personality Dimension," *J. Abnorm. Soc. Psychol.*, XLVIII (1953), 163–172.

[24] H. J. Eysenck, "Type-Factors in Aesthetic Judgments," *Brit. J. Psychol.*, XXXI (1941), 262–270.

[25] F. Barron and G. S. Welsh, "Artistic Perception as a Factor in Personality Style: Its Measurement by a Figure-Preference Test," *J. Psychol.*, XXXIII (1952), 199–203.

traits.[26] Using a group of graduate students as subjects, he found the following polarities in these three domains. At one pole there is (1) preference for simple, regular, predictable figures, (2) preference for themes dealing with religion, authority, and tradition in art choices, and (3) avowal of such traits as being contented, conservative, peaceful, stable, thrifty, moderate, and conscientious. At the other pole there is a cluster consisting of (1) preference for complex irregular figures, (2) preference for radically experimental, sensual, esoteric, primitive works of art, and (3) avowal of such traits as being gloomy, pessimistic, bitter, dissatisfied, emotional, unstable, opinionated, and temperamental.

Further findings reported by Barron about the graduate students were based on staff ratings made by experienced psychologists. They revealed that people who preferred the simple figures were evaluated as being natural, likable, straightforward, and lacking in duplicity; they were rated high on good judgment, adjustment, and abundance values. On the contrary, people who preferred the complex figures were judged to be low on abundance values and high on deceitfulness. Abundance values were defined as representing a sense of security and optimism regarding the future with a lack of fear of being deprived or exploited. Barron speculated that the high clinical ratings on deceitfulness, in conjunction with avowal of traits such as pessimism, dissatisfaction, and pleasure seeking, suggested early oral deprivation and the lack of development of infantile trust. In other words, those people who preferred the complex figures might be individuals in whom basic trust had been less well developed. In this connection, Barron said, "It is this lack of infantile trust (as Erikson names it) that leads to adult duplicity and craftiness. One aspect of complexity then (and perhaps a penalty sometimes attaching to it) is, to render it in a common phrase, a sort of 'two-facedness,' an inability to be wholly oneself at all times. The more simple, natural, and likeable person finds it easier to be always himself."[27] These findings, then, suggest a relationship of complexity to character traits derived from experiences during the oral stage of development.

In speculating about the development of creativity and originality frequently found in the complex individuals, Barron said, ". . . a person must have more commerce with himself and his feeling states and less with the environment during childhood if later he is to have sufficient communication with his own depths to produce the original thought. In this view, originality evidenced in maturity is to some extent dependent upon the degree to which the person in early childhood was faced with a complicated relationship to the maternal source of supply, combined with his capacity to persist at and eventually to achieve some mastery of this earliest problem situation."[28]

[26] Barron, *op. cit.*
[27] *Ibid.*, p. 166.
[28] *Ibid.*, p. 167.

In another discussion, Barron further speculated about similarities and differences between highly creative original thinkers, who tend to prefer complex perceptual situations, and individuals suffering from severe psychopathology. He emphasizes that in the mentally ill there is an ego failure and inability to distinguish between subject and object, between inner and outer sources of experience. In the creative person, however, the distinction has been developed, although it may have come out of childhood circumstances which are ordinarily pathogenic. Once the adequate resolution has been attained, it is maintained with great confidence. According to Barron, "The creative genius may be at once naïve and knowledgeable, being at home equally to primitive symbolism and to rigorous logic. He is both more primitive and more cultured, more destructive and more constructive, occasionally crazier and yet adamantly saner, than the average person."[29]

The matter of similarities between extremely creative thinkers and severely disturbed individuals has been given further consideration in a recent paper by MacKinnon, who said, "In view of the often asserted close association of genius with insanity it is also of some interest to inquire into the psychological health of our creative subjects."[30] In this study of highly successful creative architects, MacKinnon noted that on personality assessment instruments, such as the MMPI, they tended to have high scores on personality characteristics of depression, hysteria, paranoia, schizophrenia, and the like. He emphasized, however, that these elevated scores did not have the same meaning for these subjects, who were functioning effectively in their personal and professional lives, as they would for hospitalized mental patients. Thus MacKinnon said, "It must also be noted, however, that in the self-reports and in the MMPI profiles of many of our creative subjects, one can find rather clear evidence of psychopathology, but also evidence of adequate control mechanisms, as the success with which they live their productive and creative lives testifies."[31]

In summarizing findings from the intensive programs of personality assessment conducted at the Institute for Personality Assessment and Research, MacKinnon said, "If one considers for the moment the meaning of these preferences on the art scale, on the mosaic test, and on the scale that measures preference for perceptual complexity, it is clear that creative persons are especially disposed to admit complexity and even disorder into their perceptions without being made anxious by the resulting chaos. It is not so much that they like disorder per se, but that they prefer the richness of the disordered to the stark barrenness of the

[29] F. Barron, "Originality in Relation to Personality and Intellect," *J. Personality,* XXV (1957), 739–742. See also Chap. 10 of the present book.

[30] D. W. MacKinnon, "The Nature and Nurture of Creative Talent," *Amer. Psychologist,* XVII (1962), 484–495. See also Chap. 11 of the present book.

[31] *Ibid.,* p. 488.

simple. They appear to be challenged by disordered multiplicity which arouses in them a strong need which in them is serviced by superior capacity to achieve the most difficult and far-reaching ordering of the richness they are willing to experience."[32]

All in all, then, there seem to be complicated interrelationships among the variables of preference for complexity, tolerance of ambiguity, originality, creativity, and psychopathology. It appears that fundamental to all of these intellectual and personality processes are early experiences in the parent-child relationships. In both effectively creative individuals and emotionally incapacitated persons, there appear to have been similar inconsistencies and disturbing complexities during the oral phase of psychosexuality, with consequent similarities in certain personality characteristics in adulthood. Moreover, in both highly creative individuals and psychotic patients, there is personal preference for perceptual complexity and a tolerance of ambiguity. In one instance, however, the individuals have developed the ability to handle their inner strivings and interactions with the outer world in a satisfactory manner, while in the other case there is extreme ineffectiveness in coping with the complexities of inner needs and the demands of social living.

The reasons why phenomenal complexity during the formative stages of child development in some cases leads to successful creative productivity in adulthood and in other instances eventuates in a life wasted in the confines of a mental institution are far from adequately understood. It may well be that a concept such as "competence" and research on the development of a "sense of competence" during childhood, as White has recently advocated,[33] will somehow help to clarify, integrate, and advance psychological knowledge about these perplexing matters.

In order to increase understanding of such complex and multi-determined phenomena, the science of human behavior needs advances in methods of assessment as well as in theoretical concepts. Toward this goal, the theories and speculations of the creative thinker who enjoys puzzling over the intricacies and ambiguities in human personality must be united with the controlled methodology, rigor, and objectivity of the experimental investigator. With such a unified approach, it seems highly probable that strategic contributions in the future will come from experimental studies of personality that attempt to investigate phenomena which approximate in complexity, poignancy, and interest the kinds of events that are encountered in everyday life.[34]

[32] *Ibid.*, p. 489.

[33] R. W. White, "Competence and the Psychosexual Stages of Development," in M. R. Jones, ed., *Nebraska Symposium on Motivation* (Lincoln: University of Nebraska Press, 1960), pp. 97–141. See also Chap. 3 of the present book.

[34] The data utilized in this paper were gathered while the author was a staff member of the Harvard Psychological Clinic Annex, working as a research associate with Prof. Henry A. Murray.

8: THE COPING FUNCTIONS OF THE EGO MECHANISMS

Theodore C. Kroeber

In at least one important way the contributions of psychology to the study of lives has remained incomplete. Over the years, despite a growing interest in the study of healthy, effective people, the concepts used by psychologists have tended to be best suited to aberrant or neurotic behavior. A real study of lives demands more; it demands a rich and varied conceptual scheme. Most especially it needs concepts tailored for healthy as well as sick people. The purpose here is to introduce a model whereby certain behaviors may be conceptualized in positive as well as negative terms. This is a model which takes advantage of the most widely used theory of personality—psychoanalysis. The focus here is on the operation of the ego and on an extension of the concept of defense mechanisms to include behaviors that are particularly relevant to an active, effective person dealing with demands, often conflicting, of a biological, psychological, or social nature. To this sort of ego behavior is attached the word "coping," and such behavior is compared and contrasted with the defensive behavior familiar in psychoanalytic literature as the ego mechanisms of defense.

BACKGROUND

A need for a better way to deal with active, healthy conflict-solution and problem-solving has been present since the early years of psychoanalytic theorizing. The pure libido theory, with its image of man as a driven and impotent victim of his own instincts, could not have survived outside the confines of the analytic chamber, even had it been able to survive there. To a certain extent the defections of both Adler and Jung centered on this point, although their proposals were in favor of alternate drives rather than a rethinking of ego functions. More than one author has alluded to Freud's essentially pessimistic outlook on the behavior of human beings. Even his attention to the ego and his elaborations of ego psychology were not to change this impression materially. For example,

Horney comments, "Freud's pessimism as regards neuroses and their treatment arose from the depths of his disbelief in human goodness and human growth. . . . The instincts which drive [man] can only be controlled, or at best 'sublimated.' "[1] Nevertheless, the importance of Freud's stubborn insistence on ideas that were bound to be unpopular and of his early refusal to make them palatable should not be minimized. Only thus did they stay current long enough to live past the effects of the shock which they had produced and so pass into more general acceptance.

The revival of psychoanalytic interest in the ego is described by Anna Freud as follows: "When the writings of Freud, beginning with *Group Psychology and the Analysis of the Ego* and *Beyond the Pleasure Principle*, took a fresh direction, the odium of analytic orthodoxy no longer attached to the study of the ego and interest was definitely focused on the ego-institutions."[2] This interest centered upon the defensive functions of the ego, upon its mediating role between id and superego, and upon its protective measures against internal and external threat. The development of the ego psychology of psychoanalysis was completed, according to Rapaport, in the period 1937 to 1946 when "the psychosocial referents crystallize in the work of Horney, Kardiner, and Sullivan on the one hand, and in that of Erikson and Hartmann on the other. A system of multiple levels of analysis evolves, including the dynamic, economic, structural, genetic, and adaptive levels, whose foundations had already been built in the earlier phases."[3]

Nevertheless, psychoanalysis waited to attack the problems of health and remained less interested in health than in problems of neurosis. Freud had, to be sure, indicated all along his awareness of normal functioning and in *Inhibition, Symptom and Anxiety* in 1926 discussed the connections between "normal" and "pathological" defense mechanisms. Still in 1937 Anna Freud could say:

> Since the theory of psychoanalysis is based on the investigation of the neuroses it is natural that analytic observation should, throughout, have been primarily focused on the inner struggle between the instincts and the ego of which neurotic symptoms are the sequel. The efforts of the infantile ego to avoid "pain" by directly resisting external impressions belong to the sphere of normal psychology. Their consequences may be momentous for the formation of the ego and of character, but they are not pathogenic. When this particular ego function is referred to in clinical analytic writings,

---

[1] Karen Horney, *The Neurotic Personality of Our Time* (New York: W. W. Norton Co., 1937).

[2] Anna Freud, *The Ego and the Mechanisms of Defense* (London: Hogarth Press, 1937), p. 4.

[3] David Rapaport, "The Structure of Psychoanalytic Theory," *Psychological Issues*, II, No. 2 (1960), 19.

it is never treated as the main object of investigation but merely as a by-product of observation.[4]

Even though the new ego psychology has had trouble reorienting itself from a preoccupation with pathology and with its etiology, its major concerns have been to conceptualize nonneurotic, adaptive functioning. Although it is generally conceded that such functioning rests on ego structures, there is confusion as to the source of these structures and an absence of any adequate description of them. It is with both these questions—the source and the nature of adaptive ego structures —that recent psychoanalytic ego psychologists—especially Hartmann, Kris, Loewenstein, and Rapaport—have wrestled. Rapaport in summarizing the status of the work on the first of these problems says:

> To begin with, psychoanalytic theory assumed that all psychologically relevant structures arise in ontogeny. But at present some of these structures are considered to be congenitally given. This shift has two implications: *first,* that such constitutionally given apparatuses as motility, perceptual system, memory system, thresholds are psychologically relevant; *second,* that the ego does not derive from the id, but rather both emerge from the common undifferentiated matrix of the first extrauterine phase of ontogenesis. While originally all structures were considered to be related to drive and conflict, it is now assumed that the inborn ego apparatuses enter conflicts as independent factors and that their function is not primarily dependent on drives.[5]

Rapaport goes on to describe further complexities of the relation of drive and ego structure and in particular points out that the energy supply of these apparatuses remains a problem that has not so far been satisfactorily solved. Further, he continues, there is the complexity that certain ego structures ". . . can and often do undergo 'a change of function' and become means of action and adaptation in the service of the ego."[6] This ego autonomy is seen as akin to Allport's concept of functional autonomy.

With regard to the nature of the ego structures of adaptive behavior there has been more agreement. Psychoanalysis has always put the burden on sublimation. Perhaps Fenichel says it most economically: "The successful defenses may be placed under the heading of sublimation."[7] Even the most recent writings do not seem to go much further than this. Hartmann speaks of both defensive and nondefensive ego functions;[8]

[4] Freud, *op. cit.,* pp. 74–75.
[5] Rapaport, *op. cit.,* pp. 54–55.
[6] *Ibid.,* p. 56.
[7] Otto Fenichel, *The Psychoanalytic Theory of Neurosis* (New York: W. W. Norton Co., 1945), p. 141.
[8] Heinz Hartmann, "Notes on the Theory of Sublimation," in *Psychoanalytic Study of the Child* (New York: International Universities Press, 1955), X.

but sublimation and neutralization, which he sees as essentially synonymous, are the only specific processes he connects with nondefensive functioning, and sublimation is also retained as a defensive measure. Although Kris does not go any further in specifying more complexity in adaptive functioning than Hartmann, he makes a useful distinction between neutralization, a relevant energy transformation, and sublimation, a displacement of goal—a distinction which will be kept in the model proposed below, though presented in a different form. Perhaps creative activity has provided the clearest example of the shortcomings of the psychoanalytic model as regards nondefensive behavior. Kris recognizes some of the difficulties which face psychoanalytic theory with respect to creative activity: "The specific functions of ego autonomy in this connection have certainly not been sufficiently explored."[9] Kubie in his recent book, *The Neurotic Distortion of the Creative Process,* contends that an individual's creativity is necessarily less than it might be when it primarily serves the function of resolution of unconscious conflict.[10] Kubie would relate creativity to the free use of preconscious processes, an idea which finds a clear echo in the concept of playfulness proposed below. Both of Kubie's points would seem to argue for nondefensive ego functions.

Interestingly enough, clear suggestions for greater complexity of adaptive ego functioning can be found in the earlier psychoanalytic literature. Anna Freud may serve as an example. "All the other defensive measures which, like reversal and turning against the subject, entail an alteration in the instinctual processes themselves have their counterpart in the ego's attempts to deal with the external danger by actively intervening to change the conditions of the world around it. Upon this last side of the ego's activities I cannot enlarge here."[11]

This suggestion of a duality in function of the ego mechanisms is discussed more specifically by Lampl-de Groot, whose paper the author did not see until the work reported here was completed, but which offers, at least in general outline, a startlingly similar proposal. Lampl-de Groot discusses the confusion in psychoanalytic literature over defense, asking, "Is defense in itself a pathological phenomenon or are we entitled to speak of 'normal' defense mechanisms and defensive processes?"[12] She suggests "that we view the neurotic defense mechanisms as pathologically exaggerated or distorted regulation and adaptation mech-

[9] Ernst Kris, "Neutralization and Sublimation," in *ibid.,* p. 31.

[10] Lawrence Kubie, *The Neurotic Distortion of the Creative Process* (Lawrence, Kansas: University of Kansas Press, 1958).

[11] Freud, *op. cit.,* p. 141.

[12] Jeanne Lampl-de Groot, "On Defense and Development: Normal and Pathological," in *Psychoanalytic Study of the Child, op. cit.,* XII, 114.

anisms, which in themselves belong to normal development."[13] In a general way she indicates that the ego may be influenced to adopt what is here called coping rather than defensive ways of handling conflict. In summation she says, "In analysis we should try to give the patient's ego the opportunity for abolishing the pathological, rigid employment of the mechanisms in the neurotic conflicts, and should try to open ways for their regulative, constructive use in order to promote a harmonious after-development and unfolding of the total personality."[14]

THE MODEL

In essence the proposal here is that the mechanisms of the ego be thought of as general mechanisms which may take on either defensive or coping functions. The ten general ego mechanisms discussed here may be considered to be inborn potentialities for behavior. Just like other ego capacities, such as appear in memory or perception, these would be subject to genetic influence and individual variability. Also like other ego capacities, these ten would be subject to ontogenetic development, with all that that implies as to vicissitudes of situation, conflict, choice, and both internal and external pressure, as well as the possibility, at least in some instances, of emergent or discontinuous development. The familiar and useful defense mechanisms are taken as definitions of the defensive use of the ego mechanisms—indeed, it was *from* these "ego mechanisms of defense" that the ten general mechanisms were inferred —and ten corresponding coping behaviors are proposed. It is suggested that for any given individual, situation, or time the ego mechanisms may be utilized in either their coping or their defensive form or in combinations of both. The criteria for the distinction are as follows.[15]

Characteristics of Defensive Ego Behavior	Characteristics of Coping Ego Behavior
Rigid, compelled, channeled, perhaps conditioned	Flexible, purposive, involving choice
Pushed from the past	Pulled toward the future

[13] *Ibid.*, p. 117.

[14] *Ibid.*, pp. 125–126.

[15] From these criteria it can be seen that "mechanism" as a word, implying as it does the automatisms of a machine, seems more appropriate to defensive functioning than to coping behavior—and "defense mechanism" is already a well-established part of the language. Even though some more neutral word like "process" or "technique" might be more suitable as a single designation for both defensive and coping manifestations, if this model has lasting merit the author suspects that "defense mechanism" and "coping mechanism" will be the chosen form of discussing the behaviors.

Essentially distorts the present situation	Oriented to the reality requirements of the present situation
Involves a larger component of primary process thinking and partakes of unconscious elements	Involves a larger component of secondary process thinking and partakes of conscious and preconscious elements
Operates as if it were necessary and possible wholly to remove disturbing affects; may involve magical thinking	Operates in accordance with the necessities of the individual, to meter the experiences of disturbing affects
Allows impulse gratification only by subterfuge or indirection	Allows impulse satisfaction in open, ordered, and tempered ways

It should be evident that there are differences between coping mechanisms and the autonomy of the conflict-free ego sphere as presented in particular by Hartmann, Kris, and Rapaport. Their proposals involve only one, or at best two, of the coping behaviors given below. This would seem clearly insufficient to handle the complexities of human health. There is further the possibility of being misled by the phrase "conflict-free." The coping mechanisms are *neurosis-free* functions, autonomous in the sense that they are open to internal and external reality; but they may well develop from attempts to handle conflicts, and certainly they must be brought into action in dealing with day-to-day problems of living. By definition the defense mechanisms connote defense against something and imply distortions of available information. An individual with adequate defense mechanisms but nothing more may avoid the fate of hospitalization, but he is using a second-best way to handle conflicts, and a poor second at that. Thus it seems to be an insufficient description of the healthy, creative people of a society to say that their defenses are adequate. It is reasonable that the ego mechanisms, as psychoanalysis has maintained, develop in some historical order, with differentiation and effectiveness increasing with age. But while id or impulse probably accounts for a larger share of total functioning in an infant, it does not follow that internal conflict, in the psychoanalytic sense, necessitates a prior emergence of defense mechanisms from which autonomous ego functions would subsequently have to be liberated. Rather, it may be more fruitful to think of both coping and defense as rooted in the common attempts, at first relatively undifferentiated, on the part of the infant to deal with his internal and external reality to the best of his ability. It seems at least as fruitful to think of potential adaptive process going astray into neurosis as to insist on the inevitable necessity of wresting health from an otherwise implacable destiny of pathology. Both Hartmann[16] and Erikson[17] have provided frameworks for understanding the importance of social factors in the development and functioning of ego processes. These cannot be enlarged on here.

In going over the list of ego mechanisms below, the criteria given above for separation of defensive and coping manifestations should be held in mind, lest the descriptions of each pair of functions sound too repetitive or too evaluative. It will be seen that the ten ego mechanisms fall into three rough groupings. The first three have to do almost exclusively with cognitive functions and the last three almost exclusively with impulse economics. The middle four involve elements of both kinds of control and, in addition, deal respectively with perceptive, apperceptive, and time factors. In considering the action of any of the mechanisms it should be remembered that their alternative functions of defense and coping are not mutually exclusive. Any act or series of acts may involve either defensive or coping functioning, can be purely cognitive or impulse-centered, or may involve combinations of all four.

One can think of a mapping of the ego, at least as regards the ego mechanisms, in several ways. The *extent* (size, strength) of the ego would be given by the frequency and effectiveness of all mechanisms, irrespective of whether they were used in a defensive or coping manner. The *autonomy* of ego functioning would depend on the relative use of coping behaviors rather than defensive mechanisms. A *qualitative description* could be developed from a listing of preferred mechanisms or a rating of comparative use. An indication of *mental health* could be derived from the foregoing, with the addition of estimates of drive and assessment of other biological endowments and developments.

The Ego Mechanisms and Their Manifestations

Defense	Coping

1. Discrimination:
   ability to separate idea from feeling, idea from idea,
   feeling from feeling.

Isolation: the severing or keeping apart of ideas that emotionally belong together, the severing or keep-

Objectivity: the separation of ideas from feelings to achieve an objective evaluation or judgment where

[16] Heinz Hartmann, *Ego Psychology and the Problem of Adaptation* (New York: International Universities Press, 1958).

[17] Erik Erikson, *Childhood and Society* (New York: W. W. Norton Co., 1950).

ing apart of ideas and the affects corresponding to them.

situations require this sort of behavior. S can separate his feelings from each other when he is of two minds.

2. Detachment:
ability to let mind roam freely, speculate, analyze, create, without restriction from within or without.

Intellectualization (a subcategory of isolation): S retreats from the world of impulse and affect to a world principally of words and abstractions.

Intellectuality: even in an affect-laden situation, S is capable of thinking which requires impartial analysis and awareness or otherwise is freed from restrictions of environment, experience, or self, so as to allow thoughts full rein.

3. Means-End Symbolization:
ability to analyze causal texture of experience, to anticipate outcomes, to entertain alternative choices.

Rationalization: S offers apparently plausible causal content to explain behavior and/or intention, which allows impulse *sub rosa* gratification but omits crucial aspects of situation or is otherwise imprecise.

Logical Analysis: S is interested in analyzing thoughtfully, carefully, and cogently, the causal aspects of situations, personal or otherwise; proceeds systematically in his exposition.

4. Selective Awareness:
ability to focus attention.

Denial: S refuses to face thoughts, percepts, or feelings that would be painful to acknowledge. Basic formula: there is no pain, no danger. As applied to the past, the formula is: it did not happen that painful way at all.

Concentration: S is able to set aside recognizably disturbing or attractive feelings or thoughts in order to stick to the task at hand. Can turn to those feelings, thoughts, or percepts at will.

5. Sensitivity:
in direct relationships, apprehension of the other's often unexpressed feelings or ideas.

Projection: S unrealistically attributes an objectionable internal

Empathy: S sensitively puts himself in the other fellow's boots; he is

tendency to another person or persons in the environment instead of recognizing it as part of himself.

able to imagine how the other fellow feels, and experiences this *en petite* himself. Allows for relationships that take account of feelings of others.

6. Delayed Response:
ability to hold up decision, to time-bind tension due to noncommitment, complexity, or lack of clarity.

Doubt and Indecision: inability to resolve ambiguity. S doubts the validity of his own perceptions or judgments, is unable to make up his mind, and is unable to commit himself to a course of action. He hopes that problems will solve themselves or that someone will solve them for him. States situations or feelings, then qualifies them to meaningless death.

Tolerance of Ambiguity: ability to cope with cognitive and affective complexity or dissonance. S is capable of qualified judgments; he is able to think in terms of "both-and," as well as "either-or." S does not need to commit himself to clear-cut choices in complicated situations where choice is impossible.

7. Time Reversal:
ability to replay or recapture experiences, feelings, attitudes, ideas of the past.

Regression: S resorts to evasive, wistful, ingratiating, age-inappropriate behavior to avoid responsibility, aggression, and generally unpleasant demands from others and self and to allow concomitant indulgence.

Playfulness (regression in the service of the ego): S utilizes feelings and ideas that are not directly ordered or required by the practical, immediate elements of the situation and that belong to past experience, to add to his solution of problems, his handling of situations, and his enjoyment of life. He essentially utilizes his preconscious functioning in a rich and flexible way.

8. Impulse Diversion:
ability to modify aim or object of an impulse.

Displacement: S temporarily and unsuccessfully represses unacceptable impulses or affects in relation

Sublimation: S finds alternate channels and means which are socially accepted, tempered, and satis-

to their original objects or situations, but these find expression in some other situation. May occur as a temporal displacement or as an object displacement.

fying for expression of primitive impulses.

9. Impulse Transformation:
   ability to appropriate some energy from an impulse by disguising it through symbolization as its opposite.

Reaction Formation: a personality change involving transformation of impulses and affects into their opposites, resulting in more or less permanent alteration of behavior with occasional breakthrough of the original impulses.

Substitution: the appropriation of energy from primitive impulses in a secure manner so that tempered and domesticated opposites are evident.

10. Impulse Restraint:
    ability to control impulse by inhibiting expression.

Repression: the total inhibition of affect and/or idea. Repressed material is revealed only by symbolic manifestations.

Suppression: impulses are held in abeyance and controlled until the proper time and place, with the proper objects.

SOME RESULTS OF A PILOT STUDY

In 1957–1960 a Ford Foundation grant financed a twenty-year follow-up study of the adolescents originally involved in the Oakland Growth Study. This follow-up provided the opportunity and subjects for an initial test of the ego model just proposed. For this pilot study there were available, in the summer of 1960, the records of thirty-nine men and thirty-three women between the ages of thirty-eight and forty, all of whom had participated in the full program of the follow-up, which included interviews and testing. It was decided to attempt to rate presence, extent, defensiveness, and copingness of the ego mechanisms from the interview data and to test such appraisal by recourse to some other material gathered independently of the interviews. For the latter material the Rorschach test was selected, as it was then already scored and was immediately available.

The interviews had been transcribed from tapes dictated by the interviewers. Dictation was done after each two-hour session. On the average, each subject participated in four sessions, for an average of eight hours of intensive, skilled interviewing. There was an elaborate outline for these interviews, but it was used more as a guide to topics to be raised than as something to be rigidly followed question by question. About one third of the outline referred to the adolescent period of the subject's life, about one third to his earliest years, and one third to his adult years, current situation, and future plans.

To establish ratings for the ego mechanisms, the descriptive phrases for the defense and coping manifestations were recast into more operational form by adding examples, qualifying phrases, or explanatory paragraphs for highs and lows, which would put the definitions specifically in the framework of the interview typescripts. It was typical that the handbook was more elaborate on the coping than on the defense side, since coping was a less familiar concept. As an example of the rater's handbook, here are the working definitions for the defensive and coping aspects of detachment:

Intellectualization: A subcategory of isolation. Retreat from the world of impulse and affect to a world principally of words and abstractions. Pedantry; S thinks and talks on a level of abstraction inappropriate to the situation, uses jargon, is unable to be specific where this is called for; or S is pedantically overdetailed and overprecise. Pseudo-intellectuality.

Intellectuality: S is capable of detachment in an affect-laden situation which requires impartial analysis and awareness, or he is otherwise detached from restrictions of environment or experience or self so as to allow thought free rein. S articulates and symbolizes feelings so that they contribute appropriately to the wealth and richness of his cognitive processes. S invests considerably in intellectuality as a means of coping with life and as a source of satisfaction. This is a cathexis of things intellectual.

Subjects high on this variable show a strong intellectual investment, which would be demonstrated in interest, for example, in the scientific procedures and results of the Growth Study, and this interest would not be used as a defensive measure in regard to the interviewing. S would be able to articulate specifically his adolescent experience as separate but contributing to his present self. Subjects low on this variable would indicate a lack of detachment and overinvolvement with their present experience in the interview, so that the scientific goals would not be noted and S's reaction would be primarily to the immediate personal questioning of the interviewer. Evidence for this quality might lie in kind and extent of reading material, quality and quantity of interest and activity in arts, movies, and the like.

Each subject was rated by the person who interviewed him as well as by a second staff member. All staff members who did rating had had extensive training and experience in clinical work. The procedure was to read the entire transcript and then to assign a rating of 1 to 5 for each of the ten defense mechanisms and each of the corresponding ten coping mechanisms. The quantification of the general ego mechanisms themselves was accomplished by simply adding the ratings of their defensive and coping manifestations. The reliability of these ratings of defense and coping was checked by comparing the judgments of interviewer and rater. Since the scale that was used for rating was only a 5-point one, any defense or coping mechanism could, across the sample, have a range of only 5 points. In view of this limited range, the reliability could be assessed by looking at absolute differences between ratings of the two judges on each subject. Since each judge could award a rating of 1 to 5 for each subject and since judges were independent of each other, it was possible to compute chance expectancies for differences between ratings and to use x^2 to test for any observed departure from these expectancies. Thus for example:

Defense Mechanism No. 1: Isolation (Men, N = 39)

Absolute difference in ratings between judges	Observed frequency	Chance expectancy
0	11	7.8
1	21	12.5
2	7	9.4
3	0	9.3
4	—	—

In the example above, x^2 is 17.0, yielding a probability of chance agreement below .001. This pattern of relation between observed and chance frequency in difference between ratings was similar for all defense and coping ratings. The levels of probability ranged from .005 to well below .001 for men, and from .060 to below .001 for women. On the ten ratings of defense and the ten ratings of coping behaviors, 78 per cent of the pairs of ratings of women and 85 per cent of the pairs of ratings of men fell within a single rating point of each other. With the ten general ego mechanisms (sum of defense rating and coping rating, and thus with a potential range of nine) 81 per cent of the ratings of women and 89 per cent of men were within two points of each other. There was no doubt that, by and large, the ratings showed inter-rater reliability. In the work reported below the judges' ratings were combined to give a composite score.

As mentioned earlier, the independent measure most readily available for a first examination of the ego model was the Rorschach test. Administration of this test had been conducted by a staff member who took no part either in the interviewing or in the rating of the ego mechanisms and who, indeed, was not even acquainted with the ego model. Scoring of the Rorschach was accomplished by three judges. The first of these carried out a routine Klopfer-style scoring using the transcription of the taped sessions and the location chart provided by the tester. A second rater scored all tests on the Klopfer-style elements as well as some special ratings necessary for this study. A third rater (part of this study) scored a sample of thirty subjects on these special ratings. For reliability the scores of the first two raters on Klopfer-style elements were compared for thirty subjects. The special ratings by the second and third raters were compared on another sample of thirty subjects. In general, it seems that the reliability was far from that with which one might hope to work. Although it is true that the Rorschach is notoriously diffident about yielding reliable results, there were some places where even simple counting seemed to have broken down. Furthermore, the Rorschach protocols themselves were disappointingly unsystematic as to amount of data available, a situation apparently due to a casualness in administration or recording that was hardly appropriate for research purposes.

Nevertheless, there were sufficient Rorschach data for a pilot study. In all, out of thirty-two scores or ratings checked for reliability, nine were either unreliable or did not show statistical levels of significance. Of the remaining twenty-three, fifteen gave product moment correlations between .54 and .99. The rest yielded x^2's with probability levels from .060 to .001. Neither the Rorschach data nor their reliability was ideal, but both were sufficient for their purpose here.

A series of predictive hypotheses had been cast to relate ego mechanisms and Rorschach data. Using the definitions contained in the ego model, an attempt was made to predict a behavioral consequence in the Rorschach test situation. It was to meet the demands of some of these hypotheses that the special ratings of the Rorschach situation, such as "affective enjoyment of the test," had been attempted. Forty-two of these hypotheses were tested. In the space here available, it is not possible to present each hypothesis, along with the rationale for it, the statistics used in testing it, and the various outcomes. Therefore, only the hypotheses and their fates are listed below.

1. *Discrimination*
   There should be a positive relationship between rating of discrimination and number of D's. $p < .05$

   Isolation
   There should be a positive relationship between rating of isolation and tendency to give part responses for common wholes. $p < .01$

Objectivity
High objectivity would go with medial number of D responses.

As predicted, but not statistically significant

2. *Detachment*
There should be a positive relationship between ratings on detachment and number of responses on the Rorschach.

p <.001

Intellectualizing
Ratings on intellectualizing should be positively related to presence of technical content in Rorschach.

p <.01

Intellectuality
Ratings on intellectuality should be positively related to ratings on intellectual and cognitive enjoyment of Rorschach.

p <.005

Ratings of intellectuality should be related positively to intelligence test scores.

p <.001

3. *Means-End Symbolization*
Where there were high ratings on means-end symbolization, one should find logical handling of the inquiry, causal explanations for perceptions.

Not tested; material not available

Rationalization
No hypothesis.

Logical Analysis
High ratings on logical analysis should show a positive relationship to quality and amount of elaboration of good F responses.

As predicted, but not statistically significant

4. *Selective Awareness*
People rated high on selective awareness should show fewer FC, CF, and C responses.

p <.05

Denial
Subjects rated high on denial should show a high number of noncolored F responses to colored areas of Rorschach cards.

Hypothesis reversed, p <.001

Concentration
Rating of concentration should correlate positively with ratings on extent of attention focused on task in Rorschach.

As predicted, but not statistically significant

5. *Sensitivity*
Ratings of sensitivity should be positively related to rating of subject's sensitive reaction to the examiner's avoidance of giving specific instructions.

No test made, material not available

Ratings of sensitivity should be positively related to number of Fc responses on Rorschach.

p <.05

Projection
High ratings on projection should appear for subjects rated high on suspicious extratest behavior. — As predicted, no statistical test

There should be a positive relation between ratings on projection and reaction time. — $p < .05$

Empathy
Ratings of empathy should show positive relation to amount of H in Rorschach. — $p < .02$

Ratings of empathy should be positively related to number of M responses on Rorschach. — $p. < .001$

6. *Delayed Response*
Subjects rated high on delayed response should show longer reaction times, over-all. — As predicted, but not statistically significant

Subjects rated high on delayed response should show longer response times to noncolored cards. — $p < .02$

Doubt and Indecision
A positive relationship should obtain between doubt and indecision and ratings of amount of ambivalence shown in approach to percept formation in Rorschach. — No relationship evident

People rated high on doubt and indecision should take more time than average per response. — As predicted, but not statistically significant

Though repression may show a slight relation to average time per response, a combination of repression and doubt should show a positive relationship with average time per response. — $p < .05$

Tolerance of Ambiguity
Ratings of tolerance of ambiguity should be related positively to ratings on successive restructuring of areas. — As predicted, but not statistically significant

Ratings of tolerance of ambiguity should be positively related to ratings of affective enjoyment of the test. — No relationship evident

7. *Time Reversal*
Ratings of time reversal should show positive relation to rating of affective enjoyment of the test. — As predicted, but not statistically significant

Regression
Ratings of regression should be positively related to number of infantile themes in Rorschach. — As predicted, but not statistically significant

Playfulness

Ratings of playfulness should be positively related   p <.05
to number of original responses given in Rorschach.

8. *Impulse Diversion*

Ratings of impulse diversion should be directly re-   No test;
lated to number of H responses with extrapunitive   Rorschach
themes.   unreliable

Ratings of impulse diversion should be directly re-   p <.01
lated to number of FM responses on Rorschach.

Displacement

Ratings of displacement should be positively related   As predicted,
to card rejection.   but not statisti-
                                                             cally significant

Sublimation

Ratings of sublimation should be positively related to   Hypothesis
number of M responses.   reversed,
                                                             p <.05

High ratings on sublimation will be positively related   p <.002
to a large number of M responses only if in combination with high ratings on playfulness.

Playfulness and sublimation in combination are re-   p <.05
lated to M production.

9. *Impulse Transformation*

Ratings of impulse transformation should be positively   p <.05
related to form level.

Reaction Formation

Subjects rated high on reaction formation should   p <.03
show Rorschach records characterized by high num-
ber of responses and relatively few determinants.

Substitution

Ratings of substitution should be positively related to   p <.03
number of FM Responses.

10. *Impulse Restraint*

Rorschach records of subjects rated high on impulse   As predicted,
restraint should be characterized by low number of   but not statisti-
responses and high number of determinants.   cally significant

Repression

Ratings on repression should be related to a ratio of   p <.01
Σ C to Σ M, where high repression would go with
Σ C $>$ Σ M, low repression with Σ C $<$ Σ M.

Suppression

Ratings of suppression should be positively related to   Hypothesis
per cent of non-F-extended.   reversed, but
                                                             not statistically
                                                             significant

At this point it should be emphasized that a detailed examination of these findings and of the bivariate distributions which gave rise to most of them shows that the relationships, in general, are not of a high order, even some of those which were statistically significant. On the other hand, the current of the data was clearly in the predicted direction, as the summary below shows.

TABLE 1

SUMMARY OF SUCCESS OF PREDICTIONS

Statistically significant and supportive findings	21	
Supportive findings, but not statistically significant	12	
Total supportive		33
Findings counter to prediction, but not statistically significant	3	
Findings counter to prediction, statistically significant	2	
Total nonsupportive		5
Not tested	4	
		4
Total number of hypotheses	42	42

The summary shows that thirty-three of the thirty-eight findings were in the direction predicted by the hypotheses, and approximately two thirds of these were statistically significant at the .05 level or less. Or, to put it another way, twenty-four of the thirty-eight findings were statistically significant, twenty-two of these following the prediction and two running counter to prediction. Of the remaining fourteen findings, twelve run in the direction of prediction, a result itself unlikely to have occurred by chance. For this first stage of investigation these would seem to be reasonably encouraging findings and strong enough evidence to pursue the work further.

DISCUSSION

Because it is the model of functioning that is here the central matter, not its experimental validation, which is still in a preliminary stage, it seems appropriate to raise some problems of the ego model and to mention some of its implications. The relation of the ego mechanisms to intelligence, to each other, and to identification and identity formation will be considered.

Beyond the necessity to assess the effect of intelligence on the data here, especially the Rorschach data, it is of importance to investigate some of the general relationships of intelligence to these ego mechanisms. While it is usually conceded that intelligence is a product of both biological endowment and ontogenetic development, we have implicitly allowed the idea of intelligence as a capacity to dominate our thinking. Most especially, we tend to think of the cognitive processes involved in taking intelligence tests as separate from personality processes. This sort of compartmentalization is illogical, and the work of Honzik, Mac-Farlane, and Allen[18] has clearly shown a relation between fluctuations in I.Q. and fluctuations in factors in the child's life history, factors which were either disturbing or stabilizing. Intelligence should show positive correlations with those ego mechanisms mentioned earlier as cognitive (detachment, means-end symbolization, discrimination) and little correlation with those concerning impulse economics (impulse diversion, impulse transformation, impulse restraint). Further, it seems reasonable to expect the coping side of cognitive ego mechanisms to reflect intelligence test scores more accurately than the defensive side. If the interdependence of intelligent behavior and ego mechanisms can be demonstrated, the examination of the two in concert could shed light on many problems, such as school performance, for which only intelligence tests have heretofore been available.

Interrelationships of defense mechanisms have been a focal point of much clinical observation and a source of diagnostic lore. For example, obsessive-compulsive functioning generally is thought to show isolation, intellectualizing, doubting, and reaction formation. However, the coping function of the same mechanisms—objectivity, intellectuality, logical analysis, and substitution—would identify quite another sort of person, even though the ego mechanisms used were the same in both cases—i.e., discrimination, detachment, means-end symbolization, and impulse transformation. It would seem that it is no accident, after all, that many graduate students, demonstrably intellectual, logical, and objective, turn up at university mental health clinics showing obsessive-compulsive features. In another vein, it may well turn out that the operation of some coping mechanisms may offset or reverse others that are used defensively. Or, again, the examination of patterns of coping and defense mechanisms in relation to sex, occupation, social position, etc. may also be ultimately rewarding. Finally, that perennial favorite,

[18] M. P. Honzik, J. W. MacFarlane, and J. Allen, "The Stability of Mental Test Performance between Two and Eighteen Years," *The Journal of Experimental Education* (December 1948), 309–324.

research in psychotherapy, may receive impetus from considerations such as these. Instead of being described simply in terms of symptoms and defensive operations, patients may also be described in their coping aspects. Therapy may consist not only in relieving symptoms and freeing energy from defensive operations, but also in helping the patient to channel this energy in coping ways, something that has seldom been systematically investigated. In all of the above, the indices mentioned earlier, such as total ego, coping and defense ratio, and estimate of drive potential, may be of real value. An informal statement of relationship can be expressed thus:

$$\text{Mental Health} = f\left(\frac{\text{sum C}}{\text{sum D}}, \text{E}, \text{Dr}\right),$$

where sum C represents the sum of ratings of coping mechanisms; sum D, the sum of ratings of defense mechanisms; E, the total of general ego mechanisms (themselves sums of their coping and defensive parts); and Dr, an estimate of drive. This formulation assumes that the absolute amount of energy available (Dr) is crucial to an estimate of over-all functioning; that size of ego is important only when considered in relation to energy potential; and that the ratio of coping to defense mechanisms will reveal how the ego is controlling or channeling or utilizing that energy. Such a conception of mental health would imply that high energy availability, coupled with channeling and control through adequate coping mechanisms, would lead to the greatest potential for creative and productive use.

Identification, identity, and identity formation have been of increasing interest in recent years. Adolescence is the crucial period in which the identity process either crystallizes or fails to do so. No one has been more eloquent or more influential in developing this interest than Erik Erikson. Indeed it was in large part the idea of studying some of his conceptions of identity formation and testing their implications for adults that encouraged the development of this ego model. That, however, is a story in itself which cannot be told here. Still, a simple example may indicate at least one direction of thought. Identification seems inevitably to invoke particular content—particular feelings about particular individuals—but the process of identification may well be subsumed under impulse diversion. If identification is a specific form of impulse diversion involving a specific content, then one would not only expect to obtain correlations between measures of identification and impulse diversion, but also to account for "good" as contrasted with "neurotic" identification by noticing the degrees of substitution or displacement. Other mechanisms may also be factors in this. For example, sensitivity may relate to the ease of establishment of transference relationships and to the well-known variability in this matter, even among apparently equally trusting people.

A final note on general methodology: it has become increasingly obvious to the author that not even the smallest part of this work can be discussed without reference to the matrix from which it was drawn. Considerations such as those outlined in this extension of psychoanalytic theory seem a natural outcome of problems that arise in such long-range personality studies as the Oakland Growth Study. A complex involvement with the same individuals over time, a broad range of subjects and procedures, and a focus on crucial problems all require conceptualizing lives in a rich and diversified manner. It was in this spirit and under these pressures that this model was created. One would like to believe that the hypotheses advanced here would help clarify thinking about the ego and facilitate research. Whether they do or not, it is the conviction of the author that it is only from far-reaching studies that useful extensions of ego psychology will come. The present results have so far been sufficiently promising to justify further investigation.[19]

[19] This paper was drawn from a progress report prepared jointly by the present author and Norma Haan and submitted to the director of the Institute of Human Development, University of California, in the fall of 1960. The ego model and pilot study were a result of a collaboration between the authors of the progress report. Mrs. Haan is in the process of publishing work of her own which utilizes the ego model.

9: ORIENTATIONS TOWARD DEATH
A Vital Aspect of the Study of Lives

Edwin S. Shneidman

It is both stimulating and depressing to contemplate the fact that at this period in man's history, when, at long last, one can find a few genuine indications of straightforward discussions and investigations of death, these pursuits come at the time of man's terrible new-found capacity to destroy his works and to decimate his kind. For these reasons, it may be said that a special kind of intellectual and affective permissiveness, born out of a sense of urgency, now exists for man's greater understanding of his own death and destruction.

For the past few years, a number of us engaged in activities related to the prevention of suicide have habitually looked upon instances of suicidal phenomena as manifestations of a major scourge, involving, as they inevitably do, untimely death for the victim and generally stigmatized lives for the survivors. My own special interest in the classification of death phenomena is one outcome of this group concern with suicidal behaviors.[1] The purpose of this chapter is to stimulate a rethinking of conventional notions of death and suicide. A further purpose is to attempt to create a psychologically oriented classification of death phenomena—an ordering based in large part on the role of the individual in his own demise.

Reflections on death, including suicide, are found in some of man's earliest written works. Death and suicide have been depicted and reified in various ways; numerous misconceptions have grown up around these

[1] At the Suicide Prevention Center (supported by the U. S. Public Health Service) and at the Central Research Unit for the Study of Unpredicted Deaths (supported by the Veterans Administration)—both in Los Angeles. The group includes Norman L. Farberow, Robert E. Litman, and Norman Tabachnick. Some of the efforts of this group are reflected in the following: E. S. Shneidman and N. L. Farberow, eds., *Clues to Suicide* (New York: McGraw-Hill, 1957), and N. L. Farberow and E. S. Shneidman, eds., *The Cry for Help* (New York: McGraw-Hill, 1961). This chapter was written while the author was a U. S. Public Health Service Special Research Fellow (1961–1962), in the Department of Social Relations, Harvard University, studying with Henry A. Murray.

topics. These proliferated intellectual overgrowths are not the specimens that we wish to describe here. Rather, we have to see them as encumbering underbrush that must be cleared away before we can come to the heart of the problem. This is the task to which I now turn.

"IDOLS," OR FALSE NOTIONS ABOUT DEATH AND SUICIDE

This section might have been entitled "A Few Aphorisms Concerning the Interpretation of Suicide and the Nature of Death." Such a heading would, of course, be a minor variation of a theme in Bacon's *Novum Organum*. As in Bacon's day, there are "idols and false notions which are now in possession of the human understanding." Bacon enumerated four classes of "idols" (or fallacies): Idols of the Tribe, Idols of the Cave, Idols of the Market Place, and Idols of the Theater. Of particular interest to us in the present context are the Idols of the Cave —"the idols of the individual man, for everyone . . . has a cave or den of his own, which refracts and discolors the light of nature."[2] In respect to suicide and death each person figuratively builds for himself, in relation to the cryptic topics of life and death, his own (mis)conceptual vault of beliefs, understandings, and orientations—"Idols of the Grave," as I will call them. Further, I would propose five subcategories of these Idols of the Grave, specifically as they concern: (1) the role of classification or taxonomy in treating dying or suicidal people; (2) the classification of suicidal phenomena; (3) the relationships between suicidal and death phenomena; (4) the classification of death phenomena; and (5) the concept of death itself.

The Idol That Maximally Effective Programs of Prevention and Treatment Can Be Developed in the Absence of Taxonomic Understanding

Although one's associations to the word taxonomy—the discipline whose purpose it is to develop concise methods for classifying knowledge —are primarily to the fields of botany and zoology, I wish to focus on the role of taxonomy in the healing arts and sciences. It has been axiomatic in these disciplines that definitive therapies or cures stem from accurate diagnosis and that accurate diagnoses can hardly exist in the absence of meaningful (including taxonomic) understanding of the phenomena. Before one can meaningfully and efficiently treat, protect, and help, one must understand; paradoxically, however, the heart of understanding lies in meaningful classification. In the area of mental health (especially in the areas concerning death and suicide), meaningful taxonomies would seem to be the professionals' *sine qua non* for effective

[2] Francis Bacon, *Novum Organum*, Aphorisms XXXVIII, XXXIX, XLII, and LIII.

diagnosis, prevention, and treatment. All this is not to imply that there have not been classifications of death and suicidal phenomena but rather to suggest that we must continue to attend to the classificatory aspect of our enterprise if we mean to increase, over the years, our effectiveness —an effectiveness which must rest on expanded understanding.

The Idol That the Present Classifications of Suicidal Phenomena Are Meaningful

The use of an illustration may be the best introduction to this topic. A woman of around thirty years of age was seen on the ward of a large general hospital after she had been returned from surgery. She had, a few hours before, shot herself in the head with a .22 caliber revolver, the result being that she had enucleated an eye and torn away part of her frontal lobe. Emergency surgical and medical procedures had been employed. When she was seen in bed subsequent to surgery, her head was enveloped in bandages, and the appropriate tubes and needles were in her. Her chart indicated that she had attempted to kill herself, the diagnosis being "attempted suicide." It happened that in the next bed there was another young woman of about the same age. She had been permitted to occupy the bed for a few hours to "rest" prior to going home, having come to the hospital that day because she had cut her left wrist with a razor blade. The physical trauma was relatively superficial and required but two stitches. She had had, she said, absolutely no lethal intention, but had definitely wished to jolt her husband into attending to what she wanted to say to him about his drinking habits. Her words to him had been, "Look at me, I'm bleeding." She had taken this course after she had, in conversation with her husband, previously threatened suicide. Her chart, too, indicated a diagnosis of "attempted suicide."

Common sense should tell us that if we obtained scientific data from these two cases—psychiatric anamnestic data, psychological test data, etc.—and then grouped these materials under the single rubric of "attempted sucide," we would obviously run the risk of masking precisely the differences which we might wish to explore. Common sense might further tell us that the first woman could most appropriately be labeled as a case of "committed suicide" (even though she was alive), and the second woman as "nonsuicidal" (even though she had cut her wrist with a razor blade). But, aside from the issue of what would be the most appropriate diagnosis in each case, it still seems evident that collating these two cases—and hundreds of similar instances—under the common heading of "attempted suicide" might definitely limit rather than extend the range of our potential understanding.

Individuals with clear lethal intention, as well as those with ambivalent or no lethal intention, are currently grouped under the heading of attempted suicide: we know that individuals can attempt to attempt, attempt to commit, attempt to be nonsuicidal. All this comes about largely because of oversimplification as to types of causes and a confusion between modes and purpose. (The law punishes the holdup man with the unloaded or toy gun, precisely because the victim must assume that the bandit has, by virtue of his holding a "gun," covered himself with the semantic mantle "gunman.") One who cries "help" while holding a razor blade is deemed by society to be suicidal. Although it is true that the act of putting a shotgun in one's mouth and pulling the trigger with one's toe is almost always related to lethal self-intention, this particular relationship between method and intent does not hold for most other methods, such as ingesting barbiturates or cutting oneself with a razor. In most cases the intentions may range all the way from deadly ones, through the wide variety of ambivalences, rescue fantasies, cries for help, and psychic indecisions, all the way to clearly formulated nonlethal intention in which a semantic usurpation of a "suicidal" mode has been consciously employed.

It may not be inaccurate to state that in this century there have been two major theoretical approaches to suicide: the sociological and the psychological, identified with the names of Durkheim and Freud, respectively. Durkheim's delineation of etiological types of suicide—anomic, altruistic, and egoistic—is probably the best-known classification.[3] For my part, I have often felt that this famous typology of suicidal behaviors has behaved like a brilliantly conceived sociologic motorcycle (anomie) with two psychological sidecars, performing effectively in textbooks for over half a century, but running low on power in clinics, hospitals, and consultation rooms. This classification epitomizes some of the strengths and shortcomings of any study based almost entirely on a social, normative, tabular, nomothetic approach. It is probably fair to say, however, that Durkheim was not so much interested in suicide per se, as he was in the explication of his general sociological method.

Freud's psychological formulation of suicide, as hostility directed toward the introjected love object—what I have called "murder in the 180th degree"—was more a brilliant inductive encompassment than an empirical, scientific particularization.[4] This concept was given its most far-reaching exposition by Karl Menninger, who, in Man Against Himself, not only outlined four types of suicide—chronic, focal, organic, and

[3] Émile Durkheim, Suicide, trans. John A. Spaulding and George Simpson (Glencoe, Ill.: The Free Press, 1951), originally published as Le Suicide (1897).
[4] Sigmund Freud, "Mourning and Melancholia," Collected Papers (London: Hogarth Press, 1924), IV, 162–163; and "The Psychogenesis of a Case of Homosexuality in a Woman," ibid., II, 220.

actual—but also proposed three basic psychological components: the wish to kill, the wish to be killed, and the wish to die.[5]

Neither of these two theoretical approaches to the nature and causes of suicide constitutes the classification most common in everyday clinical use. That distinction belongs to a rather homely, supposedly common-sense division, which in its barest form implies that all humanity can be divided into two groupings, suicidal and nonsuicidal, and then divides the suicidal category into committed, attempted, and threatened.[6] Although the second classification is superior to the suicidal-versus-nonsuicidal view of life, that it is not theoretically nor practically adequate for understanding and treatment is one of the main tenets of this chapter. It may well be that the word suicide currently has too many loose and contradictory meanings to be scientifically or clinically useful.

The Idol That Living and Dying Are Separate

Living and dying have too often been seen erroneously as distinct, separate, almost dichotomous activities. To correct this view one can enunciate another, which might be called the psychodynamics of dying. One of its tenets is that, in cases where an individual is dying over a period of time, which may vary from hours to years in persons who "linger" in terminal illnesses, this interval is a psychologically consistent extension of styles of coping, defending, adjusting, interacting, and other modes of behavior that have characterized that individual during most of his life up to that time. Feifel says, "A man's birth is an uncontrolled event in his life, but the manner of his departure from life bears a definite relation to his philosophy of life and death. We are mistaken to consider death as a purely biological event. The attitudes concerning it and its meaning for the individual can serve as an important organizing principle in determining how he conducts himself in life."[7] How an individual dies should no less reflect his personal philosophy, the goodness of his personal adjustment, his sense of fruition, fulfillment, self-realization. Feifel further states that ". . . types of reactions to impending death are a function of interweaving factors. Some of the significant ones appear to be . . . the psychological maturity of the individual; the kind of coping techniques available to him; variables of religious orienta-

---

[5] Karl Menninger, *Man Against Himself* (New York: Harcourt, Brace & Co., 1938).

[6] This important distinction was made by Norman L. Farberow in 1950, "Personality Patterns of Suicidal Mental Hospital Patients," *Genetic Psychology Monographs*, XLII (1950), 3–79, and supported in 1954 by A. Rosen, W. M. Hales, and W. Simon, "Classification of 'Suicidal' Patients," *Journal of Consulting Psychology*, XVIII (1954), 359–362.

[7] Herman Feifel, ed., *The Meaning of Death* (New York: McGraw-Hill, 1959), p. 128.

tion, age, socio-economic status, etc.; severity of the organic process; and the attitudes of the significant persons in the patient's world."[8]

Dr. Arthur P. Noyes is reported to have said, "As we grow older, we grow more like ourselves." I believe that this illuminating but somewhat cryptic remark can also be taken to mean that during the dying period, the individual displays behaviors and attitudes which contain great fealty to his lifelong orientations and beliefs. Draper says: "Each man dies in a notably personal way."[9] Suicidal and/or dying behaviors do not exist *in vacuo,* but are an integral part of the life style of the individual.[10]

The Idol That the Traditional Classification of Death Phenomena Is Clear

The International Classification of the Causes of Death lists 137 causes, such as pneumonia, meningitis, malignant neoplasms, myocardial infarctions[11]; but, in contrast, there are only four commonly recognized *modes* of death: *natural death, accident, suicide,* and *homicide.* In some cases, cause of death is used synonymously to indicate the natural cause of death. Thus, the standard U. S. Public Health Service Certificate of Death has a space to enter cause of death (implying the mode as natural) and, in addition, provides opportunity to indicate accident, suicide, or homicide. Apparently, it is implied that these four modes of death constitute the final ordering into which each of us must be classified. The fact that some of us do not fit easily into one of these four crypts is the substance for this section.

The shortcoming of the common classification is that, in its oversimplification and failure to take into account certain necessary dimensions, it often poses serious problems in classifying deaths meaningfully. The basic ambiguities can be seen most clearly by focusing on the distinctions between natural (intrasomatic) and accidental (extrasomatic) deaths. On the face of it, the argument can be advanced that most deaths, especially in the younger years, are unnatural. Perhaps only in the cases of death of old age might the termination of life legitimately

8 *Ibid.,* p. 126.

9 George Draper, C. W. Dupertuis, and J. L. Caughley, *Human Constitution in Clinical Medicine* (New York: Hoeber, 1944), p. 74.

10 A practical extension of this belief is contained in the "psychological autopsies" that the professional staff of the Suicide Prevention Center conducts in connection with the Los Angeles County Coroner's Office in the certification of equivocal or possible suicidal deaths. See Theodore J. Curphey, "The Role of the Social Scientist in the Medicolegal Certification of Death from Suicide," and Edwin S. Shneidman and Norman L. Farberow, "Sample Investigation of Equivocal Suicidal Deaths," in *The Cry for Help, op. cit.,* pp. 110–117 and 118–128, respectively.

11 *International Classification of Causes of Death.*

be called natural. Let us examine the substance of some of these confusions. If an individual (who wishes to continue living) has his skull invaded by a lethal object, his death is called accidental; if another individual (who also wishes to continue living) is invaded by a lethal virus, his death is called natural. An individual who torments an animal into killing him is said to have died an accidental death, whereas an individual who torments a drunken companion into killing him is called a homicidal victim. An individual who has an artery burst in his brain is said to have died with a cerebral-vascular accident, whereas it might make more sense to call it a cerebral-vascular natural death. What has been confusing in this traditional approach is that the individual has been viewed as a kind of biological *object* (rather than psychological, social, biological organism), and as a consequence, the role of the individual in his own demise has been omitted.

The Idol That the Concept "Death" Is Itself Operationally Sound

We come now to what for some may be the most radical and iconoclastic aspect of our presentation so far, specifically the suggestion that a major portion of the concept of "death" is operationally meaningless and ought therefore to be eschewed. Let the reader ask the question of the author: "Do you mean to say that you wish to discuss suicidal phenomena and orientations toward death without the concept of death?" The author's answer is in the affirmative, based, he believes, on compelling reasons. Essentially, these reasons are epistemological, that is, they have to do with the process of knowing and the question of what it is that we can know. Our main source of quotable strength—and we shall have occasion later to refer to him in a very different context—is the physicist Percy W. Bridgman. Essentially, his concept is that death is not experienceable, that if one could experience it, one would not be dead. One can experience another's dying and another's death and his own dying—although he can never be sure—but no man can experience his own death.

In his book *The Intelligent Individual and Society,* Bridgman states this view as follows:

> There are certain kinks in our thinking which are of such universal occurrence as to constitute essential limitations. Thus the urge to think of my own death as some form of my experience is almost irresistible. However, it requires only to be said for me to admit that my own death cannot be a form of experience, for if I could still experience, then by definition it would not be death. Operationally my own death is a fundamentally different thing from the death of another in the same way that my own feelings mean something fundamentally different from the feelings of another. The death of another I can experience; there are certain methods of recognizing death and certain properties of death that affect my actions in the

case of others. Again it need not bother us to discover that the concept of death in another is not sharp, and situations may arise in practice where it is difficult to say whether the organism is dead or not, particularly if one sticks to the demand that "death" must be such a thing that when the organism is once dead it cannot live again. This demand rests on mystical feelings, and there is no reason why the demand should be honored in framing the definition of death. . . . My own death is such a different thing that it might well have a different word, and perhaps eventually will. There is no operation by which I can decide whether I am dead; "I am always alive."[12]

This pragmatic view of death—in the strict philosophical sense of pragmatism—is stated most succinctly (in a side remark about death) by the father of pragmatism. Peirce, in discussing metaphysics, says:

> We start then, with nothing, pure zero. But this is not the nothing of negation. For *not* means *other than,* and *other* is merely a synonym of the ordinal numeral *second.* As such it implies a first; while the present pure zero is prior to every first. The nothing of negation is the nothing of death, which also comes *second to,* or after, everything.[13]

In literature this concept of death as nothingness seems to have appeared early and remained.

Two further thoughts on death as experience. Not only, as we have seen, is death misconceived as an experience, but (a) it is further misconceived as a bitter or calamitous experience, and (b) it is still further misconceived as an *act,* as though dying were something that one had to do. On the contrary, dying can be a supreme passivity rather than the supreme act or activity. It will be done for you; dying is one thing that no one has to "do."[14]

In addition to this philosophical aspect of the situation, there is also the reflection that one's own death is really psychologically inconceivable. Possibly the most appropriate quotation in this connection is from the twentieth-century giant of depth psychology. In his paper on "Thoughts of War and Death," Freud wrote:

> Our own death is indeed unimaginable, and whenever we make the attempt to imagine it we can conceive that we really survive as spectators. Hence the psychoanalytic school could venture on the assertion that at bottom no one believes in his own death, or to put the thing in another

---

[12] Percy W. Bridgman, *The Intelligent Individual and Society* (New York: Macmillan, 1938), p. 168. See also pp. 168–173 and Percy W. Bridgman, *The Way Things Are* (Cambridge, Mass.: Harvard University Press, 1955), pp. 234–235.

[13] *Collected Papers of Charles Sanders Peirce,* ed. Charles Hartshorne and Paul Weiss (Cambridge, Mass.: Harvard University Press, 1931–1958), VI, 148.

[14] I am indebted to Prof. Abraham Kaplan of the Philosophy Department of U.C.L.A. for this insight and information.

way, in the unconscious every one of us is convinced of his own immortality.[15]

Indeed, the word "death" has become a repository for pervasive
logical and epistemological confusions—"Idols of the Dead." The first
order of business might well be to clarify the concepts presently embedded in our current notions of death. For my part, I would wish to
eschew, where possible, the concept of death and, instead, use concepts
and terms which are operationally viable. This is the text of the present
section, the content of the next section, and the burden of this essay.

CESSATION, TERMINATION, INTERRUPTION, AND CONTINUATION

In the preceding section, I have been critical of some current concepts relating to suicide and death. In this section I wish to propose a
tentative psychological classification of all behaviors involving demise.
Two sets of key concepts are involved: the first is made up of the terms
cessation, termination, interruption, and continuation; the second, of the
terms intentioned, subintentioned, unintentioned, and contraintentioned.
At this point, our first tasks are those of definition.

Cessation

The key concept in this chapter is the idea of "cessation."[16] In this
context, cessation has a psychological, specifically introspective referent.
Our definition of "cessation" is that it is the stopping of the potentiality
of any (further) conscious experience. "Death"—some form of termination—is the universal and ubiquitous ending of all living things; but only
man, by virtue of his verbally reportable introspective mental life, can
conceptualize, fear, and suffer cessation. Cessation refers to the last line
of the last scene of the last act of the last drama of that actor. It should
be immediately obvious that different individuals—and any particular
individual at different times—can have a variety of attitudes and orientations toward their cessations. The next section contains an explication
of possible orientations toward cessation. Cessation is used here not as
a synonym for the word death, but rather as its operationally defined

---

[15] Sigmund Freud, "Thoughts on War and Death," *Collected Papers, op. cit.,*
IV, 304–305. And Miguel de Unamuno, who is probably as nonpsychoanalytic as
it is possible for a cultivated twentieth-century human to be, says, in his chapter
entitled "The Hunger for Immortality" in *The Tragic Sense of Life* (p. 38): "It is
impossible for us, in effect, to conceive of ourselves as not existing, and no effort is
capable of enabling consciousness to realize absolute unconsciousness, its own
annihilation."

[16] The term "cessation" is used in this present sense by Bridgman on at least two
occasions, both in *The Intelligent Individual and Society* (New York: Macmillan,
1938), pp. 169, 225.

substitute. Also, in order to have a shorthand term for cessation, I shall use the term "Psyde," referring, so to speak, to the demise of the psychic processes—the final stopping of the individual consciousness, as far as we know.[17]

Termination

The concept of "termination"—which is defined as the stopping of the physiological functions of the body—is needed because there can occur the stopping of the potentiality of conscious experience (cessation) which is not temporally coincident with the stopping of the functions of the body. Our shorthand word for termination is "Somize," referring to the demise of the soma. Consider the report of the following incident: A young man was, while riding as a passenger on a motorcycle, hit by an automobile and thrown several yards through the air. He landed on his head at a curbside. At the hospital, this case was regarded as remarkable, because, although his skull was crushed and although he showed no evidence of any conscious experience and even had a rather complete absence of reflexes, he was kept alive for many days by means of intravenous feeding, catheter relief, and many other life-extending pieces of mechanical apparatus. Eventually he "expired." The conceptual point to be made in this context is that he suffered cessation the moment that his head hit the pavement. So, although he had ceased, he had not terminated, in that he continued to breathe. No one would have thought to suggest that he be buried or cremated as long as he was still breathing. A further point can be made: the operational definition (or criterion) for termination can be put at the stopping of the exchange of gases between the human organism and his environment, i.e., an individual may be said to be terminated when, if a mirror is put to his mouth, there is no frosting on the glass—the subsequent growth of his beard or other activities do not matter.[18] If cessation relates to the psychological personality, then termination has to do with the biological organism. It is useful to distinguish between cessation and termination. We all know that it is possible for an individual to put a gun to his head, planning to "blow his brains out" (termination) and yet *believe* that he will be at his own funeral, that he will be able to check whether or not his widow follows the instructions in his suicide note (without cessation). In order not to be entrapped by the confusion that exists in many minds concerning these two concepts, we must clarify them in our own.

---

[17] I am indebted to Prof. James Diggory, of the Psychology Department of the University of Pennsylvania, for suggesting this term to me.

[18] "I know when one is dead and when one lives; She's as dead as earth. Lend me a looking glass; If her breath will mist or stain the stone, Why, then she lives." *King Lear*, Act V, Scene 3.

Interruption

The third concept of this group is that of interruption, which relates not to termination but to cessation. If cessation has to do with the stopping of the potentiality of any conscious experience, then interruption is in a sense its opposite, in that "interruption" is defined as the stopping of consciousness with the actuality, and usually the expectation, of further conscious experiences. It is a kind of temporary cessation. The best example of an interruption state is being asleep; others are being under an anaesthetic, in an alcoholic stupor, in a diabetic coma, in an epileptic seizure, and, on another level, being in a fugue, amnesic, or dissociative state. The primary purpose of introducing the notion of interruption states is to provide a concept whereby data—especially those which could be obtained from experimental situations—might serve as paradigms, analogues, models, or patterns for certain cessation conditions. For example—and more will be said about this later—it might be possible to devise paradigms having to do with sleep behavior that will give us fresh leads and new insights into suicidal behaviors, which a direct approach would not yield.

Continuation

When one works with suicidal people clinically and investigates, through "psychological autopsies," cases of suicide, one often gets the impression that individuals who, in point of fact, have killed themselves, have not necessarily "committed suicide." That is to say, in some cases, it seems that the person's intention was not to embrace death but rather to find surcease from external or internalized aspects of life. In the context of this chapter, we shall call the process of living "continuation." "Continuation" can be defined as experiencing, in the absence of interruption, the stream of temporally contiguous conscious events. From this point of view, our lives are made up of a series of alternating continuation and interruption states.

One might find a group of nonlethally oriented "suicide attempters" —each of whom wished to postpone cessation—who, individually, might manifest quite different patterns of orientation toward continuation. The nuances of these patterns might well include the following: (a) patterns of ambivalence (coexistent wishes to live and to die, including rescue fantasies, gambles with death, and cries for help); (b) the state of hopefulness or hopelessness, and accompanying feelings of psychological impotence; (c) patterns of self-righteousness, indignation, inner resourcefulness, defeat, and ennui; (d) orientations toward the next temporal interval, whether one of blandness, inertia, habit, interest, anticipation, expectation, or demand; (e) intensity of thought and action in relation to continuation, ranging from absent (no thought about it), through fleeting fantasy, concern, obsession, and rash behavior outburst, to deliberate performance. Continuation is the converse of cessation. It would be important to know, in any particular case, how an individual's attitudes toward continuation interacted with his orientations toward cessation. In addition to this, we could say that a comprehensive study of suicidal phenomena should include concern for nonsuicidal phenomena and such perverse questions as what a specific individual has to live for or why a specific individual does not commit suicide.

BASIC ORIENTATIONS TOWARD CESSATION

The operation which gives meaning to the phrase "basic orientation toward cessation" has to do with the role of the individual in his own demise. By "role of the individual" is meant his overt and covert behaviors and nonbehaviors which reflect conscious and unconscious attributes relevant to his cessation. These include at least the following: his attitudes and beliefs about death, cessation, hereafter, and rebirth; his ways of thinking; his need systems, including his needs for achievement, affiliation, autonomy, and dominance; his dyadic relationships, especially the subtleties of dependencies and hostilities in relation to the significant people in his life; the hopefulness and hopelessness in the responses of these people to his cries for help; the constellation and balance of ego activity and ego passivity; his orientations toward continuation states. To know these facts about a person would well require a comprehensive psychological understanding of his personality.

Four subcategories relating to the role of the individual in his own demise are suggested: intentioned, subintentioned, unintentioned, and contraintentioned.

Intentioned

By intentioned, I refer to those cases in which the individual plays a direct and conscious role in his own demise. These cases do not refer to persons who wish for "death" or termination, but rather to those who actively precipitate their cessation. (Of course, cessation cannot be avoided by anyone. The entire issue is one of timing and involves postponing and hastening.) In terms of the traditional categories of death, no presently labeled accidental or natural deaths would be called intentioned, some homicidal deaths might be called intentioned, and most (but, importantly, not all) suicidal deaths would be called intentioned. In relation to the term "suicide," intentioned cases may be said to have *committed* suicide. Using the word "Psyde" to represent cessation, we can list a number of subcategories: (1) Psyde-seekers; (2) Psyde-initiators; (3) Psyde-ignorers; and (4) Psyde-darers.

1. *Psyde-seeker.* A Psyde-seeker is one who, during the time that he

can be so labeled, has consciously verbalized to himself his wish for an ending to all conscious experience and behaves in order to achieve this end. The operational criteria for a Psyde-seeker lie not primarily in the method he uses—razor, barbiturate, carbon monoxide—but in the fact that the method *in his mind* is calculated to bring him cessation; and, whatever his rescue fantasies or cries for help may be, he does the act in such a manner and site that rescue (or intervention) is realistically unlikely or impossible. In all, he has a predominantly unambivalent intention or orientation toward cessation during that period. The phrase "during that period" is meant to convey the notion that individuals' orientations toward cessation shift and change over time.[19] A person who was a Psyde-seeker yesterday and made a most serious suicidal act then, could not today be forced to participate in activities that might cost him his life. It is known clinically—as supported by our experience at the Suicide Prevention Center—that many individuals are "suicidal" for only a relatively brief period of time; so that if they can be given appropriate sanctuary, they will no longer seek Psyde and will wish to continue to live as long as possible.

2. *Psyde-initiator*.[20] A Psyde-initiator is a Psyde-seeker, but sufficiently different to warrant a separate label. A Psyde-initiator believes that he will suffer cessation in the fairly near future—a matter of days or weeks—or he believes that he is failing and, not wishing to accommodate himself to a new (and less effective and less virile) image of himself, does not wish to let "it" happen to him. Rather, *he* wants to play a role in its occurrence. Thus he will do it for himself, at his own time, and on his own terms. In our investigations at the Veterans Administration Central Research Unit for the Study of Unpredicted Death we find, on occasion, a case in which an older person, hospitalized in a general medical hospital, in the terminal stages of a fatal disease will, with remarkable and totally unexpected energy and strength, take the tubes and needles out of himself, climb over the bed rails, lift a heavy window, and throw himself to the ground several stories below. What is most prototypical about such an individual is that, when one looks at his previous occupational

---

[19] The Psyde-states described herein are meant to describe only the *current* status (vis-à-vis cessation) of the individual. Thus, one would, in any complete description of an individual, need also a biphasic taxonomy which describes the relatively chronic, pervasive, characterological, "presuicidal" aspects of his psychological make-up.

[20] This concept of the initiator was developed primarily by Mrs. Calista V. Leonard of the staff of the V. A. Central Research Unit and is described in her article, "A Theory of Suicide: The Implementor" (unpublished paper, Veterans Administration Central Research Unit, Los Angeles, 1962). See also the section on the unaccepting patient in E. S. Shneidman, N. L. Farberow, and Calista V. Leonard, "Suicide-Evaluation and Treatment of Suicidal Risk Among Schizophrenic Patients in Psychiatric Hospitals," *Medical Bulletin MB-8* (Washington, D.C.: Veterans Administration, Department of Medicine and Surgery, 1962).

history, one sees that he has never been fired—he has always quit. In either case, the person ends up unemployed, but the role he has played in the process is different.[21]

3. *Psyde-ignorer.* Consider the following suicide note: "Good-by, kid. You couldn't help it. Tell that brother of yours, when he gets to where I'm going, I hope I'm a foreman down there; I might be able to do something for him." Although it is true that suicide notes which contain any reference to a hereafter, a continued existence, or a reunion with dead loved ones are relatively very rare (see Appendix to *Clues to Suicide*), it is also true that some people who kill themselves believe, as part of their total system of beliefs, that one can effect termination without involving cessation. They seem to ignore the fact that, so far as we know, termination always involves cessation. One can note that even those in our contemporary society who espouse belief in a hereafter as part of their religious tenets, still label a person who has shot himself to death as suicidal. This is probably so primarily because, whatever *really* happens after termination, the survivors are still left to live (and usually to mourn) in the undeniable physical absence of the person who killed himself. Thus, this subcategory of Psyde-ignorer, or, perhaps better, Psyde-transcender, contains those persons who, from our point of view, effect their own termination and cessation but who, from their point of view, effect only their termination and continue to exist in some manner or another.

This paragraph is not meant to necessarily deny a (logical) possibility of continuation after cessation (life after death), but the concept of Psyde-ignoring (or something similar to it) is a firm necessity in any systematic classification of this type; otherwise we will put ourselves in the untenable position of making exactly comparable (a) a man's shooting his head off in the belief and hope that he will soon meet his dead wife in heaven and (b) a man's taking a trip from one city to another with the purpose and expectation of being reunited with his spouse. Obviously, these two acts are so vastly different in their effects (on the person concerned and on others who know him) that they cannot be equated. Therefore, independent of the individual's convictions that killing oneself does not result in cessation but is simply a transition to an-

---

[21] Three very different examples of Psyde-initiators—all eminent men—are contained in the following: Lael Tucker Wertenbaker, *Death of a Man* (New York: Random House, 1957), pp. 174–81; Leicester Hemingway, *My Brother, Ernest Hemingway* (New York: World, 1962), p. 283; and Gerald Holton, "Percy Williams Bridgman," reprinted in the *Bulletin of the Atomic Scientists,* XVII, No. 2 (February, 1962), 22–23. It is interesting to contrast Hemingway's attitude toward his failing body with that of Dr. Hans Zinsser: *As I Remember Him* (Boston: Little, Brown and Co., 1940), pp. 200–201.

other life, we must superimpose our belief that cessation is necessarily final as far as the human personality which we can know is concerned.

4. *Psyde-darer.* A Psyde-darer is an individual who, to use gamblers' terms, bets his continuation (i.e., his life) on the objective probability of as few as five out of six chances that he will survive. Regardless of the outcome, an individual who plays Russian Roulette is a Psyde-darer at that time. In addition to the objective probabilities that exist, the concept of a Psyde-darer also involves subjective probabilities of the same order of magnitude. Thus, a person with little skill as a pilot who attempts to fly an airplane or one with unpracticed co-ordination who attempts to walk along the ledge of a roof of a tall building may be classified as a Psyde-darer. The rule of thumb is that it is not what he does, but the background (of skill, prowess, and evaluation of his own abilities) against which he does it, that matters. In a sense the Psyde-darer is only a partial, or fractional, cessation-seeker; but since each lethal fraction contained within the gambling situation is completely lethal, it seems most meaningful to classify such an act within the intention category.

Subintentioned

Subintentioned cessation behaviors relate to those instances in which the individual plays an indirect, covert, partial, or unconscious role in his own demise. That individuals may play an unconscious role in their own failures and act inimically to their own best welfare seem to be facts too well documented from psychoanalytic and general clinical practice to ignore. Often cessation is hastened by the individual's seeming carelessness, imprudence, foolhardiness, forgetfulness, amnesia, lack of judgment, or other psychological mechanisms. This concept of subintentioned demise is similar, in some ways, to Karl Menninger's concepts of chronic, focal, and organic suicides, except that Menninger's ideas have to do with self-defeating ways of continuing to live, whereas the notion of subintentioned cessation is a description of a way of stopping the process of living. Included in this subintention category would be many patterns of mismanagement and brink-of-death living which result in cessation. In terms of the traditional classification of modes of death (natural, accident, homicide, and suicide), some instances of all four types can be subsumed under this category, depending on the particular details of each case. In relation to the term suicide, subintentioned cases may be said to have *permitted* suicide.

Subintentioned cessation involves what might be called the psychosomatics of death: that is, cases in which essentially psychological processes (like fear, anxiety, derring-do, hate, etc.) seem to play some role in exacerbating the catabolic or physiological processes that bring on termination[22] (and necessarily cessation), as well as those cases in which the individual seems to play an indirect, largely unconscious role in inviting or hastening cessation itself.[23] The Psyde groups for the subintentioned category are, tentatively, as follows: (1) Psyde-chancer; (2) Psyde-hastener; (3) Psyde-capitulator; and (4) Psyde-experimenter.

1. *Psyde-chancer.* The Psyde-darer, Psyde-chancer, and Psyde-experimenter are all on a continuum of chance expectation and chance possibility of cessation. The difference lies in the combination of objective and subjective probabilities. If a Psyde-darer has only five chances out of six of continuing, then a Psyde-chancer would have chances significantly greater than that, but still involving a realistic risk of cessation. It should be pointed out that these categories are largely independent of the method used, in that most methods (like the use of razor blades or barbiturates) can, depending on the exact place of the cut, the depth of the cut, and the realistic and calculated expectations for intervention and rescue by others, legitimately be thought of as intentioned, subintentioned, unintentioned, or contraintentioned—depending on these circumstances. Individuals who "leave it up to chance," who "gamble with death,"[24] who "half-intend to do it" are the subintentioned Psyde-chancers.

2. *Psyde-hastener.* The basic assumption is that in all cessation activities the critical question (on the assumption that cessation will occur to everyone) is when, so that, in a sense, all intentioned and subintentioned activities are hastening. The Psyde-hastener refers to the individual who unconsciously exacerbates a physiological disequilibrium so that his cessation (which would, in ordinary terms, be called a natural death) is expedited. This can be done either in terms of the "style" in which he lives (the abuse of his body, usually through alcohol, drugs, exposure, or malnutrition) or, in cases where there is a specific physiological imbalance, through the mismanagement of prescribed remedial procedures. Examples of the latter would be the diabetic who "mismanages" his diet or his insulin, the individual with cirrhosis who "mismanages" his alcoholic intake, the Berger's disease patient who "mismanages" his nicotine intake. Very closely allied to the Psyde-hastener is the Psyde-facilitator, who, while he is ill and his psychic energies are low, is somehow more-than-passively unresisting to cessation, and "makes it

[22] See, for example, J. A. Gengerelli and F. J. Kirkner, eds., *Psychological Factors in Human Cancer* (Berkeley: University of California Press, 1953).

[23] See M. E. Wolfgang, "Suicide by Means of Victim-Precipitated Homicide," *Journal of Clinical and Experimental Psychopathology and Quarterly Review of Psychiatry and Neurology*, XX (1959), 335–349.

[24] See J. M. A. Weiss, "The Gamble with Death in Attempted Suicide," *Psychiatry*, XX (1957), 17–25.

easy" for termination (and accompanying cessation) to occur. Some un-expected deaths in hospitals may be of this nature. The excellent recent paper of Weisman and Hackett explores this area.[25]

3. *Psyde-capitulator.* A Psyde-capitulator is a person who, by virtue of some strong emotion, usually his fear of death, plays a psychological role in effecting his termination. In a sense, he gives in to death or he scares himself to death. This type of death includes voodoo deaths; the type of death reported among Indians and Mexicans from southwestern U. S. railroad hospitals, where the patients thought that people who went to hospitals went there to die, and being hospitalized was thus cause in itself for great alarm; and some of the cases reported from Boston by Weisman and Hackett. All these individuals play a psychological role in the psychosomatics of their termination and cessation.

4. *Psyde-experimenter.* A Psyde-experimenter is a person who often lives "on the brink of death," who consciously wishes neither interruption nor cessation, but—usually by use of (or addiction to) alcohol and/or barbiturates—seems to wish a chronically altered, usually befogged con-tinuation state. Psyde-experimenters seem to wish to remain conscious but to be benumbed or drugged. They will often "experiment" with their self-prescribed dosages (always in the direction of increasing the effect of the dosage), taking some chances of extending the benumbed con-scious states into interruption (coma) states and even taking some chances (usually without much concern, in a kind of lackadaisical way) of running some minimal but real risk of extending the interruption states into cessation. When this type of death occurs, it is traditionally thought of as accidental.

Unintentioned

Unintentioned cessation describes those occurrences in which, for all intents and purposes, the person psychologically plays no significant role in his own demise. He is, at the time of his cessation, "going about his business" (even though he may be lying in a hospital), with no conscious intention of effecting or hastening cessation and no strong conscious drive in this direction. What happens is that "something from the outside"—the outside of his mind—occurs. This "something" might be a cerebral-vascular accident, a myocardial infarction, a neo-plastic growth, some malfunction, some catabolism, some invasion—whether by bullet or by virus—which, for him, has lethal consequences. "It" happens to "him." Inasmuch as all that anyone can do in regard to cessation is to attempt some manipulation along a temporal dimension

[25] Avery D. Weisman and Thomas P. Hackett in "Predilection to Death: Death and Dying as a Psychiatric Problem," *Psychosomatic Medicine*, XXIII, No. 3 (May 1961), 232–256.

(i.e., to hasten or to postpone it), one might suppose that unintentioned is synonymous only with "postponer," but it appears that there are other possible attitudes—welcoming, accepting, resisting, disdaining, etc.—all within the unintentioned category.

In terms of the traditional categories of death, most natural, accidental, and homicidal deaths would be called unintentioned, and no presently labeled suicidal deaths would be so called. In relation to the term "suicidal," unintentioned cases may be said to have *omitted* suicide.

The Psyde categories for unintentioned cessation are: (1) Psyde-welcomer; (2) Psyde-acceptor; (3) Psyde-postponer; (4) Psyde-disdainer; and (5) Psyde-fearer.

1. *Psyde-welcomer.* A Psyde-welcomer is one who, although playing no discernible (conscious or unconscious) role in either hastening or facilitating his own cessation, could honestly report an introspective position of welcoming the end to his life. Very old people, especially after a long, painful, debilitating illness, report that they would welcome "the end."

2. *Psyde-acceptor.* The slight difference between a Psyde-welcomer and a Psyde-acceptor lies in the nuance of activity and passivity that distinguishes them. The Psyde-acceptor is one who has accepted the imminence of his cessation and "is resigned to his own fate." In this, he may be relatively passive, philosophical, resigned, heroic, realistic, or mature, depending on "the spirit" in which this enormous acceptance is made.

3. *Psyde-postponer.* Most of the time most of us are acute Psyde-postponers. Psyde-postponing is the habitual, indeed the unthinking, orientation of most humans toward cessation. The Psyde-postponer is one who, to the extent that he is oriented toward or concerned with cessation at all, wishes that it would not occur in anything like the foreseeable future and further wishes that it would not occur for as long as possible. (This Psyde-postponing orientation should not be confused with the ubiquitous human fantasies of immortality.)

4. *Psyde-disdainer.* Some individuals, during those moments when they consciously contemplate cessation, are disdainful of the concept and feel that they are above being involved in the cessation of the vital processes that it implies. They are, in a sense, supercilious toward death. It may well be that most young people in our culture, independent of their fears about death, are habitually Psyde-disdainers, as well they might be—for a while.[26]

5. *Psyde-fearer.* A Psyde-fearer is one who is fearful of death and of the topics relating to death. He may literally be phobic about this

[26] See P. Schilder and D. Wechsler, "The Attitudes of Children toward Death," *Journal of Genetic Psychology*, XLV (1934), 406–451, and Maria Nagy, "The Child's View of Death," in H. Feifel, ed., *op. cit.*, pp. 79–98.

topic.[27] He fights the notion of cessation, seeing reified death as a feared and hated enemy. This position may be related to conscious wishes for omnipotence and to great cathexis to one's social and physical potency. Hypochondriacs, fearing illnesses and assault, are perhaps also Psyde-fearers. (A person who, when physically well, is a Psyde-fearer might, when physically ill, become a Psyde-facilitator.)

Imagine five people, all older men on the same ward of a hospital, all dying of cancer, none playing an active or unconscious role in his own cessation. Yet it is still possible to distinguish among them different orientations toward cessation: One wishes not to die and is exerting his "will to live" (Psyde-postponer); another is resigned to his cessation (Psyde-acceptor); the third is disdainful of what is occurring to him and will not believe that death can "take him" (Psyde-disdainer); still another, although not taking any steps in the direction of hastening his end, does at this point in his illness welcome it (Psyde-welcomer); and the fifth is most fearful about the topic of death and the implication of cessation and forbids anyone to speak of it in his presence (Psyde-fearer).

Contraintentioned

It is, of course, possible to shout "Fire!" in the absence of a conflagration, or "Stop thief!" in the absence of a crime. It is also possible, figuratively or literally, to shout or to murmur—the intensity of the cry does not seem to matter in some cases—"Suicide!" in the clear absence of any lethal intention. (I shall, of course, eschew the words "suicide attempt" and "suicide threat," having already indicated that either of these can range from great lethal intent, through ambivalent lethal intent, to no lethal intent.) One common result of shouting "Fire!" or "Stop thief!" is that these calls mobilize others; indeed, they put society (or certain members of society) in a position where it has no choice but to act in certain directions. An individual who uses the semantic blanket of "suicide!" with a conscious absence of any lethal intention, I shall term as one who has employed contraintentioned—advertently noncessation—behavior. From a strictly logical point of view, it might be argued that contraintentioned behaviors belong within the unintentioned category. I believe, however, that there are sufficient reasons to warrant a separate category, if only to point up the fact that individuals can usurp the labels and the semantic trappings of death, especially of suicide and, at the same time, have a clear, conscious intention not to commit suicide and not to run any risk of cessation.

Among the contraintentioned individuals there are, by definition,

[27] For example, W. A. Swanberg in *Citizen Hearst* (New York: Scribners, 1961, p. 455) says: "Hearst . . . had a violent aversion for mortality, and there was an unwritten law never to mention death in his presence."

no cessation or related post-mortem states and hence no comparable traditional modes of death. In relation to the term suicide, contra-intention cases may be said to have *remitted* (in the sense of having "refrained from") suicide.

The Psyde subcategories that we distinguish among the contra-intentioned cases are (1) Psyde-feigner and (2) Psyde-threatener.

1. *Psyde-feigner.* A Psyde-feigner is one who feigns or simulates what appears to be a self-directed advertent movement toward cessation. Examples are the ingesting of water from a previously emptied iodine bottle or using a razor blade with no lethal or near-lethal possibility or intent. Psyde-feigning involves some overt behavior on the part of the individual.

2. *Psyde-threatener.* A Psyde-threatener is a person who, with the conscious intention of avoiding cessation, uses the threat of his cessation (and the other's respect for that threat) with the aim of achieving some of the secondary gains which go with cessation-oriented behavior. These gains usually have to do with activating other persons—usually the "significant other" person in the neurotic dyadic relationship in which the individual is involved.

Two additional comments, both obvious, should be made about contraintentioned behavior. The first is that what are ordinarily called "suicide attempts" may range in their potential lethality from absent to severe.[28] I do not wish to imply for a moment that all so-called suicide attempts should be thought of as contraintentioned; quite the contrary. Thus, each case of barbiturate ingestion or wrist cutting, or even of the use of carbon monoxide in an auto, must be evaluated in terms of the details of that case, so that it can be assessed accurately—as of that time —in terms of its intentioned, subintentioned, unintentioned, and contra-intentioned components. The second comment is that those who work with people who have "attempted suicide," especially those people seen as having manifested contraintentioned behavior, must guard against their own tendencies to assume a pejorative attitude toward these behaviors. It is all too easy to say that an individual *only* attempted suicide or to dismiss the case as beneath the need for human compassion, if one assesses the act as contraintentioned. It should be obvious that no act which involves, even merely semantically, cessation behavior is other than a genuine psychiatric crisis. Too often we confuse treatment of suicidal individuals with attending to the physical trauma, forgetting that meaningful treatment has to be essentially in terms of the person's personality and the frustrations, duress, fears, and threats which he ex-

---

[28] At the (Los Angeles) Suicide Prevention Center, the staff has evolved procedures for assessing "suicidal potentiality." See Robert E. Litman and N. L. Farberow, "Emergency Evaluation of Self-Destructive Potentiality," and Norman D. Tabachnick and N. L. Farberow, "The Assessment of Self-Destructive Potentiality," in *The Cry for Help, op. cit.*

periences in his living relationships. An unquestioned contraintentioned act merits fully as much professional attention as any other maladaptive behavior; a cry for help should never be disregarded, not only for hu-
... reasons, but also because we know that the unattended cries
... ne more shrill, and the movement on the lethality scale
... unfortunately, in the lethal direction.

... protested, inasmuch as the assessments of these inten-
... Psyde categories involve the appraisal of *unconscious*
... workers (especially lay coroners) cannot legitimately
... he kinds of psychological judgments required for
.... To this, one answer would be that coroners
... ry are making judgments of precisely this nature
... eek. In the situation of evaluating a possible suicide,
... n acts (sometimes without realizing it) as psychiatrist
... ist and as both judge and jury in a quasijudicial way. This
... certification of death as suicide does, willy-nilly, imply some
... s or reconstruction of the victim's motivation or intention.
... these judgments—perhaps more coroners ought to use the cate-
... of "undetermined"—is an inexorable part of a coroner's function. My position is that it is much better for these psychological dimensions to be made explicit and an attempt, albeit crude, be made to use them, than to have these psychological dimensions employed on an implicit and unverbalized level. The dilemma is between the polarities of a usable, oversimplified classification, on the one hand, and a complex, but more meaningful classification, on the other. The goal would be to try to combine greatest usefulness with maximum meaningfulness.

AN EXAMPLE OF AN EQUIVOCAL DEATH

It might be most appropriate to conclude this chapter by presenting, by way of example, some excerpts from a singularly interesting case. The study I have chosen is taken from a uniquely comprehensive study of death and lives by Herman Melville. It is the case of the equivocal death—was it accident, suicide, or what?—of Melville's tortured, obsessively possessed, fury-driven, cetusized man: Captain Ahab of the "Pequod."[29]

The procedure called the "psychological autopsy" (used at the

[29] The reader is referred to Henry A. Murray's masterful psychological studies of Melville: "In Nomine Diaboli," in *Moby-Dick Centennial Essays* (Dallas: Southern Methodist University Press, 1953), pp. 3–29, originally published in *New England Quarterly*, XXIV (1951), 435–452; Milton R. Stern, ed., *Discussions of Moby Dick* (Boston: D. C. Heath and Company, 1960), pp. 25–34; and Richard Chase, ed., *Melville: "A Collection of Critical Essays"* (Englewood Cliffs, N.J.: Prentice-Hall, Inc., 1962), pp. 62–74; and his "Introduction" to Melville's *Pierre, or The Ambiguities* (New York: Hendricks House, 1949), pp. xiii-ciii.

Suicide Prevention Center) involves obtaining psychological data about
the behaviors and statements of the deceased in the days before his
death, from which information an extrapolation of intention is made
over the moments of, and the moments directly preceding, his cessation.
In the case of Captain Ahab, I shall proceed as though I were preparing
a report for an imaginary Nantucket coroner, including some sort of
recommendation as to what labelings would be the most appropriate on
his imaginary death certificate. The focus will be an attempt to come
to some kind of resolution concerning Ahab's intention types and Psyde
categories. But first, some facts: specifically how did the end of his life
occur?

Facts

For Ahab's death, we have the following account (from Chapter
135) of his last actions: "The harpoon was darted; the stricken whale
flew forward; with igniting velocity the line ran through the groove;
—ran foul. Ahab stooped to clear it; he did clear it; but the flying turn
caught him round the neck, and noiselessly as Turkish mutes bowstring
their victim, he was shot out of the boat, ere the crew knew he was
gone. . . ." On first thought, it might sound as though Ahab's death
were pure accident, an unintentioned death, the cessation of a Psyde-
postponer; but let us see where our second thoughts lead us. Perhaps
there is more.

Background

It is possible to view *Moby Dick* as a great, sonorous Mahlerlike
symphony—*Das Lied von der See*—not primarily about the joy of life
nor the pessimism engendered by a crushing fate, but rather as a dramatic
and poetic explication of the psychodynamics of death. And, within the
context of this thought, is it not possible that Moby Dick, the great
white whale, represents the punishment of death itself? In Chapter 28,
when Ahab makes his first appearance on the "Pequod" at sea, the word
"white" is used three times in one paragraph to describe Ahab: a head-
to-toe scar on Ahab's body, "lividly whitish"; an allusion to a "white
sailor," in the context of Captain Ahab's being laid out for burial; and
"the barbaric white leg upon which he partly stood." Everywhere, reference to the pallor of death; and if there is still any question, the case for
"white death" is made explicit in the discussion of the whiteness of the
whale (Chapter 42), in which we are told: "It cannot well be doubted,
that the one visible quality in the aspect of the dead which most appals
the gazer, is the marble pallor lingering there; as if indeed that pallor
were as much like the badge of consternation in the other world, as of
mortal trepidation here. And from that pallor of the dead, we borrow

the expressive hue of the shroud in which we wrap them. Nor even in our superstitions do we fail to throw the same snowy mantel round our phantoms; all ghosts rising in a milk-white fog—Yea, while these terrors seize us, let us add that even the king of terrors, when personified by the evangelist, rides on his pallid horse."

And if the great white whale is death, then is not the sea itself the vessel of death? Melville sets this tone for his entire heroic narrative in his stunning opening passage:

> Call me Ishmael. Some years ago—never mind how long precisely—having little or no money in my purse, and nothing particular to interest me on shore, I thought I would sail about a little and see the watery part of the world. It is a way I have of driving off the spleen, and regulating the circulation. Whenever I find myself growing grim about the mouth; whenever it is a damp, drizzly November in my soul; whenever I find myself involuntarily pausing before coffin warehouses, and bringing up the rear of every funeral I meet; and especially whenever my hypos get such an upper hand of me, that it requires a strong moral principle to prevent me from deliberately stepping into the street, and methodically knocking people's hats off—then, I account it high time to get to sea as soon as I can. This is my substitute for pistol and ball. With a philosophical flourish Cato throws himself upon his sword; I quietly take to the ship. . . .

And again, much later, in the description of the blacksmith (Chapter 112), we read:

> Death seems the only desirable sequel for a career like this; but Death is only a launching into the region of the strange Untried; it is but the first salutation to the possibilities of the immense Remote, the Wild, the Watery, the Unshored; therefore, to the death-longing eyes of such men, who still have left in them some interior compunctions against suicide, does the all-contributed and all-receptive ocean alluringly spread forth his whole plain of unimaginable, taking terrors, and wonderful, new-life adventures; and from the hearts of infinite Pacifics, the thousand mermaids sing to them— "Come hither, broken-hearted; here is another life without the guilt of intermediate death; here are wonders supernatural, without dying for them. Come hither! bury thyself in a life which, to your now equally abhorred and abhorring, landed world, is more oblivious than death. Come hither! put up *thy* grave-stone, too, within the churchyard, and come hither, till we marry thee!"

If any case is to be made for subintention—Psyde-chancing, Psyde-hastening, Psyde-capitulating, Psyde-experimenting behavior patterns— then, at the least, two further background issues need to be involved: the concept of unconscious motivation and the concept of ambivalence. Ahab's chronicler would not have, in principle, resisted the concept of subintention, on the grounds of its involving unconscious motivation, for (in Chapter 41) he says:

Such a crew, so officered, seemed specially picked and packed by some infernal fatality to help him to his monomaniac revenge. How it was that they so aboundingly responded to the old man's ire—by what evil magic their souls were possessed, that at times his hate seemed almost theirs; the White Whale as much their insufferable foe as his; how all this came to be—what the White Whale was to them, or how to their unconscious understandings, also, in some dim, unsuspected way, he might have seemed the gliding great demon of the seas of life—all this to explain, would be to dive deeper than Ishmael can go. The subterranean miner that works in us all, how can one tell whither leads his shaft by the ever shifting, muffled sound of his pick?

That which is most sharply and most accurately characteristic of the subintentioned person—namely, the ubiquitous ambivalence, the pervasive psychological coexistence of logical incompatibles—is seen vividly in the following internal dialogue of life and death, of flesh and fixture, (as reported in Chapter 51) within Ahab:

Walking the deck with quick, side-lunging strides, Ahab commanded the t'gallant sails and royals to be set, and every stunsail spread. The best man in the ship must take the helm. Then, with every mast-head manned, the piled-up craft rolled down before the wind. The strange, upheaving, lifting tendency of the taff-rail breeze filling the hollows of so many sails, made the buoyant, hovering deck to feel like air beneath the feet; while still she rushed along, as if two antagonistic influences were struggling in her—one to mount directly to heaven, the other to drive yawningly to some horizontal goal. And had you watched Ahab's face that night, you would have thought that in him also two different things were warring. While his one live leg made lively echoes along the deck, every stroke of his dead limb sounded like a coffin-tap. On life and death this old man walked.

And within Ahab, toward Moby Dick, there were deep ambiguities.

Method

In any psychological autopsy it is important to examine the method or the instrument of death and, especially, the victim's understandings and subjective estimations of its lethal works. Ahab was garroted by a free-swinging whale-line. We are warned (in Chapter 60) that ". . . the least tangle or kink in the coiling would, in running out, infallibly take somebody's arm, leg, or entire body off . . ."; we are forewarned ". . . of this man or that man being taken out of the boat by the line, and lost"; and we are warned again, "All men live enveloped in whale-lines. All are born with halters round their necks; but it is only when caught in the swift, sudden turn of death, that mortals realize the silent, subtle, ever-present perils of life." Ahab knew all this; nor was he a careless, accident-prone man. The apothecary knows his deadly drugs; the sportsman knows the danger of his weapons; the whaler captain— that very whaler captain who, instead of remaining on his quarter-deck, jumped to "the active perils of the chase" in a whale-boat manned by his "smuggled on board" crew—ought to know his whale-lines.

Questions

Having described the precise circumstances of Ahab's death, and having mentioned some background issues deemed to be relevant, I would now pose some questions concerning his demise: Was Ahab's death more than simple accident? Was there more intention than unintention? Was Ahab's orientation in relation to death entirely that of Psyde-postponing? Are there discernible subsurface psychological currents that can be fathomed and charted, and is there related information that can be dredged and brought to the surface? Specifically, can Ahab's death be described as victim-precipitated homicide; that is, is this an instance in which the victim stands up to subjectively calculated overwhelming odds, inviting destruction by the other? Let us see.

Extracts

Ahab led a fairly well-documented existence, especially insofar as the dark side of his life was concerned. *Moby Dick* abounds with references to various funereal topics: sleep, coffins, burials, soul, life-after-death, suicide, cemeteries, death, and rebirth.

But—as in a psychological autopsy—we are primarily interested in interview data from everyone who had known the deceased, especially in what our informants can tell us about Ahab's personality, insofar as his orientations toward death are known. It should be recognized that in some important ways Captain Ahab's psychological autopsy will be a truncated and atypical one, especially with respect to the range of informants; there is no information from spouse, parents, progeny, siblings, collaterals, neighbors; there are only mates, some of the more articulate shipboard subordinates, captains of ships met at sea, and, with terrifying biblical certitude, Elijah.

As we know, all the possible informants, listed below, save Ishmael, perished with Captain Ahab and are technically not available for interview. Only Ishmael's observations are direct; all else is secondhand through Ishmael, colored by Ishmael, and perhaps with no more veridicality than Plato's reports of Socrates. We shall have to trust Ishmael to be an accurate and perceptive reporter.

Our primary informant, Ishmael, reflected about Captain Ahab in twenty-five separate chapters (specifically chapters 16, 22, 27, 28, 30, 33, 34, 36, 41, 44, 46, 50, 51, 52, 73, 100, 106, 115, 116, 123, 126, 128, 130, 132, and 133). Starbuck, the chief mate of the "Pequod," is next: there are nine separate encounters with, or reports about, his captain (in chapters 36, 38, 51, 118, 119, 123, 132, 134, and 135). Next is Stubb, the second mate, with seven separate anecdotes (to be found in chapters 28, 31, 36, 73, 121, 134, and 135). All the others are represented by one or two bits of information apiece: Elijah (in chapters 19 and 21); Gabriel of the "Jeroboam" (Chapter 71); Bunger, the ship's surgeon of the "Samuel Enderby" (100); the blacksmith (113); the Captain of the "Bachelor" (115); Flask, the third mate (121); the Manxman (125); and the carpenter (127).

Knowing that the limitations of space simply do not permit me to document the essence of each informant's remarks, either with appropriate quotations or abbreviated résumés, how can I summarize all the data? Perhaps my best course would be to concentrate on the general features that one would look for in any psychological autopsy. Thus, the information distilled from interviews with Ishmael, Starbuck, Stubb, and all the others, might, in a dialogue of questions and answers, take the following form.

(1) Hidden psychosis? Not at the beginning of the voyage, but certainly at the end (and indeed from Chapter 36 on—"the chick that's in him picks the shell. 'Twill soon be out."), the madness in Ahab was blatant, open, known. His monomania was the official creed of his ship. Along with his other symptoms, his psychiatric syndrome was crowned with a paranoid fixation. But what matters in Ahab is not so much the bizarrely shaped psychological iceberg which many saw above the surface, but rather the hugeness of the gyroscopically immovable subsurface mass of other-destruction and self-destruction. We know the poems about fire and ice. Ahab is a torrid, burning, fiery iceberg. (2) Disguised depression? Ahab was openly morbid and downcast. His was not exactly psychotic depression, nor can we call it reactive depression for it transcended the bounds of that definition. Perhaps best it might be called a "character depression," in that it infused his brain like the let-go blood from a series of small strokes in the hemisphere. (3) Talk of death? The morbid talk of death and killing runs through reports about Ahab like an *idée fixe*. (4) Previous suicide attempts? None is reported. (5) Disposition of belongings? Ahab, after forty solitary years at sea, had little in the way of self-possessions or interpersonal belongings. His wife, he said, was already a widow; his interest in the possible profits from the voyage was nil; his withdrawal from meaningful material possessions (and his loss of joy with them) is perhaps best indicated by his flinging his "still lighted pipe into the sea" and dashing his quadrant to the deck —both rash acts for a sailor-captain.

In Ahab's conscious mind, he wanted to kill—but have we not said that self-destruction can be other-destruction in the 180th degree? Figuratively speaking, the barb of the harpoon was pointed toward him; his brain thought a thrust, but his arm executed a retroflex. Was his death "accident"? If he had survived his psychodynamically freighted voyage and had returned unharmed to Nantucket's pier, *that* would have been true accident. Men can die for nothing—most men do; but some few big-jointed men can give their lives for an internalized something: Ahab would not have missed this opportunity for the world.

What further evidence can be cited bearing on the issue of sub-intentioned cessation? With his three harpooners before him, with their harpoons turned up like goblets, Ahab (in Chapter 36) commands them, in this maritime immolation scene, as follows: " 'Drink, ye harpooneers! drink and swear, ye men that man the deathful whaleboat's bow—Death to Moby Dick! God hunt us all, if we do not hunt Moby Dick to his death!' " Kill or be killed; punish or be retributed; murder or suicide—how the two are intertwined.

In Ahab's case, we have no suicide note or other holograph of death, but, *mirabile dictu,* we do have (in Chapter 135) Ahab's last thoughts:

> I turn my body from the sun. . . . Oh, lonely death on lonely life! Oh, now I feel my topmost grief. Ho, ho! from all your furtherest bounds, pour ye now in, ye bold billows of my whole foregone life, and top this one piled comber of my death! Towards thee I roll, thou all-destroying but unconquering whale; to the last I grapple with thee; from hell's heart I stab at thee; for hate's sake I spit my last breath at thee. Sink all coffins and all hearses to one common pool! and since neither can be mine, let me now tow to pieces, while still chasing thee, though tied to thee, thou damned whale! *Thus,* I give up my spear!

What is to be particularly noted in this is the prescience of Ahab. "I spit my last breath at thee," he says. How does he know that it is to be his *last* breath? Where are the sources of his premonitions? What are the contents of his subintentions? Does this not remind us of Radney, the chief mate of the "Town-Ho" (Chapter 54) who behaved as if he "sought to run more than half way to meet his doom"? Is this not exactly what the tantalizer says to his "all-destroying but unconquering" executioner in cases of victim-precipitated homicide?

Recommendation

It is suggested that Captain Ahab's demise was goal-seeking behavior that made obsessed life *or* subintentioned death relatively unimportant to him, compared with the great press for the discharge of his monomania of hate. He dared, and made, that murderous death-white whale kill him. He could not rest until he was so taken. (Did Satan *provoke* God into banishing him?) Ahab invited cessation by the risks that he ran; he was a Psyde-chancer. He permitted suicide. Consider Ahab's psychological position: what could he have done, to what purpose would any further voyages have been, if he *had* killed the symbol of his search? It was, from Ahab's point of view, the time; and in his unconscious wish, it was the "appropriate death." *In nomine ceti albini!*

CREATIVE PROCESSES IN PERSONALITY
Part III

As we have seen, Murray considers creativity an intrinsic property of living systems. This property is manifested in the earliest cellular activity of the embryo, and it plays a characteristic part in all proactive, as contrasted with reactive, behavior. In human lives, there are creative elements even in what we regard as commonplace activities—planning the best way to mow a hayfield, settling a wrangle among children, finding a turn of phrase in conversation. But the attention of psychologists has been drawn particularly to what we might call conspicuous creativeness, to works of high imagination in the arts and sciences. In his introductory chapter to this section, Barron reminds us that "the problem of psychic creation is a special case of the problem of novelty in all of nature." It is the special case, however, that has been most intriguing to Freud, to Murray, and to a growing number of psychologists prepared to approach the problem through controlled investigation.

As much by illustration and allusion as by argument, Barron's chapter draws attention to the deeply paradoxical nature of creative thinking. In the interests of survival and practical achievement, we look for repetitions and similarities, doing our best to maintain environmental constancies and adapt ourselves to environmental requirements. To this end, we name, generalize, and form concepts, but in so doing we move away from the immediacy of experience toward a world of bloodless abstractions. Too great a sacrifice to practicality may block the springs of creativeness; in Carl Jung's terms, the conventional *persona* may suppress the vital *anima*. Creativity is favored by a turn back to the less-structured, more primitive, more diffuse aspects of one's psychic life—by turning away from what we have learned to consider useful and virtuous. In psychoanalytic language, the ego and supergo must be suspended in favor of the id. But here the paradox returns. The regression, as Ernst Kris suggested, must be in the service of the ego; diffusion must give way again to integration and sustained attention if the new experience is to be captured for communication to others.

What are the characteristics of people who possess the paradoxical attributes of creativity? We assume that innate skills have something to do with it, but Barron's chapter suggests that patterns of personality may also be involved. This possibility is investigated in the chapters by MacKinnon and Stein. MacKinnon reports on an investigation of a large group of architects, Stein on a group of industrial research chemists; in both cases, ways were found to divide the groups into more creative and less creative members. Both studies used self-rating procedures to secure from the subjects their conceptions of themselves. In Stein's study, the variables were taken directly from Murray's list of needs given in *Explorations in Personality.*

MacKinnon's chapter shows that the most creative architects rate themselves in such a way as to suggest a strong ego which is in good touch with the id. They are independent, self-accepting, deeply immersed in their work, and guided by standards of their own. The less creative architects emphasize conscientiousness and ability to work with people; they appear to be dependent on others, suggesting a strong superego that often dominates the ego. It is easy to conclude that people who are oriented so strongly toward social adjustment might lack the boldness required to surrender themselves to diffusion and might thus not dare drink at the springs of creativity. This inference seems to be strengthened by a similar finding in Stein's chapter with respect to less creative industrial chemists. It is to be noted, however, that the more creative chemists differ in some respects from the creative architects, the differences having a probable relation to the conditions of their work.

The reader will observe that the variable described by Sanford in the first chapter of this book—impulse expression—reappears in slightly altered form in these chapters on creativity. In Davids' paper (Chapter 7), several connections between tolerance of ambiguity and creative freedom are pointed out. But, if a warning against generalizing too rapidly is needed, it is provided by Bellak's account of Somerset Maugham (Chapter 6), whose creativity and personality do not seem to stand in the expected relation.

Stein's chapter includes a study of Peace Corps volunteers, intended, like Murray's *Assessment of Men,* to be of value in selection for field duty. Interest centers on effectiveness in work done largely with people, a quality that bears comparison with the sense of interpersonal competence discussed in Chapter 3.

In the final essay of this section, Wyatt develops the theme that recollection of the past, whether it be done by historians for nations or by psychoanalytic patients for themselves, always involves a kind of creative reconstruction under the guidance of present needs. Each age rewrites history in its own terms, and each individual reconstructs his past in the terms set by his present concerns and prospects for growth. If the past makes *us,* says Wyatt, we also "make *it* by putting it together in thoughtful reflection."

10: DIFFUSION, INTEGRATION, AND ENDURING ATTENTION IN THE CREATIVE PROCESS

Frank Barron

1

In the midst of the spectacle of the world there are a few people who always stand a bit aside and muse upon the passing show. They give to its every particular their sustained present attention, thus rescuing a part of the spectacle from time's erosion. What they save may be called eternal; for the object of their attention has been that which abides when time and particulars have passed. We call them artists or poets if they not only give their enduring attention to what abides through the cycles of change but in addition make a social communication of their vision and create a new form in which the essence of the particulars is conveyed so that at least one other person may be given to see what the artist has seen.

The study of individual human lives offers to the psychologist this valuable possibility. Psychology, if it holds itself apart from vulgar curiosity and from dehumanizing generalization, can be a sacred discipline devoted to the celebration of the human spirit. For myself this realization came in the midst of all the numbers and the mannered positivism that the Psychology Department of the University of Minnesota offered to the graduate student's view in 1942 and a while thereafter. The realization was communicated to me and to other graduate students there by Richard M. Elliott, chiefly through the agency of an "introductory" course I have never forgotten: biographical psychology. Professor Elliott made the course turn upon two major contributions to the study of lives, given to the world in just the preceding decade by two most remarkable innovators in the realm of psychology, Henry A. Murray and H. G. Wells. The required reading for the course consisted of just two books: *Explorations in Personality* and *Experiment in Autobiography*. Explorations and experiments, bold forays in uncharted psychological territory, predictions of the unlikely, and a sense always of something mysterious lying behind the mechanical, of transcendent possibilities presaged by the course of current events—these were the offerings of the two works which first commended to my own attention the study of lives.

II

The mother of the Muses is Mnemosyne, who gave to her nine daughters the power to sing and dance and paint and play; to imagine, to create, to speak the true names of things. Memory is attention which endures, which envisions both backwards and forwards, which can shine upon deep recesses filled and perhaps half-forgotten long ago; it is made up of intuitions as well as representations, feelings perhaps but faintly perceived, odors, sights, sounds, hesitancies, judgments—all the thoughts that go into the making up of mind.

But it is a healthful practice to unname once we have named, lest we lose too much of the reality which for convenience we have given a name to. What we call memory is a vast process, billions of acts of attention. We gauge a man's scope in part by the range of his attention, not only over the objects in his present ken, but over all that has ever occurred to him. One of the most ancient and persistent of religious ideas is that through constant and honest attention to all the acts of one's life one can escape the cycle of birth and death; the Buddha at his death is said to have had present in his consciousness the totality not only of his final incarnation but of all the incarnations through which he had passed. The great act of attention is all-inclusive; the more of life that is remembered and brought to bear upon the present moment in living expression, the higher the grade of being. Humanity thus rises to divinity, and within divinity itself many grades of refinement are traditionally recognized, based upon the universality and enduringness of attention.

Psychoanalysis partakes in this religious tradition in its application to individual psychotherapy of the notion of honest and unremitting attention to all the details of past and present which are potentially accessible to consciousness. The "repetition compulsion" is the psychoanalytic analogue to imprisonment in the cycle of death and rebirth; the neurotic "dies" to no avail, he runs his compulsive course to his particular form of repeatable ruin without ever knowing what is happening. "Unhappy he who dies to himself unknown," goes an old Latin proverb. "The sumless tale of sorrow is all unrolled in vain," says Housman.[1] Only the unrepressed and "undefended" life can lead to true death, so that nothing need be repeated. Grief at loss is total only if finality is experienced. It is always "the unexperienced" that presses for expression and calls for a resetting of the switches for the same old run.

[1] A. E. Housman, "The First of May," *Last Poems* (New York: Henry Holt and Son, 1922), p. 68.

These are thoughts from Professor Elliott's lectures and the writings of Wells and of Murray, and thoughts too from my own reflections on the lives I have studied in the years since then.

One need not look far to see the influence of *Explorations* upon theory and method in the study of personality. Happily enough, even the numbers are not so inhuman when animated with lively theory, and psychological measurement today owes much to that immensely provocative work. Psychological biography has profited most of all, and a later work edited by A. Burton and R. E. Harris, *Clinical Studies of Personality*, exhibits in advanced professional technique the gains to formulation of case histories which *Explorations* presaged.

The contribution of H. G. Wells to psychology may be less apparent, but he bears rereading by the psychologist, and his notion of "the open conspiracy," with its emphasis upon the free and full exchange of information and the breaking down of barriers to communication, accords quite well with the picture which recent psychological research has given us of the creative society and the creative individual.

III

The problem of psychic creation is a special case of the problem of novelty in all of nature. Wherever we look, we see repetition and similarity, and the perception of one thing as being like another is the basis of our ability to avoid unpleasant contingencies and to entertain those which will aid our survival or give us pleasure. Novelty and uniqueness, from this point of view, offer a threat to our power to anticipate events.

At the same time, the most pleasurable of anticipations is the anticipation of something new. We speak of routine as deadening; we are happy to think that our day may hold a pleasant surprise in store for us; we feel wonder, awe, or delight when a new view magnificently reveals itself to us. The great song of woe is Ecclesiastes, for the Preacher has given mighty attention to the spectacle: and, behold, "that which increaseth knowledge increaseth sorrow"; "there is nothing new under the sun"; "of making many books there is no end"; "that which is crooked cannot be made straight"; "all, all is vanity."

At the opposite pole from this is the beautiful curiosity of children, for whom the world is new, full of surprises, offering itself to be explored and played with. The baby opens his eyes, as the very universe itself over eons must have grown able to see, and the show is on. To innocence the spectacle is enthralling; to disillusioned experience the world is jaded. So it seems that the first time around is always the best.

In this, memory shows another face. In a sense, the beginning of death is remembering. To remember is first of all to compare what is present with what is past, for the purpose of matching one with the other in a way that may lead to adaptive action. This very beginning of integration has in it, however, the seeds of death. It is based on all those generators of efficiency—division, compartments, differentiation, classification—and on logic, attention, judgment—the insurers of the development of structure, which weighs down the heart and anchors it to time, and thence to diffusion and to dissolution. But *there* precisely is the ultimate paradox in one of its guises; for the moment of complex and creative integration is life at its best—high life, when the heart is light and the fancy is free and we have all the time in the world. There are at least two sides to everything, and whether we see things as running down or running up depends in part on how we look at phenomena.

IV

Whether we should stop, if we can, the vivid moment and give thought to it or stop thought, if we can, and let vivid detail come helter-skelter is not a matter of choice, however fondly the one sentiment or the other is embraced by philosophers. The invincible Irish yearning for a glimpse behind the veil animated Bishop Berkeley's lifelong quest for a magical drug that could kill thought while leaving the thinker otherwise the same; the Celts had long used mead for no sensual aim, but simply to escape thought. Acute sensibilities always experience as antispirit anything which partakes of the mechanical, and that aspect of thought which is capable of being reproduced mechanically is known as a form of prison. But the middle ranges of sensibility always strike a compromise for economy's sake, so that the unique image and the best first meaning that can be assigned to it seem to occur simultaneously and without friction. And so time passes normally and is felt to be an ordinary and proper condition of existence. Only when abstraction in a completely ordered construction has left sensible detail utterly behind, as in Einstein's attempt at a general field theory, or when the spectacle has in every vivid detail claimed the full attention of the fully open eye, as in Buddha's emptiness—only then is time no longer a condition of experience.

I recently learned in Dublin that I have never been drunk, or, as the more pleasant Irish pronunciation has it, "thrunk." A group of Dublin bloods had come noisily into the bar of the Gresham Hotel, where I had quietly and by myself been sipping a fine glass of Jameson. As I sat there for about half an hour with my one glass, they neatly and ostentatiously each downed five or six glasses in rapid succession. It was an occasion of some sort, and there was much talk of fighting. When I finished my glass and ordered another, however, they became silent and I realized that they had stopped to notice me. "You there now," a tall young man in their midst suddenly addressed me sharply, "have y'ever been thrunk?" I sat and thought about that for a moment, and then said, perhaps a bit sadly but to give them a bit of their own back nonetheless, "There've been times when I've thought I've been thrunk, but I've always been thrunk at the time." Silence again for a while, on the part of all. No one looked at me. Then in slow tones came the verdict, delivered quietly to no one in particular: "The man's never been thrunk."

On the occasion of my visit to Dublin I spent several days with the great Irish writer Sean O'Faolain, who may outlast the lot of them when it comes to communicating the concentration of feeling and the lack of interest in external variety which is so characteristic of the brooding Irish spirit outside Dublin. O'Faolain had spoken of his own wondering at the absolute lack of interest the Irish had shown in the approaches of European civilization. Was Ireland dead or just dreaming, passing sleep-time with visions that themselves knew no schedule of actualization? Yeats had written, "We Irish, born of that ancient sect, But thrown upon this filthy modern tide. . . ." Yet the prediction of Renan a century earlier—that should the Irish harden themselves for entry into the world of intellect and practical affairs, they would have a brilliant though brief blooming—had in a sense already been borne out. The Celtic Renaissance, with its shining roster of writers and thinkers from Shaw through Yeats to O'Casey, was a genuine variegated flowering.

And in America there had been an odd encounter between the gentleness, idealism, and almost incredible lack of practicality of the Irish when they arrived and the challenge of a new culture in which the cultivation of self-interest and the relentless seeking of personal advantage was most generously rewarded. Not many accepted the challenge totally, but in national and state politics we are seeing today some of the resultant force. Harvard University, by a geographical accident, participated in the encounter between Irish immigration and the New World. As psychologists we may note in passing that the first American ancestor of the James family, another William James, amassed from nothing at all one of the greatest personal fortunes in the America of his day. One of his thirteen children, Henry James, Sr., and the remarkable children of Henry and Mary Walsh made their mark through a distinctive combination of passionate otherworldliness and disciplined attention to the facts. F. O. Matthiessen summed up his description of Henry James, Sr., by quoting the witty phrase of Annie Fields (meant to be heard rather than read) that James was "aninted with the Isle of Patmos," and added: "Concord and Boston were familiar enough with apocalyptic, if somewhat thin-blooded Yankees. But Henry James, Senior, was unique in that circle in being not only apocalyptic, but also full-bloodedly Hibernian."[2]

But all such entries into action must set in motion the inevitable cycle

[2] F. O. Matthiessen, *The James Family* (New York: Alfred A. Knopf, 1947), p. 16.

of integration and dissolution, and to one who has spent time on the western and northern coasts of Ireland there comes some feeling of regret and sadness to see such a form of purity going down. The dreams there are not for psychoanalytic ears. After seeing O'Faolain, I had on that same trip gone to the northern tip of County Donegal to visit my grandmother's brother, then ninety-three years old. He was a fiery and proud old fellow, and the morning after my first night in his cottage he waited, dressed in his best, for me to wake and have breakfast. I had dreamed it seemed a million dreams, and my head was buzzing with them. I told him so and asked him then whether he had had any dreams that night. He looked at me not unkindly, but his reply was firm: "Nay, young man, there'll be none of that. Ye'll get no dreams out of me." Charles Boyle his name was; he died a year later, and his last words were, "Thank God for giving me such a long life."

V

In the spate of spying and lying with which we so ignominiously brought the decade of the fifties to a close—a decade which for the University of California began with a "loyalty oath" requiring faculty members to agree in writing not to think certain possible thoughts about Communism—there did occur one refreshing episode. This episode involved the great Negro trumpeter, Louis Armstrong, who during a good-will tour through the Near East was suddenly, in the aftermath of the U-2 debacle, barred from one country as an American spy. Mr. Armstrong was questioned closely about this by a corps of international newsmen shortly after, and his reply was in the classic vein and worthy of his Muse: "Who, me spy? Man, I got no time to spy!"

Perhaps the decade is not best understood as one of stagnation, however. Certain forms of power were solidifying their position, and for the moment it meant a reduction in freedom of movement and in the entertaining of radically new possibilities. Yet this is an old story. There seems to be an essential and continuing tension between the establishment and maintenance of environmental constancies and the interruption of achieved equilibriums in the interest of new experience. The creative process itself embodies this tension, and persons who distinguish themselves in artistic and scientific creation exemplify an incessant dialectic between integration and diffusion. In the sequence of related acts which result in the creation of something new, there occurs consistently a rhythmic alternation and a genuine resolution or synthesis of certain common antinomies. Apparently contradictory principles of action, thought, and feeling, which usually must be sacrificed one to the other, are instead expressed fully in one sequence, the dialectic leading at special moments to an unusual integration.

VI

Perhaps the most basic antinomy psychologically is the distinction between self and not-self. It is fundamental to common sense and may be thought of as the first achievement of the ego or the beginning of perceptual structure. All of logic and of causal thinking begins with this distinction and its corollaries. Whether things are going on inside us or outside us is the first distinction we must make. With that established, space and time can take on separate existence; distinct events at specific space-time co-ordinates can be described; reasons can be given for the occurrences we discriminate; and, above all, our self belongs to us alone, our mind is distinct and separate from other minds.

Paranoia is the most vivid pathological manifestation of a breakdown in the ability to maintain the distinction between what is inside the self and what is outside it. But paranoia bears a puzzling relationship to certain intense experiences of a religious, transcendental, or mystical nature, whose existence we know best from the reports of outstandingly sane men. The common feature in such experiences is the feeling of unity with the entire universe, utter merging of the self in the infinite, a relinquishing of the experience of boundedness and separateness of subject from object.

From my own recent research, mostly with writers, though some painters and musicians took part as well, I can contribute two observations which bear upon the psychology of such states and their relationship to creativity. The first of these observations comes from a study of creative writers, conducted at the Institute of Personality Assessment and Research. The basic research method employed was to compare a group of writers nominated by qualified critics and scholars as "original and creative artists" with an approximately equal number of writers who could be considered representative successful writers but whose primary aim in writing was not to create a work of art. Many techniques of comparison were employed, and many questions were asked and the answers compared. One set of questions was designed to elicit accounts of the sort of unusual experience we are here discussing, in which a mystical sense of unity with the universe occurred vividly. Nearly 40 per cent of the group of representative successful writers reported having had such experiences, and over 50 per cent of the specially selected group of creative writers reported similar experiences.

Until recently the prevalence of such apparently unusual states of mind was not fully appreciated, but most newspaper readers know that only this year these mystical experiences have received a kind of certification of statistical normalcy. The Gallup Poll reported in April of 1962, just in time for Easter, that fully 20 per cent of all adult Americans have experienced such feelings. The day after the appearance of the Gallup report I heard some psychiatrists who were discussing the survey allude dis-

consolately to "the psychotic core in everyone," but those poor fellows
have a cross of their own to bear in attempting to be utterly rational so
many hours of the day. Whether or not the world is fundamentally odd, it
is certain that people are. A temporary abandonment of the distinction
between subject and object can be a great and freeing delight, for though
we make our antinomies for profit, we suffer a loss with them as well.

A fairly representative Yankee from Concord, Massachusetts, in a
philosophic poem to Brahma, expressed this sort of insight well. Here are
some of his lines:

> If the red slayer think he slays
> Or if the slain think he is slain
> They know not well the subtle ways
> I keep, and pass, and turn again.
>
> Far and forgot to me are near
> Shadow and sunlight are the same
> Forgotten gods to me appear
> And one to me are shame and fame.
>
> They reckon ill who leave me out
> When me they fly, I am the wings
> I am the doubter and the doubt
> And I the hymn the Brahmin sings.[3]

And Wystan Hugh Auden in his "New Year Letter, 1940" has things
to say with which Ralph Waldo Emerson might have agreed.

> How hard it is to set aside
> Terror, concupiscence and pride
>
> .   .   .   .   .   .
>
> How hard to stretch imagination
> To live according to our station.
>
> For we are all insulted by
> The mere suggestion that we die
> Each moment and that each great I
> Is but a process in a process
> Within a field that never closes.[4]

Auden's words suggest also a related distinction and common antinomy: one is either controlling matters or not controlling them. It is
repugnant to good sense to believe that one can control and yet be controlled by what he is controlling, or that we cannot change anything

---

[3] Ralph Waldo Emerson, "Brahma," in Richard Aldington, ed., *The Viking Book
of Poetry of the English-Speaking World* (New York: Viking Press, 1946), p. 807.
[4] © 1941 by W. H. Auden. *The Collected Poetry of W. H. Auden* (New York:
Random House, 1945), p. 265. Reprinted in the United States by permission of
Random House, Inc., in the British Commonwealth, by Faber and Faber Ltd.

without being changed by our act of changing. Yet any competent psychotherapist knows that in working to change his patients he has been changed, and if he is really good he has probably been changed nearly as much as his patients have. Military geniuses have often expressed themselves as being aware that they were the slaves of their followers; the poet Goethe said, "I did not make my songs; my songs made me," and there are many proverbs on the subject of love between man and woman which observe that when things are really right it is not always clear who is who.

Masculine and feminine are related to the antinomies of dominance and submission, activity and passivity. From birth to maturity, male human beings tend to become more masculine in their habits of mind, and female human beings tend to become more feminine. Although this is partly a function of differences in hormonal constitution, there is little doubt that a certain sharpening and accentuation of characteristic features occurs in a purely psychological way. Masculine and feminine are genuine psychological antinomies. The sphinx is one of the eternal symbols of resolution and paradoxical combination; perhaps another is the gracious but mocking smile of Buddha which, like the smile of the Mona Lisa, is an expression of enigma; and angels are characteristically androgynous. Even the person of Christ has been so interpreted by the remarkable Russian Orthodox Catholic mystic, Nicholas Berdyaev, in his germinal contribution to the psychology of creativity, *The Meaning of the Creative Act*. A few years ago the great Mexican muralist Sequeiros had a home in Mexico City, whose main room was dominated by a giant portrait of his own muscular arms and his wife's beautiful face, with a suggestion of swelling breasts, mostly out of sight, and a suggestion also of the haunches of the beast. Male and female, animal and human, a hint too of the presence of the god: in certain *symbols* all this may be attempted and the common antinomies allowed simultaneous, resolving expression.

VII

To enjoy the advantages of sanity and at the same time have access to the arcane pleasures popularly imputed to psychosis has been the goal of many men through the ages. Plato has unfortunately been vastly misunderstood in the passage so frequently quoted in which he links poetic inspiration to "madness." The Greeks were fully aware of the dreariness and stultification of human potentiality represented by psychosis; the "madness" which they praised was always something added, a gift from the god, and not, as we know psychosis to be, something subtracted. It was an extension of consciousness in the presence of an already existing clarity and coherence of perception; furor or frenzy were certainly not of its essence, although they might indeed play a part if Dionysus had a hand in the game. Ancient Greece appears to have been a sunny and pleasant place, easy to sport about in as well as to imagine and construct in. We should not be surprised, therefore, if some of the divinities turned out to be riffraff, however delightful, and if a few were even given to tantrums and dramatic excesses; the divine madness could take all the forms which human attention could afford.

To express this in the terms of our modern psychology, it appears that creative individuals have a remarkable affinity for what in most of us is unconscious or preconscious. A certain amount of semantic confusion has resulted from the use of terms like subconscious and unconscious in theoretical frameworks other than the Freudian, and it is probable that some of the introspective accounts by great innovators and creators, in which they speak of influences from the unconscious, coincide with the psychoanalytic notion of easy recombination of ideas in the preconscious. Nevertheless, it is clearly true that the creative individual is able to find hints of emerging form in the developmentally more primitive and less reasonably structured aspects of his own mental functioning.

This refusal to be content with the basic and immediately adaptive perceptual constancies leads at times in creative persons to real psychological imbalance. There is reason to believe that many creative individuals deliberately induce in themselves an altered state of consciousness in which the ordinary boundaries of experience are broken. This may be achieved by allowing psychoticlike material to have its way with them for a time, or it may be achieved through trance states, feelings of being possessed, mystical experience, falling in love, drunkenness, drug intoxication, or even excesses of intuition—the mundane madness; these, in company with dreams, the drift of symbols through our minds when we are thinking of something else, restful regressions, and the refusal of the psyche to work, are states of diffusion which serve as counterstatements to no longer fully satisfactory integrations. In them there is a repudiation or rejection of commitment and of attention to the project of maintaining the self as it is in the world; there is a return to possibility, the alternatives are invited back. And then, like breathing in and breathing out, diffusion slowly gives way again to the integrative tendencies, and if the sequence has been a creative one, we see a form that had not been before.

VIII

Mysticism has characteristically served a practical aim: the attainment of a feeling of rapport or actual identity with a transcendent power or a form of being higher and more subtle than ordinary sensibility can reach. In doing so, it does not eschew the use of ordinary reason in the development of the prologue to the mystical act itself; a comprehensive though sometimes unrecognized rational structure is basic as a point of departure for the most advanced and highly developed forms of mysticism, such as we see in Plotinus and in Eckhardt. The church has traditionally been wary of its mystics, though tolerant of them so long as they did not prove dangerous to themselves or to the business of the day. This is eminently consistent with Roman Catholic theology, with its emphasis upon the union of the divine and the human in the organic body of the church. Disease and malformations are to be expected in the natural course of events in the development of the human form, and the thing to do is watch them and take measures against them only if they become a persistent sore point or an actual danger to the organism. Mysticism in these terms is best understood as an altered state of consciousness, which can be expected to occur regularly though infrequently in the body of the church and it is indeed rather interesting and at times salutary and valuable, even though it is psychically a rarified condition which unless surrounded by the safeguards of doctrine, dogma, ethical practice and approved ritual and symbol, may become aberrant.

Disciplined mysticism is in this sense analogous to the creative use of material from the personal and collective unconscious; what the church refers to as "spiritualism and related errors" is akin to exploring the collective unconscious without bringing to bear upon the mass of perceptions and potentialities there the faculties of attention, discrimination, judgment, and the responsibility for shaping the nascent forms for entry into consciousness.

The concepts of discipline, responsibility, and committed, enduring attention are all too often left out of account in descriptions of the creative process, simply because what so often first impresses us in the personality of the creative artist or scientist is unconventionality, self-assertiveness, independence of judgment, impulsiveness, a skipping wit, and a tendency to take lightly what most of the rest of us are wont to take seriously. Emerson was once upbraided by some of his neglected unasked-for followers for not having met his responsibilities as a leader, and he replied quite simply: "I have other responsibilities." This is perhaps a bit too grand, but the fact is that the artist submits his will to a purpose beyond himself in a manner complete enough for the humblest monk.

Widespread seeking for mystical experience or altered states of consciousness has historically been a mark of dissatisfaction with the prevailing culture, an indication that important human needs were not being met or that precious potentialities were left to die at birth. The prevalence today of the use of drugs that produce psychological effects is one of many indications that there is much amiss in the relationship of the collective ego to the problems posed by external reality. Most of this vast traffic in drugs stems unquestionably from pathology, although in religious and scientific explorations with the so-called psychodelic drugs, we can clearly see evidences of a creative groping toward new understandings and a more inclusive form of integration of which the collective ego may be capable.

In its pathological form, the yearning for the experience of mystical unity and fullness is a consciously despairing response to a sense of inner hollowness and personal isolation and impotence, just as the desire for a disordering or deadening of the senses through drugs may arise from crippled affect and from an inability to function in a normal and emotionally satisfying way. To wish to be "high" because not to be high means to be low or to wish to be "turned on" because not to be turned on means to be turned off (the very terminology reflects the despair to which mechanism leads) is an unmistakable sign of loss of normal function in perception and feeling.

The creative aspect of experimentation and exploration with the psychodelic drugs lies in the possibility they provide of permitting a great many individuals to know, firsthand and as a result of conscious decision by the normal ego, the vast ranges and reaches of possible human experience which the normalizing function itself tends to exclude, except on rare occasions, from individual consciousness. The recent chemical synthesis of drugs which place such experience within the reach of many individuals presents the psychologist with an unusual opportunity and a very serious responsibility. The responsibility itself is unusual in kind, and it may prove to be one of those "other responsibilities" to which Emerson referred in rejecting more conventional demands.

IX

Let us say it once again, more briefly. In the creative process there is an incessant dialectic and an essential tension between two seemingly opposed dispositional tendencies: the tendency towards structuring and integration and the tendency towards disruption of structure and diffusion of energy and attention. The marks of integration are: (1) differentiation and discrimination: (2) classification in the interest of prediction (which would include broadly all sorts of communions, amalgamations, and incorporations for the sake of increasing power); and (3) establishment of perceptual constancies, or selective perceptual adaptions (taking of habits, establishment of sovereignties).

When differentiation has occurred, the original walls now enclose more than one chamber. In human beings, of course, the chambers are numbered in the billions, and the human brain is the most elegant of mansions. Differentiation, together with adaptive dispositional tendencies that make discrimination possible, permits the focusing of energy at a single point; in a sense, the organism becomes able to face things, to attend. Moreover, and this we usually do not think of, differentiation means that individual death is in the offing; the rule is that whatever grows must die. The very act of establishing a class brings a sort of death to all the unique attributes of the objects classified, although at the same time it gives new power because it is a step towards regularity and law. In human relationship, itself a form of classification, by making common cause we gain strength individually from the new unit and bring a new form of being into existence, though at the cost of some unassimilable unique attributes of each individual.

This fact of existence leads to one of the basic paradoxes of human development: the more fully developed and finely articulated we become, the less the *possibility for alternative integration*. But one of the amazing features of the human brain is that it permits the possible to survive alongside the actualized; whatever is potential in mind is not damaged by not being actualized, even though in the individual life there may not be time enough for a return to bypassed possibilities.

Genius is nothing if not naïve, and the interesting fact for creativity about conditions that bring about diffusion is that very often they restore a certain naïveté of perception. One of the poets who served as a subject in my study of creative writers was at that time in his early fifties and was the father of three young children, the products of what for him was a late and very happy marriage. He felt that he had been unexpectedly blessed, that he had been "lucky" after a turbulent and changeful youth and early middle age. Yet as he told me of this good fortune and of his pleasure in his home and family, he added musingly, half to himself, "I wonder whether I'll ever write anything really new from now on. I don't think I could ever throw myself away again."

What this man meant by "throwing himself away" is what in this context we mean by permitting diffusion to occur in the service of a need for an enrichment of conscious experience—a need which is felt with such intensity that the individual is willing to "die unto himself," i.e. to permit an achieved adaptation or state of relative equilibrium to perish. And there are no guarantees that something better will thereby be arrived at. Looking backwards from the end point of the creative process, we are inclined to say, "Ah, yes, it had to be so; the chance had to be taken; the chalice could not be passed; the agony was necessary for the redemption and the resurrection." But facing forward in time we see only risk and difficulty, and if we have not the courage to endure diffusion ("suffer death") we cannot achieve the new and more inclusive integration ("gain the light"). The expansion of consciousness requires the temporary abandonment of certain ego structures, at least the crustier outside ones which are farthest from the core of what William James called "the transcendental ego" (which I conceive of as "inside" or "within" in the same sense in which Christ spoke of the kingdom of God as "within").

The appositeness to psychology of these religious metaphors and personifications (as well as the use I have made of them in this attempt at a naturalistic account of certain aspects of the creative process) is an interesting fact in itself. There need not be any fundamental oppositions between science, art, and religion; all are "mind at work," though each assumes a different posture. A link perhaps is provided by a common Latin root: *pono, ponere, posui, positus*. Postulate, posture, pose, posit, position: what each signifies is a form of local integration. And human intellection as a whole, we may guess, is itself only a partial integration. Science, art, and religion may then be understood as differentiated and valid expressions of possibilities actualized in our *local form of mind*.

This emphasis upon shifting patterns of diffusion and integration gives us a somewhat restless view of the creative process if we omit enduring attention. And in the individual life, after all, there is something good to be said for knowing when to take in sail. Psychological growth too has its pathological aspect, and there is a cancerous kind of ego expansion which occurs when no bounds to individuality are recognized. One of the characteristics of normal tissue is that it contains intrinsic and inherent restraints upon its own growth. Surely something of the same sort exists in normal psychological development. To each of us is given a span of attention and a span of years, and both are brief but wondrous. The enduringness of attention through the cycles of change enables us to complete the whole.

The mythical celebrator of all the comings and goings is Orpheus, born of the union of Zeus with one of the daughters of Memory. "Once and for all, it's Orpheus where there's song," writes Rilke in his *Sonnets*. The concluding sonnet of the cycle, Number 29 of Part II, as translated by C. F. MacIntyre, expresses beautifully, with the freedom of poetic genius, some of the relationships I have here tried haltingly to describe.

> Still friend of many distances, feel yet
> how your breathing is augmenting space.
> From the beamwork of gloomy belfries let
> yourself ring. What devours you will increase
>
> more strongly from this food. Explore and win
> knowledge of transformation through and through.
> What experience was the worst for you?
> Is drinking bitter, you must turn to wine.
>
> Be the magic power of this immense
> midnight at the crossroads of your senses,
> be the purport of their strange meeting.
>   Though
>
> earth itself forgot your very name,
> say unto the tranquil earth: I flow.
> To the fleeting water speak: I am.[5]

[5] Rainer Maria Rilke, *Sonnets to Orpheus,* trans. C. F. MacIntyre (Berkeley: University of California Press, 1960), p. 113. Permission to reprint in the United States and Canada granted by the University of California Press. Permission to reprint in the British Commonwealth (except Canada) granted by The Hogarth Press, Ltd.

11: CREATIVITY AND IMAGES OF THE SELF

Donald W. MacKinnon

In 1943, G. W. Allport noted that "one of the oddest events in the history of modern psychology is the manner in which the ego (or self) became sidetracked and lost to view."[1] Surveying the various conceptions of the ego in the psychological literature, he urged the readmittance of the ego to good standing in psychology and optimistically predicted that "ego-psychology in the twentieth century will flourish increasingly. For only with its aid can psychologists reconcile the human nature that they study and the human nature that they serve."[2]

Allport's prophecy was a self-fulfilling one, for the very clarity and force with which he stated the case for the ego stirred psychologists to consider again its role in behavior.

It was not true, of course, that the ego had been completely lost to view during its period of neglect by American academic psychologists. McDougall never wavered in his insistence that the master sentiment in man, most determinative of all his behavior, is the sentiment of self-regard.[3] But McDougall was more British than American, and his purposivism never won wide acceptance in the United States. It must be remembered also that during this time the psychoanalysts continued to be concerned with ego function or, more properly speaking, with ego dysfunction, for it was the relatively weak egos of psychoneurotic patients that were their main concern. Although they conceptualized a trait of ego strength, it was ego weakness which they described repeatedly and in detail. In the 1940's, following the publication in 1939 of Heinz Hartmann's paper, "Ich-Psychologie und Anpassungsproblem,"[4] psychoanalysts began to think of the ego as developing simultaneously with the id, instead of de-

[1] G. W. Allport, "The Ego in Contemporary Psychology," *Psychol. Rev.*, L (1943), 451.

[2] *Ibid.*, p. 476.

[3] William McDougall, *The Energies of Men* (New York: Scribners, 1933).

[4] Heinz Hartmann, "Ich-Psychologie und Anpassungsproblem," *Internationale Zeitschrift für Psychoanalyse und Imago*, XXIV (1939), 62–135.

veloping out of it, and to recognize that ego functions are not necessarily outgrowths of conflict. Whereas previously ego function was conceived to be largely a matter of ego defenses at work, in recent years the constructive, integrative, and adaptive functions of the ego have been increasingly emphasized and studied by psychoanalysts.

Although academic psychologists have obviously been less concerned with pathological ego functioning than have the psychoanalysts, they, too, were once concerned with the negative, unhealthy, and destructive aspects of personality. But, like the psychoanalysts, they have shifted their interest, both in their theoretical writing and in their experimental researches, to a more recent emphasis upon the positive, healthy, and constructive factors in the structure and functioning of persons. If one were to seek to fix in time and place this shift in interest, its most important beginnings would be found in the work of Allport[5] and of Murray[6] at Harvard in the 1930's.

There is no intention to review here the history of personality theory and research, but merely to note as has Sanford, that among the major developments in this field since 1937 have been an increased awareness of the complexity of personality; a decreasing accent upon motives, accompanied by an increasing emphasis upon cognitive variables as the significant variables of personality; an increasing holistic orientation; and a trend toward thinking about higher things.[7] The present chapter, which reports some results of a study of the ego in creative process and the self-images of creative persons, exemplifies several of these new emphases in personality theory and research.[8]

EGO AND SELF IN CREATIVE PROCESS

The history of the concepts of ego and self has been a long and con- ... e, but there is today rather general agreement upon the sense in which each is to be used in psychological theory. In a functionalist psychology of personality the ego is conceived to be a system of regulating functions—inhibition, reality testing, decision-making, scheduling, etc.— which serve to integrate the subsystems of personality. On the one hand, it effects adjustment of the individual to the situation in which he finds him-

[5] Gordon W. Allport, *Personality,* "A Psychological Interpretation" (New York, Holt, 1937).

[6] Henry A. Murray *et al., Explorations in Personality* (New York: Oxford University Press, 1938).

[7] Nevitt Sanford, "Personality: Its Place in Psychology," in Sigmund Koch, ed., *Psychology,* "A Study of a Science" (New York: McGraw-Hill, v. d.), Vol. 5.

[8] The study reported here is part of a larger investigation of the creativity of American architects, conducted in collaboration with Wallace B. Hall. It is, in turn, part of a still larger investigation of creative work and creative workers in the arts, sciences, and professions which has been carried out at the Institute of Personality Assessment and Research of the University of California, Berkeley, and supported in part by funds granted by the Carnegie Corporation of New York. The statements made and views expressed are, however, solely the responsibility of the author.

self and, on the other hand, it permits the individual to express himself in creative actions which change the environment and contribute to the actualization of himself through the development and expression of his potentialities. In contrast to the ego, the self is conceived of as an individual's system of perceptions, conceptions, and images of himself as a person. The two systems are intimately related; the regulating functions of the ego are obviously influenced by the complex of percepts, concepts, and images which constitute the self, while the content of awareness that the perceiving individual thinks of as his self is clearly influenced by the quality and quantity of the functioning of his ego.

This is the rationale that led us in our study of creative persons and the creative process to hypothesize that the creativeness with which persons perform in their professional roles is a function of their images of themselves as individuals and as professional practitioners.

THE SUBJECTS

The subjects whose creativity and images of the self are here reported are 124 American architects. Forty of them, constituting a nationwide sample and here designated as Architects I, were selected by a panel of five professors of architecture at the University of California, Berkeley, for the unusual creativeness they had shown in the practice of their profession.

The second group, Architects II, consists of forty-three architects so chosen as to match Architects I with respect to age and the geographic location of their practice. Each of them met the additional requirement that he had had at least two years of work experience and association with one of the originally selected creative architects.

The third sample, Architects III, was also chosen to match Architects I with respect to age and geographic location of practice, but, unlike Architects II, the forty-one men in this group had never worked with any of the Architects I.

Architects I, II, and III were selected in this manner in hopes of tapping a range of creative talent sufficiently wide to be fairly representative of the profession as a whole. To determine whether or not we had succeeded, ratings on a seven-point scale of the creativity of all 124 architects were obtained from six groups of architects and architectural experts: the five members of the original nominating panel at the University of California, nineteen professors of architecture distributed nationwide, six editors of the major American architectural journals, thirty-two Architects I, thirty-six Architects II, and twenty-eight Architects III. The mean ratings of creativity for the three groups are shown in Table 1. The differences are in the expected direction and are statistically highly significant.[9]

[9] For a fuller description of the selection of the three groups and their differ-

TABLE 1

MEAN RATINGS OF CREATIVITY ON SEVEN-POINT SCALE
OF 124 ARCHITECTS

Groups rated	Mean rating	SD	t-Ratio	p-Value
Architects I	5.46	0.43		
			10.795	.001
Architects II	4.25	0.56		
			4.908	.001
Architects III	3.54	0.74		

It should be noted, however, that the three samples show an overlap in their judged creativity; they are not discontinuous groups, but, combined, approximate a normal distribution of judged creativeness ranging from a low of 1.9 to a high of 6.5 on a seven-point rating scale.

In view of the approximately normal distribution of the rated creativity for the total sample of 124 architects and with the further evidence that Architects I, II, and III do indeed represent significantly different levels of creativity, we can proceed to examine differences in the self-imagery of architects in relation to differences in their level of creativeness by two major means: (1) computing the correlations between external judgments of creativity and various facets of self-imagery for the total sample of 124 architects, and (2) comparing differences of means of various aspects of self-imagery among Architects I, II, and III.

IMAGE OF THE SELF AS PERSON

A major technique employed for the recording of the architects' images of themselves was the Gough Adjective Check List.[10] Upon its first administration each architect was asked to check on this list of three hundred adjectives those which he judged to be most descriptive of himself, and upon its second presentation to check those which would describe him if he were the person he would like to be. The two images thus obtained were, first, the image of the *real self* and, second, the image of the *ideal self* or *ego ideal*.

Adjective Descriptions of the Real Self

Table 2, which lists the fourteen adjectives checked as self-descriptive by 80 per cent or more of all three groups of architects and the frequency with which they were checked by each of the groups, shows what is common to the architects' self-imagery regardless of the level of their creative-

entiating characteristics, see D. W. MacKinnon, "The Personality Correlates of Creativity: A Study of American Architects," in *Proceedings of the XIV International Congress of Applied Psychology, Copenhagen 1961* (Copenhagen: Munksgaard, 1962), II, 11–39.

[10] Harrison G. Gough, *The Adjective Check List* (Palo Alto: Consulting Psychologists Press, 1961).

s. The adjectives are favorable without exception. The differences in
-imagery among the three groups are, by the nature of the data, slight
at most merely suggestive. Architects I, more often than either Archi-
II or III, see themselves as imaginative, active, and idealistic; Archi-
I, as compared with both Architects I and III, see themselves most
as civilized, serious, and fair-minded; and Architects III, more
the other two groups, see the adjective "conscientious" as most
-scriptive.

TABLE 2

THE FOURTEEN ADJECTIVES CHECKED AS SELF-DESCRIPTIVE BY
80 PER CENT OR MORE OF ALL THREE GROUPS OF ARCHITECTS
AND THE FREQUENCY WITH WHICH THEY WERE
CHECKED BY EACH

Architects I		*Architects II*		*Architects III*	
Adjective	*Per cent*	*Adjective*	*Per cent*	*Adjective*	*Per cent*
imaginative	98	civilized	95	conscientious	98
active	92	conscientious	93	honest	95
honest	92	honest	93	cooperative	93
idealistic	90	serious	93	intelligent	93
civilized	88	capable	91	reasonable	93
conscientious	88	fair-minded	91	civilized	90
intelligent	88	imaginative	91	capable	90
reasonable	85	intelligent	91	fair-minded	85
fair-minded	85	friendly	86	friendly	85
capable	82	reasonable	86	healthy	85
cooperative	82	idealistic	84	imaginative	83
friendly	80	active	81	serious	83
healthy	80	cooperative	81	active	80
serious	80	healthy	81	idealistic	80

The differences in self-imagery among the three groups are more
clearly revealed by the data presented in Table 3. Here the adjectives
checked as self-descriptive by 80 per cent or more of one group, but by less
than 80 per cent of one or both of the other groups, are listed.

Architects I, more often than either Architects II or III, see themselves as inventive, determined, independent, individualistic, enthusiastic,
and industrious; more often than Architects II they say they are adaptable,
and have wide interests; and more often than Architects III they describe
themselves as artistic, progressive, and appreciative. A strikingly different
image of the self is held by both Architects II and III, who more often
check as self-descriptive the adjectives responsible, sincere, reliable, dependable, clear-thinking, tolerant, and understanding. More often than
Architects I, Architects II say they are forgiving, kind, sensitive, rational
and alert; and Architects III, more often than Architects I, say they are
peaceable, good-natured, moderate, steady, practical, and logical.

TABLE 3

ADJECTIVES CHECKED AS SELF-DESCRIPTIVE BY 80 PER CENT OR MORE OF ONE SAMPLE BUT BY LESS THAN 80 PER CENT OF ANOTHER

Checked by ≧ 80 per cent of I, but < 80 per cent of III	Checked by ≧ 80 per cent of I, but < 80 per cent of II	Checked by ≧ 80 per cent of II, but < 80 per cent of I	Checked by ≧ 80 per cent of III, but < 80 per cent of I
* inventive	* inventive	† responsible	† responsible
* determined	* determined	† sincere	† sincere
* independent	* independent	† reliable	† reliable
* individualistic	* individualistic	† dependable	† dependable
* enthusiastic	* enthusiastic	† clear-thinking	† clear-thinking
* industrious	* industrious	† tolerant	† tolerant
artistic	adaptable	† understanding	† understanding
progressive	interests wide	forgiving	peaceable
appreciative		kind	good-natured
		sensitive	moderate
		rational	steady
		alert	practical
			logical

* Checked by ≧ 80 per cent of I, but < 80 per cent of II and III
† Checked by ≧ 80 per cent of II and III, but < 80 per cent of I

In summary, architects, regardless of the level of their creativeness, tend to think well of themselves, but the quality of the self-image of highly creative architects differs from that of their less creative colleagues. Where the former more often stress their inventiveness, independence, and individuality, and their enthusiasm, determination, and industry, their less creative colleagues are impressed by their own virtue and good character and by their rationality and sympathetic concern for others.

It is well known that persons differ widely in the number of adjectives which they check as self-descriptive. Gough reports that in an earlier studied sample of 1,364 men the range in number checked was from 13 to 298, with a mean of 99.[11] In the development and standardization of some twenty-three variables to be scored on the Adjective Check List (ACL) it was obvious that the total number checked would act as a response-set artifact unless controlled in deriving standard scores on the several variables. Using the standard score conversion tables in the ACL Manual, which take into account the number of adjectives checked, it is possible to compare any individual's score or the mean score of any group on any of the variables of the ACL with the mean of the standardizing sample.

The mean standard scores for the three groups of architects on the twenty-three dimensions of the Adjective Check List are plotted on the profiles of Figure 1.

The first variable on the profile sheet is total number of adjectives checked (No Ckd). Though Architects I and II both score higher (53) on this dimension than Architects III (50), the differences are not significant. And in the total sample creativity is not significantly related to the number of adjectives which architects check to describe themselves.

The second variable of the ACL, defense (Df), provides a measure of the defensiveness or guardedness with which one fills out the check list. There is a tendency for the less creative architects to be more defensive in describing themselves; Df correlates −.21 with rated creativity in the total sample.[12] This greater defensiveness of the less creative architects is not surprising in view of their more frequent attribution to themselves of virtue and good character (see Table 3).

The scores on the next two variables of the ACL, the number of favorable adjectives checked (Fav) and the number of unfavorable adjectives checked (Un-Fav), also reveal a more defensive attitude on the part of the less creative architects. Though the mean score on favorable adjectives checked progresses from Architects I (48) to Architects II (51) to Architects III (52), these differences are not significant, nor in the total

[11] Harrison G. Gough and Alfred B. Heilbrun, Jr., *Manual for the Adjective Check List* (Palo Alto: Consulting Psychologists Press, Inc., 1963). Reproduced by special permission.
[12] For $N = 124$, $r_p.05 = .18$, $_p.01 = .23$.

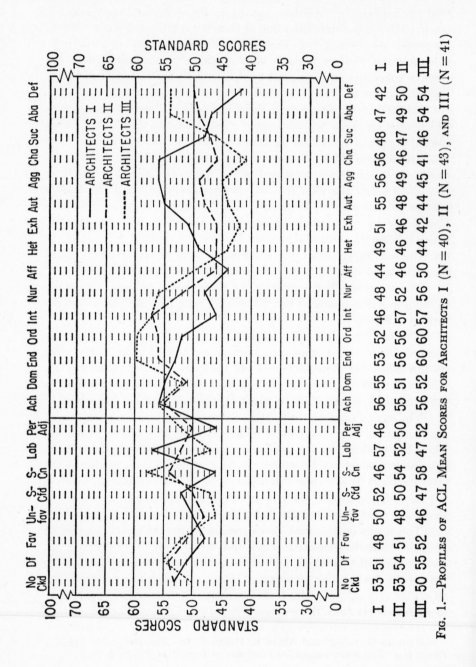

Fig. 1.—Profiles of ACL Mean Scores for Architects I (N = 40), II (N = 43), and III (N = 41)

sample does rated creativity correlate significantly with the number of favorable adjectives checked.

On the other hand, the number of unfavorable adjectives checked correlates +.28 with rated creativity for the total sample, and the mean score on unfavorable adjectives checked for Architects I is significantly different ($\leqslant$.01 level) from the mean score for Architects III (46). It is not that highly creative architects are more self-critical than people in general (their standard score is 50), but that the less creative architects are less inclined than their more gifted peers to admit flaws in their character armor.

With respect to self-confidence (S-Cfd) the three groups of architects do not differ significantly one from another, nor in the total sample is self-confidence as measured by the ACL scale significantly correlated with rated creativity; but in self-control (S-Co) the groups do differ, with Architects I scoring below the profile mean (46) and Architects II (54) and Architects III (58) scoring above the mean.

This is congruent with the findings reported above, since high scorers on the self-control scale, according to Gough, "tend to be serious, sober individuals, interested in and responsive to their obligations. They are seen as diligent, practical, and loyal workers. At the same time there may be an element of too much control, too much emphasis on the proper means for attaining the ends of social living. Thus the highest level of ego integration which involves recognition and sublimation of chaotic and destructive impulses, along with the allosocial and life-giving dispositions, may be denied to these individuals."[13] In light of this description it is interesting to note that in the total sample of architects self-control correlates −.40 with rated creativity.

It is the other way around with lability (Lab) as measured by the ACL, Architects III scoring below the standard score mean at 47, Architects II just slightly above the mean at 52, and Architects I well above the mean at 57, the differences being significant ($\leqslant$.01 for I *vs.* III $\leqslant$.05 for I *vs.* II and II *vs.* III). Gough's description of high and low scorers on the lability scale, written long before the present study and without benefit of any of the data here presented, has a prophetic ring. Or if one prefers a more restrained formulation, the differential scores of the three groups of architects constitute an impressive cross-validation of Gough's original study which led him to write:

> Although there is a facet of high ego strength in this scale, an adventurous delighting in the new and different and a sensitivity to all that is unusual and challenging, the main emphasis seems to be upon an inner restlessness and an inability to tolerate consistency and routine. The high scoring subject is seen favorably as spontaneous, but unfavorably as excitable, tempera-

[13] Gough and Heilbrun, *op. cit.*

mental, restless, nervous, and high-strung. The psychological equilibrium, the balance of forces, is an uneasy one in this person and he seems impelled toward change and new experience in an endless flight from his perplexities.

The low scorer is more phlegmatic, more routinized, more planful and conventional. He reports stricter opinions on right and wrong practices, and a greater need for order and regularity. He is described by observers as thorough, organized, steady, and unemotional.[14]

It is, then, not surprising to find that in the total sample of architects lability correlates +.29 with rated creativity.

On the personal adjustment scale (Per Adj) Architects I score below the profile mean (46), Architects II at the mean (50), and Architects III above it (52). The differences are significant ($\leq$.01 level) between groups I and III and between groups I and II ($\leq$.05 level), but not between groups II and III. The scale, according to its author, measures an attitudinal set of optimism, cheerfulness, an interest in others, and a readiness to adapt to the social situation.

The high scoring subject [writes Gough] is seen as dependable, peaceable, trusting, friendly, practical, loyal, and wholesome. He fits in well, asks for little, treats others with courtesy, and works enterprisingly toward his own goal. He may or may not understand himself psychodynamically, but he nonetheless seems to possess the capacity for "love and work" which is the sought-for outcome of such understanding.

The subject low on the personal adjustment scale sees himself as at odds with other people and as being moody and dissatisfied. . . . What appears to begin as a problem in self-definition eventuates as a problem in interpersonal living.[15]

This description of the low scorer seems too extreme to be fully applicable to Architects I, though in terms of conventional adjustment and unquestioning acceptance of social norms and standards there is no doubt, as evidence reported elsewhere clearly indicates, that more creative architects are less conforming ("well-adjusted") than their less creative colleagues.[16] It is interesting to note, then, that personal adjustment as measured by the ACL scale correlates −.33 with rated creativity in the total sample of architects.

The next fifteen dimensions on the ACL are the need scales developed by Heilbrun[17] to measure variables first conceptualized by Murray.[18] Heilbrun, following Edwards[19] in his development of the Personal Prefer-

[14] Loc. cit.
[15] Loc. cit.
[16] MacKinnon, op. cit.
[17] Gough and Heilbrun, op. cit.
[18] Murray, op. cit.
[19] Allen L. Edwards, Edwards Personal Preference Schedule Manual (New York: Psychological Corporation, 1954).

ence Schedule, refers to the conceptualized dimensions as manifest needs within Murray's need-trait system. To be sure, eleven of the fifteen variables—abasement, achievement, affiliation, aggression, autonomy, deference, dominance, exhibition, nurturance, order, and succorance—were listed by Murray as manifest needs. Murray also described need sex, but did not use the term heterosexuality to designate it. Change, endurance, and intraception are terms used by Murray, but they were described by him as general traits or attributes, not needs.

Whether the variables measured by the Heilbrun scales are manifest needs may be a somewhat academic question. They are all dynamic variables of personality conceptualized by Murray, and no serious injustice is done to Murray's system when Heilbrun refers to the scales he has developed for the ACL as scales measuring need dispositions.

It is of interest to note first those variables on which architects of different levels of creativeness do not differ. All three groups are above the standard score mean on achievement (Ach) and dominance (Dom) and below the mean on succorance (Suc). Their mean scores on these dimensions are not significantly different one from another. Considering the nature of their profession, the success with which they practice it, the demands it makes upon them, and the kinds of relationships they must establish with clients and builders, this is as one would expect.

Of the remaining scales there are five on which Architects I score higher than Architects II, and Architects II higher than Architects III— namely, heterosexuality (Het), exhibition (Exh), autonomy (Aut), aggression (Agg), and change (Cha). On all but the first of these dimensions Architects I score above the profile mean, while Architects II and III have mean scores below it; and on each of the dimensions the difference in the mean score between Architects I and Architects III is significant at the $\leq.01$ level, with the exception of heterosexuality, where the difference is significant at or beyond the .05 level. In addition, each of the scales, except for heterosexuality, correlates ($\leq.01$ level of significance) with rated creativity in the total sample of 124 architects: exhibition, $+.38$; autonomy, $+.37$; aggression, $+.36$; and change, $+.46$.

All three groups have mean scores below 50 on heterosexuality (I, 49; II, 46; III, 44), and in the total sample, heterosexuality is not significantly correlated with the criterion.

On seven of the Heilbrun scales the relative position of the three groups is just the reverse, Architects III scoring higher than Architects II, who, in turn, score higher than Architects I. These are the scales for endurance (End), order (Ord), intraception (Int), nurturance (Nur), affiliation (Aff), abasement (Aba), and deference (Def); and the difference in mean score between Architects III and Architects I on each of these scales is significant (.01 level). Where exhibition, autonomy, aggression, and change are positively correlated with rated creativity in the total sample of 124 architects, these variables are negatively correlated with creativity: endurance, −.25; order, −.33; intraception, −.40; nurturance, −.31; affiliation, −.25; abasement, −.21; and deference, −.36.

The negative correlations of abasement, affiliation, deference, and nurturance with creativity are as one would predict. Some question might, however, be raised about the inverse relationship of endurance, order, and intraception with creativity.

It would appear that the type of endurance tapped by the Heilbrun scale involves working uninterruptedly at a task until it is finished, sticking to a problem even though one is not making progress, and working steadily at a single job before undertaking others. Endurance of this short-range type is not so characteristic of the highly creative person as is endurance over long periods of time, even a lifetime, with much more flexibility in behavior and variation in specific means and goals. In the life-history interview, for example, the more creative architects, more often than those less creative, report turning to another activity when seriously blocked in a task and returning later to it when refreshed, whereas less creative architects more often report working stubbornly at a problem when blocked in their attempts at solution.

On several measures of psychological-mindedness, creative architects, like creative persons in many other fields, score higher than their less creative colleagues.[20] One might, then, expect them to score higher on intraception. In both psychological-mindedness and intraception there is a subjective concern with others and an interest in their make-up and motivations; but the measures of psychological-mindedness, for example the Py-scale of the California Psychological Inventory,[21] tap more the intellectual, cognitive, and conceptual concern with psychological problems and processes, whereas the intraception scale of the ACL places more emphasis on the feeling of concern with others and the desire to support and help them. Note, for example, these adjectives which are scored plus by the intraception key: considerate, fair-minded, forgiving, sympathetic, tolerant, understanding. In view of this difference between the measures of psychological-mindedness and intraception and the primary interest of architects in the design of material things and in the arrangement of external spaces, the negative correlation of intraception with architectural creativity is easily understood.

---

[20] D. W. MacKinnon, "What Makes a Person Creative?" *Saturday Review*, Feb. 10, 1962, pp. 15–17, 69.

[21] Harrison G. Gough, *California Psychological Inventory Manual* (Palo Alto: Consulting Psychologists Press, 1957).

As for the negative correlation of order with creativity, this is highly congruent with a large body of data obtained in our own studies as well as in those of others at the Institute of Personality Assessment and Research.[22] These data indicate a strong preference on the part of highly creative persons for richness and complexity of stimulation; they prefer the challenge of disorder to the barrenness of simplicity.

We do well to remind ourselves that the variables of personality measured by the Heilbrun scales of the ACL, which so effectively predict creativity, are based upon images of the self which subjects reveal to us through the checking of those adjectives which they consider most descriptive of themselves. It is remarkable that so simple a device as a list of three hundred adjectives can reveal so much about a person. That it can do so is due in large part to the fact that a person's self-image is not a static concept but the focus of a constellation of dispositional trends— needs and their associated affects—in the person. If we know the nature of this constellation, what Murray and Morgan earlier would have called the sentiment *ad* the self,[23] we are in a fair way to predict the behavior of an individual and even so complex an aspect of his behavior as the creativeness with which he practices his profession.

Adjective Descriptions of the Ideal Self

We have already seen that architects in general tend to think well of themselves; yet in spite of their highly favorable self-images, they are not entirely self-satisfied. They check some unfavorable adjectives as self-descriptive, though considerably less frequently than more favorable ones. But the clearest evidence of their dissatisfactions with themselves is to be found in the discrepancies between the adjectives they check to describe the ideal self and those checked when describing the real self.

Table 4 lists those adjectives checked by 80 per cent or more of Architects I when describing the ideal self and checked at least twenty percentage points less often when describing the real self. The percentages of subjects checking each adjective when describing his real self and his ideal self, and the discrepancy between the two percentages are shown both for single adjectives and for groups of adjectives.

---

[22] MacKinnon, "The Personality Correlates of Creativity: A Study of American Architects," *op. cit.*, but especially Frank Barron, "The Needs for Order and for Disorder as Motives in Creative Activity," in C. W. Taylor (Principal Investigator), *The Second Research Conference on the Identification of Creative Scientific Talent* (Salt Lake City: University of Utah Press, 1958), pp. 119–128.

[23] Henry A. Murray and Christiana D. Morgan, "A Clinical Study of Sentiments," *Genet. Psychol. Monogr.*, XXXII (1945), 3–149, 153–311.

TABLE 4

ADJECTIVES CHECKED BY 80 PER CENT OR MORE OF ARCHITECTS I, WHEN DESCRIBING IDEAL SELF, WHICH HAD BEEN CHECKED AT LEAST TWENTY PERCENTAGE POINTS LOWER WHEN DESCRIBING THE REAL SELF

Personal attractiveness	Percentage ideal	Percentage real	Percentage discrepancy
attractive	90	30	60
charming	90	30	60
good-looking	82	25	57
Average	87	28	59
Self-confidence			
adventurous	100	78	22
confident	98	62	36
courageous	98	58	40
masculine	90	70	20
optimistic	88	68	20
self-confident	88	68	20
strong	82	35	47
daring	80	32	48
Average	91	59	32
Maturity			
natural	92	68	24
humorous	88	62	26
mature	85	50	35
Average	88	60	28
Intellectual competence			
alert	100	78	22
clear-thinking	98	68	30
thoughtful	95	72	23
resourceful	92	68	24
logical	88	65	23
thorough	85	50	35
versatile	82	62	20
witty	80	42	38
Average	90	63	27
Good social relations			
generous	92	72	20
kind	92	70	22
considerate	88	68	20
forgiving	88	68	20
sociable	88	65	23
sympathetic	88	68	20
affectionate	85	65	20

patient	85	55	30
tactful	85	65	20
warm	82	62	20
Average	86	64	22
High level of energy			
enterprising	92	70	22
energetic	90	70	20
Average	91	70	21
Sensitiveness			
sensitive	95	75	20

These adjectives fall into certain natural groupings, which reveal areas of personal functioning in which creative architects feel least satisfied with themselves and most desirous of change. Above all they wish for greater personal attractiveness, checking markedly more often for the ideal than the real self the adjectives attractive, charming, and good-looking. The average discrepancy scores for these adjectives between the real and the ideal is fifty-nine percentage points. Secondly, they desire greater self-confidence, checking with a mean discrepancy score of 32 the adjectives adventurous, confident, courageous, masculine, optimistic, self-confident, strong, and daring. The cluster with the next largest average discrepancy score (28)—natural, humorous, and mature—suggests a desire for greater maturity of mind and spirit. The creative architect would also ideally have greater intellectual competence—would like to be more alert, clear-thinking, thoughtful, resourceful, logical, thorough, versatile, and witty than he sees himself as being.

It is in the realm of his social relations and interpersonal reactions, however, that the creative architect finds the largest number of favorable adjectives that he wishes were descriptive of him. Ideally he would be more generous, kind, considerate, forgiving, sociable, sympathetic, affectionate, patient, tactful, and warm. Ideally, too, he would have a higher level of energy (energetic, enterprising) and he would also be more sensitive.

Since the intelligence of Architects I as measured by the Terman Concept Mastery Test correlates −.08 with their rated creativity, it is questionable whether Architects I would be more creative if their intelligence could somehow be increased, and it is paradoxical that they wish for themselves so many of those mild and gentle traits of social and interpersonal behavior which their less creative colleagues see as so characteristic of themselves.

Actually, discrepancies between adjectives checked to describe the real self and those checked to describe the ideal self reveal all three groups as desiring more personal attractiveness, self-confidence, maturity, and intellectual competence; a higher level of energy; and better social relations. As for differences between the groups, however, Architects I would ideally be more sensitive; and Architects II and III both wish for opposites if not incompatibles—they would ideally be more original but at the same time more self-controlled and disciplined.

Aside from these qualitative differences and similarities in adjectives checked by the three groups of architects in describing themselves as they are and as they would ideally be, there is the question as to whether the groups differ with respect to the degree to which they see themselves as approximating their ideal selves. The mean correlation of adjectives checked to describe the real self with adjectives checked to describe the ideal self is for Architects I +.44, for Architects II +.48, and for Architects III +.53.

On this dimension Architects I are not significantly different from Architects II nor Architects II from Architects III. Architects I are, however, significantly different ($\leq$.05 level) from Architects III, seeing themselves as approximating their ideal selves less closely than the group of architects who are the least creative. Here again is evidence of a greater defensiveness on the part of the less creative architects and a willingness on the part of their more creative colleagues to recognize and to admit a greater discrepancy between themselves as they are and as they would ideally be.

IMAGE OF THE SELF AS ARCHITECT

Having seen how creative architects and their less creative colleagues perceive themselves as persons and having seen, too, what additional virtues they would wish to possess, we may now inquire as to how they see themselves in their professional role of architect and how closely they perceive themselves as approximating their ideal for the profession.

To obtain these images of themselves we first asked each architect to sort fifty statements, describing talents, skills, interests, values, work habits, and points of view of architects, into five categories ranging from those most characteristic to those least characteristic of him, the number of statements to be sorted into each category being prescribed in a quasi-normal distribution (5, 10, 20, 10, 5). Compositing the sortings made by all the architects in each group yields a ranking of the statements from those most characteristic to those least characteristic; in other words, their group images of themselves as architects.

Later each architect was asked to sort the fifty statements again, this time so sorting them as to describe the ideal architect. Again compositing separately those sortings made by each group yields a ranking of the statements from those most characteristic to those least characteristic of the ideal architect as the group imagines the ideal architect to be.

The composite rankings of the fifty statements made by Architects I, II, and III in describing themselves as architects are shown in the first three columns and those made by the three groups in describing the ideal architect are given in the next three columns of Table 5.

A first impression of differences in the architects' professional self-images may be gained by noting the item which each group sorts as most saliently descriptive. For Architects I it is their aesthetic sensitivity and respect for artistic standards. For Architects II it is the holding of exceptionally high standards of professional performance for oneself as well as for others and a superior ability in evaluating and judging architectural plans. For Architects III it is their sense of responsibility and, like Architects II, their superior ability in evaluating and judging architectural plans. Items ranked first by one group are not given markedly discrepant placement by the others—there is fairly good agreement among all three groups as to what most characterizes them as architects—but what *is* revealed by the first-placed items is so congruent with other facets of their self-images as to deserve special notice.

Three of the five statements sorted as most characteristic by Architects I are also placed high by the other two groups, but the other two statements are given radically different ranks by Architects II and III. The item, "Reacts to architectural problems; immediately generates a great number of ideas," is given a rank of 2.5 by Architects I but receives ranks of 19 and 21 from Architects II and III. The statement, "Is interested in philosophical problems which arise in architecture," which holds fifth rank for Architects I is ranked 25 and 30.5 by Architects II and III. The differential placement of these two items suggests an absorbingly deep interest and involvement of the self in architecture on the part of the more creative architects—interest and involvement which are much less pronounced in their less creative colleagues. It is as though the architectural apperceptive mass of creative architects is so rich and so active that their reaction to any architectural press is immediate, deep, and far-ranging.

At the other end of the distributions, namely, the five items sorted as least characteristic, there is even better agreement among the three groups of architects. The only difference to be noted is a rather pronounced tendency for Architects I to disclaim any "special talent for solving organizational problems" (rank of 46), whereas Architects II and III less often deny organizational skills (ranks of 39.5 and 33).

Several instances of Architects III stressing their strong sense of responsibility have been observed. It is of some interest to note how they, as compared with the other two groups, sort the items which refer to an architect's responsibility to his client, to his profession, and to society. These three statements and their placement by the three groups are presented in Table 6.

TABLE 5

Q-Sortings for Self as Architect and for the Ideal Architect

	Item ranking for self-description			Item ranking for ideal architect		
	Group			Group		
	I	II	III	I	II	III
Five statements most characteristic						
Takes an aesthetic view; is especially sensitive to matters of form and coherence in architectural problems.	1	3	10	1	2	6
Has exceptionally high standards of professional performance for himself as well as others.	2.5	1.5	3.5	4	3	1
Reacts quickly to architectural problems; immediately generates a great number of ideas.	2.5	19	21	13	11	7.5
Has a lively sense of intellectual curiosity and inquiry, a desire to know and to understand.	4	5.5	7	5	4	7.5
Is interested in philosophical problems which arise in architecture.	5	25	30.5	7	20	24
Ten statements somewhat characteristic						
Has strong powers of spatial visualization.	6	5.5	14	2	1	4
Has a broadly based, responsible, and comprehensive approach to architectural problems.	7	7	1.5	3	5	2
Is good at evaluating architectural plans; able to diagnose strong and weak points in a plan quickly and accurately.	8	1.5	1.5	15	8	3
Grasps other people's ideas quickly; often long before they finish explaining them.	9	4	6	19.5	18.5	20.5

Is creative in anything he tries, whether in architecture or not.	10	15.5	15	8	7	10.5
Is stimulating to other people; seems to catalyze others into more original and productive endeavor than they would otherwise achieve.	11	26.5	36.5	14	10	13
Has a "sense of destiny" with respect to his own professional career, an inner conviction of the worth and validity of his own efforts.	12	28.5	26	10	12	17.5
Has a balanced, critical view of architecture.	13	12.5	5	16	16	10.5
Is a perfectionist; devotes endless attention to matters of design, planning, detailing, industrialization, technology, etc.	14	33	26	6	13	9
Has a knack for improvising quick solutions in architectural trouble spots.	15	11	11	26	24	19

Twenty neutral, or middle-category, statements

Is flexible and adaptable in his thinking; able to shift and to restructure easily.	16.5	17.5	8.5	17	18.5	16
Pursues details and ramifications of architectural problems with great thoroughness.	16.5	20	16.5	12	17	20.5
Has an active, efficient, well-organized mind.	19	10	12.5	11	6	5
Is a driving, indefatigable architect; cannot stop thinking about a problem until it is resolved.	19	33	28	26	14	17.5
Is only satisfied with new and original solutions to design problems.	19	35	38.5	23	29	31.5
Is intellectually gifted.	21	14	41.5	9	9	12
Works best under pressure.	22	17.5	19	33	35	34.5
Dislikes and avoids administrative details connected with architectural projects.	23	37	36.5	38	41	40.5
Can imagine enjoying lines of work other than architecture.	24	21	17	39	38	38
Prefers to work on problems which lend themselves to elegant and exact solutions.	25	33	29	19.5	32	27

TABLE 5 (*Cont'd.*)

Q-SORTINGS FOR SELF AS ARCHITECT AND FOR THE IDEAL ARCHITECT

	Item ranking for self-description			Item ranking for ideal architect		
	Group			Group		
Twenty neutral, or middle-category statements (cont'd)	I	II	III	I	II	III
Primarily an "idea man"; prefers to turn his rough sketches over to someone else for systematic working-out of the details.	26	36	44	35	34	37
Seeks out the help and advice of other people when he hits a trouble spot in his own work.	27	9	12.5	24	29	33
Can take other people's ideas and concepts and fashion them into practical architectural designs and programs.	28	8	3.5	28	15	14
Prefers to work alone; is not a team man.	29	41	40	36	40	40.5
Has strong professional biases; is vehement in his disapproval of certain expressions and types of solutions.	30	38	45	41	39	44
Is aware of his own professional limitations; does not attempt what he cannot do.	31.5	15.5	21	33	36	36
Subordinates everything to his architectural goals; puts architectural values above all others.	31.5	47	41.5	18	21	26
In his practice places responsibility to his clients above all else.	34	12.5	8.5	30.5	22.5	15
Productivity runs in cycles.	34	31	38.5	42	42	42

Statement						
Tends to be hypercritical of the work of other architects.	45	45	45	47	45	34
Ten statements somewhat uncharacteristic						
Has a special talent for solving technological problems.	29.5	29	22	26	39.5	36
Is neat and orderly in his habits and manner of work.	28	33	30.5	21	22.5	37
Emphasizes structural requirements of his designs more than their aesthetic aspects.	34.5	37	40	23	42.5	39.5
In his practice places responsibility to society above all else.	31.5	22.5	21	34.5	28.5	39.5
Makes a serious effort to keep up with current publications and the literature in architecture.	23	25	37	24	22.5	39.5
Performs at less than his full capacity.	43	46	46	30.5	24	39.5
Is somewhat distractible; requires optimum conditions for concentration.	46	44	43	34.5	42.5	42
Has an exceptionally good memory.	29.5	29	29	32	30	43
In his practice places responsibility to his profession above all else.	22	26	33	18	26.5	44.5
Is erratic in his architectural output; varies from work of excellent quality to work of marginal or even inferior worth.	48.5	47	47	43	46	44.5
Five items least characteristic						
Has a special talent for solving organizational problems.	25	29	26	33	39.5	46
Is relatively uninformed on most subjects other than his architectural specialty.	48.5	48	49	48	48	47
Prefers not to tell anyone about his architectural ideas and plans until his work is finished.	39	43	44	46	44	48
Tends to slight the contributions of others; takes undue credit for himself.	50	50	48	50	49	49
His interests in architecture lie within a rather narrow range.	47	49	50	49	50	50

TABLE 6

Item Ranking for Self-Description and for Ideal Architect by Architects I, II, and III
of Statements Referring to Responsibility

Statements	Item ranking for self-description			Item ranking for ideal architect		
	Group			*Group*		
	I	*II*	*III*	*I*	*II*	*III*
In his practice places responsibility to his clients above all else.	34	12.5	8.5	30.5	22.5	15
In his practice places responsibility to his profession above all else.	44.5	26.5	18	33	26	22
In his practice places responsibility to society above all else.	39.5	28.5	34.5	21	22.5	31.5

It is clear that Architects III take their responsibilities seriously, first to the client (rank of 8.5), then to the profession (18), and lastly to society (34.5). The more concrete and immediately present the individual or the group, the greater the sense of responsibility which Architects III feel toward them. There is a hint that their strong sense of responsibility is experienced as something of a burden, possibly as an inhibitor of their creativity. At least they picture the ideal architect as one in whom the sense of responsibility to the client and to the profession would be somewhat less emphasized, these items receiving ranks of 15 and 22, respectively, in their image of the ideal. Only the sense of responsibility to society would be more emphasized in the ideal architect, moving from a rank of 34.5 to a rank of 31.5.

In contrast, the more creative Architects I see a sense of responsibility to others as much less emphasized in their character. Of the three responsibilities, that to the client comes first (34), then responsibility to society (39.5), and in last place responsibility to the profession (44.5). In his picture of the ideal architect, the creative architect sees each of these responsibilities as more important. It is interesting to note, though, that strongest would be the responsibility to society (21), then responsibility to the client (30.5), and finally responsibility to the profession (33).

In general, and as one would expect, Architects II, in their attitudes toward these responsibilities in themselves and in the ideal architect, are intermediate between Architects I and III.

Though a sense of responsibility to the client, to society, and to the profession is less salient in the self-imagery of more creative architects as compared with those whose creativity is judged to be less, one can hardly think of Architects I as an irresponsible group or as persons who would see themselves as lacking a sense of responsibility. The question then arises as to what they do feel is their greatest responsibility as architects, and the answer can be sought in an analysis of their Q-sortings of descriptions of themselves and of the ideal architect, and the corresponding descriptions given by Architects II and III.

In the search for differences, analysis is restricted to those items whose placement by Architects I is separated by at least ten ranks from their placements by both Architects II and III.

It is at once apparent that creative architects feel their primary responsibility is to their own high standards of what is right and proper in architectural design. About these standards and their ability to meet them they have no serious doubts. They see themselves as perfectionists, devoting endless attention to matters of design, planning, detailing, individualization, industrialization, technology, etc. (14, 33, 26).[24] Not only do they

[24] The three figures in parentheses here and those in the ensuing discussion indicate the ranks of the relevant items in the Q-sortings of Architects I, II, and III.

see themselves as perfectionists, but they also recognize that they are hyper-critical of the work of others (34, 45, 47). They are convinced of the worth and validity of their own efforts; indeed they report a "sense of destiny" with respect to their career in architecture (12, 28.5, 26). Convinced that they can accomplish anything they set out to do, they tend less often than their colleagues not to recognize their own professional limitations and consequently may attempt the impossible (31.5, 15.5, 21). In contrast to their colleagues, they more often report putting architectural values above all others, subordinating everything to their architectural goals (31.5, 47, 41.5). They also more often see themselves primarily as idea men content to leave the systematic working out of details to others (26, 36, 44), and they much more often claim to be satisfied only with those ideas which are new and original solutions to design problems (19, 35, 38.5).

Although they believe they influence and help colleagues to be more creative in their endeavors (11, 26.5, 36.5), creative architects do not easily, willingly, or often find that they can accept ideas and help from others in working out their own architectural solutions. In contrast to them, their less creative colleagues report more often being able to take other people's ideas and concepts and fashion them into practical architectural designs and programs (28, 8, 3.5); and when blocked in their work less creative architects more frequently seek the help and advice of others (27, 9, 12.5).

The independence with which creative architects work is revealed in their expressed dislike and avoidance of administrative work (23, 37, 36.5) and in the frequency with which they assert that they are not team men but prefer to work alone (29, 41, 40). Indeed, they see themselves as much less interested than their colleagues in making a serious effort to keep up with current publications and the literature in architecture (39.5, 22.5, 24).

Finally, we may note that architects in general feel that their memory is not exceptionally good. This is especially true of the more creative archi-tects (43, 30, 32), who also less often than their colleagues think of them-selves as neat and orderly in their habits and manner of work (37, 22.5, 21).

Having examined the images which architects of different levels of creativeness have of themselves in their professional role, we may now ask what, if any, is the relation between satisfaction with one's own professional image and one's creativity.

To begin, we may note that, of the three groups, only Architects I place in first rank in describing the self the same item which they rank

---

The first figure, 14 in the present case, is to be found in the first column of Table 5 and identifies the item which justifies the statements and conclusions made in the text.

first in describing the ideal, namely, "Takes an aesthetic view; is especially sensitive to matters of form and coherence in architectural problems." Creative architects are agreed that the most salient trait of the ideal architect is an aesthetic view and sensitivity to matters of form and coherence. This is the trait which they also see as most characteristic of themselves.

Architects II see themselves as most characterized by high standards of professional performance and superior ability in judging and evaluating architectural plans, but in describing the ideal they give first rank to the item "Has strong powers of spatial visualization." For them the most valued trait of the ideal architect is an intellectual skill rather than an aesthetic sensitivity.

Architects III see their most characteristic traits to be a broadly based, responsible, and comprehensive approach to architectural problems and a superior ability to judge and to evaluate architectural plans; they place in first rank as most characteristic of the ideal architect one of the items which was tied for first place in the self-description of Architects II: "Has exceptionally high standards of professional performance for himself as well as others."

Here again we see differences among the three groups of architects which are highly congruent with the differences revealed in other analyses. Architects I see as most characteristic of themselves and of the ideal architect some inner artistic standard of excellence and a sensitive appreciation of the fittingness of architectural solutions to that standard.

Architects II apparently place more stress upon the efficient execution of architecture, seeing as most saliently characteristic of the ideal architect the possession of that intellective ability, "strong powers of spatial visualization," which clearly is so crucial to the effective practice of architecture.

Architects III, unlike both Architects I and Architects II, choose as most characteristic of the ideal architect not the meeting of one's own standard but rather the standard of the profession. Once again they show that strong sense of responsibility to the group rather than to themselves or to some inner ideal of perfection which is uniquely theirs.

Finally, we may inquire more generally whether architects in the three groups differ in the degree to which their self-image approximates their image of the ideal for the profession, and we may note that there is a slight tendency for the more creative architects to think more highly of themselves as architects than either of the other groups. Using as scores the correlation of an architect's Q-sorting to describe himself as an architect with his Q-sorting for the ideal architect, the mean score for Architects I ($+.51$) is higher ($\leqq.10$) than for the less creative architects (Architects II, $+.41$; Architects III, $+.40$).

The tendency of creative architects to think especially well of themselves as architects is, however, perhaps most vividly illustrated by the extremely large number of them who, in rating their own creativity and the creativity of the other architects in the total sample, give themselves the highest rating of 7: 43 per cent of Architects I in contrast to 6 per cent of Architects II and 9 per cent of Architects III.

EGO FUNCTIONING, SELF-IMAGERY, AND CREATIVITY

There have emerged from the foregoing analyses three rather distinct pictures of personality, each characterized by its own level or degree of creativity and by its own style or quality of self-imagery and ego functioning. The data leave little doubt of the mutual dependence of ego and self and the crucial role of both in determining the level of creativeness with which a person practices his profession, in the present instance that of architecture.

One is struck by the accuracy of self-perception, by the degree to which architects see themselves as they really are, and by the remarkable consistency with which they conform in their thought and in their behavior to the type of person they see themselves as being.

The creative architect thinks of himself as creative, and his image of what a creative architect is, as well as his image of what a creative architect should be, exert a far-ranging influence upon what he thinks and what he does in his practice.

Above all else he thinks of himself as imaginative; unquestionably committed to creative endeavor; unceasingly striving for creative solutions to the difficult problems he repeatedly sets for himself; satisfied only with solutions which are original and meet his own high standards of architectural excellence; aesthetically sensitive; an independent spirit free from crippling restraints and impoverishing inhibitions; spontaneous; forthright; and self-accepting. He has a sense of destiny about his career as an architect.

The picture which the relatively uncreative architect holds of himself and conveys to others is in striking contrast. Where the creative architect is most impressed by his imagination and inventiveness, the less creative architect sees himself as most saliently conscientious, responsible, and sincere. In his professional role he prides himself on his ability to get along with others and to accept and work over their ideas and concepts. He thinks of himself as most importantly a team man; and it is clear that both as an architect and as a person he is strongly oriented to others, emotionally dependent upon them, and overly accepting of the values and judgments of his profession and of society.

The third picture is perhaps understandably much less sharp and distinctive than are the pictures of the highly creative and relatively uncreative architect. Just as his creativity is of an intermediate degree, so his perceptions of himself as a person and as an architect tend to fall between the self-perceptions of those more creative and of those less creative than himself. It is clear, however, that his self-imagery in both roles tends to approximate more closely that of the less creative architects. But with respect to two traits, his image of himself is clearly different from the self-image of those more as well as less creative: more often than both Architects I and Architects III, Architects II see themselves as intellectually gifted (21, 14, 41.5) but as performing at less than full capacity (39.5, 24, 30.5). There is a hint here, strongly supported by other assessment data, that the architects of intermediate creativity are indeed intellectually gifted (it is interesting to recall that they see as most characteristic of the ideal architect an intellective ability—strong powers of spatial visualization), but that more than the other two groups they suffer from neurotic conflict.

What is most impressive about Architects I is the degree to which they have actualized their potentialities. They have become in large measure the persons they were capable of becoming. Since they are not preoccupied with the impression they make on others or the demands that others make on them they are freer than the other two groups to set their own standards and to achieve them in their own fashion. It is not that they are socially irresponsible but that their behavior is guided by aesthetic values and ethical standards which they have set for themselves and which have been effectively integrated into their images of themselves and of their ideals. They are perhaps the prototype of the person of strong ego. Confident of themselves and basically self-accepting, they are to an unusual degree able to recognize and give expression to most aspects of inner experience and character and thus are able more fully to be themselves and to realize their ideal.

Architects III, on the other hand, appear to have incorporated into their egos and into their images both of the person they are and the person they would like to be, the more conventional standards of society and of their profession. More dependent upon the good opinion of others for their own good opinion of themselves, their goals and ideals are to an important degree those of the group rather than uniquely their own. Whereas the egos of Architects I are on more intimate terms with the id, the egos of Architects III are more at home with their superegos. It is not that Architects III experience more conflict than Architects I, but that, whereas Architects I have decided that where id was ego shall be, Architects III have determined that superego shall be where ego might have been. The egos of Architects I are characterized by effective integration of the id, but the egos of Architects III are distinguished by a more marked integration of the superego. Architects III see themselves as men of conscience: 98 per cent of them say they are conscientious; 93 per cent of them also check conscientious when describing the person they would wish to be.

Architects II, by and large less creative than Architects I but more creative than Architects III, show an overlapping of traits with both of the other groups and consequently appear to experience more conflict than either of them. If one takes ego strength as determined by the Minnesota Multiphasic Personality Inventory as a measure of id-ego-superego integration, Architects II are less integrated and in more conflict than Architects I, since they earn a score of 48 as against Architects I's score of 50 on ego strength, a difference in score significant at or beyond the .05 level.

In focusing upon images of the self we have ignored many traits and dispositions which clearly determine the limits within which one is creative. In any complete discussion of the determinants of creativity their role would have to be considered. Yet quite apart from these, the relationships which have been demonstrated between the self-images and creativity of architects stand in their own right as compelling testimony to the dynamic character of the self in determining the person that an individual becomes.

12: EXPLORATIONS IN TYPOLOGY

Morris I. Stein

It was when I was a psychological interne that I first read *Explorations in Personality*.[1] Even before opening the book, two things made immediate and lasting impressions: the book had *Explorations* in the title, and the seal on the jacket with the ever-present whale contained the inscription, "Let not him who seeks cease until he finds, and when he finds he shall be astonished." Then I arrived at the Harvard Psychological Clinic. (Somehow to say "Harvard" alone would be inappropriate, because life centered so much around the yellow house on Plympton Street.) Here at Henry Murray's informal seminars the foundations were laid for my future interests—T.A.T., assessment, and creativity. But, more important, here was the source of stimulation and inspiration for new explorations and new surprises. Henry Murray is thus responsible not for the results of my explorations, but the direction they have taken.

IN DEFENSE OF TYPES

In the spirit of this occasion I would like to present the beginnings of a recent exploration in which Murray's system of needs plays a central role. The venture is concerned with a topic that is currently out of fashion—typologies. Some of the reasons why they are out of fashion relate to the criticism of previously existing typologies. Others relate to the fact that, for the past several decades, psychologists have been trained in emulating the models of the physical sciences and so concern themselves with the relationships between variables. And finally, without attempting to exhaust the list of criticism, typologies are, for some, "undemocratic." Nevertheless, matters of fashion should not be permitted to stand in the way of an exploration.

[1] Henry A. Murray *et al.*, *Explorations in Personality* (New York: Oxford University Press, 1938).

The stimulus for this exploration came out of the following experiences. After completing several studies in which I was concerned with the variables that might differentiate between two groups, it was apparent that the significance of a variable in the context of one personality was somewhat different or even very different from its significance in another context. For example, let us say that need achievement was the differentiating variable. For one individual it may have an aggressive and forceful quality, whereas for another it lacks any compulsive quality and is indeed associated with playfulness and pleasure. An individual's personality is reflected not in his separate motives but in the organization of his motives. Differences of organization become important, especially if one is interested not only in understanding but in predicting behavior and is concerned with the conditions under which certain behaviors will become manifest. One way of coping with this problem is through the fullness of the case study, but this has the disadvantage of being rather cumbersome when one has to deal with large numbers of individuals. Consequently, it seemed that some compromise had to be effected between nomothetic and idiographic approaches.

Another experience that stimulated this exploration was related to assessment. In assessment, where one is concerned with the differences between groups that vary in the degree to which they achieve a criterion or standard of performance, one frequently finds that there are different ways of achieving the same criterion. For example, in differentiating between successful and unsuccessful students, one of the things that often stands out is that there are various pathways to success. One student achieves it by memorizing course content, and another learns and integrates the material. There is no single profile of *the* successful student, just as there is no profile of *the* creative individual. It is probably more accurate to say that regardless of the criterion there are several profiles of the individuals capable of achieving it. Once again, what I have said is not too startling since it is consistent with the principle of equipotentiality.

Let me continue with an observation from another area. In an experimental investigation of efficiency in problem solving, it was apparent that subjects would follow different kinds of approaches.[2] One subject would try to "pull the answer" out of the problem; another would "feel" his way through and appear to trust his intuition in making his decisions; and a third appeared to be hoping that through some random movements he might so manipulate the stimuli that the solution would occur to him—as indeed, for some, it would. From these observations it appeared as if one subject followed the principles of reinforcement, while another followed

[2] Sidney J. Blatt and Morris I. Stein, "Efficiency in Problem Solving," *Journal of Psychology*, XLVIII (1959), 193–213.

the principles of Gestalt psychology. It was also apparent that their behaviors were congruent with the different types of personalities involved, but these differences would not stand out in the final result, where only separate variables were related to the criterion.

The problem is more pervasive. We also encounter it when we survey the various theories of personality and the conflicts between theorists. Some of the diversity and conflict arises because of differences in the types of individuals studied. Maskin points out that "Freud used hysteria as the model for his therapeutic method, depression as the basis for his later theoretical conjectures. Adler's clinical demonstrations are rivalrous, ineffective, immature character types. Jung's examples were restricted to a weary, worldly, successful, middle-aged group. Rank focused upon the conflicted, frustrated, rebellious artist aspirant. Fromm's model is the man in a white collar searching for his individuality. And Sullivan's example of choice is the young catatonic schizophrenic."[3] Types, then, are implicit in our theorizing; might it not be worthwhile to make them explicit and, in doing so, might we not be better able to integrate our knowledge?

TYPES BASED ON SELF-IMAGES

Because of the potential significance a knowledge of types has for both research and theory but with full awareness that types are out of fashion, this exploration was begun. Its aim was to learn whether a typological system based on self-images could satisfy, at least initially, some minimal criteria and whether it could be useful in illuminating some problems that are encountered in applying psychological knowledge. Among the minimal criteria for useful types were the following: they should be internally meaningful and consistent; they should be relatively independent of each other; they should be differentially related to other criteria; and they should have different developmental histories. Assessment methodology was selected to explore the usefulness of types.

The types are based on two different populations. One consists of a group of 116 Ph.D. chemists employed in industrial research organizations. The other is a group of eighty Peace Corps volunteers.

The group of 116 chemists, who were in their mid-thirties and came from three different industrial organizations, participated in a study of creativity. They were divided into three categories. One was a group of men regarded as "more creative" by virtue of the ratings they obtained from their superiors, peers, and subordinates. The second was a group of "less creative" men selected by the same procedure. Both groups represented approximately the upper and lower 20 per cent of the available

[3] Meyer Maskin, "Adaptations of Psychoanalytic Technique in Specific Disorders," in Jules H. Masserman, ed., *Science and Psychoanalysis*, Vol. III: *Psychoanalysis and Human Values* (New York: Grune and Stratton, 1960), pp. 321–352.

chemists in their organizations. There was a "middle group" which remained undefined, and this makes up the third subgroup.

The Peace Corps volunteers consist of a group of eighty young men in their mid-twenties who were assessed for assignment to a newly developing country. All but one of them have some college education, and about half completed college. At the time they applied to the Peace Corps, they had no idea whether they would be accepted, where they would be sent, or what they would do. From the large number who had applied, eighty were screened as acceptable for further training and selection for a community development project. At the conclusion of the training program and the second stage of the screening process, sixty-two men were selected for the project. The men rejected included those who had educational difficulties or personality problems, as judged by the training and assessment staffs. After assessment, the sixty-two selected men were assigned in two-man teams to various communities where, together with a local co-worker, they would work with the local populace in building roads, schools, aqueducts. What is probably more critical, they participate in teaching the villagers how they can better their lot by virtue of their own efforts. These volunteers were studied during the training program and after they had been in the field for six months. They will continue to be studied at periodic intervals in the future.

Both populations were used to investigate the value of typology. Our explorations have not proceeded so far as to enable us to investigate all the same issues with both groups. But with both the chemist and the Peace Corps populations we inquired as to the types of individuals that made them up and the degree to which they were independent of each other. With both groups we were also interested in the relationships between the types and some criterion—creativity for the chemists and effectiveness after a six-month period for the Peace Corps volunteers. In these instances, we were especially interested in learning whether the obtained data would be consistent with the principle of equipotentiality—namely, that different types might be able to achieve the same criterion. With the chemists we inquired further into the relationships between the types and one critical antecedent factor; with the Peace Corps volunteers we inquired into some issues that arise in assessment—the problem of risk in selection and the problem of change over time in the field.

The method for obtaining the information on which the types are based is a self-description questionnaire, consisting of twenty paragraphs, each describing the manifestations of a different need after Murray. It includes the following needs: abasement, achievement, affiliation, aggression, autonomy, blamavoidance, counteraction, defendance, deference, dominance, exhibition, harmavoidance, infavoidance, nurturance, order, play, rejection, sentience, sex, and succorance.[4] The test was initially developed for use with the chemists, and the needs were selected because they were regarded as potential inhibitors or facilitators of creative activity. In responding to the questionnaire, the subject is asked to rank the needs from 1 to 20, from the one which is most descriptive of himself (rank of 1) to the one which is least descriptive (rank of 20).

As I have said in discussing the problems that stimulated this exploration, the functional significance of a need is dependent on the context in which it appears. It is the ranking procedure just described which makes it possible to highlight individual organizational systems. Previously I gave the example of two types of achievements—one with an aggressive and the other with a playful component. These differentiations are possible when, in one ranking, need achievement and aggression appear close together and, in the other, they are not only far apart but play is ranked close to achievement. A ranking procedure is also consistent with Murray's theoretical formulations in which he points out how needs may fuse with each other or may be subsidiary to one another. This condition might not be satisfied with other theoretical frameworks.

The potential significance of the questionnaire is based on the assumption that the picture an individual has of himself will have an effect on how he will behave. It also assumes that the twenty different needs are shared by all individuals to a greater or lesser extent and that the needs may be manifest in a variety of ways. It is further assumed that individuals vary in their need hierarchy. Theoretically, there are many ways of ranking the twenty paragraphs and many patterns are possible, although I shall consider only the nine types found in our data.

The questionnaires were administered separately to the two groups. The individual rankings of all subjects were intercorrelated in each group, and separate Q-analyses were computed. The principal components of each of the intercorrelation matrices were extracted and rotated via the Varimax method to yield simple structures. The data for the chemists yielded a five-factor solution, and the data for the Peace Corps population a four-factor solution. To arrive at a picture of the types, subjects who loaded highest on each of the factors were selected as type definers, and their mean ranking of the needs was used in establishing the need hierarchy for the type. In the chemist population 78 out of the 116 men were type-definers (26 for Type A, 16 for Type B, 13 each for Types C and D, and 10 for Type E). Out of the eighty Peace Corps volunteers, forty-six

---

[4] The descriptive paragraph for need abasement, as an example, is: "I passively submit to external forces. I accept injury, blame, criticism, and punishment. I surrender. I am resigned to fate. I admit my inferiorities, errors, wrong-doings, or defeats. I blame myself."

TABLE 1

NEED HIERARCHIES AMONG THE FIVE TYPES
FOUND IN THE CHEMIST POPULATION

Type A	Type B	Type C	Type D	Type E
Achievement	Affiliation	Achievement	Achievement	Achievement
Affiliation	Blamavoidance	Counteraction	Affiliation	Counteraction
Play	Counteraction	Autonomy	Counteraction	Affiliation
Counteraction	Order	Aggression	Order	Autonomy
Sentience	Achievement	Dominance	Nurturance	Nurturance
Dominance	Deference	Defendance	Defendance	Order
Order	Infavoidance	Rejection	Dominance	Sentience
Exhibition	Harmavoidance	Order	Exhibition	Sex
Autonomy	Nurturance	Affiliation	Autonomy	Succorance
Sex	Play	Sex	Deference	Deference
Deference	Defendance	Harmavoidance	Aggression	Dominance
Nurturance	Autonomy	Infavoidance	Play	Defendance
Harmavoidance	Abasement	Play	Harmavoidance	Infavoidance
Defendance	Sentience	Exhibition	Succorance	Blamavoidance
⌈Aggression ⌉*	Sex	Blamavoidance	Infavoidance	Play
⌊Infavoidance⌋	Succorance	Sentience	Blamavoidance	Rejection
Rejection	Exhibition	Succorance	Sentience	Aggression
Blamavoidance	Rejection	Deference	Rejection	Abasement
Succorance	Dominance	Nurturance	Abasement	Harmavoidance
Abasement	Aggression	Abasement	Sex	Exhibition

* The bracketed needs represent ties.

were type-definers (19 in Type I, 12 in Type II, 10 in Type III, and 5 in Type IV). Since the order in which the needs appear in tables 1 and 2 are based on the absolute values of the needs within types, one must be cautioned that in comparing types a need may appear in the same ordinal position, although its absolute value may be different in each instance.[5]

[5] A more complete presentation of the statistical analysis is reserved for another communication.

TABLE 2

NEED HIERARCHIES AMONG THE FOUR TYPES
FOUND IN THE PEACE CORPS POPULATION

Type I	*Type II*	*Type III*	*Type IV*
Affiliation	Affiliation	Achievement	Nurturance
Nurturance	Achievement	Affiliation	Play
Counteraction	Sentience	Counteraction	Sex
Achievement	Sex	Dominance	Affiliation
Deference	Autonomy	Nurturance	Autonomy
Sex	Counteraction	Order	⌈ Sentience ⌉ *
Order	Nurturance	Exhibition	⌊ Succorance ⌋
Succorance	Play	Sex	Exhibition
Blamavoidance	Dominance	Deference	Counteraction
Play	Rejection	Defendance	Order
Dominance	Succorance	Play	Abasement
Harmavoidance	Order	⌈ Aggression ⌉ *	Defendance
Infavoidance	Deference	⌊ Autonomy ⌋	Deference
Sentience	Blamavoidance	Sentience	Dominance
Exhibition	⌈ Harmavoidance ⌉ *	Rejection	Infavoidance
Defendance	⌊ Defendance ⌋	Succorance	Achievement
Autonomy	Aggression	Harmavoidance	Blamavoidance
Rejection	Infavoidance	Abasement	Harmavoidance
Abasement	Exhibition	Infavoidance	Aggression
Aggression	Abasement	Blamavoidance	Rejection

* The bracketed needs represent ties.

In each population, eighteen needs were found to differentiate significantly among the types by analysis of variance. To condense the data and to investigate which of the needs contribute most to the uniqueness of the type, the average ranking of a need in one type was compared with its average ranking in all other types, for a total of thirty-six comparisons. Only those needs were then retained for which there were differences of one standard deviation or more in twelve or more comparisons. This analysis yielded twelve critical needs: nurturance, deference, autonomy, aggression, blamavoidance, sentience, play, sex, dominance, achievement, exhibition, and succorance. The intercorrelations of the ranks for each of the types were calculated to investigate the degree of resemblance between types both within and between populations. Within populations there is a great deal of independence. The highest intercorrelation among the chemist types was .41, and among the Peace Corps types it was .45. Higher intercorrelations were obtained between populations, and if one selects a correlation of .80 as a criterion of identity, then it might be said that two types (II and E) are subtypes of a larger type.

TYPES AMONG INDUSTRIAL CHEMISTS

The type descriptions focus on the dynamic interrelationships between the needs, but they should be regarded with caution, for at the moment they are tentative. Complete and thorough descriptions will be possible only after more intensive study. It should be remembered, furthermore, that the type descriptions are based on self-descriptive data and hence refer to self-images; whether and to what extent these self-images are consistent with other types of personality data is an issue that will not be dealt with here. In writing these descriptions we were, however, aided by some knowledge of several individuals who were type-definers and by experience with the questionnaire administered to persons who had also taken rather complete batteries of clinical tests. To avoid the problem of "freezing" their identities in terms that might become clichés, the types are not named. As has been indicated above, the types found among the chemists are identified by letters, and those among the Peace Corps volunteers by Roman numerals.

Type A

The individuals who compose this type are achievement-oriented. But their ambitions and aspirations are not so intense that they overlook interpersonal relationships. They like to be with others and enjoy cooperating with them. They trust others and in turn are loyal to their friends. Although they may want to please others and win their affection, they are not inclined to be submissive nor are they inclined to avoid situations in which they might lose the love of others. Although their social relationships are obviously not without warmth, they are not likely to become involved with others by showing intense sympathy, nor is it very characteristic of this group to go out of its way to support or comfort others. When the occasion demands, members of this type can be critical of others without feeling that they have to be unduly sensitive to others' feelings. By the same token, members of this type do not look to other people for advice, guidance, and emotional support. Indeed, this type ranks need succorance lower than do any of our eight other types.[6] Although it is uncharacteristic of individuals of this type to submit passively to external forces and to surrender or resign to fate, they are not insistent upon expressing their autonomous strivings. They can accept restrictions and probably effect compromises. Among the other characteristics of persons in this group is the fact that they appear capable of accepting their libidinal strivings, and that their aggressive needs appear to be under integrative control. Unlike our other types of creative individuals but like Type IV among the Peace Corps population, the men of Type A can do things for fun and without purpose. They enjoy play and relaxation. They like to laugh, they are easygoing, and can be lighthearted and merry. These men also seek out and enjoy sensuous impressions and aesthetic feelings. Possibly it is this combination of need play and need sentience which gives the impression that members of this type may be characterized as open to new experiences. They can selectively filtrate the most important factors from these experiences and so maintain mastery and control of their environments in an orderly and organized fashion which is more flexible than constricting. All this is not to say that members of this type are without anxieties. Although the sources of their anxieties are not clear and although they may not experience very intense anxiety, it is conceivable that they may become anxious when their freedom is interfered with or when they find themselves lacking in resources to solve the problems that confront them.

Type B

The men in this group find it most important to please others and win their affection. Such behavior comes at the cost of their own spontaneity. They are so insecure that they will seek out many relationships and not be discriminating in their choice of friends. They will avoid situations in which they might lose others' love or in which they might be blamed for their actions. They are not likely to be assertive, forceful, or severe with others. Indeed, they have difficulty in dealing with their aggressive feelings. This type ranks blamavoidance higher and aggression and dominance lower than any of the other eight types. They strive to be inoffensive by avoiding hurting other people's feelings and by striving to overcome their own weaknesses. In social relationships they are likely to appear apprehensive and inhibited. Although they try to maintain their self-respect at a high level, they seem to be lacking in internal sources of evaluation. They probably function best in well-structured situations where they can tell what is required of them. These requirements they will try to fulfill in a

[6] In a description of a type, the term "lower" refers to a rank that is closer to the least descriptive end of the continuum (toward a rank of 20) and the term "higher" refers to the most descriptive end of the continuum (toward a rank of 1).

reasonable but not necessarily outstanding fashion, for their drive to succeed is not very strong. Nor are they likely to stray far from what they know, since doing so might expose their inadequacies and possibly make them vulnerable to attack.

Type C

This type, like Type A, is also achievement-oriented. But, unlike a man in Type A who combines achievement with affiliation and play, a man in Type C is more driven, and his ambition has a more hostile quality about it. He ranks aggression higher than do any of the other eight types. Achievement may be so important to him that, when he fails in an undertaking, he returns to master it and so to demonstrate that he has few, if any, weaknesses or that he will not allow fears to stand in his way. In this sense, he may be both counteractive and counterphobic. He will be inclined to be defensive, on his guard against criticism, and argumentative in support of his own position. He is likely to perceive others as obstacles to be removed, ignored, or surpassed. He is critical and discriminating in his choice of friends, and he may well be inclined to be snobbish, disgusted, and bored with other people, rather than comforting and supportive. He ranks need nurturance lower than any of the eight other types and therefore is likely to reject others whom he regards as inferior. Because his autonomous needs are high, he is not one to bow to custom or conform to tradition. He likes to dominate situations, and he prides himself on being free and acting according to impulse. The impulses he expresses are likely to be aggressive ones. He is prone to conflict with his superiors, for he does not necessarily respect them; and he is unlikely to fulfill their requests unless he believes they foster his own ends. In this regard he is more extreme than our other types, for he ranks need deference lower than all of them. As one studies the hierarchy of needs within this type, one cannot help but gain the impression that men in this type are compensating for inferiorities and weaknesses.

Type D

The first three needs of this type are achievement, affiliation, and counteraction. Unlike Type C, however, the achievement of a man in this type is not colored by intense personal pressures; and unlike Type A, his achievement is not characterized by playfulness or enjoyment. Indeed, this type is not inclined to express his libidinous strivings. He ranks need sentience and need sex lower than do the other eight types. For a man in this group, there seems to be a moral commitment to work. In his work as in his other habits he is likely to be neat and precise, and he enjoys arranging and organizing things. Such emphasis on order protects him from criticism and blame. Members of this type do not see themselves as giving in to external forces easily. Rather, they view themselves as controlling their environments just as they control themselves. Men in this type will work together with others in a cooperative enterprise, taking more satisfaction in the efficient accomplishment of a task, however, than in the sharing of feelings. These men are inclined to help others who need their aid. And, on such occasions, one has the impression that their aid stems more from an ethical code than from compassionate feeling. One also has the impression that they have incorporated the values of others rather than finding their own, and those which they have accepted they seek to perpetuate. An individual in this type accepts "the tried and the true," and when he does occasionally venture forth on his own, he does not deviate markedly from the *status quo*. Finally, should anyone frustrate this man's style of life, it is likely that his equanimity will be disturbed and the aggression that was previously channeled into work will be provoked.

Type E

A man of this type is achievement-oriented as are the men in Types A, C, and D. However, whereas Type A has a playful attitude in his achievement orientation and desires positions in which he can be dominant, Type E has little need to be the center of things so long as he is free to do what he wants. In contrast to Type C, who is primarily concerned with his own goals and regards others as sources of frustration, Type E is both more affiliative and more nurturant. And, whereas Type D pursues his goals by checking out the tried and the true, Type E is more inclined to accept his own hunches. Type E differs from all types (including those just mentioned) by placing more emphasis on resisting coercion and restrictions. The members of this type avoid relationships in which they might be dominated; rather, they prefer relationships which are marked by cooperation and trust. They are sympathetic persons; they will help others and not dominate them. They regard themselves as independent and free to act according to their impulses. In satisfying their impulses, however, they will not be exhibitionistic. Indeed, they rank need exhibition lower than do any of the other types. Furthermore, in being independent there is something of a serious or stable cast to their activities, for they rank need play lower than do all of the other types. Although a man in Type E is fairly well organized, the order he achieves does not stem from any attempt to impose structure on his environment, but rather from his capacity to "sense" and "feel" his environment. He enjoys these experiences and does not hesitate to follow his impressions.

These, then, are the five types we found among our 116 chemists. If they are meaningful and useful, then we should say that they differ on a variety of characteristics other than those covered by the twenty needs.

Such an investigation is currently under way, but I shall limit myself here to several points relating the types to creativity.

It will be recalled that the 116 chemists were made up of three sub-groups. One was a group of "more creative" men $(N = 31)$, the second was a group of "less creative" men $(N = 34)$, and the third or middle group $(N = 51)$ was undefined. Judgments of "more" and "less" creativity were based on ratings obtained from the men's superiors, colleagues, and subordinates. Since our type-definers in the chemist population do not include all persons studied, we also find a decrease in the number of "more" and "less" creative individuals among our type-definers. The data indicate that among the type definers there are twenty-three more creative and twenty-five less creative individuals.

The first question we may ask is how are these persons distributed among the types. We find that more and less creative men appear in all types, which is consistent with the principle of equipotentiality. Of the twenty-three more creative men, 48 per cent are of Type A, 9 per cent of Type B, 34 per cent equally divided between Types C and D, and 9 per cent of Type E. Of the less creative men, 16 per cent are of Type A, 36 per cent of Type B, 12 per cent of Type C, 24 per cent of Type D and 12 per cent of Type E. Thus, the largest proportion of more creative men appears in Type A, and the largest proportion of less creative men appears in Type B. Type A also yields a larger ratio of more creative to less creative individuals. In all the other types combined there are almost equal proportions of more and less creative subjects $(x^2 = 7.84, p < .02)$.

In a further analysis of the data, all 116 chemists were categorized by creativity status ("more," "less," and undefined) as well as by their relative loadings on Factors A and B. Analysis of these data indicated that a significantly larger proportion of "more" creative individuals were among those men whose factor loadings were above the median on Factor A and below the median on Factor B, whereas a larger proportion of "less" creative individuals showed the reverse pattern $(x^2 = 18.45, p = < .01)$. Thus, we find a differential relationship between the types and an important aspect of behavior.

Another criterion of the meaningfulness of types is that they should be related to antecedent data and biographical information. There is much biographical information that we have on the types, which will be analyzed in the future. At present, we should like to present data on only one aspect of parent-child interaction for the two types, A and B, on which we have most data.

In attempting to understand how "more creative" individuals develop, we investigated the possibility that they were exposed to complexity early in life. One source of early complexity is the extent to which the subject perceived the mother as inconsistent in relation to himself. It was assumed that an inconsistent mother might be frustrating to the child and that the child, to structure his own environment or to satisfy his needs, would be thrown more onto his own resources than a child reared in a consistent environment; and that this experience of using his own resources would stand him in good stead in future creative work. Obviously, one kind of experience alone would be insufficient to develop a "more creative" adult. Other conditions must also exist, but first it would be necessary to establish the importance of inconsistency.

To gather the necessary data, a questionnaire entitled "Interpersonal Relations in Childhood" was utilized. In this questionnaire subjects were asked to rate on a 7-point scale the degree of consistency or inconsistency they recall having perceived in their mother. The item read, "As a child I felt my mother was," and then the rating was to be indicated on a continuum that ranged from "very consistent" to "very inconsistent."

When the data for all the "more" $(N = 31)$ and all the "less" $(N = 34)$ creative men among the 116 chemists were analyzed, it was found that the former did indeed regard their mothers as less consistent $(H = 5.04, p = <.05)$. Consequently, if inconsistency of the mother was related to creativity status, it should also differentiate between the Type A and Type B groups. Here we find a trend in the direction of the hypothesis. The Type A group does tend to rate their mothers as less consistent than does the Type B group $(H = 2.65, 10 > p > .05)$.

It was previously indicated that Types A and B differ in their relationships to creativity status. Let us now ask what is there about the A typological vector that enables individuals who load heavily on this factor to be regarded as "more creative" and what is there about the B typological vector that would limit or restrict creative activity? For the discussion of these relationships it must be borne in mind that both "more" and "less" creative groups conduct their activities in industrial research environments where they must fulfill scientific, professional, administrative, employee, and social roles.[7] Placed in this context it soon becomes apparent that the groups are differently disposed to fulfilling their various roles, and in what follows are several suggestions that will be investigated in the future.

A Type A person, oriented to achievement and willing to cooperate with others, appears well suited to carry out his activities within the organized social system of an industrial laboratory. The fact that he trusts others probably aids him in communication. He can accept information from others and at the same time discuss his own ideas and findings with them, so that he might profit from constructive criticism. At the same time, he is not an abasive individual; he does not submit to others and probably

[7] Morris I. Stein, "The Roles of the Industrial Researcher" (unpublished).

does not passively accept others' ideas, for he has internalized criteria for reacting to and evaluating problems. It is this same lack of submissiveness which is probably involved in his capacity to question existing data and theories. In pursuing the unknown and seeking novel accomplishments he is further aided by the fact that need play is rather high. He can engage in activities that have no immediate purpose and so can break down existing *Gestalten* into their component parts, which he studies to see how they can, through some reintegrative process, be developed into new and useful ideas. In this activity, he is also aided by his aesthetic sensitivity, which enables him to differentiate between the unnecessary or irrelevant and so arrive at more elegant solutions to problems. His behavior is goal-directed. He is not oriented to avoiding situations or being blamed for his actions; he is confident in what he does and not bothered by the ambiguity generated when an existing structure is disrupted. The fact that he is capable of impulse acceptance suggests that internal boundaries are relatively flexible, and thus they may be capable of "regression in service of the ego."[8] He is probably motivated in his search for novelty to demonstrate his mastery and control of his environment, and what he generates in this regard he presents to others in a forceful and masterful fashion. Finally, he can assume positions of leadership where he is responsible for the activities of others.

Type A, characterized by striving and internal freedom which appear well organized and purposeful, seems to be capable of fulfilling the scientific, professional, administrative, and social roles in the industrial research organization. Members of this type would probably have difficulty, however, in fulfilling the employee role.

By contrast to Type A, consider Type B and his capacity to fulfill the role requirements. Type B appears to lack the freedom and spontaneity to disrupt existing products, processes, and ideas. Being more oriented to avoidant behavior, he is likely to find his security in what exists and will not deviate markedly from what confronts him. Consequently, he will encounter problems in fulfilling both the scientific and professional roles. In these roles he will be further incapacitated by the emphasis men of this type place on people rather than objects, theories, and ideas. Both in working on his research and in the fulfillment of the administrative role, he will encounter problems because he finds it difficult to be assertive. He might produce creative products if he were a member of a team in which another individual offered many ideas from which he could select one tenable and worthy of testing. Even under such circumstances he would require reassurance, probably frequently, that what he had done was appropriate. After several such experiences a man of this type might be

[8] Ernst Kris, *Psychoanalytic Explorations in Art* (New York: International Universities Press, 1952).

able to go off on his own, provided he still had a supportive environment. In view of his emphasis on affiliation, his low need rejection, his blam-avoidant attitude, and his desire to make up for his shortcomings, a man of this type seems to be better suited for the fulfillment of social and employee roles.

There are too few men in Types C, D, and E to allow for much discussion. However, some speculation, which may lead to hypotheses for future test, is in order. Further study of the men in Type C may indicate that they may have difficulty fitting into an organizational framework. Their needs autonomy, aggression, and dominance may handicap them in relating to others. The intensity of their behavior also suggests that creative members of this type may "burn themselves out before their time." One might also venture the hypothesis that this group, under periods of stress, may experience psychosomatic ailments. These individuals are likely to be more capable of dealing with ideas and thus are better oriented to fulfilling the scientific role, but they will chafe at the bit when they have to fulfill social and employee roles. They will likely "drive" their subordinates and so have problems with the administrative role. And, finally, they may have difficulty in taking orders from their superiors.

Type D, with his emphasis on achievement, affiliation, order, and nurturance, may find the administrative role most to his liking. In addition, he will probably tolerate and not too grudgingly acquiesce to the employee and social roles. But, because his needs dominance and exhibition are high, he hopes not to stay in the confinement of these two roles for very long but to rise in the organization. He is well organized and probably good at translating scientific data to the company client. He lacks, however, the spontaneous and "creative" spark in the fulfillment of scientific and professional roles that is evident in Type A. It may be hypothesized that those of Type D who are regarded as creative have achieved their novel products and processes through problem solving or a trial-and-error approach.

The men of Type E will be aided in fulfilling the scientific and professional roles by their emphasis on achievement, autonomy, and their aesthetic attitude. They will also be able to fulfill the social role but are likely to get too involved with people because their needs affiliation and nurturance are rather high. This consideration would also affect them if they were in administrative positions. However, they may have difficulty in attaining these positions, since they are not very dominant or exhibition-istic. In all likelihood, it may be that they can achieve such positions in research organizations, where their superiors look for people who have valuable ideas but are not likely to push themselves forward.

These, then, are some speculations as to how and why the types may manifest differential effectiveness in fulfilling their roles, and especially why the men of Type A may be better disposed to creative activity in industrial research organizations than are members of other types.

There are several other aspects of the relationship between creativity status and typology that should not be overlooked. As was pointed out previously, the data indicate that there is no single psychological picture of *the* individual who is regarded as more creative; more creative persons appear in all types. Future research may bring to light the different processes these individuals follow in producing novelty. Moreover, being of a type (at least insofar as self-images are concerned) does not guarantee that an individual will produce creative products. The type indicates only that individuals who make it up may possess some of the necessary conditions for creativity. There is much more to be considered about the individual and about the transactions between the individual and his environment before completely accurate predictions can be made.[9]

The data also indicated that *within* a type one finds both "more" and "less" creative individuals. This, again, may be a function of many factors. At the moment, inspection of the similarities and differences between individuals within a type suggests that the less creative individuals may be positive or negative exaggerations of the critical features of the type, or they may be conflicted about the type they represent. With regard to the matter of conflict, one must bear in mind that the types relate to self-images. Thus, it is conceivable that an individual may try to be of a type of self-image but have difficulty in carrying it off. Stating this point differently, it is suggested that in a "pure" type there is internal dynamic equilibrium. Those who are not of a pure type may be under strain. To investigate this point further, it would be critical to have additional clinical data on the types and especially to investigate the behavior of individuals who are congruent or incongruent with regard to typologies based on both clinical data and self-images.

For a typological system to have significance, as we pointed out earlier, it has to satisfy certain criteria. Thus far, utilizing the data of "more" and "less" creative individuals it has been possible to show that the types are independent and meaningfully related to significant aspects of behavior. For at least two of them it was also pointed out that they tend to differ on a critical developmental variable. Finally, several hypotheses were suggested that require further investigation.

TYPES AMONG PEACE CORPS VOLUNTEERS

The final criterion for our types is that they must enable us to cope

[9] Morris I. Stein, "A Transactional Approach to Creativity," in C. W. Taylor, ed., *The 1955 University of Utah Research Conference on the Identification of Creative Scientific Talent* (Salt Lake City: University of Utah Press, 1956), pp. 171–181.

better with certain research problems. The problems on which it is hoped that they will cast light are in the area of assessment.

Assessment may be regarded as composed of two major phases, diagnostic and predictive. In the diagnostic phase one seeks to learn as much as one can about the individual. Using this information and, where possible, knowledge of the situation in which the individual will be placed, the assessor then attempts to predict how well the individual will perform. The prediction is not a probability statement but is first manifest in the individuals accepted and rejected and is later checked by field data. The predictive aspect is actually the risk-taking part of the assessment process. One of the problems in assessment is to know which individuals are the risks and, if they are, whether the risk is worth taking. Another problem in assessment arises after an individual has been selected for an undertaking: to what extent will he change as a result of his new experiences and in what direction will these changes occur?

The assessment of the Peace Corps volunteers provided an opportunity to investigate these problems. It will be recalled that these volunteers were a group of young men who were screened from a much larger group as having the potential for work in a newly developing country. Final decisions as to who would go overseas were made at the end of a training period. Not all those accepted for training were selected for overseas duty, so that it was possible to use acceptance-rejection rates as reflections of risk. Furthermore, since data are available on the men after they had been in the field for six months, it has been possible to inquire whether these risks were worth taking. Finally, some of the field data may also be used to learn something about the changes that have taken place in the men.

It should be pointed out that the self-description questionnaire was administered to the men at the beginning of their training and that it figured very little, if at all, in the assessment proceedings. A Q-analysis of the data yielded four types. The average rankings of these types appear in Table 2 and the description of each of them follows.

Type I

The individual in this type appears to be dedicated to other people. He enjoys being with and working with other people. In doing so, he finds greatest satisfaction in assisting helpless individuals and in supporting, comforting, and protecting others. The average rank for need nurturance in this type is higher than for all other types. A man of this type is sympathetic. He avoids hurting others and he will not be critical or severe in his interpersonal relationships. For him, need aggression is his lowest need. Compared to the others we studied, a person of this type is lowest on autonomy and highest on deference. Consequently, he appears to be one who is relatively lacking in independence. He can be dominated by others and is likely to accept restrictions placed on his behavior. Indeed, he will strive to conform to others' wishes; when he knows what they want, he will try to fulfill their requests.

Type II

Members of this type also enjoy being with people and working with them. Unlike members of Type I, however, they place greater emphasis on need achievement. In striving to attain their goals, these men are likely to follow internal frames of reference. They believe they know what is best. They want to follow their own inclinations and in so doing would be inclined to come into conflict with authority. They are sensitive, aware of both internal needs and external stimuli. Compared to the other three types, they are more likely to seek out and enjoy sensuous impressions and to enjoy aesthetic feelings. Their average rank for need sentience is higher than for the three other types. But, since need order appears low in their hierarchy of needs, they may find themselves frustrated in utilizing their aesthetic impressions constructively. Left to their own devices, members of this type are likely to leave a situation which is not to their liking, rather than cope with the difficulties they encounter, and to seek a new environment which will give them greater satisfaction. The need hierarchy for this type correlates most highly with Type E in the chemist population. Type II differs from Type E in that he is more likely to give in to impulse expression and is lower on control features than Type E.

Type III

An individual of this type aims to get things accomplished. He enjoys working with others, but it is most important to him to be in control of the situation. Compared to the three other types, the average rank for need achievement and need dominance is highest in this type. A man of this type sees himself as confident and likes to influence others, but at the same time he is aware of others' needs and can be quite nurturant and sympathetic. He is inclined to be systematic in what he does and to accept responsibility. He is not likely to avoid situations because he might be blamed for his actions. Compared to the three other types, average rank for need blamavoidance is lowest in this type. A man of this type gives higher priority to fulfilling goals than to satisfying his impulse life. When he does satisfy his impulses, he will do so in a socially acceptable and approved manner, rarely overindulging himself, for he would not like to appear inferior. He gives the impression that he will strive to be upright and sincere in whatever he does by following a code that he has been taught.

Type IV

The top ranking need of this type is nurturance. A person in this group enjoys going to the aid of helpless individuals with whom he can be supporting and comforting. Compared to the other types of individuals, the average rank for need achievement in this group is lowest. For a member of this type, need nurturance serves the function of finding other individuals with whom he can share experiences in which impulse needs were frustrated and perhaps also the function of staving off any restriction or punishment that he might encounter for indulging his impulse needs. Need play and need sex are not only ranked high within this type but the average ranks on these needs are higher than for any other type. A man of this type is not very discriminating in his interpersonal relationships, for rejection is his lowest ranked need. Indeed, a member of this group likes to have others around him so that he can be seen and heard, can entertain and amuse. In this he also differs from the other types for, on the average, he ranks need exhibition higher than they do. At the same time, he also needs others to provide him with affection and tenderness. In this too he differs from the other types, for his average rank for need succorance is higher than the others. He will seek out others who will provide him with sympathetic understanding and possibly some direction and leadership, but not domination, for this man prides himself in not being abasive or submissive to others. He is not very well organized, for he sees organization as coercive and does not see order as allowing for freedom. Nor is he an achieving person for, compared to the other types, his average rank for need achievement is lowest. He gives the impression that he regards himself as a free soul who would be just as happy to see others go their own way too. Underneath it all he may be thankful that others are more organized, because it is through their presence that he can go off and satisfy his own impulses. Finally, if others are kindly disposed toward him and provide him with leadership in a permissive atmosphere, he will under these conditions be able to develop and achieve goals.

These, then, are the four types we found among the eighty men who were accepted for further training and selection. Let us now turn to the several questions to which we sought answers. The major question of risk is broken down into three subquestions: If an individual is of a type, what are the probabilities that he will be accepted for overseas duty? Do their anticipated problems differ from those actually experienced in the field? How effective are these types in the field? With regard to the second major question of change we inquired whether changes appeared in the men's values—specifically, authoritarian values. Answers to these questions would contribute to a better understanding of assessment procedures and some of the difficulties usually encountered therein.

It will be recalled that the type analysis was based on eighty men, forty-six of whom were type definers. The largest number of type definers (nineteen) were categorized as Type I, and approximately 80 per cent, or fifteen, were accepted. Type II contains the second largest group of type definers (twelve) ; half of them were accepted and half rejected. Ten men were categorized as Type III, and all were accepted. Finally, Type IV contains five men, three of whom were accepted and two rejected. In other words, if a man was of Type I or III, the probabilities were good that he would be accepted for overseas duty. However, if he was of Types II or IV, the probabilities were about equal that he would be accepted or rejected.

If one assumes a relationship between the self-images of these types and behavior during training and interview, then it is likely that members of Type I impressed the assessment staff with their affiliative and nurturant needs and the likelihood that they would be most congruent with the service orientation of the Peace Corps. Type III may have impressed the assessors with his confidence and assertiveness and the likelihood that he would be action-oriented and capable of implementing the Peace Corps program. Types II and IV may have presented more serious problems. Compared with the other types, Types II and IV rank needs related to impulse-life higher and they appear to be less socialized, less directed, and less likely to fit in with requests for conforming behavior. Since these individuals are more self-directed and given to basic need satisfaction, they do pose serious problems when one has to predict their behavior in situations about which one has relatively little information. The question is, however, was the decision to accept or reject Types II and IV made solely on the basis of whether or not the self-directed aspect of their personalities came through during the interview situation? This question we are unable to answer at the present time.

The type analysis has so far highlighted the question of potential risk for overseas duty. We shall later present data that will tell us whether these risks were worth taking. But let us first inquire into the difficulties the men said they experienced after they had been in the field for six months.

During the training period in the United States the volunteers were presented with a check list on which they could indicate the intensity with which they anticipated problems in the field (lonesomeness, living in a strange surrounding, etc.). After they had been in the field for six months, the group was asked to indicate the degree to which it had actually experienced these same difficulties. On the first administration of the test, Type I anticipates most difficulty, Types III and IV follow, and Type II anticipates least difficulty. On the second administration of the check list, after a six-month period in the field, the data of Types I, III and IV stay relatively the same; there is no appreciable change between the intensity of their anticipated and experienced problems. However, the one type that shows the largest increase in intensity between anticipated and experienced problems is Type II ($t = 3.29$, $p = <.05$). Furthermore, the discrepancy indicates that this type of individual may underestimate the problems he might encounter in the field. These data also support the previous point that men of Type II are among the greater risks. However, the fact that a man is a risk may or may not be related to his effectiveness in the field, as we shall see.

To obtain a global measure of effectiveness in the field after a six-month period, ratings were collected from the men's supervisors on a seven-point scale ranging from 0 for "very poor" to 6 for "outstanding." A minimum of three ratings was available for each man. Analysis of the data indicates that the average (median) effectiveness ratings for Types I and III, the "least risk" types, were lower (2.75 and 2.58, respectively) than the effectiveness ratings for Types II and IV (3.25 and 4.00, respectively). Although these differences are not statistically significant, the trend is in favor of the greater risk types. One wonders, therefore, whether the Types II and IV who were rejected might not have been worthy candidates for overseas assignment.[10]

The last question to which we turn is, what kinds of people change while in the field and, if they do change, in what direction. An answer to this question would obviously be of value to areas other than assessment. It would be applicable to studies in therapy and to studies investigating the effects of education. In this exploration we investigated the change in values. Specifically, we inquired into the change of F-scale scores for our population of Peace Corps volunteers over a period of six months. The brief version of the F-scale, developed by Daniel J. Levinson, was administered both during training and in the field to all available Peace Corps volunteers, and the intercorrelation between the two administrations was .82. A regression equation was calculated, and the deviation between a man's actual score on the second administration and his expected score was obtained. Analysis of these data indicated that compared to all other groups Type III changes most from what one would expect. And, unlike the other three types which tend to obtain lower F-scale scores after their field experience, members of Type III tend to obtain higher F-scale scores than one would expect.

It will be recalled from the descriptions of the Peace Corps types that Type III differed from the others in several important respects. Their

[10] Inspection of other data on the relationships among types, difficulty of assignment, and over-all effectiveness of those volunteers already in the field suggests that, in future research, we may learn more about the overseas conditions under which the rejected Types II and IV might have been effective.

average ranks for needs achievement and dominance were higher and their average ranks for needs play and sex were lower than those found in other types. In a sense, the men of Type III are more forceful and more action-oriented than the other persons studied. When such individuals confront a situation in which they have to wait patiently for the development of results, is it not possible that they would think how much more they could accomplish if they could have more control and be more authoritarian? Might this not also change their value system? We hope to learn more about these individuals when they are revisited and we shall be especially interested in learning whether their reactions were short-lived or whether the early changes were reinforced.

Summarizing the assessment study, it may be said that the typological analysis has highlighted those men who are potential risks and the reasons why they might be so. It has also suggested that some of these risks might have been worth taking. And, finally, it has been helpful in studying problems of change.

CONCLUSION

This completes the description of our exploration to date. As in all explorations, one cannot tell where it will finally lead. For the moment, at least, it has been helpful in integrating a body of data and in illuminating some problems. It has been possible to provide tentative descriptions of individuals, based on the dynamic interrelationships between their needs. These descriptions provide a more meaningful basis for differentiating among individuals than is provided when one focuses solely on the discrete variables on which they differ and so loses sight of the persons involved. By bringing to light the varieties of individuals who can achieve the same criterion, our exploration has cautioned us against the errors that arise from being inconsistent with the principle of equipotentiality. Finally, not only has our exploration been helpful in clarifying some problems in assessment procedures, but it has also furthered our understanding of individuals who are involved in two types of cultural change.

There is still much to be done. There is still the need to explore whether the types we found differ in behavioral characteristics other than those we considered; and there is still the need to investigate the relationships between types based on self-images and those based on other personality data. Should our efforts continue to be meaningful and productive, one cannot help wondering if they might not also be useful in other areas. Is it not possible that we could further our understanding of human behavior if we explored how different types of individuals learn, perceive, solve problems, etc.? No doubt there is much reluctance to consider typologies in the light of history, and no doubt it may be impossible to meet all the desirable criteria for a typological system.[11] Avoidance of these problems, however, not only delays the development of a classification system that would foster progress in personality research, as it has in other sciences; but it also delays the integration of available knowledge. As we continue our efforts in understanding man, let us not overlook the varieties of men.[12]

[11] Isidor Chein, "Personality and Typology," *Journal of Social Psychology*, XVIII (1943), 89–109.

[12] Parts of this research were supported by the Carnegie Corporation and by the Peace Corps. I am grateful to John Neulinger, I. Chein, S. Schachter, and J. Colmen for their critical reactions and suggestions.

13: THE RECONSTRUCTION OF THE INDIVIDUAL AND OF THE COLLECTIVE PAST

Frederick Wyatt

When the paradoxes of intellectual history are considered, the alienation of psychology from history should be given a prominent place. Psychologists might explain this alienation by saying that psychology has a long past but a short history. It has little investment in history (they might expound) and so does not care very much for it. But as we move into the second century of acknowledged psychology, this argument no longer holds up. More likely, the lack of interest in its own history reflects a limitation characteristic of the orientation of modern psychology. With a few notable exceptions, it has stayed away from subjects for which its methods are unsuitable, the historical determination of human conduct being one of them. It would not be incorrect, therefore, to say that history as a dimension of human experience has little range in present-day psychology, which is interested in its own history only in a desultory fashion, as a polite gesture to the grandfathers, so to speak.[1] If judged by publications, psychology would appear to have no perception of the significance of universal history for the understanding of present-day conduct—nor, simply, of how much psychology there is in history.

On a more general plane we may also have to ask why various disciplines prefer to concentrate on favorite approaches and methods, thereby barring other possibly fruitful ways of looking at the same thing. History, for instance, could profit from the specifics of psychology; psychology from the broad perspectives of history.[2] On a still more universal level we shall finally have to consider the naïve objectivity which dominates all scientific efforts at a certain stage. In the early phases of scientific development everything observed is regarded as an indigenous part of the objects under

[1] A change in this condition is in the offing thanks to the efforts of men like A. B. Carlson (editor of the recently created "Newsletter for the History of Psychology") and R. Watson.

[2] F. Wyatt, "A Psychologist Looks at History," *J. Social Issues,* XVI (1962), 182–190.

study, whether they be stars or human events. If the sun rises and sets, it is indeed the sun that moves and not the observer. In the next stage of development and as a result of more circumspect observations, science proceeds to locate back in the observer what he had at first projected onto the object of his researches. Not only attributes like space and causality, but size and motion turn out to be *his* contribution, rather than a natural quality of what he had been studying. Psychology, for instance, came to acknowledge rather late how much our own conscious and unconscious wishes affect whatever we are investigating. Nor does recognition of this kind come about without resistance. Since it upsets both the accustomed order of things and man's idea of his own superiority, he does not much care for the encroachment. The more science takes account of the function of the observer, the more relativistic and roundabout it must necessarily become. Relativism increases complexity and enhances confusion in an observer who is out for certainty; the result of this progression is that knowledge becomes an elusive problem and insight an interminable process. Like other more or less scientific disciplines, psychology is reluctant to admit for itself the common limitations of all inquiry. History, possibly a sadder and, at any rate, an older and wiser discipline, has accustomed itself to enduring uncertainty. However, it shows no more inclination to associate with psychology than vice versa.

Yet history and psychology obviously have a great deal in common. Both deal with human experience and conduct:[3] one with its concrete incidents, the other with the principles underlying it. History, perhaps without explicit awareness, has always used some kind of psychology for its presentation. Without continuous reference to what moves man to act and makes him behave as he does, the writing of history could not advance a step. Psychology, on the other hand, inasmuch as it concerns itself with people in real life situations, had to become historical once it grew out of its early peripheral reactionism. As soon as it began to ask why a person acts right now in one way and not in another, psychology had to think in terms of processes and developments.[4] The advent of psychoanalysis deepened and extended the historical dimension and gave it a significance it had not had before; not only the beginnings but the major determinants of present conduct were now to be sought in the individual's past. Both history and psychology deal as a matter of course with the reconstruction of past events. By definition, neither has direct access to the past. History is

---

[3] Since history continuously engages in extrapolating the motives and aims of personalities and in interpreting the meaning of events, it cannot be said to deal with behavior in the sense of reinforcement theory. For further discussion of this point see: F. Wyatt, "Phantasy, the Ego and the Thematic Apperception Test," *J. Projective Techniques*, XII (1957), 130–160; and F. Wyatt, "A Psychologist Looks at History," *op. cit.*

[4] According to Maurice Merleau-Ponty, man is an *"idée historique."*

accustomed to reconstructing it from oblique records and from inferences drawn from a variety of material objects and circumstances. Psychoanalytic psychology depends for its reconstructions as much on a progression of remembering as on inference. This investigation of the individual past transcends itself continuously as it progresses: constructions or inferences about past events lead to more remembering, or at least to responses which may be used to amend and modify the earlier constructions, thereby eliciting new memories.[5] The purpose here is to examine the logic of the reconstructions of both history and psychology and their ultimate validity.

THE AUTHENTIC PAST

The traditional view of history is that of a complete set of facts, the "past" as hidden behind a fog of oblivion and yet-undiscovered documentation. The supreme job of history writing, therefore, would be to give back to the present this lost world, which must be assumed to exist in some kind of ontological space—perhaps as St. Augustine imagined it. A classical, though of course realistic, expression of this viewpoint may be found in Ranke's much-quoted adage that the task of history writing is to establish *"wie es denn eigentlich gewesen"*[6] (freely translated, "how it *really* was when it happened"). This must obviously mean that among many *uneigentliche,* or "false," views of the past there is one *eigentlicher,* or "authentic," one and that diligent search will bring it forth.

The great question here is whether this authentic past, suspended in some kind of timeless arrest, makes any possible sense. It may seem a little startling, but it is philosophically no more than a commonplace that we can speak of the past only when it is revived in somebody's present thinking. Such thinking, however, will depend on that person's own memories and on the memories of others. In the case of a past long vanished, it will have to depend entirely on documents that represent the repositories of such memories and on relics of the past left in the debris of time. All evidence of this kind is, to varying degrees, oblique, including the most personal memoirs, on which we may sometimes chance. No report can possibly contain the full complexity of a living event. The historian must gather, compile, assemble many different reports in order to reconstruct a semblance of the original event. The person who was actually there was constrained not only by fortune (which allowed him to see one side to the exclusion of others) but also by a whole host of biases ranging from the traditional values of his culture and the cognitive categories of his time to the most personal idiosyncrasies. This has not kept historians

---

[5] Sigmund Freud, "Constructions in Analysis" (1938), *Collected Papers* (New York: Basic Books, 1959), Vol. V, pp. 358–371.

[6] H. Ranke, *Geschichte der romanischen und germanischen Völker von 1494 bis 1514* (3rd ed.; Leipzig: 1885), pp. v-viii. Reprinted in F. Stern, ed., *The Varieties of History* (New York: Meridian Books, 1956).

from recognizing certain facts with considerable, though scarcely complete, objectivity; but it still leads to many differences when these facts are finally arranged in a larger context. "Context" implies "meaning." In order to be meaningful at all, facts need to be organized into a context. The chimera of a complete past which investigators might rediscover also implies that, with the diligent search for facts, the context, or meaning, of it will evolve by itself.[7]

For example, that Caesar crossed the Rubicon is a fact. The records of it may not be impeccable. Fortunately, they are in this case supported by geography. Since he was in Gaul before, he must have crossed that river in order to move on to Rome. Although the crossing is a fact, it is in and by itself no more than a triviality. Any significance that it may have for the historian endeavoring to bring some order into the course of Roman events derives from the meaning which it may give to previous and later events. Caesar may have been ferried across the river in a barge, or may have forded it on horseback, or may have been carried across piggyback lest he get his feet wet. He may have decided long before coming to the river that the chips were down or only sometime afterward in conjunction with some obscure exigency; and he may not have thought of the terse and slightly banal phrase of the die that had been cast (*alea jacta est*) until much later, when he had had time to work out his own myth. The fact of the river-crossing becomes significant only because it has the symbolic connotation of an allegory; it alludes to a meaningful context and, again by allusion, was used to represent that context. The fact of the Rubicon-crossing itself is of interest only in the context of Caesar's quickening decision to take his chances and defy the legal authority of his country. In order to establish this context, of course, facts like this, as well as many others, were necessary. The context itself, however, is the contribution of the historian. As we shall see, context is always tentative. If new facts were uncovered or if it were possible to establish a more plausible context on the basis of new insights—for example, by advances in the understanding of the motives of conduct—the meaning of this episode would change, and its history would have to be rewritten.

Historical records, therefore, are not only oblique but by their very nature sporadic or fragmentary. They may *lead* to a context, but they do not *possess* one a priori. One might say that history, qua history, does not

[7] After struggling for centuries to contain speculation and begin with empirical observation, the social sciences find themselves now in the paradoxical situation of making something of facts which cannot be made from them—namely, categories, contexts, and universal frames of reference. See also P. Gardiner, *The Nature of Historical Explanation* (London: Oxford, 1952). Faith in facts can be as uncritical as faith in the deductive power of ideas. Empiricism, ironically, shows an inclination at present for giving itself over to a mystique of facts. The circle closes, for in effect *and* intent this brings up something very much like the speculative dogmatism that empiricism once set out to liquidate.

really exist when it occurs. The purpose of history writing is to grasp and describe changes in human affairs. It traces an event from the origins, or causes, through its gradual unfolding, until such an event has run its course and has been taken over and incorporated by other events. Obviously, it is the historian who decides what an event is and when it has spent itself. Even though he is guided (not always to his greatest advantage) by much broader, collective notions of what events are supposed to be—a conquest accomplished, a war ended through a victorious battle, a prominent person ascending officially to some institutional rank—these notions are subject to change without notice. It can be said, therefore, that the historian describes events as he conceives of them and closes his account of change when he feels that, for the time being, he has reached the limits of his task. In this sense history becomes apparent only as it has time to unfold. Like the curve which will combine various entries on a graph into a meaningful whole, history can be plotted only after a variety of entries has been made so that different contexts can be tried for fit. History is *not* the search for the Augustinian specter, for the authentic reality of the past, *das eigentlich Gewesen*. Instead, it is an unending enterprise, a persistent effort to give plausible form to an array of data, a form which continuously needs to transcend itself in the light of new data, to the end of attaining a more comprehensive, more plausible context.[8]

A HISTORICAL PARABLE

I should like to illustrate this view by means of a historical parable. Let us suppose that King Croesus of Lydia, after being defeated and captured by Cyrus of Persia, had had the inclination to reflect upon his fate. Inevitably his thoughts turned to the oracle of Delphi, whose prophecy he had followed at the cost of his own undoing. "Either I must have utterly misunderstood it," he ruminated, "when those priests told me that I would destroy a great empire if I crossed the Halys River; or the oracle is a pious fraud, as some of my court philosophers hinted anyway." As a child of his time, the king inclined to the former view, even in defeat; as a political personality, he also wondered for a moment whether he might not have underrated that Persian upstart, Cyrus. Croesus, of course, had many more personal and idiosyncratic thoughts, and their schemata were, naturally, filled with the memory of faces and conversations; but the dimensions of his thinking were clearly defined by his time and place.

We, however, *do* want to go further than he was able to do in his reflections, and in order to examine the nature of historical evidence *in praxi*, we shall borrow H. G. Wells's Time Machine for a scientific expedition. Thus equipped, we shall send a team of social scientists to Lydia, twenty-

---

[8] For a similar view see H. J. Muller's immensely stimulating, argumentative book *The Uses of the Past* (New York: Oxford University Press, 1952).

six centuries back in time, shortly before the fateful involvement with
Persia. Upon returning, our field staff brings us the following information: The economist makes a strong case that the extravagant concentration of national wealth in Croesus' private treasury has for quite some
time played havoc with the economic life of Lydia. Money is in such short
supply that loan capital can be obtained only at ruinous rates of interest.
Moreover, Croesus' wealth derives largely from heavy taxation which has
further reduced the capital needed for new enterprises. The impression is
that the country is fast approaching economic stagnation. At this point the
sociologist takes over and reports that the oppressive economic conditions
of the country are causing apathy among the citizens and poor morale
among the king's scantily equipped and badly paid soldiers. The arbitrari-
ness of his policies, together with oppressive taxation—in short, the hopelessness of the whole situation—are about to bring Lydia to the brink of
anomie. Then the psychologist comes in and presents the results of a
series of personality studies of the king and his advisers. He concludes that
the king's overweening preoccupation with money (based, without doubt,
on an unusually strong anal fixation) has further increased his drive for
omnipotence. Even more than other potentates, Croesus needs to control
everybody and everything and must have his way in every decision. This
has tragic consequences for the conduct of the cold war with Persia. The
king arbitrarily dismisses facts he doesn't like, as well as the advisers who
brought them to his attention. The psychologist then predicts that because
of his obsessive-compulsive character Croesus is prone to rely for his decisions on portents and superstitions. He cannot be at all expected to
approach realistically the problems of his high office and so is not likely
to cope with them successfully.

As frequently happens, the psychologist in his clinical zest overlooked
certain cultural patterns; but we cannot deny that he offered a plausible
interpretation of a personality and its bearing on a noted historical event.
If we are not satisfied with the import of the Delphic oracle for the down-
fall of the Lydian Empire, we shall have to ask ourselves what a contemporary observer, clear-eyed and impartial, could have known about
these events, if he were of a perceptive and judicious mind and so placed as
to see and hear more than anybody else in the state. Let us also for the
moment assume that the findings of our social science team were not
merely plausible but true. Even the most diligent contemporary observer
could not have grasped the economic and social causes of Lydia's down-
fall. No such data would have been available to him simply because the
concepts that would have guided him toward the data did not yet exist.
Although in *our* view of Lydian history there must have been economic,
social, and psychological problems, nothing indicates that at that time
they would have made sense to anybody in Lydia. The causes com-

pounded with their results might have been dimly perceived and called *moira*, or *hubris*, or perhaps even human folly; but they could not have been organized in the frame of reference that we would, as a matter of course, employ today in order to grasp the meaning of these events of social interaction and disruption. In the days of Croesus they could neither be identified nor understood. It is not saying too much that, for all practical purposes, they did not exist.

One could claim, therefore—I believe with considerable justification—that those who were present to witness *das eigentlich Gewesen,* the authentic events, while they were occurring, knew *less* about them than do we, historians of a later day. Their contexts were limited and almost always misleading. The significance of the processes, of which they witnessed a segment here, a segment there, escaped them because the drift and drama of the whole thing were still too close and too inchoate to be discerned; nor could they grasp what we now consider the causes and motives of the events before their eyes. Since the scientific study of human conduct is of such recent origin, our age has concepts and principles of interaction at its disposal which were not available to former ages. There are undoubtedly many instances in recorded history when the point I made about the limitations of eyewitnesses does not hold. There are also many events and periods for which so few data are available that the participants, in spite of all the previously argued strictures, must have known more than we now do simply because we know almost nothing. But this does not affect the principle. It is very unlikely that the end of the Lydian Empire was brought about by a king's acting upon the ambiguous words of an oracle. More likely, it followed from a complex of causes in which economic, social, and psychological factors merged with yet others.

All this affords us a grave conclusion: there is no authentic past to be retrieved. We have to reconstruct it, quite properly, in our own image. Reconstruction means to find a context which integrates all relevant data. Context usually derives from the historian's preferred theories and from those values and sentiments in which all theories are ultimately embedded. It follows that each age writes its own history. To philosophers of history (like Croce or Collingwood) this idea is neither new nor is it as paradoxical as it may sound on first hearing.[9]

AN INSTANCE OF INTERPRETATION AND ITS RATIONALE

I should like to demonstrate this process of reconstruction by reporting briefly a recent study by William Willcox and myself on Sir Henry

[9] B. Croce, *History,* "Its Theory and Practice," trans. D. Hinslee (New York: Harcourt Brace & Co., 1921), and R. G. Collingwood, *The Idea of History* (Oxford: Oxford University Press, 1946).

Clinton, an eighteenth-century English general.[10] He was definitely not among the prima donnas of history, but having been first the deputy commander and eventually the commander-in-chief of the British forces during the American War of Independence, he stood close enough to the hub of history to merit attention. For what he called the "American Rebellion" was almost from its beginning part of the incessant power struggle of European nations.[11] Clinton, of course, could not know that the war which he directed for four years stood also at the beginning of more momentous developments than he himself witnessed. Professor Willcox, who edited the Clinton papers, described him in the introduction to this publication as sometimes appearing like two different men: "One is the military rationalist, reserved and dignified; the other is torn between timidity and aggressive self-confidence as if the furies were at work on his psyche. The interaction between the two is the clue to Clinton's generalship." Clinton's military autobiography is "his apologia for a career that failed. But the failure, in the last analysis, came from a cause that he would have died rather than admit. His nemesis was himself."[12]

There is scarcely anything more frustrating than to report the breadth and subtlety of biographical material in a few formulalike sentences. Just that, however, is necessary here for reasons of space. Clinton's personal problems showed up, when he had to collaborate with equals and superiors, in his endless argumentativeness and morose sensitivity and in an astounding lack of tact and of realistic timing. They showed themselves further in his generalship as a persistent incongruity between bold planning and the overcautious execution of these plans, and they made themselves known in his inclination to procrastinate and in his utterly unrealistic conception of time. At the core of Clinton's neurotic difficulties is his relationship to authority: he craved and fought for positions of leadership, but once in them he obviously feared power and attempted in many ways to resign from it. As a whole, either Clinton's conduct must appear as irrational, inconsistent, and inexplicable, or we must assume that his motives were not the manifest ones of which he talked, but entirely different ones of which he was largely unconscious.

This hypothesis led us to examine the data of Clinton's life history in terms of psychoanalytic psychology of personality. A methodology was worked out designed to check the flights of interpretative fancy, while defining levels of plausibility. The interpretation of an historical person-

---

[10] F. Wyatt and W. Willcox, "Sir Henry Clinton: A Psychological Exploration in History," *William and Mary Quarterly*, XVI (1959), 3–26.

[11] W. Willcox, ed., *The American Rebellion*, "Sir Henry Clinton's Narrative of His Campaigns, 1775–1782, with an Appendix of Original Documents" (New Haven, Conn.: Yale University Press, 1954).

[12] *Ibid.*, pp. xii and li, respectively.

ality is obviously handicapped by the absence of that continuous process of response, recollection, and reorganization for which the conditions of psychoanalytic psychotherapy provide. The therapist always receives new material, which enables him to test and correct his own interpretative conclusions. In the psychoanalytic study of an historical record the major question is how to compensate for the self-transcendence that is built into the therapeutic process. In clinical perspective Clinton's problem was that of an obsessive-compulsive personality troubled by ambivalence and unconscious guilt. Against these affects he attempted to protect himself by costly defensive maneuvers, which interfered with his official role and perhaps also with his private life. Psychological interpretation added no new facts to Clinton's history. It may have succeeded, however, in suggesting a degree of meaningful coherence in Clinton's conduct and in making unexpected sense of much contradiction and senseless caprice.

The hypothesis of unconscious motives and conflicts puts most of the facts of his personal and professional history into a meaningful context. It makes no other assumption but that Clinton must have been subject to the kind of motivation which we now regard as universal, even though in his day nobody would have fully comprehended it. Many of Clinton's actions and recorded character traits have an almost symptomatic quality. On their own they seem to point to the syndrome described before. We can also be sure that the data have not been falsified to fit our case: those who reported them could scarcely have shared our bias. We even had an advantage over the self-corrective transcendence of psychotherapy, in that we could examine the observations of many different people about the war, about Clinton's generalship, and about his personality. On the other hand, Clinton's symptoms might still refer to entirely different motives from those we have inferred. Inevitably, we had to include in our conjectures events of which little is known. Without particularly forcing them we extrapolated what, to us, they implied; but with equal ease they might also be made to mean something entirely different. However, the over-all consistency of events in Clinton's life seems to attest the validity of our interpretation. It cannot be easily dismissed that he spoke and acted over and over again in a manner which psychoanalysis, nearly a century and a half later, has shown to refer to the same psychological condition and the same core of motives. To be sure, if new materials bearing upon Clinton's life history were discovered, our interpretation might well have to be changed. Equally, if somebody came out with principles of human conduct more comprehensive or more incisive than those now at our disposal, a new, more unifying, and more consistent interpretation would have to replace ours. The same applies *mutatis mutandis* to large segments of acknowledged history.

RECONSTRUCTION IN PSYCHOTHERAPY

But what about the feeling of absolute certainty regarding one's own past? Is it not extravagant to claim that the past of a living individual is no more definite than that of a long-forgotten people centuries or millennia ago? The difference is indeed undeniable, for the reconstruction of the individual's past will in most (though not in all) instances be easier and may well turn out to be more complete. Usually, more observations by others will be available in the case of a recent than in the case of the long bygone past, although these observations too may not always contribute as much as we expect. But above all, an individual who lives among us and whose history is to be uncovered can be asked questions; he can be induced to recall what does not occur to him right away. At any rate, there will be more material and it will be imbued with a much greater feeling of certainty. Does this mean that the individual's past thirty years ago is fundamentally different from that three thousand years before our time? Is there any reason to think that the recent past more than the remote past exists in and by itself to a greater degree, independent of our endeavor to reconstruct it? The principle that any past event in order to "exist" again must first be remembered, is certainly not affected by the *recency* of that event. Psychoanalytic psychotherapy shows, if nothing else, that most ready memories are inaccurate. Even the defenders of manifest memory— that it is just what it claims to be and no less—do not assert that an individual can remember all the events of his life. The same must apply to those who now remember the past actions of a living person and may thereby want to help him to remember them himself.

But there is still the stubborn unflinching certainty: "Of course my past exists and goes on existing! I have a past as surely as I have myself!" This is an elementary conviction before and beyond all reasoning, and it cannot be glibly discounted. Was there really such a man as Caesar? Over the years I have read countless references to him, but there still is no comparison between the sureness of Caesar's past and mine. Most of the events of my own past are charged with feeling—sad or happy, elating or embarrassing. Caesar's life carries none of these affects for me, or only in a derived and secondary manner, when he has been adopted into my own personal experience as, for instance, through the medium of art. At any rate, *all* my memories have a quality distinguishing them from anything else: they pertain to *me;* they *are* me. They are endowed with a unique feeling-tone finding expression in the word "I" that prefaces any statement of the subjective past. The problem therefore is not *why* we are so sure of our own past; that sureness springs directly from the way every person experiences his own memories. But being so sure of our past, why should we so often be wrong in recollecting it? In other words, when our own past seems to us to have remained somewhere as a fixed entity, an autonomous body of past events preserved, as it were, in the brine of memory—why is it so often manifestly false and, on closer scrutiny, hardly autonomous at all? The answer psychoanalysis has offered represents, therefore, a contribution to man's self-knowledge on a much more general and more philosophical level than first intended. These memories were subjected to conflicting psychological demands: some of the demands were more concerned with anguish and the protection against it; others with pleasure and self-enhancement; and still others with order and consistency. In order to be adapted to these pressures, the memories were subtly transformed over time and molded into their present appearance. We must conclude that the individual past, too, is not a relic carried along from early to late, a reliable testimony as to *wie es denn eigentlich gewesen*. Quite the contrary: it is part and parcel of the living present, continuously affected by its concerns. The subjective certainty of one's own past, however, points to all kinds of things of psychological import, to some of which I shall return later.

All this gives us no cause to *doubt the past*. Everything speaks for it, not least of all that it continues as an integral part of the individual's present scope of experience. The attempt here is not to prove that in an ontological sense there is no past; that would be patently absurd. All I wish to propose is that for all practical purposes the past exists only when we re-create it by training our thinking on it, or that the past as individual and collective history cannot be recovered but has to be reconstructed.

Let us now compare historical reconstruction with that kind of reconstruction continuously undertaken in the uncovering of individual history in psychoanalytic psychotherapy. The major source of data in this instance is the memory of the patient who has subjected himself to recalling the past under the conditions of transference. Occasionally these data can be cross-checked against the memories of other persons. Even then the check will at best simply confirm the outline of an event.[13] Yet the idea of an *authentic* past may prove as useful here as it did in history, for we have no more grounds for accepting any assertion about the psychological past than we have about the historical past. The psychoanalytic reconstruction of the individual past may or may not have outside checks available; it has, in any case, the perpetual self-transcendence of emerging memories and of recurring need patterns as they manifest themselves through the transference.

Once their interest has been aroused, patients, beginning at a certain stage of therapy, will often look for external evidence for those construc-

[13] E. E. Haggard, A. Brekstad, and A. G. Skard, "On the Reliability of the Anamnestic Interview," *J. Abnormal and Social Psychology*, LXI (1960), 311–318. See also Note 5 and S. Freud, "Further Recommendations in the Technique of Psychoanalysis. Recollection, Repetition and Working Through," *Collected Papers, op. cit.*, Vol. II, pp. 366–376.

tions of their past which have begun to play a part in therapy. The intent is usually to confirm hunches or fill in stubborn gaps of memory. Sometimes the patient's own recall can be supported by the remembrances of other people; more often a version of the past will then be offered to the patient, which, like an alien ornament, does not fit into his design. The reason for making such constructions follows from the technique of psychotherapy. The recall of past events depends on so many psychological conditions that the method of free association by itself would never bring out certain key memories. (This goes to show that silence may be golden, but that, in therapy at least, it is not enough for attaining the desired aims.) Interpretation is therefore a very general name for a variety of therapeutic actions which have in common only that the therapist "intervenes" by establishing a relationship between various statements the patient has previously produced.[14] In so doing the therapist arrives at the proposal of a *meaning*. In the vast majority of interpretations this proposition is purely heuristic. It has the quality of a working hypothesis which may or may not be confirmed by the patient's subsequent responses. As a construction, it is almost always incomplete and imperfect. Its chief aim, in fact, is to solicit material in the light of which it can then be modified or further extended. It is as if the therapist had said: "Well, let's see what happens if we put things together *this* way. That is what I think it means; let's try it out and see now how it fits!" The criticism so frequently leveled against interpretation in therapy, that it is based on insufficient evidence, therefore misses the point entirely. Most interpretations are both more and less than assertions about the patient's past experiences. Far from pretending a certainty, they are devices to search out and arrive at plausible constructions. Why this helps toward realizing the aims of therapy is a question for the theory of psychotherapeutic endeavors and does not concern us here.

We may, however, reflect on what it means that psychotherapy nearly always has to make do with such an incomplete and uncertain account of the past. I mentioned before that many patients, after the initial gambit is over, begin to search for objective confirmation of childhood events. Parents can contribute data about nursing, intercurrent childhood diseases, moves, and absences. "You know what my mother said?" the patient will report. "My sister was born *before* we moved to Jefferson Boulevard and while we were still living on Peachtree Avenue." Informants are usually much less reliable when it comes to assessing the "objective" meaning of such events. Inevitably their own attitudes are involved, their unconscious ambiguities and self-protective stances, as well as the repressions and transformations of their own memories. Witnesses of the patient's past, in short,

[14] For a definition of therapeutic action, see F. Wyatt, "Therapeutic Effort and Therapeutic Situation," *Amer. J. Orthopsychiatry*, XVII (1957), 616–620.

are subject to the same major liabilities when the reality of the past is concerned as is the patient himself. Everybody's past is differentially forgotten and repressed; what is retained of it is inevitably subject to continuous modification. If our patients (which is only a roundabout way of saying everybody when properly studied) do not remember the authentic past, this must be due, above all, to the condition under which it was first experienced. Children do not differentiate facts from fantasy. More correctly, the so-called objective reality and their own fantastic elaborations of it are for them a global, as yet undifferentiated whole.[15] It will be the most important task of their development to differentiate fact from fantasy. The adults who observed them while they were children and who tell them many years later "how it really was" were, of course, not so much affected by the convergence of fantasy and reality as was the child. This is no reason to assume, however, that they now have reality by the ears. Carrying the memories of their past with them, they too, naturally, have subtly transformed it over the years.

It might be argued here that there are, after all, objective facts in the individual's past, as in the history of mankind, and that it does not matter whether in one instance they are correctly remembered or not. In principle, they could have been recorded and so preserved. Isn't the family album of photographs such a record, or, among the more affluent set, the movies father took when the children were small? The answer is that there are, of course, "objective" facts. The move from Peachtree Avenue to Jefferson Boulevard is such a fact. If it had been forgotten by all, it could still be retrieved from the registry of deeds, exactly as historians do in order to establish a grid of facts for the past they wish to re-create. The birth of the little sister is another indisputable fact. Mother might vaguely recall now that her older child seemed quite forlorn and for a while acted strangely, just around that time when sister was born. If mother was given to preserving memories, she might even have kept a diary and might find an entry of that date with some details.

Such a fact may attain crucial significance when it comes to reconstructing the past. The birth of a baby sister will be a key fact, and even the move from Peachtree Avenue may link together, or help define, other data.[16] In and by themselves, the move and the birth of the sibling are isolated events culled from their contexts. They do *not* represent the individual's past—as the more naïve factualist would have it—but an abstraction. It takes little introspection to see that we do not experience life

---

[15] E. G. Schachtel, *Metamorphosis* (New York: Basic Books, 1959). See especially Chapter 12, "On Memory and Childhood Amnesia."

[16] For a critical discussion of the problems inherent in the attempted reconstruction of early childhood and of the principles of psychological genesis to be derived therefrom, see R. Ekstein and L. Rangell, "Reconstruction and Theory Formation," *J. Amer. Psychoanalytic Association*, IX (1961), 684–697.

in terms of unrelated episodes as they appear in a birth register or in a register of deeds. When transmitted by memory, these abstractions tell us more of the slow, spontaneous reorganization of that memory over time than about the real experiences from which it was distilled. It would not do to regard such fragments as "history"; but they are indeed indispensable markers for the construction of history. The past with which the psychotherapist is concerned is the context and meaning of the childhood events to which I referred before. Offering his reconstruction of the past, the therapist might say: "When your sister was born, you felt left out and uncared for. You did all kinds of things to express your hurt and to make them understand you, but they didn't. The whole episode was so distressing that you forgot some of the painful details and without knowing it shifted their weight to other seemingly trivial events which you can still remember now. Afterward you moved the whole episode to a later stage of your life, again without being clearly aware of the shift, as if you wanted to express mutely that it was too difficult an event to cope with when it really happened."[17] The therapist's interpretation would still remain incomplete and incorrect. Even after the interpretation has been recast in the light of new material, we have no reason to think that we have recaptured the past. The process turns into an endless regression until we acknowledge that the past of our patient exists only insofar as he remembers it and insofar as its contexts and meanings can be reconstructed under the particular conditions of therapy.

Another example may illustrate this point. The patient, a man who is about to turn thirty, glories at the beginning of the hour in recalling that he defied the therapist by cancelling the previous session at the last moment and by not calling for another appointment even though he had offered to do so. He then indicates that he is full of vindictive and defiant thoughts against the therapist. Suddenly his attitude changes, however. He is sorry about what he just said and wants to make sure that he doesn't really mean any of it. He speaks about liking the therapist's office and that he could easily go to sleep right now, as if his mother were sitting at his bedside. Then he presses the therapist to make some comment and complains that he doesn't get anything for his money or that all this is a game and that he doesn't really take it seriously.

A little later the therapist points out the three stages in the patient's communication: first, defiance; next, a show of affection as a preface to asking for love; finally, the complaint that he does not receive what he wants most. The therapist relates these stages to the events in the patient's

---

[17] The selection of this instance from a case in therapy was not intended to parallel Freud's own paradigm so closely; but the choice can hardly have been accidental, as I saw when, some time after I had written this essay, I again read the paper, "Constructions in Analysis," *op. cit.*

early childhood which they reflect, together with the patient's reaction to them. In his communications, however, only a few recollections have come up so far to substantiate the therapist's conjecture. Manifestly, the patient has talked mostly about his preferred position in the family as the eldest of several siblings. He has spoken a good deal about his successes in gaining the affection of others and about his erotic involvements in which he presented himself either as an evildoer or as the victim of seduction. The therapist acts on the assumption that the patient, then a little boy, may have been aware that his father for a time paid more attention to somebody else than to him, as might have been the case with a younger sister. Under the impact of the anguish, envy, and humiliation this experience caused him, the patient seems to have repressed it. Forced and prompted by subsequent events, he worked over the memory until it finally turned into the image of himself which he reported in the initial phase of therapy. The sentiments which the patient is now experiencing in the transference offer guidelines for the reconstruction of the original event, which is repeated in many variations, as if the patient were improvising upon a set theme. Other of his statements refer to incidents in the following years when one or another element of the primal event was revived and re-experienced in a variety of different situations. If the patient's response endorses the therapist's conjecture, the patient will for the first time *know* what has happened in his own past, instead of just living it or suffering it in terms of specific incidents—but even more by grasping their context and thus realizing their significance.

The conviction of one's own past as a complete repository of things that have happened, even though they are now unknown, is nevertheless invincible and inexorable. And for good reason. Such conviction represents the continuity of the self, which is an indispensable aspect of experiencing oneself as an integrated person, or of "being normal." The sense of a meaningful continuity is therefore as "true" as it is necessary. We need the feeling of order and continuity so as to cope with the unending onslaught of external and internal experiences. We therefore have to impose our order on their flux and, if we cannot grasp continuity, make it up in some fashion ourselves. The sureness of "I was" is a necessary component of the sureness of "I am," or, better, of "I am something that makes sense to myself and to others." Neither, however, bears out the idea of an *authentic* past. It may not be too difficult to explain how that idea came about; but the reasons for its occurrence can hardly be used to justify it. The past as history, as a coherent account of events, their sequence, interdependence, and significance comes into being only when it is reconstructed in an ever-renewed present.

Not all reconstructions are equally good; that they are reconstructions of the past does not free them from the obligations of rational responsibility. I have used the word plausible to describe the scope of reconstruction for integrating available data into a meaningful context after they have been critically examined. The context depends not only on *facts,* those relics and dry bones of history, but on individual and cultural sentiments, on categories of knowledge, and especially on the prevalence of psychological and sociological theories. Reconstructions are therefore subject to continuous change. They are, according to the model of individual psychotherapy, self-transcendent in the light of new data and new viewpoints. However, plausibility as it is used here does not imply license for any idea just because it yields some kind of context or succeeds in putting data together in an accommodating manner. The gratification over having created a context is first of all that of the individual who credits himself with this achievement. The context is of *his* choice and making and so has inevitably been directed by predilections of which he will be largely unconscious. To give meaning to events is an act involving the entire man, his reason and culture, his needs and archaic secrets, his self-restrictions and flight from internal dangers. The study of so-called projective techniques in our day has shown this in neat focus, even though man's perennial effort in the arts to give form and purposeful order to his private fantasies has been demonstrating the same point since the dawn of civilization.[18]

The job of reconstruction, if it aims to transform subjective experience into insight relevant for others, must therefore begin with the checks and cautions through which rationality raises itself into science. It must accustom itself also to dwelling on the sharp edge of paradox by striving for what appears at that moment the most comprehensive context, while knowing at the same time that it will, of necessity, soon be transcended. For the analysis of the historical past is not more interminable than is, in Freud's great phrase, the analysis of the individual past. If you think this uncertainty trying, consider that the past not only makes *us,* but that we, literally, make *it* by putting it together in thoughtful reflection. It seems to me that only in this way is the past really retrieved: when it is revived again, right now, as we try once more to reconstruct it.

---

[18] See H. A. Murray *et al., Explorations in Personality* (New York: Oxford University Press, 1938) for the understanding of fantasy as self-manifestation which has informed our approach to it ever since.

VALUES IN PERSONALITY
Part IV

Science has had trouble with values. The scientist, setting himself the worthy goal of objectivity, which requires the overcoming of personal idiosyncrasy and preference, came to think of values mainly as sources of error, if not of opposition to the very cause of science. Overlooked in this understandable attitude was the fact that objectivity is itself a human value, one to which devotees make great sacrifices in discipline and self-denial. A considerable campaign has nevertheless been necessary to secure the admission of values as a proper object of scientific study. Murray's thinking along this line was in close tune with that of his friend and colleague, anthropologist Clyde Kluckhohn. Unwilling to see science neglect a topic of such vast social consequence, these two labored together to make values intelligible as objects of study in personality, society, and culture.

The first chapter in this section addresses itself to the definition of values. Brewster Smith reviews "a variety of distinguishably different and worthy concepts" that have become attached to the term and undertakes to clear a path through the thicket by adopting a restrictive definition emphasizing "conceptions of the desirable that are relevant to selective behavior." He then develops a modest taxonomy of values and some thoughts on their origins in early life. The chapter is constantly pointed toward research on personal values.

Wilson's chapter combines the study of values with the analysis of literary products. He examines four works of Albert Camus—two novels, *The Stranger* and *The Plague,* and two philosophical essays, *The Myth of Sisyphus* and *The Rebel.* When Camus was the age of Inburn (Chapter 2), he perhaps presented a similar picture of alienation, but Wilson traces an evolution of his outlook that ends with the conception of personality as creative struggle.

The next chapter is also in the spirit of a case study. Holt gives us a fragment of Freud's ever-fascinating intellectual biography, concentrating on the scientific climate that surrounded his years as a physiologist and his first attempts to construct a system of psychology. It becomes evident that Freud selected materialism and the concept of energy, rejecting other possibilities, because they were in accord with his basic values; his conceptions of the desirable were clearly relevant to his selective behavior. It is a special merit of this chapter that it reminds us how long ago Freud made the conceptual choices that are still apparent in psychoanalytic theory.

In Chapter 17 Tomkins discusses in more general terms the relation between personality and ideology. On the side of the person, he says, there is an ideo-affective position which is the consequence of his whole history of affective experience. When ideologies—organized systems of ideas— come to his notice, there will be a selective "ideo-affective resonance" that precipitates a marriage between his ideo-affective position and its soul mate among ideologies. It is thus that Inburn resonated to his friend's alienated cynicism and that Freud cast his lot with materialistic determinism. Tomkins then spreads a broad canvas and paints the far reaches of a basic dimension in ideology and personality. Nicknamed "left" and "right," the ends of this dimension can be characterized according to the principal location of value—whether it is felt to reside in the individual, in his needs and satisfactions and happiness as ends in themselves, or whether it is found in something outside the individual, such as custom, principle, or the requirements of the group. This variable reappears in many spheres of thought, and people are inclined to lean consistently to left or right with respect to any ideologies with which they are familiar. Readers will find it intriguing to cast Tomkins' dimension back over the preceding chapters, relating it to what has been said about impulse expression, tolerance of ambiguity, and especially the differences between more creative and less creative people.

In the final chapter, Erikson takes up the many versions of the Golden Rule as attempts to regulate the deep moral conflict between self-interest and the interests of others. He calls attention to the somewhat inauspicious origins of morality in childhood and adolescence, with their temptations to self-righteousness and absolutism, but he also points out the mutuality between mother and child in which each mobilizes and strengthens the other. Mutuality, with respect for the uniqueness of each party—as it is seen, for example, in the relations of mother and child, of lovers, and of physician and patient—can become the basis for mature ethics that might gradually extend to groups and nations.

14: PERSONAL VALUES IN THE STUDY OF LIVES

M. Brewster Smith

This essay is a much-delayed response to a personal challenge from Henry A. Murray, a challenge of at least ten years' standing, to develop some incipient ideas about the formulation of personal values as a topic for personological and social-psychological inquiry. Characteristically, Harry gave enthusiastic support when I first broached the subject; a larval idea can only bask in the glow of his warm receptiveness and is even tempted to fancy itself a butterfly. In the cold awakening that so often follows such a self-indulgent episode, however, the larval state of the ideas was all too apparent; they have been in indefinite pupation ever since.

I still have no butterfly to present. But a number of considerations now lead me to accept the challenge all the same. The topic of values has certainly attracted much more attention in the intervening years than it previously enjoyed; among major efforts, there are the recent book-length bibliography by Albert and Kluckhohn,[1] the comparative cultural studies by Kluckhohn and Strodtbeck[2] and by von Mering,[3] and the factor analytic research stemming from Charles Morris' scheme.[4] If anthropologists and sociologists concerned with cultural values as focuses of personal and cultural integration have been the largest contributors to this literature, psychologists have also found themselves talking more frequently about values—as features of the philosophical boundary that sets the terms of

---

[1] Ethel M. Albert and Clyde K. M. Kluckhohn, *A Selected Bibliography on Values, Ethics, and Esthetics in the Behavioral Sciences and Philosophy, 1920–1958* (Glencoe, Ill.: The Free Press, 1960).

[2] Florence R. Kluckhohn and Fred L. Strodtbeck, *Variations in Value Orientations* (Evanston, Ill.: Row, Peterson, 1961).

[3] Otto von Mering, *A Grammar of Human Values* (Pittsburgh: University of Pittsburgh Press, 1961).

[4] Charles W. Morris, *Varieties of Human Value* (Chicago: University of Chicago Press, 1956).

professional decisions[5] or as ingredients of accounts that propose to describe the functioning person.[6]

But the increased currency of explicit value concepts among psychologists and social scientists has unfortunately not been accompanied by corresponding gains in conceptual clarity or consensus. We talk about altogether too many probably different things under one rubric when we stretch the same terminology to include the utilities of mathematical decision theory,[7] fundamental assumptions about the nature of the world and man's place in it,[8] ultimate preferences among life styles,[9] and core attitudes or sentiments that set priorities among one's preferences and thus give structure to a life.[10] And, at the same time, we are embarrassed with a proliferation of concepts akin to values: attitudes and sentiments, but also interests, preferences, motives, cathexes, valences. The handful of major attempts to study values empirically have started from different preconceptions and have altogether failed to link together to yield a domain of cumulative knowledge.

These observations would be grounds for avoiding the topic entirely, except for the fact that each new topic to which I turn seems to transmute itself into one in which questions of values are inescapable. In our study *Opinions and Personality*,[11] carried out at the Harvard Psychological Clinic with the inspiration of Murray's example and tradition, Jerome S. Bruner, Robert W. White, and I found in the personal values of our subjects a level of analysis that seemed peculiarly advantageous for discerning inner coherence among their political opinions. Subsequent concern with the concept of mental health convinced me that this embarrassingly unsatisfactory term barely conceals an almost pure value problem.[12] And in my current explorations of patterns of coping and adjustment in the intercultural situation of Peace Corps service, questions of value commitment arise centrally once more. My fate, apparently, is to be haunted by the problem of the psychological status of personal values, which keeps bobbing up like King Charles' head. This may be an auspicious occasion to face the problem more frontally.

[5] See, e.g., C. Marshall Lowe, "Value Orientations—An Ethical Dilemma," *American Psychologist*, XIV (1959), 687–693.

[6] See, e.g., David C. McClelland, *Personality* (New York: William Sloane, 1951).

[7] Cf. Ward Edwards, "The Theory of Decision Making," *Psychological Bulletin*, LI (1954), 380–417.

[8] F. Kluckhohn and Strodtbeck, *op. cit.*

[9] Morris, *op. cit.*

[10] Gordon W. Allport, *Personality*, "A Psychological Interpretation" (New York: Holt, 1937).

[11] M. Brewster Smith, Jerome S. Bruner, and Robert W. White, *Opinions and Personality* (New York: John Wiley and Sons, 1956).

[12] M. Brewster Smith, "Mental Health Reconsidered: A Special Case of the Problem of Values in Psychology," *American Psychologist*, XVI (1961), 299–306.

At present, one may hope that a tentative armchair analysis will be fruitful. Thanks in part to the naturalistic study of lives that Murray pioneered, we have the advantage of considerable familiarity with values in relation to personality. Contemporary systematic thinking about "personality in nature, society, and culture" (to echo the title of a book in which Murray was centrally involved) also gives us the beginnings of a framework with which a developed conception of personal values must eventually articulate. This essay attempts to develop a few distinctions and to point to a few of the relationships of values to the framework of thinking about man in society which may make one direction of conceptualization more profitable than another. In keeping with the preliminary character of what I am attempting, I will not try to cover systematically the substantial literature of discussion and the smaller literature of research on values. Any headway we can make toward greater conceptual clarity should have implications for methods and directions of research, in an area in which choice of method has seemed haphazard and direction often lacking.

SELECTING A CONCEPTION OF VALUE

The first and crucial step in picking a way through the confusion that has enveloped discussions of values is to identify an unequivocal core meaning. Of course, semantic decisions of this sort are in a sense arbitrary. Like Humpty-Dumpty, one may use words as one pleases, so long as one uses them consistently. Yet, unless one is content to live in a Humpty-Dumpty world—an unfavorable environment both for efficient communication or for the cumulative advance of articulated knowledge—one had best take pains about the decision. The conception of values that I am approaching pays due regard to contemporary usage but also is selected with other essential criteria in mind.

To be useful in the study of lives, a conception of values should include in its reference at least some of the important human phenomena that one encounters when one sees people valuing, caring, committing themselves, judging as better or worse. A meaning should be found, if the term is to be at all serviceable, that falls within the vaguely bounded area of discourse evoked by such situations. And further, the use of a special term, rather than others more firmly grounded in general psychological theories not specifically human in reference, will be most clearly justified if it refers to distinctively human phenomena within this broader area— phenomena, that is, that are not exhausted by more general terms like motive, incentive, and valence, which apply equally at human and infra-human levels.

A further strategic consideration stems from the fact that value terminology has become prevalent in a wide range of social or behavioral sciences besides psychology: sociology, cultural anthropology, economics, political science. There is at least the basis for hoping that value can become one of the important concepts that potentially link different levels of organization and analysis and can therefore play a central part in a developing general science of social man. The hope may be illusory, for the seeming convergence on terminology may merely hide basically divergent meanings: loose efforts at integrating the social sciences too often hinge on the slippery use of terms. In searching for a core meaning of value, however, I will be seeking one that is primarily relevant for personology but also engages with issues and concepts of anthropology and sociology— one that meets the needs of the social psychologist concerned with the development and functioning of the person in his social and cultural context.

Some Alternatives

Before these criteria can be brought to bear, we need to map out, in a preliminary way, some of the major alternatives that are available in recent usage. Because of the prevalent confusion, my final preference will be for a well-bounded, specific meaning that does not pretend to include many of the referents to which the term has been applied. But the preliminary task of mapping requires starting with a highly general conception that embraces most of the meanings in which "value" has been employed. Such a conception, it seems to me, is that of selective behavior—in which a person chooses, rejects, takes interest in, approves, disapproves—with respect to a physical, social, or ideal object.

Whenever we talk about values and valuing, we are confronted—in actuality, in principle, or in retrospect—with persons engaged in processes of selection or choice with respect to objects. We employ the terminology of values as a conceptual handle for discerning and dealing with regularities in this behavior. The selective behavior may be instrumental to attaining some further object or state of affairs beyond that to which it is immediately oriented, or it may be consummatory, an end-term in the behavioral sequence. Or the behavior under inspection may rather be talk about such encounters.

The search for underlying constancies in the flux of behavior turns the theorist, like the Everyman of Heider's "commonsense psychology,"[13] to attend to properties that he attributes to the polar components of the behavioral situation: person and object. So the major cleavage in the use of the term value divides those who focus on the person and his dispositions, on the one hand, and those who apply the term to properties of the

[13] Fritz Heider, *The Psychology of Interpersonal Relations* (New York: John Wiley and Sons, 1958).

object of choice, on the other. For the first group, values are subsumed in one way or another under attitudes, the most general term for personal dispositions toward a psychological object or class of objects. For the second, value is or results from properties of the object that evoke selective behavior—either intrinsic properties of the object or, more commonly, functional properties that emerge in relation to the motivation of the person who is in commerce with it.

In the early years of empirical social research, W. I. Thomas in his methodological introduction to *The Polish Peasant* introduced just this distinction with the complementary terms, attitude and value.[14] For Thomas, attitude refers to any disposition of a person toward an object, while any object becomes a value by virtue of being the target of a person's attitude. Here the term value is used very generally and is located explicitly at the object pole. Similarly employing the term for concepts anchored in the object of choice are the economists, when they deal with the value of an object, either in the marketplace or in its utility for particular persons.

Theorists concerned with personological problems have sometimes applied the term to classifications of the objects or goals of behavior. Thus, Lasswell[15] and Murray[16] offer classifications of sought-for goals under this rubric; and Ralph K. White's *Value Analysis* is also a catalogue of goals or end-states toward which motivated behavior may be directed.[17] Still others employ terms other than value for related concepts having to do with choice-evoking properties of the object: thus Lewin's valence,[18] Freud's cathexis,[19] and the concepts of reward or incentive value which are current in the psychology of learning.

More characteristically, however, students of personality have understandably been preoccupied with dispositions of the person, and when they have used the term value, they have had some class of evaluative attitude in mind. Here the influence of Gordon Allport and, through him, of Spranger's now-familiar typology of aesthetic, theoretical, economic,

---

[14] W. I. Thomas and Florian Znaniecki, *The Polish Peasant in Europe and America* (Boston: Badger, 1918–1920), Vol. I.

[15] Harold D. Lasswell, "Describing the Content of Communications," in Bruce L. Smith, Harold D. Lasswell, and Ralph D. Casey, *Propaganda, Communication, and Public Opinion* (Princeton, N.J.: Princeton University Press, 1946).

[16] Henry A. Murray, "Toward a Classification of Interactions," in Talcott Parsons and Edward A. Shils, eds., *Toward a General Theory of Action* (Cambridge: Harvard University Press, 1951), p. 463.

[17] Ralph K. White, *Value Analysis*, "The Nature and Use of its Methods" (Glen Gardner, N.J.: Libertarian Press, 1951).

[18] Kurt Lewin, *A Dynamic Theory of Personality* (New York: McGraw-Hill, 1935).

[19] Sigmund Freud, "On Narcissism: An Introduction," in James Strachey, ed., *Standard Edition of the Complete Psychological Works of Sigmund Freud* (London: Hogarth Press, 1957), XIV, 73–102.

political, social, and religious values has been substantial.[20] *A Study of Values* in the Allport-Vernon[21] and the Allport-Vernon-Lindzey[22] versions was for years the only standardized instrument that purported to measure personal values. Its considerable predictive power, as shown for example in studies of creativity and of vocational choice, attests to the fact that it measures something that is humanly important. In the test-oriented field of personality research, its sheer availability, as well as its real merits, led to its widespread use; and its general use, in turn, has tended to center the meaning of personal values, for the student of personality, on essentially the sort of thing that the Allport-Vernon-Lindzey version measures. Spranger's original formulation, in the Germanic spirit of *Verstehen,* has generally been lost to view, and the concept of personal values has come to mean, in common usage, highly general orienting preferences, which are usually assigned a relatively central and hierarchically superior status in the organization of personality.

The view of personal values as general and hierarchically important attitudes, as components of a personal philosophy of life, has also been promulgated in recent research on the psychology of opinions and attitudes. I adopted this usage in an early paper,[23] and it was followed by Bruner, White, and myself in our collaborative work.[24] In a parallel line of development, Daniel Katz and his students at the University of Michigan employed a closely similar conception in their functional theory of attitude structure and change.[25] Assuming that values are more general and central than other attitudes, they show that a person's attitude on a specific issue can be predicted from a joint knowledge of his hierarchy of values and of the instrumental relationship that he perceives between his values and the issue in question;[26] moreover, changes in perceived instrumentality induced by persuasive communication result, in turn, in corresponding changes in attitude.[27] In this framework of analysis, values are

[20] Edouard Spranger, *Types of Men,* trans. P. J. W. Pigors (Halle: Niemeyer, 1928).

[21] Philip E. Vernon and Gordon W. Allport, "A Test for Personal Values," *Journal of Abnormal and Social Psychology,* XXVI (1931), 233–248.

[22] Gordon W. Allport, Philip E. Vernon, and Gardner Lindzey, *A Study of Values,* "A Scale for Measuring the Dominant Interests in Personality" (Rev. ed.; Boston: Houghton Mifflin, 1951).

[23] M. Brewster Smith, "Personal Values as Determinants of a Political Attitude," *Journal of Psychology,* XXVIII (1949), 477–486.

[24] Smith, Bruner, and White, *op. cit.*

[25] Cf. Daniel Katz and Ezra Stotland, "A Preliminary Statement to a Theory of Attitude Structure and Change," in Sigmund Koch, ed., *Psychology,* "A Study of a Science," Vol. 3: *Formulations of the Person and the Social Context* (New York: McGraw-Hill, 1959), pp. 423–475.

[26] Milton J. Rosenberg, "Cognitive Structure and Attitudinal Affect," *Journal of Abnormal and Social Psychology,* LIII (1956), 367–372.

[27] Earl R. Carlson, "Attitude Change Through Modification of Attitude Structure," *Journal of Abnormal and Social Psychology,* LII (1956), 256–261.

inherently supraordinate to the attitudes under study, but a more precise definition of values, which would distinguish them from other general attitudes, is not required. Some people may well ask whether an additional term is really necessary in this context; the same relationships could very likely be expressed in a terminology of attitudes varying in generality-specificity and related hierarchically to one another.

To round out this sketch, we must finally take notice of a kind of usage that fits the scheme more awkwardly: the phenomenological approach that uses the object language to refer to properties of the phenomenal world of the experiencing subject. For the psychologist not reared to this intellectual tradition, the "objective" givenness of values emphasized by Köhler[28] may seem confusingly subjective. He is essentially concerned with the descriptive fact that within the psychological world of the experiencing person, values like beauty or repulsiveness are immediately given properties of the psychological object and are not perceived as arising from his own subjective tastes. Depending on one's preferred theoretical strategies, one may elect to emphasize or to ignore such a phenomenological observation; in any event, Köhler's descriptive point is compatible with an explanatory account that treats values as functional properties that objects acquire, in part, by virtue of their relationships to dispositions of the behaving person.

Personal Values as Standards of the Desirable

The foregoing excursion among some of the options offered by recent usage establishes, if nothing else, the need for explicit decision concerning terminology on the part of anyone who would contribute to this area; a variety of distinguishable and worthy concepts have become attached to the single term. It is time to declare my choice.

My starting point will be the definition given by Clyde Kluckhohn, which has had considerable currency:

> A value is a conception, explicit or implicit, distinctive of an individual or characteristic of a group, of the desirable which influences the selection from available modes, means, and ends of action.[29]

Let us put aside for the time being some of the particulars in this definition. Our main interest will be in personal values, so we can set aside the question of the various ways in which values may be "characteristic of a group." We might also do well to postpone facing the difficulties hidden in the phrase, "which *influences* the selection . . ."; the nature of the influence is a matter to be explored. The possibility should also be left open that a person's "conceptions of the desirable" may sometimes play a merely

---

[28] Wolfgang Köhler, *The Place of Value in a World of Facts* (New York: Liveright, 1938).

[29] Clyde K. M. Kluckhohn, "Values and Value Orientations in the Theory of Action," in Parsons and Shils, eds., *op. cit.*, p. 395.

retrospective role in criticizing or justifying his previous selective behavior. The core of Kluckhohn's definition that I would presently stress, then, is its focus on a particular class of personal dispositions: *conceptions of the desirable that are relevant to selective behavior.*

Personal values in the present sense are attitudes, in the sense of object-directed personal dispositions. But they are a special kind of attitude, functioning as standards by which choices are evaluated. Personal values pertain to the desirable, the preferable, rather than to the merely desired or preferred; to the realm of "ought" rather than that of "is" or "want." As standards against which specific choices are tested they have at least to some degree the hierarchically superior status customarily ascribed to personal values. As I will point out later, they are also often central in the organization of personality, to the extent that they are constitutive of the self. But not all central and hierarchically superior attitudes are personal values in the sense of this definition. One may have highly general preferences, consistencies that underlie many occasions of choice, yet these preferences need not necessarily carry the cachet of preferability. An aspect of the commonly noted erosion of values that has accompanied the shift from absolutism to relativism in our modern culture is surely a shift from the "objective" requiredness of the desirable (ought) to the merely desired (want). It is a significant difference.

I want therefore to highlight rather than to slip past the lack of exact fit between the present conception and that underlying the Allport-Vernon-Lindzey *A Study of Values.* According to the operations of item-checking that go into determining a set of scores on this instrument, it gets at consistent patterns of verbally expressed preferences, just as do the Kuder Preference Record[30] and the Strong Vocational Interest Blank.[31] Very likely, these preferences are often sustained by convictions about the preferable, but the content of the items does not guarantee that such is the case, and there are no external checks to give us this assurance. Similarly with respect to Morris' "Paths of Life."[32] Again the respondent is asked to rank his preferences among complex and widely varying life styles, without any guarantee that the preferences reflect adherence to standards of preferability.

Here I had best pause. The Allport-Vernon-Lindzey is a justly respected test, with which personologists are closely acquainted through long use; and Morris' "Paths" has likewise attracted a good deal of recent interest. It is well enough to establish that the operations involved in these

[30] G. Frederic Kuder, *Kuder Preference Record* (Chicago: Science Research Associates).
[31] Edward K. Strong, Jr., *Vocational Interest Blank for Men, Revised* (Stanford, Calif.: Stanford University Press).
[32] Morris, *op. cit.*

instruments do not correspond precisely to the definition I derive from Clyde Kluckhohn; but why should one prefer the definition to the instruments? It begins to look like a case of everyone out of step but Johnny.

I don't at all intend to disparage the importance of measuring patterns of fundamental preference, as part of the descriptive task of mapping variations in personal philosophy. My objection is simply that these instruments do not come to grips with the distinction that I am presently insisting on. It remains to support my contention that the distinction is worth making.

One ground for the distinction is phenomenological: simply pointing to the vivid qualitative difference commonly evoked by the words "desired" and "desirable." The ensuing section will look more closely at this phenomenal contrast and some possible bases for it. Another reason reverts to one of the criteria touched upon at the outset: reference to distinctively human phenomena within the broader area of selective dispositions. The peculiarly human aspect of selective behavior would seem to be precisely the universal occurrence of standards of the desirable, of "oughts" and "thou shalt nots." Preference and desire and cathexis—motivation and attitude—can be found in a wide range of animal behavior, though of course only one species is capable of completing *A Study of Values*; it is personal values in the sense of Clyde Kluckhohn's definition that pose the challenging theoretical problem at the human level. A final line of justification, to be developed subsequently, is that the conception favored here is fruitful of relationships linking personality to society and culture—relationships of a sort that tantalize the social psychologist.

To fuse preferability with preference for purposes of the descriptive measurement of personality is natural enough, since the distinction is an analytical rather than an empirical one; if we give credence to the sort of strain toward consistency in cognition emphasized by Heider[33] and Festinger,[34] there is reason to expect people more often than not to prefer what they think preferable, and vice versa. So the student of the architecture of personality may often safely neglect the distinction, unless he is concerned with the genesis and functional correlates of the peculiarly human aspect of human valuing.

Similarly, the anthropologist concerned with the analysis of culture patterns can make other fusions. Thus Clyde Kluckhohn moves quickly from his definition of values to the consideration of "value orientations," which he defines as

. . . generalized and organized conception[s], influencing behavior, of nature, of man's place in it, of man's relation to man, and of the desirable

[33] Heider, *op. cit.*

[34] Leon Festinger, *A Theory of Cognitive Dissonance* (Stanford, Calif.: Stanford University Press, 1957).

and nondesirable as they may relate to man-environment and interhuman relations.[35]

Values—as one concretely encounters them, that is—are embedded in a context of fundamental assumptions, "existential," or "is," rather than "ought" propositions. If one is interested in the comparative study of cultural ethos, one has to deal with this fusion of the existential and the normative, just as would be the case in the study of personal philosophies of life. Florence Kluckhohn and her collaborators have pursued the systematic study of value orientations so conceived with much empirical ingenuity.[36] For other theoretical purposes, however, it seems essential to cleave here to the narrower conception of values isolated from the core beliefs with which they are likely to be closely linked.[37]

THE PHENOMENAL OBJECTIVITY OF VALUES

The crux of the present conception of values, then, is the word desirable. As Kluckhohn elaborates, "The desirable . . . is not restricted to what is commonly designated as the 'moral.' It includes the aesthetic and those elements of the cognitive which reflect appraisal. The cue words are 'right' or 'wrong,' 'better' or 'worse.' "[38] All of these words carry for us the connotation that standards apart from personal whim are being applied; in Köhler's sense, "objective" considerations are brought to bear on matters of choice. As with Köhler, the objectivity involved is that of the phenomenal world of the experiencing person. For further clarification of distinctions in this taken-for-granted but elusive realm, it will be profitable to turn to Heider's perceptive analysis of "commonsense psychology" —in this case, his treatment of the concept of "ought."[39]

Heider starts with the Wertheimer-Köhler-Asch conception of requiredness, introduced to describe a situation in which we feel that "something ought to happen." "Requiredness, according to this view, is rooted in the gap or incompleteness of the situation. Acting in accordance with this implicit injunction, acting in a manner that brings about the necessary closure, then becomes identified with the right."[40] But he immediately points to the insufficiency of this interpretation:

> Yet, it is not strictly correct to equate gap-induced requiredness with ought requiredness, for clearly there may be many occasions in which the person may experience the tension of an incompleteness in the situation,

---

[35] C. K. M. Kluckhohn, *op. cit.*, p. 411.

[36] F. Kluckhohn and F. L. Strodtbeck, *op. cit.*

[37] Milton Rokeach, *The Open and Closed Mind* (New York: Basic Books, 1960).

[38] C. K. M. Kluckhohn, *op. cit.*, p. 398.

[39] Heider, *op. cit.*, pp. 218–222.

[40] *Ibid.*, p. 219.

without at the same time experiencing the tension of an ought. For instance, the person may realize that he wants *x*, the situation being incomplete in the sense that his desire is unfulfilled, and yet that he ought not to have it. Or, in interpersonal relations, the person may recognize that someone else wants *x*, but unlike the case in which *o* needs help, filling the gap by satisfying his wants does not necessarily coincide with what ought to be done.[41]

As a first approximation, Heider notes a degree of parallelism between the content of "I ought to do such-and-such" and that of "somebody wants or commands that I do such-and-such."

In the case of ought, however, it is not a particular somebody that is felt to want or command people to do *x*, but some suprapersonal objective order. It may also be experienced as a supernatural being who personifies this objective order. In any case, when *p* [the experiencing person in Heider's convention] has the conviction that he ought to do *x* he recognizes a vector in the environment, a vector which is like a wish or a demand or a requirement on the part of some suprapersonal order and which has the validity of objective existence.[42]

From this starting point, Heider goes on to identify the functional properties of "oughts," as they occur in the person's phenomenal world.

First of all, oughts are impersonal. They refer to standards of what ought to be done or experienced, standards independent of the individual's wishes. That is not to say that personal wishes do not influence the perception of ought forces; it is rather that they "should not," that in principle the ought is established by objective requirements.[43]

Moreover, oughts are dispositional in character. They refer to invariant standards, to "laws of conduct" which hold in spite of many variations in incidental or momentary factors . . . as long as differences among situations do not alter what are perceived to be impersonal objective requirements.[44]

The objectivization of ought as an impersonal, dispositional concept also implies that ought has interpersonal validity. Not only should ought disregard personal desires, not only does ought in principle appear unchanged in spite of incidental situational factors, but it is also universal and should look alike to everybody. . . . If *p* accepts the vector which is given by the objective order and acts accordingly, he feels that he is a "good" person. He may even expect praise. But if he violates the directives of this vector, he may expect punishment.

Thus we see [Heider concludes] that even in this first approximation, the meaning of ought . . . is not a mystical quality somehow attached to the word. It can be defined by investigating the functional role it plays in our thinking and our reactions. We have suggested that it can be represented as a cognized wish or requirement of a suprapersonal objective order which

[41] *Loc. cit.*
[42] *Loc. cit.*
[43] *Loc. cit.*
[44] *Ibid.,* pp. 220–221.

has an invariant reality, and whose validity therefore transcends the point of view of any one person.[45]

The suggestiveness of this phenomenological analysis for a social-psychological and developmental approach is immediately apparent. Before exploring some of the directions that it opens for inquiry, however, we need to place Heider's "ought" in firmer relation to our present treatment of personal values.

The experience of "ought," as Heider has dissected it, would seem to be a prototype of the actual, momentary occurrences of valuing in human behavior; the explicit or implicit standards according to which "ought" is experienced are values in our present sense (Heider employs the term in another way which need not concern us here). "Ought" may not exhaust the occurrences to which values pertain (for example, it seems to fit less aptly experiences of preferability in the realm of the aesthetic), but the phenomenally given objectivity and interpersonal validity that Heider finds characteristic of "ought" would seem to be true of value standards generally.

SOME TYPES OF PHENOMENALLY OBJECTIVE REQUIREDNESS

The phenomenologist may be privileged to rest content with discovering the objectivity with which values are given in naïve experience. For most psychologists, however, phenomenology is a starting point rather than a goal; one asks immediately (perhaps prematurely, the phenomenologist might say) whence the experience of objectivity arises and what difference it makes. To start in this direction of inquiry, it may be helpful to shift from Heider's concern with the features that experiences of "ought" have in common, to ask if there may not be discernible *types* of value requiredness, all experienced as in some sense objective, but perhaps with different sources and functional correlates. Several such types can be distinguished in a preliminary way.

Social Requiredness

One type that is directly suggested by Heider's discussion may be labeled social requiredness: he or they or, projectively, the gods or God require something of me. Heider began by observing the partial similarity between "ought" and someone else's wish or command; one experiences in both cases an expectation from without as to how one should act. For his purposes, Heider went on to contrast the impersonality of "ought," its phenomenal anchorage in the objective order, as compared with the personal quality of commands and wishes. But we must now note once more the similarity; demands from the other are in any event "objective" for p,

45 *Ibid.*, p. 222.

and, in important special cases, personal demands become phenomenally indistinguishable from requirements of the objective scheme of things.

Thus for the infant and young child, his parents as "others" comprise an enormous segment of his relevant world. Until the child attains a fairly sophisticated level of reciprocity, from which he can discount the "human-ness" of his parents' perspective, their wishes and demands are not merely part of the objective order as it emerges for him; they are likely to be among the most important parts to which he has to accommodate. At the beginning of personality, then, we can safely assume that social required-ness provides a basis for the experience of objective requiredness in its full force.

Another special case is that of the traditional culture in which there is a high degree of social consensus on the proper ways of acting in each of the large but finite number of situations that life offers. "They" expect such-and-such of me—but *they* are everyone (probably including the ghosts of my ancestors) ; they comprise my whole social world, and their wishes for me in effect constitute the requirements of the objective order. As in the case of the young child in relation to his parents, here, too, the person has no choice but to accept the requirements of the "others" as given.

To seek in social requiredness a principal basis for the felt objectivity characteristic of adult values is only to rephrase customary thinking about the birth of conscience in the processes of socialization. But as long as we remain on the level of social requiredness as such, the value standards in-volved in the rules set by others—parents or tradition or the Joneses—can be spoken of as personal values only in a very limited sense if at all. The person is in the last analysis oriented toward whatever "they" require; if he goes on to embrace the rules as his own, a new ingredient has entered the picture. In Kelman's terms, pure social requiredness is the sphere of compliance and identification, but not of internalization.[46]

In such an imaginary pure case of social requiredness, there is no difficulty in speaking of cultural values. Thus, the observing anthropologist looks for meaningful patterns that enable him to formulate principles and priorities underlying the many situation-bound rules of a traditional so-ciety. These are cultural values at a higher level of generality than the particular rules that specify good and proper behavior in each culturally recognized kind of situation. In learning the cultural maze while growing up, each individual also learns these rules, which have objective required-ness for him; but if he is primarily oriented to the demands of the others who carry the tradition, it could be misleading to conceive that the more

[46] Herbert C. Kelman, "Processes of Opinion Change, *Public Opinion Quarterly,* XXV (1961), 57–78.

general cultural values (as formulated by the anthropologist) are also his personal values. The rules that define what is situationally proper function as values for him, but they may well be learned as so many particulars. At this level, their significance for him depends on the actual or imagined sanctions of approval or disapproval that back them up. They are extrinsically related to his personality rather than constituents of it.

Something approximating the pure case of social requiredness doubtless occurs in the early stages of individual development, but it seems unlikely that entire societies can be fitted exactly to the type without violence to the facts. The proposed dichotomy of shame versus guilt cultures has not fared well in recent discussions.[47] Whether the pure case exists in any concrete society is immaterial, however, to the analytical utility of the distinction.

Personal Requiredness

Out of social requiredness emerges what may be called personal requiredness, under circumstances that have recently been the subject of intensive inquiry by students of socialization and personality development. The process by which the person moves from one to the other level is conventionally referred to as the "internalization" of values, a term that of course explains nothing. Currently prevalent theory can be related to my scheme if we introduce two subtypes of personal requiredness: superego requiredness and self-requiredness.

Superego requiredness may be said to characterize those standards (values) that the person holds in the fashion portrayed in the classical Freudian superego. The values are "internalized" in that their application to a person's behavior does not depend on the presence of others. But they are inflexibly held, irrationally applied, and are typically implicit, or unconscious, rather than explicitly formulated by the person who holds them. A person may feel ridden by these requirements as something alien to his self. He applies the standards in ways that involve only the most primitive cognitive discriminations. When he violates them, he is burdened with guilt. All told, standards adhered to in this fashion have the earmarks of having been laid down early in life, prior to the firm development of a reflective self. If, as Freud would have it, they are acquired primarily by a process of defensive identification, this could account for the heavy predominance of negative over positive content: "thou shalt not" over "thou shalt," guilt over positive affect.

But superego values are only one kind that involve personal requiredness, and in persons who approach more closely the commonly formulated

[47] Cf. John W. M. Whiting, "Sorcery, Sin, and the Superego," in Marshall R. Jones, ed., *Nebraska Symposium on Motivation, 1959* (Lincoln, Neb.: University of Nebraska Press, 1959).

ideals of maturity and good functioning, they fall into the background as compared with values characterized by what I am calling self-requiredness. These are standards that may be implicit but, in any case, are accessible to conscious formulation. They are actively embraced by the person and thus become constituents of the self, part of what the person feels himself to be and to stand for. Characteristically their application involves more finely differentiated cognitive discriminations than is the case with super-ego values, and they can therefore be applied with more flexibility, appropriateness, and rationality. As one measures oneself and one's behavior against these standards, his self-esteem rises or falls; at low ebb there is a sense of shame or worthlessness to correspond to the supergo affect of guilt, but the negative end of the affective spectrum does not seem to be so inherently dominant as in the case of an active superego. Since they are integrated in the self rather than sealed off in an infantile form, they are open to progressive modification and elaboration. They retain the phenomenal character of objective requiredness emphasized by Heider but are sustained by the individual's active commitment to them as the values that he chooses to live by.

Objective Appropriateness

It would best suit the biases of a social psychologist to stop taking inventory of types of requiredness and values at this point, as the stage is well set for an account that would trace all personal values to sources in social experience, along lines parallel to the theories of the self that view it as a mere looking glass of reflected appraisals, a purely social formation. But just as self theory in the Mead-Cooley tradition ignores the presocial ingredients of organic sensation and body imagery, so I fear it would be in error to claim that the objective requiredness of values can be traced exhaustively to social origins. A place has to be reserved for the role of objective appropriateness as a source of standards having the experienced quality of requiredness. Here we return to the home ground of Köhler's Gestalt account.

The "goodness" or correctness of a solution to a mathematical problem, to pick an extreme example, is objectively required in a way that depends, to be sure, on elements of convention or rules of the game, but at the same time follows ineluctably from the inherent structure of the problem. And a good performance is distinguished from a poor one, whether in the accomplishment of a skilled task, the play of a competitive sport, or the re-creation of a piece of music, according to standards somehow intrinsic to the nature of the activity, the potentialities of form that it entails. These examples have the quality of "ought" that Heider found lacking in some instances of Köhler's "gap-induced requiredness": if one sets out to solve a mathematical problem at all, one "ought" to do it correctly; if one undertakes to perform a task, one "ought' to do it as well as one can. Artists may work within the framework of a cultural style or of a set of classical rules that is fixed by convention, but the critic's judgment of artistic quality is not simply a matter of estimating the degree of fidelity with which the rules have been applied, the style exemplified. He is almost sure to be convinced that within the framework of convention, standards are nonetheless intrinsic and objective, hard as they may be to make fully explicit. What seems common to these cases is that although convention or cultural tradition sets the terms of the problem or defines the materials, modes, and ends of the activity, standards of evaluation arise that have some necessary relation to the structure of the activity and are not themselves merely conventional.

These matters are outside my competence and involve perennial questions about which controversy will not soon be exhausted. It is enough for my present purposes to leave my scheme open to the possibility that elements of objective appropriateness may combine in varying degrees with more clearly social ingredients in the actual genesis of values.

Interrelations

The distinctions I have been drawing are analytical abstractions; the requiredness that attaches to the values actually held by real people can be expected to come from mixed sources. But one may speculate, without altogether losing contact with potential facts, on the interrelations among social and personal requiredness and objective appropriateness.

Where social requiredness has the support of virtually complete consensus on the proper behavior for a stable and exhaustive inventory of culturally defined situations—or an inclusive set of rules—there is little occasion for personal requiredness to become salient, if it develops at all. Here we have the ideal type of the tradition-directed character described by Riesman.[48] As I noted earlier, one can appropriately discern a system of cultural values in such a society, underlying the interlocking set of social rules that has shaken down into coherence through long usage; but these cultural values are hardly constitutive of the individual selves of the society's members. Here perhaps lies a reason for the anomic disorganization often observed when the value system of a traditional society is broken by the radically changed circumstances and cultural intrusions occasioned by exposure to the modern world.

In changing societies where traditional social requiredness can no longer specify what is fitting and proper for a definitive inventory of situations, personal requiredness, if there is the basis for it at all, is likely to become more salient. It becomes more salient partly by default, because

[48] David Riesman, *The Lonely Crowd* (New Haven, Conn.: Yale University Press, 1950).

traditional patterns defined by specified social expectations no longer provide adequately for the predicaments of choice that life brings. And it is reinforced by success; the "gyroscope" of inner directedness, in Riesman's metaphor,[49] has cash value in such circumstances. Of the varieties of personal requiredness, superego requiredness would seem to be the more socially dependable and foolproof when the psychological conditions for its development can be maintained—but at the cost of much personal neurotic suffering and an element of social rigidity. Self-requiredness, a subtler formation, has its special vulnerability.

It is vulnerable because the degree of explicit commitment involved in consciously embracing values as part of the self casts potential doubt upon the objectivity that distinguishes values from tastes or preferences. Remember Heider's analysis of "ought" as impersonal, relatively invariant, and interpersonally valid. For our values to carry the full force of "ought," we need to believe that they have validity beyond our individual fiat, that they are as valid for others as for ourselves. Self-values have this quality of phenomenal objectivity, but it is endangered by the very failure of consensus, the prevalent relativism and pluralistic tolerance, that makes them salient. In other words, they appear to be especially susceptible to change —I was about to say deterioration—into mere tastes and preferences which, since they lack the force of "ought," can hardly play the same central role as values in personal and social integration.

In principle, one can conceive of the person who embraces his values with full commitment in the absence of consensus among his fellows or of belief in a cosmic cheering section rooting behind the scenes for the right. But few of us are like Nietzsche's Superman; all too human, we need the support of cobelievers to remain convinced that our standards are interpersonally valid.[50]

The possible ingredient of objective appropriateness continues to puzzle me. If we think of it as somehow generated by the requirements of historically conditioned human nature, as they mesh or fail to mesh with the situations that people encounter, perhaps we begin to get at intrinsic sources of values in the discovery of value "universals" that recur in most cultures[51] or by the study of directional, "progressive" trends in history in the development of value standards. Or perhaps Asch points to a more promising path when, in his intended refutation of cultural relativism, he seeks to maximize the invariance of value standards transculturally by

---

[49] *Loc. cit.*

[50] Cf. Festinger's emphasis on "social reality," as in Leon Festinger, Henry W. Riecken, Jr., and Stanley Schachter, *When Prophecy Fails* (Minneapolis, Minn.: University of Minnesota Press, 1956).

[51] Clyde K. M. Kluckhohn, "Culture and Behavior," in Gardner Lindzey, ed., *Handbook of Social Psychology* (Cambridge, Mass.: Addison-Wesley, 1954), pp. 921–976.

attributing as much as possible of the intercultural variability in value judgments to cultural differences in the real or culturally defined situation.[52] If we give the principle of invariance of values the benefit of every doubt, as Asch does, what "invariant" values do we in fact come out with from a close study of world cultures?

Granted the possible relevance of objective appropriateness, it is at least conceivable that perceived relationships of appropriateness are an important source of values in personality development, together with the influence of parental demands and expectations which we are now better able to formulate. The suggestive evidence for a core of value universals points, albeit weakly, to continued pressure from this source that partly shapes what is socially or personally required.

THE REFLEXIVENESS OF SELF-VALUES

In the study of lives, it is the self-values that call most insistently for closer investigation, both because of the central part they would appear to play in the organization and integration of the self and because of the instability to which they seem particularly vulnerable under present cultural conditions. Reverting to my previous comments about the most widely used instruments in personological research on values, both *A Study of Values*[53] and "Paths of Life"[54] aim primarily at this value sphere; although, as I noted in criticism, they do not permit a clear distinction between value standards and preferences that lack the force of "ought." New approaches are needed if we are to bring data to bear effectively on such psychologically and socially relevant questions as the conditions and consequences associated with the predominance of values or of tastes. Toward this end, the remainder of the essay is devoted to exploratory discussion of some features of self-values that we may expect on theoretical grounds. The theory I draw on is the convergent body of speculation and research concerning the self, to which sociologists,[55] psychiatrists,[56] and psychologists[57] have contributed.

As an institution of personality, the self has the peculiarity of being a subsystem (a functional construct inferred by the observer-theorist) or-

[52] Solomon Asch, *Social Psychology* (Englewood Cliffs, N.J.: Prentice-Hall, Inc., 1952).

[53] Allport, Vernon, and Lindzey, *op. cit.*

[54] Morris, *op. cit.*

[55] See, e.g., George Herbert Mead, *Mind, Self, and Society* (Chicago: University of Chicago Press, 1934). Mead was of course a philosopher, not a sociologist, but his formulations are central to the sociological analysis of the self.

[56] See, e.g., Harry Stack Sullivan, *Conceptions of Modern Psychiatry* (New York: Norton, 1953).

[57] See, e.g., Theodore R. Sarbin, "Role Theory," in Lindzey, ed., *op. cit.*, pp. 223–258; Ruth C. Wiley, *The Self Concept*, "A Critical Survey of Pertinent Research Literature" (Lincoln, Neb.: University of Nebraska Press, 1961).

ganized around a phenomenal entity existing only for the experiencing person—the self-percept or concept in the sense of the person's organized awareness of his being.[58] The inherent reflexiveness or self-reference of this subsystem (it is hard to talk of these matters without getting into verbal tangles) has been the focus of much theoretical interest.

On the one hand, there is plausible speculation concerning how it comes about, how the direct and naïve awareness of the human infant achieves the sophistication for him to view himself as an object in his phenomenal world. Mead,[59] following earlier suggestions by James,[60] Baldwin,[61] and Cooley,[62] developed the most influential formulation of this problem in his proposal that we progressively attain selfhood and a kind of objectivity through covertly or imaginatively adopting the perspective on our actions of the others with whom we interact. We eventually integrate these partial perspectives into a more stable capacity for self-objectification as we become able to take what Mead referred to as the role of the "generalized other." As noted earlier, this account neglects the contribution of direct body-awareness to the developing self-percept, but its emphasis on social intercourse as an important ingredient of reflective selfhood seems hard to contravene.

And on the other hand, theorists have devoted attention to the special role in the functioning of personality that such a reflexive self can play. For McDougall, the "sentiment of self-regard," just such a reflexive entity, did duty as replacement for the "will" of classical psychology.[63] Sociologists and social psychologists in the tradition of Mead also emphasize the adaptive and integrating value of the self, as the person comes to be able to respond symbolically to his own behavior and attributes in terms that are potentially communicable. The concept of a reflexive self is intimately linked to possibilities of self-control. And, in the personality theory of Carl Rogers, the self is explicitly at the heart of the personality system and, indeed, the source and focus of the most important human motivation.[64]

[58] M. Brewster Smith, "The Phenomenological Approach in Personality Theory: Some Critical Remarks," *Journal of Abnormal and Social Psychology*, XLV (1950), 516–522. Reprinted in Alfred Kuenzli, ed., *The Phenomenological Problem* (New York: Harper & Brothers, 1959), pp. 253–267.

[59] Mead, *op. cit.*

[60] William James, "The Consciousness of Self" in *Principles of Psychology* (New York: Holt, 1890), I, 291–401.

[61] James M. Baldwin, *Social and Ethical Interpretation in Mental Development* (New York: Macmillan, 1913).

[62] Charles H. Cooley, *Human Nature and the Social Order* (New York: Scribners, 1902).

[63] William McDougall, *Social Psychology* (15th ed.; Boston: John W. Luce, 1923).

[64] Carl R. Rogers, *On Becoming a Person* (Boston: Houghton Mifflin, 1961).

So much is essential background for approaching the reflexiveness of values that become incorporated in the self. We may begin by considering how values are probably acquired in the course of the processes of socialization that give rise to selfhood. The child before selfhood has no direct contact with values; what he encounters as he emits behavior that his significant others evaluate is sanctions: tokens, more or less explicit, more or less directly rewarding or punishing, of the approval or disapproval that he has evoked. By the time language comes into the picture (an acquisition that Mead believed to be intrinsically linked to developing selfhood), he also encounters requests and demands, and usually reasons—both for the requests made and for the sanctions administered. And he has the example of the behavior of his parents and significant others and of their accounts of themselves. These are the raw materials from the ongoing social world, out of which the child must construct his own values.

If we leave aside the part played by example and modeling, which may well become important only as the child acquires a relatively well-defined sense of self and other, the foregoing amounts to saying that the child's first acquaintance with values is mediated by the consequences of having his own behavior evaluated, usually by his parents. Just as the primitive "ought," to extrapolate from Heider's analysis, has its source in the parental request, so the initial step in the use of value standards is taken when the child covertly adopts the role of the parent and evaluates his own actions, thoughts, and characteristics as his parent has done: when he administers sanctions of approval or disapproval to himself. Like the self, then, values are essentially reflexive from the start. And in this respect they differ intrinsically from preferences or cathexes, direct orientations toward an object that do not require mediation by taking a role.

Whether or not sanctions or requests are accompanied by more or less explicit reasons understandable to the child may be decisive, determining whether the personal values he acquires in this fashion are assimilated to an increasingly autonomous self-system or embedded in the superego. The self-system is flexible, expanding, relatively integrated, and increasingly autonomous of its origins because the growing person is in continual reflexive discourse with himself through linguistic and imaginal symbols. The reasons that accompany parental sanctions or demands provide the child with symbolic handles that tie the perceived parental standard into this system and permit its continual symbolic reworking, so that the ultimate result is firmly interwoven with his developed self-concept. They also enable the child to formulate the standard for himself in a much more differentiated way than would be possible through unverbalized processes of generalization. If, on the other hand, parental evaluations come arbitrarily without intelligible reasons, the child is likely to adopt them just as arbitrarily, with little differentiation and no basis for subsequent reworking and incorporation into an autonomous self.

These are, of course, characteristics of what we call the superego. Superegolike values are to some extent inevitable from the fact that the infant receives many parental evaluations before he has become symbolically equipped to assimilate them into the self. And this isolated, persistently infantile system of child-perceived parental evaluation is also presumably stocked with evaluations that would provoke too much anxiety for verbal symbolization to be tolerable.

Conceptual Implications

If this account of the genesis of personal values in the self, elliptical as it is, comes near the truth, some consequences follow for the conceptual status of self-values and for directions in which they may fruitfully be approached in empirical research. One implication returns us to a feature of Clyde Kluckhohn's definition that we postponed considering.[65] A value, Kluckhohn asserted, is a conception of the desirable which influences selective behavior; what is the nature of the influence? Seeking a definition that would hold for both personal and cultural spheres, Kluckhohn was necessarily vague on this point. With our present attention focused on self-values, we need to be more specific. Taking self-values as inferred, symbolically formulated standards, we can be sure, a priori, only that they will influence evaluation: judging, praising, or condemning as better or worse, true or false, worthy of admiration or of contempt; evaluating the behavior of others or one's own actions and qualities. It is nearly as safe to assume that one's self-values influence his responses when he is exposed to unfavorable evaluation by others or finds his actions somehow called into question. This should follow from the context of socialization in which self-values are acquired. The child soon learns to call selectively on value standards to defend his actions when they have become suspect. "I wasn't either lying!" assumes a shared value of honesty; "I didn't mean to!" carries the implicit value that intentions count more than acts. In the long pull of maintaining "face" before others and self-esteem within, we all become thoroughly practiced in evoking values to justify ourselves. Justification (or rationalization), like evaluation, is a "self-conscious," reflective operation, which is brought to bear on behavior in retrospect.

But these influences may seem rather trivial; what counts, we may protest, is the prospective, not the retrospective. How are we to formulate the bearing of self-values on one's active choices? One alternative, that taken by French and Kahn, whose treatment of the role of values in personality I find congenial in many respects, is to say that a value may also

[65] See p. 331, *supra*.

be a motive; that when one's values influence one's choices they do so by virtue of motivational force.[66] The issues here are definitional or analytic rather than substantive, I think, but they are nonetheless real. If we are to avoid unnecessary confusion, we need to use our concepts with as rigorous consistency as we can. The concept of self-value at which we have arrived is that of a symbolically formulated standard of the desirable. A standard is not itself a motive, but in relation to other facts, it may generate motivation. For example, the discrepancy between an evaluated state of affairs and what is optimal for the person may give rise to motivation. To insist on this distinction is more than verbal quibbling. It directs us not to look for motivational and nonmotivational classes of values but to try to identify the value standards that the person has adopted, whatever they may be, and only then to inquire how their application or engagement, or its lack, is motivationally relevant.

Implications for Research

Let us finally turn briefly to some implications of this approach to personal values for research in the study of lives. A person's superego values are primitive and obscure, by definition not accessible to his reflective awareness without distortion. To infer them is a matter of subtle indirection and behavioral detection. But self-values, to the extent that they fit our definition, are ideally approached by verbal means. As ingredients of inner discourse, we can tap them through the interview and its derivatives if we enjoy good rapport with our subjects. To be sure, all verbal communication is indirect, and we can never afford to neglect the possibility of deliberate falsification or unintentional distortion as the subject's verbal behavior is shaped in part by the demands of the interview situation. But in the case of the value constituents of the self, the occasion for concealment is less than we may expect to encounter in many other private areas.

That we are tapping something "merely verbal" is no occasion for dismay: the verbal symbolism by which values are knit into the fabric of the self is a source of their importance, not a limitation. Indeed, the notion that "behavioral values" would somehow be firmer stuff than verbal values, could we only get at them, seems to me quite mistaken. Overt behavior is never a direct index of any personological variable, being a result of components attributable to personality and the behavioral situation; for the contribution of personality in this case is further resolvable into motivation and ability, and the motivation, in turn, arises only in part from the engagement of value standards. Talk is of course behavior, too, but it is be-

[66] John R. P. French, Jr., and Robert Kahn, "A Programmatic Approach to Studying the Industrial Environment and Mental Health," *Journal of Social Issues*, XVIII, No. 3 (July, 1962), 1–47.

havior from which we can infer what is revelant to know about a person's values more surely and economically than in any other way.

The more serious problem, which has yet to be solved in systematic research, is to distinguish dependably between values and preferences, between the desirable and the merely desired. Had I solved it, I should probably have been contributing substantive results rather than this essay. Progress toward a solution, however, seems promising in at least three possible directions. One is the complex, informal, recorded interview patterned somewhat after the approach that seemed fruitful in *Opinions and Pesronality*,[67] before the present distinction became critically important. Working from transcripts of such interviews, trained raters could be instructed to maintain the distinction with ascertainable and perhaps satisfactory reliability. A second approach would adapt currently available instruments, revising them to employ a consistent language of "ought," "should," and desirability rather than of wish and preference. And the third would depart from the idea that personal values are especially exposed in the context of justification. It would seek some more or less systematic way to trace a person's grounds for choice back as far as possible.

I have been struggling here with a few of the conceptual problems that have hampered progress in the investigations of personal values, in spite of considerable interest in the general topic. If we can only get a firm grasp on concepts and methods, the study of values should become a promising focus of psychological and humanistic concerns.

[67] Smith, Bruner, and White, *op. cit.*

15: ALBERT CAMUS

Personality as Creative Struggle

Robert N. Wilson

The struggle itself toward the heights is enough to fill a man's heart. One must imagine Sisyphus happy.
 —*The Myth of Sisyphus*[1]

For Albert Camus, as *The Myth of Sisyphus* makes explicit, man is alive only in his struggle, only in his defiant engagement with a world he never made but in which he must live. In pursuit of self-awareness and competence—not mastery—vis-à-vis his environment, man is not pursuing happiness but already enjoying all of that blessed condition he will ever know. For Camus happiness is recognized in activity, not achieved as a state of being; personality is renewed in process, not honed to a finished symmetry.

The life and work of Camus are made more understandable, and their implications for the study of behavior are sharpened by reference to three themes which have consistently distinguished Henry A. Murray's psychological thought: the view that personality is a lifelong dynamic process, a configuration of thoughts, feelings, actions woven into a pattern in social time and space; the belief that creative activity, especially the schooled creativity of art and science, is at once a crucial human characteristic—perhaps the most positive and durable of man's attributes—and a revealing context for the analysis of psychic functioning; the insistent assertion that imaginative literature is significantly related, in manifold ways, to the quality of human life and the effort to comprehend man's behavior.

Further, the French novelist and the American psychologist may be seen as spiritual allies despite their differing fields of endeavor, cultural backgrounds, and life courses. One is an artist, one is a scientist; one French-Algerian, one Old American; one pathetically and accidentally dead in the flush of maturity and rising powers, one enduring in youthful heart and the wisdom that knows no age. But they share a moral passion. Camus' humane concern for the survival of the individual in the modern world transcended his formally beautiful art. Murray's grasp of the possibilities of life, his nurturing devotion to young talent, his radical call for a new testament

[1] New York: Alfred A. Knopf, Inc., Vintage Books, 1959, p. 91.

to avert nuclear dissolution—these transcend his incisive exploration of personality. Still, it may be said of both men that their fundamentally moral postures are at last inseparable from their objective achievements. They *care*; and their deep absorption in the human enterprise, their rectitude in the face of existence, inform the work for which we honor them.

If psychology is defined as "the study of lives," it seems perfectly clear that the writer of fiction, especially if he is extraordinarily accomplished, can contribute much raw material to the scientific analyst. And some would contend that the artist can help the psychologist in a more profound way than by providing dramatic example or casual insight, that he can indeed help to formulate models of mental life. Among other things, the novel is precisely "the study of lives"; moreover, this study is in the best instances a coherent, serious attempt to confront the basic issues posed by human existence.

So it is with Camus as novelist and essayist: he starts from scratch and asks how a man can and should live, how he can regard himself, what stance he can take toward the physical universe, how he can work, how he can be related to other persons. Camus questions the very possibility and worth of living, and he does this in radically naked, direct fashion. Although he is by no means a formal existentialist philosopher, he adopts the attitude of deliberately naïve inquiry into the nature of reality: What is the design of the world as directly experienced? Is human life desirable, and if so how may it be conducted?

THE PHILOSOPHICAL CONTEXT

Camus begins without assumptions to guarantee the worth and meaning of personality. He perceives the universe as chaotic, without pattern and without any significance other than its day-by-day experienced meaning to the individual. He casts off the solace of religious doctrine, of political salvation, of evolutionary progress in men's affairs or in a man's internal development. He insists on a life without illusion, a life of strict honesty toward the self and stoic perseverance toward a witless universe that matches Rossetti's image of "the whirlpool's shrieking face."

In this life, personality is both ground and product of a harsh battle, it is a unique integrity to be created, renewed, rewon in a quotidian fight. Man alone is involved in a struggle without cease, a perilous war of attrition against meaninglessness, brutality, injustice, and ultimate loss of nerve. Camus exhorts us to stop the sacrifice of human beings on the altars of ideology, to live for ourselves and others but not for abstract dictates. Thus he sees personality as neither "given" nor "bought," but as an ongoing achievement. Because the odds against them are so long, right conduct and inner grace are precious trophies to be burnished and constantly retrieved from the flux of existence.

Camus cannot be understood without placing him in the context of modern European man. He is able to ask such searching questions and grapple so vigorously with social psychological problems only because he grew to manhood in a social order stripped of illusion. The stripping involved not only loss and absence, the renunciation of ancient religious and philosophical verities; it involved also the intrusion of total warfare, totalitarian politics, all the wretched spasms of man's inhumanity to man. Essentially, Camus finds that old answers have failed, old myths become less satisfying. Neither the religion of Christianity nor the ideology of Communism, he maintains, affords contemporary man a satisfactory framework for explaining life or a reliable guide for conduct toward his fellows.

Camus' days spanned the Europe of pre-1914 security, the interwar hope of political utopianism and the crushing of that hope in the torments of the 1930's, World War II with its sequels of rehabilitation and destruction. In effect, Camus says, we have been deceived. The universe is not intelligible on the basis of divine plan, and human relations are not intelligible on the basis of historical drift or ideological commandment. The issue is not that of picking up the pieces but of inventing new pieces better tailored to living beings. Camus does not despair, even when his superb intelligence gives him many reasons for despairing. Instead he faces the world; he looks within himself. He dares the most extreme questions and does not flinch from blunt answers. Above all, he continues being a man; he survives with the ironic fortitude he expressed so well: "The important thing, as Abbé Galiani said to Mme. d'Epinay, is not to be cured, but to live with one's ailments."[2]

The grandeur and excitement of Camus' conception of personality is rooted in his view of life as tentative and precarious. To him personality possesses added savor because it is so palpably life in the presence of death, existence with the omnipresent alternative of suicide. An individual, realizing that life is absurd, can get out of it; he can destroy himself, resign from the game, and end forever the struggle to understand, to create a self and a meaning. Camus argues that the question of suicide is the first philosophical issue, and perhaps it is the first psychological one as well. If the option is chosen, then obviously no other problems need be resolved. The fully aware man, in a meaningless universe, has in some sense this first great freedom to choose. His life is lived in the shadow of the choice; if he is determined to go on, one might say that he has affirmed the idea of personality and won the kernel of individual process.

Camus recommends rebellion as the proper philosophical stance toward life. The act of suicide is to him an illegitimate way out of the human predicament. Rather than voluntarily retiring from what seems to be an

[2] *Ibid.*, p. 29.

absurd situation—rational man opposed to irrational universe—the individual should rebel at lack of meaning. This rebellion is not only, or even chiefly, a defiance of political axiom or conventional authority, it is really a rebellion against indignity, against the impotent and irrational and unmanly. Camus holds counteraction to be the wise and courageous reply by the individual to all the senseless terrors of this world. Not being given a finished personality, a revealed reason for living, or an inevitable design in nature, man must create for himself his own vital rationale. His building and maintenance of a viable personality is the nobler because he recognizes the brevity of life. In the inner conviction that his days are short, his triumphs impermanent, his predicament absurd, he yet defies his condition. If he is fully aware and spiritually creative, he wins the short-run battle to be human, even as he necessarily loses the long-run battle to be fixedly right, to be in any sense immortal.

STRANGERS AND PLAGUES

The imaginative achievement of Camus' too-short career is embodied in a series of novels, plays, and essays. His version of personality and social conduct may be traced most clearly in two superb novels, *The Stranger*[3] and *The Plague*,[4] and two central essays, *The Myth of Sisyphus*[5] and *The Rebel*.[6] These writings are in the very first rank of modern European literature and made their author a Nobel laureate while he was still in his early forties. They afford us the testimony of a gifted artist on the situation we are in: What is the problem for personality, for the person-in-action? They give us also Camus' implicit conclusions about what we are to do: In the problematic circumstance of modern life, how can and should a fit individual behave? It might be said that Camus enunciates a rather special psychology, the psychology of the artist or intellectual. Yet not only does he stress the continuity between the artist and everyman, but, as we see repeatedly in history, the problems of the artist at a given time are likely to be the endemic problems of a slightly later era.

The Stranger is the short novel which first brought Camus to wide attention. It is a compact, poetic, merciless account of the absurd man in his first realization of absurdity. The hero, Meursault, has discovered the open secret that the universe is without meaning. His nihilistic response is to abolish value from his personal life, to live a hedonistic calculus but without passion. In personality Meursault is passive, a detached observer of life who satisfies his biological needs in a joyless shadow play. Ennui and fatigue, coupled with a sardonic half-interest in the motives of those

---

[3] New York: Alfred A. Knopf, Inc., Vintage Books, 1954.
[4] New York: Alfred A. Knopf, Inc., 1948.
[5] *Op. cit.*
[6] New York: Alfred A. Knopf, Inc., Vintage Books, 1956.

around him, are his abiding characteristics. Under a hot, relentless Algerian sun, in a universe as drained of vitality as it is drained of meaning, Meursault enacts a senseless career. There is no reason for him to act as he does; but in his own terms there is equally no reason for him to act otherwise.

In Camus' stranger, we find the individual who is estranged from the universe—not one who merely dislikes his part in the scheme of things, but one who denies that the scheme of nature or society, or his role in them, has any significance whatever. Meursault might say, with the Bazarov of *Fathers and Sons*: "We have nothing to boast about but the sterile knowledge of understanding, up to a certain point, the sterility of what exists."

In plot, *The Stranger* rehearses a simple, stark chain of unwitting doom. Meursault is first encountered as he reacts to his mother's death, and our first clue to his nature is that he does *not* react. He knows what he is expected to feel and to do, but he goes through the motions of mourning in a numb, trancelike state, feeling no emotion stronger than annoyance. His mother's death is an imposition upon him, since he must trouble himself to appear grieved, to accept condolence, to pretend that the end of her life and their relationship is a meaningful event. Throughout the vigil and the funeral, Meursault preserves a flat level of affect. His emotional neurasthenia is seen as he apologizes to his superior for taking time off from work to go to the funeral, as he refuses to look at his mother's body, as he plods sweating to the church. The tone is manifest in his exchange with the undertaker (Meursault is the narrator) :

> "Sun's pretty bad today, ain't it?"
> "Yes," I said.
> After a while he asked: "Is it your mother we're burying?"
> "Yes," I said again.
> "What was her age?"
> "Well, she was getting on." As a matter of fact, I didn't know exactly how old she was.[7]

Meursault proceeds to have a desultory love affair, beginning immediately after his mother's burial. Toward the girl, Marie, he again feels nothing; he sees her claim upon him as an invasion, a violation of his desire not to be engaged with the world.

When he is offered a better job, he refuses. His job means nothing more than onerous routine, an interference with sleep, and another invasion of his passive privacy. Indeed, the idea of "better" or "worse" among his activities and relationships is quite foreign to him. Anything is as good as any other thing.

Without reason, he is drawn into visiting the seaside with a casual

[7] *The Stranger, op. cit.,* p. 19.

friend who fears a violent encounter with some Arabs. He arms himself against a possible clash. Strolling the beach, he comes upon one of the Arabs. He thinks he sees the glint of a knife, and in the dizzying heat he fires and kills. Brought to trial, he offers no defense. He has seemingly murdered without motive, but his conviction and sentence to death hinge less on the act itself than on his obdurate lack of remorse. Meursault is in fact convicted *for not caring*; his guilt is in his detachment from life:

> Replying to questions, he said that I'd declined to see Mother's body, I'd smoked cigarettes and slept, and drunk *café au lait*. It was then I felt a sort of wave of indignation spreading through the courtroom, and for the first time I understood that I was guilty.[8]

At his trial, the most damning indictment against him is his disregard of social convention; his unfeeling behavior at his mother's funeral is emphasized by the prosecutor to show his essential inhumanity. Only as his execution is imminent does he begin to feel the attractions of life. Life in the presence of death takes on color, savor, a sense of purpose in his resolution to die well and justly.

Meursault is a nihilist, holding the philosophy of the ultimately estranged individual. He represents what Camus elsewhere distinguishes as two of the logical implications of nihilism: rational egoism, a strategic and utter selfishness oriented solely to the convenience and comfort of the self; and annihilation, the destruction of the existing order. All that happens in *The Stranger* is viewed entirely in its implications for Meursault, who is really unable to participate in anything that occurs outside his own musings, his internal dialogue. So self-entrapped is he that he is constantly fatigued, longing for the rest and sleep which shut out the boring, repellent world and excuse him to be alone with himself.

If Meursault is the rational egoist, he is also the agent of annihilation. His final assertion of the lack of meaning in his life is to commit a meaningless murder. Murder is the ultimate act of destruction, first of another personality and then, by inexorable implication, of the self. To Camus, murder is, like suicide, an illegitimate path of rebellion against existence. In *The Rebel* he describes it thus:

> It is the limit that can be reached but once, after which one must die. The rebel has only one way of reconciling himself with his act of murder if he allows himself to be led into performing it: to accept his own death and sacrifice.[9]

This is precisely what Meursault does. And it is senseless: the victim is a stranger to the killer, just as the killer is a stranger to the universe.

[8] *Ibid.*, p. 112.
[9] *Op. cit.*, p. 282.

Murder is the culmination of a search for total freedom of action. It is the limiting case of nihilism, expressed by the radical statement: "It is a matter of indifference to kill when the victim is already condemned to death." That is, if all men are mortal and if life has no meaning, what natural design or moral law has a murderer in fact contravened? As Meursault muses before killing the Arab: "And just then it crossed my mind that one might fire, or not fire—and it would come to absolutely the same thing."

Meursault might be seen as a skeletal personality, an individual purged of convention and delusion. He has a certain uncluttered purity; he has faced existence and cast off the trappings of older images of man. But his pristine self is without positive force; he represents the first stage of absurdity, an awareness of the plight. His single initiating act is mistaken: he has used the freedom afforded by absurd cognition in an illicit way. Meursault reconciles himself with the murderous act by "accepting his own death and sacrifice." In this acceptance he begins for the first time to feel, to have active likes and dislikes. His approaching death brings him a feeling of certainty. Somehow cleansed by his willful act and its fated consequence, he opens his heart to the "benign indifference of the universe." Meursault gains awareness of his existential freedom to choose at the moment when he is about to lose it. Paradoxically in a logical sense, but understandably from a psychodynamic viewpoint, he enjoys subjective freedom in the only well-defined social role he has ever known: the role of prisoner awaiting the guillotine. Gone are the ambiguities, the tensions of unresolved desire, the anxieties of choice.

The Stranger may represent a clearing-away of dead wood, a farewell to divinely assured man and historically complacent man. Perhaps such a destructive leave-taking is necessary to blot out traditional models of personality and traditional bondage to blind social forms. Meursault *sees* clearly although he acts wrongly. But Camus does not stop with this fearsome surgery, this devilishly bold attempt to return to the primitive issues of man's existence. *The Stranger* states the case for the individual's freedom to make himself and to find refreshment in a naïve, poetic experience of the universe—as if nature and society were truly confronted for the first time, with all patterns to be questioned, all actions newly evaluated. But Meursault's response is a monstrous error. Camus' next novel, and probably his finest, *The Plague*, is in an important sense an answer to the dilemma posed by *The Stranger*: How can the individual find meaning in an indifferent cosmos, how can he conceive his life in terms that make life preferable to death?

Meursault has simple, sensuous joys and direct perceptivity. The heroes of *The Plague* add to these rudimentary virtues a higher pair: the sense of vocation and the capacity for love. Their situation demands the exercise of devoted intelligence and energy, for it involves not merely the problems of living a normal life but also the high challenge of pestilence—the active forces of death. In explicit plot, *The Plague* is as bare and simple as *The Stranger*: an epidemic of bubonic plague is visited on the city of Oran, and the narrative tells us how various citizens behave in a situation of extreme threat. Camus makes it clear, however, that plague as physical disease symbolizes all the inhumanities and deaths to which men are recurrently exposed; the human condition is vulnerable to war, cruelty, injustice, lack of love, lack of purpose, and all these are summed up in the plague bacillus. Many persons are followed through the long months of epidemic terror, the isolation, fear, and suffering unto death. And the city itself is followed, the human community under stress in its shifting moods and colors. Basically, we are told how people respond to ultimate threat: how they live with it, fight it, die from it.

Camus traces a climactic period in the lives of lovers, criminals, priests, the young and the aged, observers, officials, and healers. Oran is walled off from the outside world, turned in upon itself to cope with a pestilence which at its peak carries off hundreds of victims each day. The first and last torments of the victims are described in brutal clinical detail, always in the context of personal history and tangible urban environment. In essence, *The Plague* is a grim morality tale, underwritten and told without pomposity or sentimentality; it is, strikingly, a morality tale in which morals are constantly offered up for testing and re-evaluation, in which codes are questioned under the last duress of imminent death. Above all, it is the story of a fight, of the strategies people adopt to combat a fierce disease that threatens each of them in its capricious path through the population of Oran.

A model of personality and a model of conduct are implicit in the leading characters of *The Plague*. The host of individuals all reveal facets of Camus' conception, but the core is most firmly embodied in two men: the physician, Dr. Rieux, who is the novel's chief figure and purported narrator; and the rather mysterious Tarrou, a person of no fixed occupation and therefore a poet or saint. Rieux and Tarrou are distinguished by a quiet heroism, an understated courage that gains an added force from contrast with the lurid ravages of the plague itself. The novel recounts the impact of disease on Oran, the disjunctions in private lives and community organization, and especially the strenuous exertions of Rieux and Tarrou in the care of the afflicted. It is overtly a losing battle; the epidemic runs a long and virulent course, the healers cannot save those they love best or even one another. But they never surrender to the plague, never cease to be rebels against death. It is just this endless rebellion in the service of life which constitutes the moral imperative for Camus: to live without appeal to absolutes of faith or reason; to see as clearly as possible; to avoid giving others pain; to fight plague wherever it appears.

The idea of personality as a process and of happiness as a by-product of struggle is integral to both *The Plague* and the brief philosophical essay *The Myth of Sisyphus*. In a sense, Sisyphus' task is a mythic analogue of Rieux's vocation of healing:

> The gods had condemned Sisyphus to ceaselessly rolling a rock to the top of a mountain, when the stone would fall back of its own weight. They had thought with some reason that there is no more dreadful punishment than futile and hopeless labor.[10]

Dr. Rieux, too, realizes that all must be done again, that the epidemic will carry off many of those he has treated and that other epidemics will occur. Yet he sees the fight against all our plagues as both necessary and intrinsically rewarding. He and Tarrou inherit Camus' notion of "humiliated thought"; they do not believe themselves utterly right, are not arrogant or all-wise. They humbly recognize that they may not always even identify the plague correctly, but Tarrou states their duty, ". . . on this earth there are pestilences and there are victims, and it's up to us, as far as possible, not to join forces with the pestilences."[11]

Fulfillment for these heroes lies in struggle. One must imagine them to be, like Sisyphus, happy. Their happiness, like his, rests on two primary supports which enable them to endure in a world without ultimate meaning or hope of ultimate achievement. Sisyphus, says Camus, glories in his freedom from illusion, in the concrete shape of his natural world, in the tangible reality of his chore. And so it is with Rieux and Tarrou: their morale is refreshed by acute awareness and by obviously important work. Both their consciousness and their labor are manifestations of love, although in modesty and toughness they do not speak of love. As Rieux, the healer, speaks of his goals, "Salvation's much too big a word for me. I don't aim so high. I'm concerned with man's health; and for me his health comes first."[12]

Tarrou, the poet who has joined in the grinding labor against the plague, speaks of his morality. It is the morality of the artist, the true perceiver, informed by love of victims and hatred of oppressors. Consciousness, by which he means the maximum of alertness, sensitivity, and knowledge, is seen as a goal for personality.

> The soul of the murderer is blind; and there can be no true goodness nor true love without the utmost clear-sightedness. . . .[13]

[10] *Op. cit.*, p. 88.
[11] *The Plague, op. cit.*, p. 229.
[12] *Ibid.*, p. 197.
[13] *Ibid.*, p. 121.

And I know, too, that we must keep endless watch on ourselves lest in a careless moment we breathe in somebody's face and fasten the infection on him. What's natural is the microbe. All the rest—health, integrity, purity (if you like)—is a product of the human will, of a vigilance that must never falter. The good man, the man who infects hardly anyone, is the man who has the fewest lapses of attention.[14]

Rieux questions him, wondering at his involvement in public health when he appears to be a man without faith or announced altruism:

Rieux: "Your code of morals? What code?"
Tarrou: "Comprehension."[15]

THE SOCIAL PSYCHOLOGY OF EXTREMITY

Camus' fiction portrays extreme situations; his men are always living in high tension, "at the stretch," as Rieux describes the sensations of an attentive plague fighter. In this vein, his imaginative work corresponds to the harsh angularity of his essays, the pushing of limits which marks the confrontation of the absurd in root philosophical terms. Distortion of reality, grotesque happenstance, the polarity of evil and holiness, a social stage denuded of the petty comforts of conventional life—all these are characteristic of modern literature in its attempt to persuade men of the enormity of their condition. It is as if the felt confusion of values, the revelation of evil in war and totalitarianism, the sense of being somehow lost in a disorganized social universe were translated into imaginative chaos and bitter unrealism.

One might suppose that in showing us a deranged world the artist is akin to the clinical psychologist, illuminating normal functioning by seizing on the accentuated lessons—and lesions—of the abnormal. Erikson has justified our concern with the atypical by recalling Freud's image of the broken crystal, which reveals its structure best in a shattered state. We have evidence, too, from studies of behavior in natural disasters such as fires and tornadoes, that the actions of men under profound stress are relevant to theories of behavior in the large.

There are at least three levels on which Camus' presentation of human extremity may be discussed: (1) as a veridical rendering, exaggerated only in superficial detail, of certain timeless problems inherent in the human condition; (2) as a reflection of issues which are specific to twentieth-century urban man, issues sharpened for us by the sacrifice of moderation and familiar habitude in fictional guise; and (3) as a study of *de facto* extremity, of the way people act in situations which are avowedly abnormal and catastrophic.

The first of these alternatives would perhaps be most appropriate to

[14] *Ibid.*, p. 229.
[15] *Ibid.*, p. 120.

Camus' explicit intent, although obviously these ways of seeing are not mutually exclusive. His protagonists are in the kinds of situations men have always been in; they differ from the classical heroes of tragic circumstance only in their extraordinary awareness of their plight, which is bound up with their terrifying freedom from dogma. They are in the plight of Oedipus, but there is no pattern of justice and injustice. They are in the plight of Job, but there is no God, however deaf. They are in the plight of Lear, but there is no accepted measure of nobility in character or value in the affairs of men. All of Camus' heroes rehearse the eternal ordeals which are inseparable from being human. Meursault, the stranger, poses the question of intelligibility in the universe: Where is the design that makes one act preferable to another? Is life to be chosen over death? Rieux, the plague doctor, announces again the problem of Job: Why should there be senseless suffering, why the death of a child from bubonic plague? In *The Plague*, too, we are asked the basic moral question: What do men owe to life, and to one another?

Underlying such traditionally formulated issues and implicit in much of Camus' work is the fundamental dualism of the human being as at once animal and angel—the dislocation between virtuosity in symbolic behavior and bondage to physiological imperatives, especially as expressed in man's persistent estrangement from the immediacies of experience. The Camus hero's task is well expressed in the ancient observation of Heraclitus, "Man is estranged from that with which he is most familiar and he must continuously seek to rediscover it." The rediscovery of the familiar in the light of cosmic indifference, the primitive seeking of a way to live, may be seen as the chief assignment of the absurd man.

Contemporary dilemmas, the second possible ordering of Camus' fictional themes, center on a truism of modern literary criticism that men exist among a confusion of values, a confusion so pronounced that some live without values. The novelist covertly and the critic overtly deplore the lack of valuative consensus in the modern world. To it they refer the anxious questioning of the self-conscious hero and the difficulty of artistic communication in a society bereft of symbolic communion. Since men no longer share a religious world view or any other consistent, received hierarchy of values, they cannot agree on the meaning of symbols or share a recognized set of terms for the interpretation of experience. The widespread apprehension of "normlessness," roughly indicated by the sociological concept of *anomie*, is at the heart of the absurd man's being; he questions all things, including the legitimacy of the questions themselves. Thus Meursault in *The Stranger* and Camus in his essays.

The social organization that is often called "mass society" is the setting for the absurd hero's interrogation of the life around him. This social web, now seemingly so dense that it stifles, now so thin that it leaves the individual gasping for sustenance, is seen as both cause and effect of the valuative breakdown. Its trite features include the depersonalization that characterizes large numbers of people engaged in relationships of a fragmented, transitory cast; in sociological terms, this is a society marked by many "secondary relationships," interpersonal contacts emphasizing a particular aspect or role of the individual—buyer and seller, for instance—at the expense of his fully unique personality. This taking of parts for wholes is often related to what Maurice Stein called "the eclipse of community," the feeling that we are not now members of one another in anything like the fashion of smaller, intimate face-to-face groupings. No one in *The Stranger,* including his mother, is at all close to Meursault; he soon discovers that people have nothing to say to one another.

There are other facets of life today which help create the sense of extremity and the burden of loneliness. We are at once overstimulated and stultified, in the popular critical view. Overstimulated by the plethora of inputs from the mass media of communication, we are unable to find a quiet place; stultified by the routine requirements of work in large bureaucracies, we are unable to exert creative will. Over all these features hovers the shadow of rapid change, as life slips through and around the person, as society changes the rules before the player has mastered the game.

Of final, special relevance today is the set of issues Erikson terms "the problem of ego identity." The question of knowing who one is, and hopefully why, gnaws the hero in fiction as in life. All of Camus' characters search for self-knowledge, regarding their identities as fleeting and their postures in the eyes of others as problematic. Individuals are unsure of "placing" themselves and others in a fluid social environment. One's work may carry a label but not a seal of worthful conviction. Personal identity, personality itself, is a struggle without end.

Finally, we may see Camus' landscape as a realistic disaster area. In this perspective the novels are instructive commentaries on social disarticulation. Disaster in *The Stranger* is personal, not mass murder and guilt, but the death of one Arab and the prospective demise of his killer. Yet the shock of disaster, the changed orientation of Meursault as temporary survivor, the coping behavior of the persons involved are illustrative of general human processes in extreme situations. *The Plague* is much more nearly an analogue of social disaster on a wide scale and is indeed almost a text for community life under duress. Here we find the slow reluctance to recognize disaster, as the pestilence is assimilated to "normal" events for as long as possible. We find the shock of definition— the plague comes to be called a plague—and the numbed acceptance of mass fatalities. There are heroism and competent adaptation; there are also cowardice, apathy, and random frenzy. Most importantly, *The Plague* reveals the way communities pull themselves together constructively under

disaster and the way individuals act with a competence and generous efficiency. Here the novelist foretells many of the generalizations which have
been more recently derived from scientific field studies of disaster. Camus
teaches what research affirms: that the stress of abnormal events calls forth
assured coping more often than panic; that the challenge of extremity may
stimulate both a firmer communal bondage and a more ample individual
capacity to deal with the environment.

The final paragraphs of *The Plague* give point to the idea that extreme situations reveal much that is positive in human character. What
Camus says here is pertinent to classical and contemporary philosophical
extremity as well as to overt disaster; it also leads us toward his conception
of personality as unresting struggle. The citizens of Oran are celebrating
the lifting of the plague:

> And it was in the midst of shouts rolling against the terrace wall in
> massive waves that waxed in volume and duration, while cataracts of
> colored fire fell thicker through the darkness, that Dr. Rieux resolved to
> compile this chronicle, so that he should not be one of those who hold
> their peace but should bear witness in favor of those plague-stricken people;
> so that some memorial of the injustice and outrage done them might en-
> dure; and to state quite simply what we learn in a time of pestilence: that
> there are more things to admire in men than to despise.
>
> None the less, he knew that the tale he had to tell could not be one of
> a final victory. It could be only the record of what had had to be done,
> and what assuredly would have to be done again in the never-ending fight
> against terror and its relentless onslaughts, despite their personal afflictions,
> by all who, while unable to be saints but refusing to bow down to pesti-
> lences, strive their utmost to be healers.[16]

CONCLUSION

It is perfectly clear that Camus as artist enunciates neither a formula
for personality nor a detailed model for conduct. His laws of human behavior are the common law of precedent, of hard-gained experience, not
the codified law of civil postulate. Yet the student of personality and
society discovers in his creations both a valid statement of existential
boundaries and a wise, fresh proposal for action.

Life is involvement. Personality is the process of being actively engaged with one's world. What Camus asks is that the individual exercise
conscious choice and that he persist in the exercise, despite his recognition
of man's frailty and his knowledge that there are no ultimate certainties
toward which he may steer. Sisyphus and Dr. Rieux are alike in their
endurance, their acceptance of a work to be done all again, and their
glorying in the struggle for its own sake. In Gordon Allport's words,
their motives are "functionally autonomous," resting not on instinctual
drive or the promise of distant applause but on intrinsic satisfactions.

[16] *Ibid.*, p. 278.

The themes of engagement and effortful choice are complemented by a stoic humanism that enjoins healing. Dr. Rieux is a symbol of this defiant refusal to neglect the daily needs of others. An admirable personality is a committed one, spending itself in the grim battle against plagues of all kinds. Camus essentially holds that the individual fulfills himself in loving devotion to other men; but this devotion is not an abstract, bloodless love geared to religious dicta or vague humanitarian sentiments. Rather, it is the watchful care and energetic construction of the man who lives every day fully, sees every choice in its charged human significance. As Camus writes in *The Rebel:*

> This insane generosity is the generosity of rebellion, which unhesitatingly gives the strength of its love and without a moment's delay refuses injustice. Its merit lies in making no calculations, distributing everything it possesses to life and to living men. It is thus that it is prodigal in its gifts to men to come. Real generosity toward the future lies in giving all to the present.[17]

The capstone of this orientation to personality and conduct is the idea of creativity. Camus takes the artist as prototype of the free man, who glories in the struggle to be alive and to clarify reality. He says the human will has "no other purpose than to maintain awareness." For him this is precisely what personality means: the fully alert man engaged in war against disorder, sloth, blindness. And this personality truly makes itself in an endless nervous process; it must do so, since it has no external props, no absolutes, no secure resting place. Awareness implies a heady freedom. Just because the modern individual is in a hard world and has foregone the soothing illusions of the past, he is free to choose. He can be self-generating, can be an exemplar of the "pro-action" that Henry Murray opposes to the traditional psychological model of reactive man. And so the creative man as Camus explains him:

> Of all the schools of patience and lucidity, creation is the most effective. It is also the staggering evidence of man's sole dignity: the dogged revolt against his condition, perseverance in an effort considered sterile. It calls for a daily effort, self-mastery, a precise estimate of the limits of truth, measure, and strength. It constitutes an *ascesis*. All that "for nothing," in order to repeat and mark time. But perhaps the great work of art has less importance in itself than in the ordeal it demands of a man and the opportunity it provides him of overcoming his phantoms and approaching a little closer to his naked reality.[18]

Camus' psychology, like Murray's, is not susceptible to easy summary. It is a protean conception of man, shrewdly cognizant of all the deficits in the human condition and still aware of the surpluses. Both thinkers empha-

---

[17] *Op. cit.,* p. 304.
[18] *The Myth of Sisyphus, op. cit.,* p. 85.

size the individual's capacity to act on his environment and to order himself toward substantial achievement. Both exalt the creative act, seeing it as the healthy essence of being human. Each has plumbed the black recesses of personality and known the shock of horror at man's inhumanity, yet held to a sturdy secular faith in the individual will. Personality is growth and constant learning, the unfinished business of every man. Camus states "the only original rule of life today: to learn to live and to die, and, in order to be a man, to refuse to be a god." Camus and Murray stress growth, openness to experience, exhibiting the true humility of the audacious questioner. And both come at the end to a profound optimism, grounded not in feckless hope, but in the deep endurance of sentient personality.

16: TWO INFLUENCES ON FREUD'S SCIENTIFIC THOUGHT

A Fragment of Intellectual Biography

Robert R. Holt

If Freud never quite expressed what Murray was to formulate with grand precision—that personology is the study of human lives, that personality is the pattern of a life as lived through time—still his thought and work formed the indispensable basis from which these bold conceptions grew. Likewise, Freud initiated the psychological study of a man through his ideas, proposing and exemplifying thematic exegesis as a way of learning more about people and their work alike—an enterprise that was elaborated, systematized, and domesticated to the grasp of the working clinical psychologist by Murray in the T.A.T. It seems appropriate here to examine, in however partial and limited a way, two themes in Freud's thought, their development across the arc of his life, and their embeddedness in the man and his milieu.

FREUD'S THREE TYPES OF THEORY

When one reviews the body of Freud's theoretical writings, one is struck by their diversity and extensiveness, as well as by the extraordinary lucidity, power, and insight of his formulations. At the risk of considerable oversimplification, I want to suggest a preliminary classification into three types of theory.[1] These in turn will lead us into an examination of some aspects of Freud's scientific training and his contact with trends or traditions of scientific thought, which may have influenced him.

First and best known is the clinical theory of psychoanalysis, with its psychopathology, its theory of psychosexual development, of character formation, and the like. The subject matter of this type of theorizing is

[1] I am not attempting a comprehensive treatment of intellectual influences on Freud, which would be much broader in scope, but merely to develop the implications of some ideas put forward by Bernfeld in "Freud's Earliest Theories and the School of Helmholtz," *Psychoanal. Quart.*, XIII (1944), 342–362. The influences of Hughlings Jackson and Herbart in particular have been neglected here.

major events in the life histories of persons, over a span of time ranging from days to decades. This theory is the everyday, working stock-in-trade of the clinician—not just the psychoanalyst, but the vast majority of psychiatrists, clinical psychologists, and psychiatric social workers. Loosely referred to as "psychodynamics," it has even penetrated into general academic psychology, via textbooks on personality.

Second, there is what David Rapaport calls the general theory of psychoanalysis, also called metapsychology. Its subject matter (processes in a hypothetical psychic apparatus or, at times, in the brain) is more abstract and impersonal; and the periods of time involved are much shorter—from microseconds up to a few minutes. The processes involved are mostly those of dreams, thinking, affect, and defense; the reasoning involved is much closer, and there is more use of theoretical models. The main works I have in mind here are the *Project for a Scientific Psychology*, Chapter 7 of the *Interpretation of Dreams*, and the metapsychological papers.

Third, there remains a considerable body of Freud's writing, about which one hears rather little these days, which might be called his *phylogenetic theory*. The subject matter is man as a species or in groups and events over periods of time ranging from generations to eons. These are Freud's grand speculations, largely evolutionary and teleological in character; they contain no explicit models of a psychic apparatus, employing instead many literary, metaphorical concepts. The principal works in question are *Totem and Taboo, Beyond the Pleasure Principle, Group Psychology and the Analysis of the Ego, The Future of an Illusion, Civilization and its Discontents,* and *Moses and Monotheism.*

It should be obvious that the dividing lines between these various types of theory are not as clear and sharp as I have implied, and any one book of Freud's may include aspects of all three kinds. For this reason I have not tried to fit a number of his most important theoretical works into this scheme. But I think it may be helpful in organizing some thoughts about the ways Freud worked as a scientist.

Note, first, that clinical contributions are among the earliest of Freud's papers that we read today, and that he continued to write in this vein all of his life. As far as the other two types of theory are concerned, however, they occupy only partly overlapping periods of time: the major metapsychological works came early, the main phylogenetic ones late. As Freud's concepts became more metaphorical and dealt with such grandiose issues as ultimate origins and the meaning of life and death, he became less concerned with portraying or systematically accounting for the course and fate of an impulse or thought. Consider, for example, the sequence from the *Project* to *The Ego and the Id*. The first work follows processes in great detail, not only through great systems of the brain, but through individual neurons. The seventh chapter of *The Interpretation of Dreams* traces the formation of a dream through a determinate sequence of systems containing less explicit pathways. In the metapsychological papers, the changes introduced into the topographic model make it no longer possible for this process of topographic regression to take place; and by the time we reach the structural model in *The Ego and the Id* there is no reference to pathways, no clear statement of how even a simple process involving perception and action traverses the newly promulgated systems of ego, superego, and id. We know that somehow they all participate, but there is no way to tell specifically *how*. That was no longer the type of conceptual problem that interested Freud.

What are the origins of these three quite different types of theory, and what can we discern in Freud's life that may illuminate the changes that took place in his preferred style of conceptualizing? In the course of attempting answers to these questions, I shall digress freely to take note of a number of other features of Freud's style of working as a scientist and shall offer further hypotheses and remarks about them.

About the clinical theory, I have least to say. I have not studied it with as intensive attention to its methodological features as I have the other two types and can only state a casual impression that in this realm Freud conceptualized in a clear and orderly manner, as well as with great originality. Because his most creative and novel contributions, as well as his most widely accepted ones, are in the clinical theory, it is hardest to trace their conceptual ancestry. Yet one can see some roots of this part of Freud's work in clinical medicine, neurology, and psychiatry, with their emphasis on molar, common-sense observation, coupled with the use of modest concepts that attempt little more than to name phenomena that have been rather directly observed. To the extent that Freud's greatly admired teacher Theodor Meynert dealt with psychiatry and not neurology, it was psychiatry of the classical descriptive variety, in which the principal method is that of following the course of an illness without any particular efforts at interfering. It was a branch of natural history in which the species being observed were psychotics of various types. Even though Freud did not spend long on his teacher's psychiatric wards, Meynert provided all his psychiatric instruction, gave him a place in his laboratory of brain anatomy, and made a powerful impression on him.[2] His other mentor, Josef Breuer, also seems to have been gifted in this type of molar observation; it was he who did the unusual thing of spending so much time with a patient, Anna O., listening to her and observing the sequence of events in her illness in a relatively noninterfering way, which enabled him to make some of the first psycho-

[2] S. Bernfeld, "Sigmund Freud, M.D., 1882–1885," *Int. J. Psychoanal.*, XXXII (1951), 204–217.

dynamic constructions. And we know that Breuer's accounts of this case had a strong influence on Freud.[3]

Freud seems not to have been particularly proud of his clinical theory. He undoubtedly had a stronger emotional investment in his two other types of scientific thinking, and he tried to translate the clinical formulations into the much more ambitious process terms, first, of his neuropsychology and, later, of his metapsychology. Both times, however, he was not satisfied with the result. Thus, he did not send to Wilhelm Fliess the later, psychopathological parts of the *Project*; and out of the original group of twelve metapsychological papers he apparently destroyed those that dealt with anxiety, conversion hysteria, obsessional neurosis, the transference neuroses in general, and paranoia, publishing only one of this kind ("Mourning and Melancholia").[4] The difficulties, I think it is fair to guess, lay not with the clinical observations and the concepts in which they were formulated but with the more abstract, general theory, which could not very well accommodate them.

Freud's more favored types of thinking—the general, or process, theorizing and the contrasting speculative-phylogenetic theorizing—derive, as I hope to show, from two contrasting trends in German thought, which might be called hard and soft: the classical, tough-minded, and highly scientific tradition of physicalistic physiology, which gave rise to process theories; and the romantic, wide-ranging tradition of *Naturphilosophie,* the principal intellectual ancestor of Freud's phylogenetic theories.

"NATURPHILOSOPHIE" VERSUS PHYSICALISM

In "An Autobiographical Study," Freud wrote about the time when he was finishing the *Gymnasium:*

> Neither at that time, nor indeed in my later life, did I feel any particular predilection for the career of a doctor. I was moved, rather, by a sort of curiosity, which was, however, directed more towards human concerns than towards natural objects; nor had I grasped the importance of observation as one of the best means of gratifying it. My deep engrossment in the Bible story (almost as soon as I had learnt the art of reading) had, as I recognized much later, an enduring effect upon the direction of my interest. Under the powerful influence of a school friendship with a boy rather my senior who grew up to be a well-known politician, I developed a wish to study law like him and to engage in social activities. At the same time, the theories of Darwin, which were then of topical interest, strongly attracted me, for they held out hope of an extraordinary advance in our understanding of the world; and it was hearing Goethe's beautiful essay on nature

---

[3] S. Freud, "An Autobiographical Study," in James Strachey, ed., *Standard Edition* (London: Hogarth, 1959), XX, 21 f.

[4] E. Jones, *The Life and Work of Sigmund Freud* (New York: Basic Books, 1955), II, 208 f.

read aloud at a popular lecture by Professor Carl Brühl just before I left school that decided me to become a medical student.[5]

"Goethe, who determined this choice," Bernfeld writes, "is a pioneer of *Naturphilosophie*—in his Scientific Essays (and in this field only) is himself a *Naturphilosoph,* though a moderate and a balanced one. The 'short incomparably beautiful essay on nature' (as Freud called it) is a sort of program of the early spirit of the German *Naturphilosophie.*"[6] This philosophy of nature, Bernfeld tells us, had had a vogue in Germany "from about 1794 to 1830," even though it was "weaker here than in England and France."[7]

The following is Bernfeld's description of this current in European intellectual life:

Naturphilosophie is the name of the pantheistic monism, close to mysticism, which, professed by Schelling, repeated, and developed by a host of writers, was eagerly accepted by the average educated man and literary ladies. The universe, nature, is one vast organism; ultimately consisting of forces, of activities, of creations, of emergencies—(all these!) organized in eternal basic conflicts, in polarity; reason, conscious life, mind, being only the reflection, the emanation, of this unconscious turmoil. These ideas have been expressed before and since, and contain the seeds of some of the scientific theories of the 19th century and of our time. But it is not the ideas which are characteristic of the movement nor the romantic temper which envelops them. This was a general European trend. What characterizes the German *Naturphilosophie* is the aspiration expressed in the name "speculative physics" (which Schelling himself gave to his endeavors) and the unbalanced, megalomanic emotionalism of the fantasy and of the style of these writers. Fechner praised "the gigantic audacity" of Oken, a prominent representative, while a sober English historian puts it thus: "They exhibit tendencies that seem foreign to the course of European thought; they recall the vague spaciousness of the East and its reflection in the semi-oriental Alexandria."[8]

"Physicalistic" physiology—although not by itself—overthrew [this] philosophy and took its place. As has happened before, the conqueror introjected the emotionalism of his victim. "Unity of science," "science," "physical forces" were not merely directing ideas or hypotheses of scientific endeavor; they became almost objects of worship. They were more than methods of research—they became a *Weltanschauung.* The intensity of this temper was varied from scientist to scientist, from place to place. In Berlin with DuBois-Reymond it was at the maximum, strangely mixed with Prussian nationalism. In Austria, *Naturphilosophie* never had much power,

[5] *Op. cit.,* p. 8.

[6] Whether or not he himself actually wrote the essay, which James Strachey tells us is unlikely, Goethe adopted its ideas and gave them the prestige of his name.

[7] Bernfeld, "Freud's Earliest Theories and the School of Helmholtz," *op. cit.,* p. 353.

[8] G. S. Brett, *A History of Psychology* (London: Allen and Unwin, 1921), III, 129.

and the physiology fanaticism was at a minimum in Vienna and with Brücke. Yet it was there.[9]

The very time that Freud lived in, then, was a transitional one, a time when the grand speculative view of nature was becoming increasingly discredited in science, at the same time that it doubtless lingered in the humanities. We know that Freud's *Gymnasium* training was primarily humanistic, and from the general facts of cultural lag it seems a safe assumption that his teachers there had formed their ideas a generation before, when the romantic ideas were more ascendant.

It is noteworthy that in the passage quoted from "An Autobiographical Study," Freud linked a reference to the excitement over Darwin's ideas, which swept Europe in the 1870's, to the lecture at which he heard the fragment on nature—a connection that is not immediately obvious. Darwin, after all, was no philosopher of nature, but a natural scientist, whose magnum opus, the *Origin of Species,* was published in 1859, when Freud was three years old. But of course the furor over Darwinism had extensive philosophical—not to say theological—involvements, and the doctrine of evolution has an undeniable grandeur of sweep, which must have revived some of the dying interest in *Naturphilosophie.* Moreover, the general concept of evolution had played a large role in the thought of Schelling and other *Naturphilosophen.* Apparently it was just these "philosophical" overtones that caught Freud's interest and invested such a potentially dull subject as comparative anatomy—the subject of Brühl's lecture—with far-reaching implications, for this discipline had supplied some of Darwin's most telling evidence. Indeed, it is hard to imagine any other time than at the crest of the excitement among educated people about Darwinism when there would have been a heavily attended, popular lecture on comparative anatomy, to which a high school student like Freud would have been drawn.

It is in a way a delightful piece of irony that his attraction to a poetic, metaphorical, and grandiosely encompassing approach to nature led Freud into medicine and thus into the University of Vienna Medical School, a hotbed of physicalistic physiology. There, in his second semester, a course in "General Biology and Darwinism" was one of his first two electives, the other being his first course in physiology with Ernst Brücke.[10]

Physicalistic physiology was in those days a fighting discipline, and the antagonist, by now nearly routed, was *Naturphilosophie.* Jones and Bernfeld both suggest that *Naturphilosophie* had made a powerful appeal to deep motivational sources within Freud, among which must be

[9] Bernfeld, "Freud's Earliest Theories and the School of Helmholtz," *op. cit.,* p. 355.
[10] Bernfeld, "Sigmund Freud, M.D., 1882–1885," *loc. cit.*

included infantile sexual curiosity and the somewhat sublimated desire for power through knowledge. Bernfeld reminds us that "Freud in his early enthusiasm for the 'physicalistic' physiology swung for a brief time into radical materialism." He threw himself wholeheartedly into the new doctrine, and we have many indications that Freud's earlier inclination towards speculative philosophy was something against which he felt a very strong need to defend himself. Jones writes that when he once asked Freud how much philosophy he had read, the answer came: "Very little. As a young man I felt a strong attraction towards speculation and ruthlessly checked it."[11] (Note Freud's equation of speculation and philosophy.) The interpretation that this implies an involvement of conflict and defense is perhaps more convincing when one reflects that Freud took no less than five courses and seminars in philosophy with Franz Brentano during his eight years in the university, when he was supposedly studying medicine. I do not mean to imply that Brentano was a *Naturphilosoph*; his Aristotelian and psychological orientation was of much more classical stamp. It seems, rather, that when Freud cast his lot with physicalism, he rejected philosophy quite generally: note the fact that the semester when he formally joined Brücke's laboratory was the last time he took a course with Brentano.[12]

For the rest of his life, Freud's expressed attitude towards philosophy was quite negative. In "Inhibitions, Symptoms and Anxiety" he remarked: "I must confess that I am not at all partial to the fabrication of *Weltanschauungen*"[13]; in the *New Introductory Lectures* he expanded on this point in a whole chapter. In his medical autobiography, after characterizing his theoretical works of the early 1920's as speculative, Freud hastened to add that he had not given up close observation of psychoanalytic material: "Even when I have moved away from observation, I have carefully avoided any contact with philosophy proper. This avoidance has been greatly facilitated by constitutional incapacity."[14] In a letter of January 30, 1927, Freud wrote, speaking about metaphysics, "I not only have no talent for it but no respect for it, either. In secret—one cannot say such things aloud—I believe that metaphysics will be condemned as a nuisance, as an abuse of thinking, as a survival from the period of religious *Weltanschauung*."[15] And to Romain Rolland, he wrote in 1929: "To me mysticism is just as closed a book as music."[16] We shall see a little later how, in Freud's thinking, philosophy came to

[11] Jones, *op. cit.*, I, 29.
[12] Bernfeld, "Sigmund Freud, M.D., 1882–1885," *loc. cit.*
[13] Freud, "Inhibitions, Symptoms and Anxiety," *Standard Edition*, XX, 96.
[14] Freud, "An Autobiographical Study," *Standard Edition*, XX, 59.
[15] E. L. Freud, ed., *Letters of Sigmund Freud* (New York: Basic Books, 1960), p. 375.
[16] *Ibid.*, p. 389.

be equated with broad, synthetic, deductive theory-formation, whereas his preferred style of scientific thinking was analytic—as surely must be suggested by the name he chose for his discipline, psychoanalysis.

Under the influence of physicalistic physiology and the Helmholtz school, Freud entered on the first great period of his scientific and professional life. From being a medical student, he moved easily into becoming a research worker in comparative anatomy of the nervous system and then into neurological practice.

For a summary of the content and spirit of physicalistic physiology, we cannot do better than turn once again to Bernfeld.

> In the sixties, that part of German university teaching which was held to be the most interesting, the most far-reaching, and the most modern, was the physiology of the Helmholtz school. It fascinated the student of that time in somewhat the same way as atom-smashing appeals to the student of today. When Freud entered the medical school in Vienna in 1873, physiology still retained that spell. Though the movement had passed its peak the physiological institute of Brücke was still very active and famous, even glamorous.

Though Helmholtz gave his name to the school, it was actually started by Emil DuBois-Reymond and Ernst Brücke, who in 1842 pledged their famous oath:

> . . . to put in power this truth: no other forces than the common physical chemical ones are active within the organism. In those cases which cannot at the time be explained by these forces one has either to find a specific way or form of their action by means of physical mathematic method, or to assume new forces equal in dignity to the chemical physical forces inherent in matter, reducible to the force of attraction and repulsion.[17]

They were soon joined by Hermann Helmholtz and Carl Ludwig; their little private club was the origin of the Berlin Physical Association (1845). "Most of its members were young students of Johannes Müller —physicists and physiologists banded together to destroy, once and for all, vitalism, the fundamental belief of their admired master." The vitalistic target is clearly implicit in the above-quoted oath. For this extraordinary little group of men, which included Freud's teacher, scientific work had much of the aura of a crusade, a glorious adventure, a daring exploratory foray into the unknown.

I think it is not too farfetched to hazard the hypothesis that one of the important underlying emotional attitudes towards his scientific work, this sense of lonely adventure, was one that Freud picked up from his teachers, perhaps by an act of identification. It was to be expressed in

[17] Bernfeld, "Freud's Earliest Theories and the School of Helmholtz," *op. cit.,* p. 348.

his writing to Fliess (in a letter of February 1, 1900) that he was "nothing but by temperament a *conquistador*—an adventurer, if you want to translate the word—with the curiosity, the boldness, and the tenacity that belongs to that type of being." In his own view of his career, as reflected in his autobiographical writings, Freud portrayed this as a role that was thrust upon him by his being rejected by his contemporaries. There are good reasons to believe, however, that he had an inner need to be just this kind of worker and that a differently constituted man might not have experienced his reception at the hands of his colleagues as nearly so much of a rejection.[18]

At a meeting of the Berlin group, when it was still more a club than a formal scientific association, on July 23, 1847, "Helmholtz read a paper on the principle of conservation of energy—with the modest purpose of giving a sound foundation to the new physiology."[19] And yet, in the opinion of Singer, "The fundamental doctrine of the 19th century, that of energy, was first clearly enunciated under that name in 1852"—five years later.[20] This is an instance of the fact that the reality of historical advance is quite different from the impression given by the texts, with their neat columns of dates when various theories began. At any rate, the concept of energy was one of the truly germinative achievements of the century, one that made an enormous impression on all the school of Helmholtz, and one that is at the root of most modern developments in engineering and physical technology.

It is easy to see the origin of the economic point of view in metapsychology in the scientific stir caused by the concept of energy. Indeed, it became a kind of hallmark of science to use this concept; a truly respectable discipline, such as Freud always wanted psychoanalysis to be, *had* to consider energies. Without a realization of this background, it is hard to understand, as one reads Chapter 7 or "Instincts and Their Vicissitudes," in *The Interpretation of Dreams,* why it is that Freud so consistently preferred to conceptualize problems that today seem clearly structural in terms of cathectic energies and their transformations (or vicissitudes).

It was not as obvious then as it is now that the core of Helmholtz's contribution was mathematical and that if energy cannot be measured, it becomes a meaningless concept. In a way, Freud may have been aware of this fact, for he usually emphasized the quantitative aspect at

[18] Cf. Ilse Bry and A. H. Rivkin, "Freud and the History of Ideas: Primary Sources, 1886–1910," in J. Masserman, ed., *Science and Psychoanalysis* (New York: Grune and Stratton, 1962).

[19] Bernfeld, "Freud's Earliest Theories and the School of Helmholtz," *loc. cit.*

[20] C. Singer, *A Short History of Scientific Ideas to 1900* (London: Oxford University Press, 1959).

least as much as the energetic when treating the economic point of view in metapsychology, and he never gave up the hope that the quantities involved might become measurable some day.

In the summary of Brücke's lectures on physiology which Bernfeld provides, I want to focus attention on one sentence: "The real causes are symbolized in science by the word 'force.' "[21] Notice also the almost exclusive emphasis on forces in the Brücke–DuBois-Reymond oath. Here is the origin of the dynamic point of view in metapsychology and of the overemphasis in psychoanalysis on dynamics, or considerations of forces.[22] If the only true causes of things were forces, then the only truly scientific approach was a dynamic one. Aside from the difficult question of measurement, the only trouble is one of neglect: a neglect of structural considerations. For forces and energies cannot exist in a structural vacuum; they must operate on masses arranged in particular organizations.

This side of things was by no means neglected in Brücke's physiology; indeed, it was a predominantly structural—that is to say, anatomical and histological—discipline. Perhaps it was because the physical structure of the organism was such an obvious fact of nature that it did not enter into the manifestoes and more ideological pronouncements. Anyway, we know it for a fact that Freud's successful early researches were all anatomical, which is to say that he was continually engaged in studying the structure of various organs, particularly the human medulla, which he studied in Meynert's laboratory. When he finally began medical practice, it was in neurology, which, as Bernfeld remarks, "demands a thorough knowledge of brain- and nerve-anatomy, and in fact was at that time, even more than it is today, merely a diagnostic application of anatomy."[23] Freud's clinical reputation began with his ability, demonstrated by autopsies, to locate lesions in the brain from a study of presenting (partly behavioral) symptoms.

Moreover, in Freud's first period of psychological theorizing, he continually relied on structural concepts; the conception of the central nervous system as understood at the time was structural. The *Project,* the finest product of his first period, has a complex and ingenious structural base. Not only did Freud distinguish major systems in the brain, but he also clearly stated that the basic unit was the neuron and worked out his explanation of processes in terms of currents of quantity transmitted along chains and networks of these physical units.

It is not difficult to show, thus, that the three major aspects of metapsychology as Freud described them in 1915, the dynamic, economic,

[21] Bernfeld, "Freud's Earliest Theories and the School of Helmholtz," *op. cit.,* p. 349.

[22] D. Rapaport and M. M. Gill, "The Points of View and Assumptions of Metapsychology," *Int. J. Psychoanal.,* XL (1959), 153–162.

[23] Bernfeld, "Sigmund Freud, M.D., 1882–1885," *op. cit.,* p. 207.

and topographic (i.e. structural) points of view, grew directly from Freud's contacts with physicalistic physiology. Unfortunately, my command of German is not good enough to allow me easy access to the works of Brücke, Meynert, and S. Exner, but the excerpts from their writings that I have read show striking parallels with many tenets of Freud's process theories. The point is perhaps most easily and convincingly made by reference to the theoretical chapter—by Breuer—in *Studies in Hysteria,* now translated. Breuer was a member of the school of Helmholtz, and he wrote with a transparently physicalistic orientation. A comparison of his theory with Freud's *Project,* or even with the seventh chapter in *The Interpretation of Dreams,* quickly shows in how many respects Freud took over concepts and a way of thinking that formed the respected and generally accepted core of contemporary neurology. The concept of a passive nervous system that strives to rid itself of externally imposed energies and the closely related ideas of the constancy principle, the pleasure principle, tension reduction, the need for a protective shield against stimuli, action and affect as phenomena of energy discharge—all derive from the heritage of physicalistic physiology. Indeed, I believe that a good case can be made that most of the inherent difficulties of Freud's general theory derive from this heritage, which he could never get rid of, and not from his original ideas. Be that as it may, I wish to emphasize the fact that a direct line of continuous influence and growth can be seen if one traces the general process theory of psychoanalysis from its neurological beginnings in the works of Freud's teachers and older colleagues, to the *Project,* and through his later metapsychological writings.

FREUD'S SCIENTIFIC TRAINING

Let us consider for a few moments the nature of the training in scientific method that Freud gained from his years in the laboratories of Brücke, Stricker, and Meynert. As is now well known, his first piece of research was literally search—for the testes of the eel in the immature specimens of that animal that alone were available. This was followed by further microscopic work on neurohistology, again with a strong evolutionary flavor: his first major paper showed a developmental link between the nerve cells of lower and higher animals, and this was followed by further important neurohistological work.

At the microscope, Freud learned to look long and patiently, to be on the watch for spurious effects produced by the observer or by his methods, to devise new techniques of avoiding such artifacts and seeing more clearly what he was after. The work also probably taught him a respect for facts and a realization that they were not always apparent at a glance or by means of the first method chosen. The techniques of control and objectivity that he learned were essentially those of the natural historian, the scientific explorer. Yet they were sufficient for the kinds of problems he was working on: establishing certain anatomical facts.

This kind of scientific work has an active, analytic and a passive, observational phase: one must dissect preparations carefully before they are ready to be scrutinized to find out what is there. Moreover, Bernfeld has pointed out in detail how, in his studies of the medulla, Freud adopted a recently developed genetic method—that of studying sections of foetal brains at various states of development, a process by which the cranial nerves can be traced to their origins.

When, later, he turned to psychological dissection and observation, Freud invented a new type of scientific control, his self-analysis, a vitally important step in fashioning him into an accurate scientific instrument. But even this revolutionary step was essentially of a piece with the controls he had used with the microscope. Like the techniques of staining tissue that he had invented, it was a way of avoiding artifacts of observation and hypothesis formation.

Though Brücke's laboratory was called physiological, we should remember that Freud did not work on problems of function and process, which would have required experimentation, but on problems of structure. "Here in the seventies the microscopic and the experimental approaches were still united."[24] Consequently, what he learned of method had less applicability to the psychological issues he was to struggle with than a physiological apprenticeship would today.

This is not to deny that Freud gained a great deal for his particular style of research from his apprenticeship. To quote Bernfeld again:

> His method was to look and listen passively, with a minimum of interference with the object. He quickly gave up the use of electrical machinery and then hypnosis because he felt clumsy and uneasy in the use of such coarsely interfering activities. Governing, curing, educating—he repeatedly confessed having no inclination for these. He liked to compare psychoanalysis to the work of the archaeologist who only removes the sediments of the ages and finds what was hidden beneath.[25]

Freud wrote to Stefan Zweig in 1931 that he had "actually read more archaeology than psychology."[26]

The essence of experiment is controlled observation under conditions of controlled "interference with the object." Bernfeld tells us that Freud made four attempts to work in this manipulative kind of way, including one experiment on cocaine using human subjects to test its

---

[24] Bernfeld, "Freud's Earliest Theories and the School of Helmholtz," *loc cit.*
[25] *Ibid.*, pp. 357 f.
[26] *Letters of Sigmund Freud, op. cit.*, p. 403.

effects on muscular performance, and all four were essentially failures. The resulting orientation away from experimentation stayed with Freud for most of the rest of his life. In 1907 he wrote to Jung: "Because I have so little hope in convincing the experts I have also, as you have correctly detected, shown only a half-hearted interest in your galvano-metric experiments."[27] Over twenty years later, he indicated to Saul Rosenzweig very little interest in the newer experiments growing out of psychoanalytic hypotheses, about which Rosenzweig had told him. They could do no harm, Freud conceded, but they were not really necessary, since the facts of psychoanalysis were already so well established by thousands of clinical observations.[28] And in 1930, he wrote to H. Löwy: "Within the methods of our work there is no place for the kind of ex-periment made by physicists and physiologists."[29]

Let us go back to the influence of *Naturphilosophie*. Several factors had conspired to drive it underground in Freud's thinking, and as long as he remained a practicing neurologist, teaching as a *Privatdozent* in the university and continuing his researches on the brain in Meynert's labo-ratory, he was safe from its dangerous seduction. Quite soon, however, this effective and respectable pattern of living and working was to be interrupted.

The disturbance, of course, was the problem of hysteria, which his practice inevitably presented. In this heyday of grand conversion hys-teria, with its spectacular paralyses, contractures, and anesthesias, a major problem of differential diagnosis in neurology was the discrimina-tion of similar symptom-pictures with and without underlying organic lesions. Freud's initial efforts to understand the mechanism of conversion followed the physicalistic line and could hardly be called psychological: a constitutional predisposition caused certain persons to channel their "strangulated affect" into somatic pathways. The affect was dammed-up, however, because there had been a traumatic (emotionally arousing) ex-perience and the patient had been prevented from discharging the rapidly accumulating energy; and this kind of trauma was undeniably psycho-logical. As early as 1893, then, Breuer and Freud were launched on psy-chological theorizing.

This development does not at first sound to us as if it necessarily opened any philosophical Pandora's box. But psychology and speculative philosophy were closely connected in Freud's mind. Remember that the psychology to which Freud was exposed in the university was largely that of Brentano and was a branch of philosophy on an equal footing

---

[27] *Ibid.*, p. 252.

[28] As L. Luborsky pointed out (in a discussion of this paper), a marked ex-ception was Freud's friendly treatment of Poetzl's tachistoscopic experiments.

[29] *Letters of Sigmund Freud, op. cit.*, p. 396.

with epistemology, metaphysics, and ethics.[30] Psychology as an experimental science was just being born in Freud's student days; even as they founded their laboratories, Wilhelm Wundt and James remained teachers and writers of philosophy, like Fechner before them. In the universities, the separation of departments of philosophy and psychology was to *begin* only a generation later, and it became complete only about the time of Freud's death. Small wonder, then, that the associationistic psychology that Freud became conversant with appeared to him as deductive and speculative as any other branch of philosophy. As we shall see, he was not unaware of the "new psychology" of the 1890's, but it had so little to offer him that he could hardly have been much impressed by its claims for recognition as a science.

THE INFLUENCE OF FLIESS

At the time he was first turning his interests from neurology toward psychological problems, Freud met his brilliant contemporary from Berlin, Wilhelm Fliess. Freud, struggling to make a living in private practice, was relatively isolated from scientific colleagues and badly in need of encouragement, an audience, someone to believe in him—and someone to give him support by example and approbation for his attempts to break through the rigid crust of conventional and accepted ways of thinking about his patients. Fliess supplied all of this. At a time when public discussion of sex was almost taboo, Fliess was developing a pansexual theory of grandiose proportions. As "brothers banding together to slay the primal father" of conservative and traditional theory in psychiatry, medicine, and psychology, they could give one another courage and a sense of not being alone and unprotected in a dangerous enterprise, so that it could become an exhilarating, even a heroic venture.

There are a number of echoes of the foundation of the Helmholtz school in this, and indeed Fliess had been trained in that tradition as well as Freud. Their awareness of their teachers' struggles may have played something of a role in their own slightly romantic conception of themselves.

Fliess was, if anything, more closely identified with physicalistic physiology than was Freud. The latter speaks in his letters of hoping to "appeal on many points to your superior scientific equipment," or says, "Perhaps you may supply me with solid ground on which I shall be able to give up explaining things psychologically and start finding a firm basis in physiology!"[31] Note the implication in this last letter, written in 1896,

---

[30] As was the psychology of Herbart, which he had been taught in *Gymnasium*, and even the experimental psychophysics of Fechner, whom Freud quoted and admired perhaps more than any other psychologist.

[31] Marie Bonaparte, Anna Freud, and E. Kris, eds., *The Origins of Psychoanalysis* (New York: Basic Books, 1954), pp. 122, 169.

of Freud's uneasiness in and ambivalence about his initial ventures into psychological explanation and away from purely neurological modes of thought. Clearly, he felt that he was treading a dangerous territory.

The reference to psychology is to what is now known as the *Project* —Freud's "psychology for neurologists." To modern eyes, this work seems at least as much neurological as psychological. But Freud wrote about it in the following manner during the months when he was thinking through the *Project* and before he had written it out:

> A man like me cannot live without a hobby-horse, a consuming passion— in Schiller's words a tyrant. I have found my tyrant, and in his service I know no limits. My tyrant is psychology; it has always been my distant, beckoning goal [compare his remarks about the lure of philosophy] and now, since I have hit on the neuroses, it has come so much the nearer. I am plagued with two ambitions: to see how the theory of mental functioning takes shape if quantitative considerations, a sort of economics of nerve-force, are introduced into it; and secondly, to abstract from psychopathology what may be of benefit to normal psychology.[32]

In another letter, he wrote:

> As a young man my only longing was for philosophical knowledge, and now that I am changing over from medicine to psychology I am in the process of fulfilling this wish. I became a therapist against my will.[33]

Again, he complains:

> This psychology is really an incubus . . . all I was trying to do was to explain defense, but I found myself explaining something from the very heart of nature. I found myself wrestling with the problems of quality, sleep, memory—in short, the whole of psychology.[34]

When he finally started writing the theory out, it was "for you to criticize" (letter of September 23, 1895). Later in the same letter, he writes: "Apart from adapting the theory to the general laws of motion, for which I count on you, I have to test it against the individual facts of the new experimental psychology." A month later, he characterizes his theorizing as "philosophical stammering," a remark which makes quite explicit his feeling of having ambivalently returned to philosophy via psychology.[35]

The role Freud assigned Fliess was reasonable enough in terms of Fliess's self-estimation and his intellectual façade. If one provisionally accepts Kris's portrayal, Fliess was a brilliant intellectual quack, an ingenious but barrenly speculative man—essentially a numerologist, who nevertheless had many of the outward trappings of the cool, logical scientist. Not only was he steeped in the Helmholtz tradition, but he had

[32] *Ibid.*, pp. 119–120.
[33] *Letters of Sigmund Freud, op. cit.*, p. 232.
[34] *The Origins of Psychoanalysis, op. cit.*, p. 123.
[35] *Ibid.*, p. 127.

something that Freud lacked: a ready facility with numbers. Fliess could dazzle his admiring friend with his calculations and formulas, seeming to prove his points conclusively by what Murray has called "the divine strategies of mathematics." And he remained firmly physiological in his orientation and the clinical application of his theories.

Freud recovered very largely from his overestimation of Fliess and markedly revised his evaluation of the latter's scientific attainments. But I cannot resist putting forward the hypothesis that when Freud rejected Fliess' number-juggling, he may have overgeneralized it somewhat—at least, in his emotional attitude—to include mathematics and the use of numbers more generally.[36] At least, I find it striking that during the 1890's there are frequent references in Freud's papers to the numbers of cases of one sort or another and the frequency with which they show given patterns of symptoms, etiological conditions, and what not; whereas thereafter such references are exceedingly rare.

Freud tells us in the letters to Fliess how poor a mathematician he considered himself; in a letter to Pfister in 1909 he complains "how difficult it is for us to imagine [large] numbers."[37] Jones agrees:

> Freud had a very orderly mind (and also orderly habits), and his power of organizing a mass of facts into a systematic grouping was truly remarkable. . . . But on the other hand he rather spurned exactitude and precise definition as being either wearisome or pedantic; he could never have been a mathematician or physicist or even an expert solver of chess problems.[38]

No doubt there were other experiences than his brush with mathematics, as personified by Fliess and the philosophers, which may have been even more important in determining his attitude toward quantification, but we know little of them. Perhaps one of the difficulties was that the kinds of things Freud would have been very much interested in measuring, like "the inherent quantitative strength of an idea," have resisted efforts at mensuration to this day.[39] Like Herbart, Freud failed to see one critical point about measurement—the fact that concrete operations

[36] Also related to Freud's antipathy to mathematics may have been its connection with mystical philosophy and metaphysical psychology: "Fechner's mind is a result of two very distinct influences—the romantic philosophy of the post-Kantian school and the scientific developments of the second quarter of the 19th century. Even the psycho-physical standpoint is an outcome of the 'Natur-philosophie'; it is a concrete instance of that ultimate unity of the sciences which the doctrine of an Absolute postulates. Mathematics and mysticism are not so very far apart by nature; Herbart is a good example of the close alliance between metaphysics and numbers." (Brett, *A History of Psychology, op. cit.,* III, 128.) Brentano, whose ideas we know Freud rejected, was also an advocate of measurement and statistics.

[37] *Letters of Sigmund Freud, op. cit.,* p. 280.

[38] Jones, *The Life and Work of Sigmund Freud, op. cit.,* I, 33.

[39] *The Origins of Psychoanalysis, op. cit.,* p. 166.

have to be specified for any quantitatively conceived concept. Therefore, since his concept of cathectic energy never included any such operations, it has never been possible to make measurements in this, the central economic concept, the very place where quantitative considerations were important for psychoanalysis.

Fliess surely deserves our gratitude for the support he gave Freud during difficult and lonely years and for encouraging him to make his initial attempt at a psychology, the *Project*. Let us return to a consideration of this remarkable work, and ask in what way, besides the mere fact that it was a psychology, it may have been a first emergence of the speculative, philosophical aspect of Freud's thought.

FROM THE GENERAL THEORY TO PHYLOGENETIC SPECULATION

Aside from its explicitly neurological character, the *Project* differs from all of Freud's other theoretical writings in three respects: (1) It attempts nothing less than the construction of a complete and comprehensive model of normal as well as pathological psychological phenomena; (2) it proceeds in a quasideductive way from (3) an initial set of clear, concise definitions. In each of these respects Freud must have thought of it as being essentially philosophical and speculative. Let me buttress this conclusion by some quotations from Freud's later writings. In his paper on narcissism, he made clear his somewhat paradoxical equation of speculation and clear definitions:

> One dislikes the thought of abandoning observation for barren theoretical controversy, but nevertheless one must not shirk an attempt at clarification. It is true that notions such as that of an ego-libido, an energy of the ego-instinct, and so on, are neither particularly easy to grasp, nor sufficiently rich in content; a speculative theory of the relations in question would begin by seeking to obtain a sharply defined concept as its basis. But I am of opinion that that is just the difference between a speculative theory and a science erected on empirical interpretation. The latter will not envy speculation its privilege of having a smooth, logically unassailable foundation, but will gladly content itself with nebulous, scarcely imaginable basic concepts, which it hopes to apprehend more clearly in the course of its development, or which it is even prepared to replace by others. For these ideas are not the foundation of science, upon which everything rests: that foundation is observation alone. They are not the bottom but the top of the whole structure, and they can be replaced and discarded without damaging it. The same thing is happening in our day in the science of physics, the basic notions of which as regards matter, centres of force, attraction, etc., are scarcely less debatable than the corresponding notions in psycho-analysis.[40]

And in *The Ego and the Id,* he equated philosophy with systematic completeness:

[40] "On Narcissism: An Introduction," *Standard Edition,* XIV, 77.

There has been a general refusal to recognize that psychoanalytic research could not, like a philosophical system, produce a complete and ready-made theoretical structure, but had to find its way step by step along the path towards understanding the intricacies of the mind by making an *analytic dissection* of both normal and abnormal phenomena.[41]

(Parenthetically, the parallel of the phrase "analytic dissection" to Freud's early scientific activities in neuroanatomy is striking.) Again: "A science based upon observation has no alternative but to work out its findings piecemeal and to solve its problems step by step."[42]

A number of other similar passages could be adduced if space permitted. From them and from the considerations presented so far, the accompanying schematic table emerges, as a reconstruction of the apparent "latent structure" of methodological ideas in Freud's mind.

TABLE 1

LATENT STRUCTURE OF FREUD'S METHODOLOGICAL IDEAS

Derived largely from philosophy, especially *Naturphilosophie:*	Derived largely from physicalistic physiology:
Philosophy, academic philosophical psychology	Physiology, neuropsychology, metapsychology
Complete, comprehensive theories with precise definitions of concepts	Partial, *ad hoc* theories with groping, imprecisely defined concepts
Deductive procedure, mathematics	Inductive procedure
Speculation, synthesis	Observation, dissection, analysis
Darwinian biology, archaeology	

If the alignments in this little table are correct, they explain some apparent paradoxes about Freud's thought. Note, first, that on the philosophical side there are both "good" and "bad" conceptions, as Freud saw them, with speculation in between. Deduction, comprehensive coverage of a theory, and rigorous definition were associated in his mind with the sterile, formalistic aspects of philosophy; they were the parts of the complex of his thought that first emerged in the *Project* and were decisively rejected by him thereafter. But Darwinian biology and archaeology, which similarly reconstructed the remote past of man by a genetic method, were empirical sciences, even though linked to the philosophical complex by their speculative method. Moreover, I have been able to find no balancing factors on the other side to play the role of anticathexis, as it were. They therefore could make it possible for Freud, finally, to indulge his long-suppressed yearning for broad, speculative theorizing. In "An Autobiographical Study," he wrote: "In the works of my later

[41] London: Hogarth Press, 1923, pp. 35 f. Italics mine.
[42] "An Autobiographical Study," *Standard Edition*, XX, 58.

years (*Beyond the Pleasure Principle, Group Psychology and the Analysis of the Ego,* and *The Ego and the Id*) I have given free rein to the inclination, which I kept down for so long, to speculation."[43]

In a sense, of course, it is only an extension of the method of genetic reconstruction to go back beyond the beginnings of an individual life and attempt to trace the development of socially shared customs in the larger life history of a people, as Freud did in *Totem and Taboo.* The conceptions of Haeckel (that ontogeny recapitulates phylogeny) and of Lamarck (that acquired characteristics may be passed on genetically) were generally known during Freud's scientifically formative years and enjoyed a far more widespread acceptance by the scientific world than they did during Freud's later years. This acceptance made it difficult for him to give them up. If the functional anthropologists had gotten to work a generation sooner and if the evolutionary approach had not been so popularized by Sir James Frazer, Freud might have been able to understand how pervasive and unconscious the patterning of a culture can be. This intricate interconnection makes it possible for culture to be transmitted via subtle and almost imperceptible kinds of learning, a fact that obviates what Freud felt was the necessity that a social psychology should postulate the inheritance of acquired characteristics.

THE CHANGE OF IDENTITY

Starting in about 1895, with his self-analysis, Freud underwent a number of remarkable changes in both his personality and his work, changes that are perceptible in his style of scientific thinking. Fliess was the last of a series of father-figures to play an important role in Freud's life, and with the termination of that complex, intimate, and dependent relationship shortly after the publication of *The Interpretation of Dreams,* the process of identity transformation came to an end (or at least passed out of its most dramatic phase). At the beginning of the transitional period, Freud's father died; by its end, he had ceased siring children himself. Freud entered this five-year period an established, respected neurologist, who had a coveted position in the university and who strove with great intensity and persistence for the prestige of an appointment as professor extraordinary. At the end, with this goal achieved, he had begun the process of withdrawal from participation in university and medical societies alike; now more truly isolated than before, he no longer had the need for a crony to be his "only audience." During this time, he wrote his last neurological papers and monographs and began publishing a new kind of scientific contribution. Thus he left behind an established place in a respected scientific discipline and established an entirely new discipline, of which he was for a while the only practitioner.

[43] *Ibid.,* p. 57.

Doubtless he got the courage to pioneer in this way in part from the fact that he had already made a series of great discoveries: the wish-fulfilling nature of dreams; the nature of the primary process, which enabled him to interpret dreams and neurotic symptoms; the Oedipus complex, and the importance of the psychic reality of incestuous fantasies as against the hypothetical trauma of actual incestuous seduction; and others. This was also the period during which he developed the basic technical procedures of psychoanalytic therapy and thus transformed himself from a neurologist trying to learn psychotherapy from an older colleague into a practicing psychoanalyst.

On the side of theory, the transition is from the *Project* to *The Interpretation of Dreams*. Part of the change, as already noted, was the abandonment of the goal of a complete psychology, deductively arrived at from a set of prior definitions, in favor of a psychology of the dream process, which attempts to stay fairly close to and build on the clinical facts, introducing approximate definitions of concepts as they are needed. There was, however, one other major change: from a theory the structural elements of which were explicitly neurological, to one that explicitly rejected such a grounding:

> I shall entirely disregard the fact that the mental apparatus with which we are here concerned *is also known to us in the form of an anatomical preparation,* and I shall carefully avoid the temptation to determine psychical locality in any anatomical fashion. I shall remain upon psychological ground, and I propose simply to follow the suggestion that we should picture the instrument which carries out our mental functions as resembling a compound microscope. . . . Psychical locality will correspond to a point inside the apparatus at which one of the preliminary stages of an image comes into being. . . . I see no necessity to apologize for the imperfections of this or of any similar imagery. Analogies of this kind are only intended to assist us in our attempt to make the complications of mental functioning intelligible by *dissecting* the function and assigning its different constituents to different component parts of the apparatus. So far as I know, the experiment has not hitherto been made of using this method of *dissection* in order to investigate the way in which the mental instrument is put together, and I can see no harm in it. We are justified, in my view, in giving free rein to our *speculations* so long as we retain the coolness of our judgment and do not mistake the scaffolding for the building. And since at our first approach to something unknown all that we need is the assistance of provisional ideas, I shall give preference in the first instance to hypotheses of the crudest and most concrete description.[44]

There is much in this famous passage that we could profitably dwell upon, but let me just briefly call your attention to the equation of analysis and dissection; the cautious emergence of speculation as a tool; the negated apology for metaphorical thinking; and the way that Freud's

---

[44] "The Interpretation of Dreams," *Standard Edition,* IV, 536. Italics mine.

wording does *not* reject the fact, although he will disregard it, that the systems he is going to describe are ultimately anatomical ones.

This last point is, I believe, often overlooked: it is easy to understand him as having turned his back entirely on what is sometimes called neuromythology and as having chosen completely abstract concepts which, like those of Kurt Lewin, are purely intervening variables and do not purport to be hypothetical constructs (to use MacCorquodale and Meehl's dichotomy[45]). Consider a later disclaimer, in "The Unconscious": "Our psychical topography has *for the present* nothing to do with anatomy; it has reference not to anatomical localities, but to regions in the mental apparatus, wherever they may be situated in the body."[46] The emphasis on the words "for the present" is Freud's, indicating that he expected the regions of the mental apparatus eventually to be definitely located in the brain.

The last quotation immediately follows this next passage, giving his reasons for abjuring neurology. A question he has been discussing is difficult

> . . . because it goes beyond pure psychology and touches on the relations of the mental apparatus to anatomy. We know that in the very roughest sense such relations exist. Research has given irrefutable proof that mental activity is bound up with the function of the brain as it is with no other organ. We are taken a step further—we do not know how much—by the discovery of the unequal importance of the different parts of the brain and their special relations to particular parts of the body and to particular mental activities. But every attempt to go on from there to discover a localization of mental processes, every endeavour to think of ideas as stored up in nerve-cells and of excitations as travelling along nerve-fibres, has miscarried completely. The same fate would await any theory which attempted to recognize, let us say, the anatomical position of the system *Cs.*—conscious mental activity—as being in the cortex, and to localize the unconscious processes in the subcortical parts of the brain.[47]

The last two sentences describe exactly what he had tried to do in the *Project* and contain a harsh judgment of it. Is it fair to say that the attempt "miscarried completely," so that Freud was justified in giving up the attempt to create an explicit neuropsychology? Not according to Karl Pribram, who says that, when a few relatively minor modifications are made to bring its neurology up to date, the *Project* becomes as sophisticated a model as anything of its kind that we have today.[48] True,

---

[45] K. MacCorquodale and P. E. Meehl, "On a Distinction between Hypothetical Constructs and Intervening Variables," *Psychol. Rev.*, LV (1948), 95–107.

[46] "The Unconscious," *Standard Edition*, XIV, 175.

[47] *Ibid.*, p. 174.

[48] K. Pribram, "The Neuropsychology of Sigmund Freud," in A. J. Bachrach, ed., *Experimental Foundations of Clinical Psychology* (New York: Basic Books, 1962).

as Freud left it, it has some internal inconsistencies, but no more than in any other work of his of comparable size. I doubt, therefore, that his dissatisfaction with it was a purely rational judgment that it could not be made to work; I am more impressed by the possibility that Freud felt a need to burn his conceptual bridges behind him, as part of an identity consolidation. He was now a psychoanalyst, not a neurologist but a depth psychologist; very well, he would now begin to think and theorize like one.

One consequence of this step was that in giving up the neuron, Freud no longer had any clear structural unit for his hypothetical systems. From time to time, when the problem demanded some such concept, he reverted to the idea of pathways without ever explicating what they were or just how they were related to the topographic systems. I suspect that his preference for dynamic and economic over structural explanations may be related to the fact that any detailed structural consideration always threatened to take him back to nerve tracts and nuclei and thus to an abandoned identity.

As we have seen, Freud now began to allow himself the use of speculation and metaphor, and once the process was begun, it continued with a slow acceleration. The sacrificed advantage of a neural model is that there are independent, nonpsychological data which must be respected by a theory and which set limits to the necessarily speculative process of constructing it. Any scientist must speculate, but he also needs to discipline the freedom of theoretical construction, and psychoanalysis had relatively few such safeguards. A model built of intervening variables has to be responsible only to the very data it attempts to explain, so that it has a necessary circularity and is not externally constrained from going anywhere that fancy leads. It is not only possible but likely, however, that Freud needed just this much freedom in order to be able to make his fundamental contributions.

His renunciation of a theory that attempts to conceptualize the whole of normal as well as abnormal behavior also bought him a new freedom. He decided to work with a minimum of assumptions and concepts, to explain one phenomenon at a time, and to let his concepts grow and change as exigencies of different problems required, as he described in the well-known opening page of "Instincts and Their Vicissitudes."[49]

If in developing a theory of one phenomenon one does not have to concern himself with the implications for all of psychology of what he proposes, his creativity will clearly be less hampered. On the other hand, a science cannot long afford to tolerate inconsistencies and contradictions but must seek ways to decide among mutually exclusive alternatives. Likewise, to attempt sharp, clear definitions will, I believe, no longer

[49] "Instincts and Their Vicissitudes," *Standard Edition,* XIV, 117.

hamper the development of psychoanalytic theory as it might have done in Freud's time, but will advance it.

In conclusion, I should like to stress one point: times have changed since Freud was actively working, and we should change too. He was never loath to give up an old idea when he saw that it proved unserviceable; there have been few scientists whose ideas underwent so many great changes over the course of time. Moreover, he was annoyed with the tendency of his followers to treat what he wrote like holy writ instead of mastering it and then going on beyond.[50] Like everyone else, Freud was a child of his time, too close to some of his own assumptions to be able to see their untenability. Others he had learned so early and in such an emotional context that it was impossible for him to change them. But we were not brought up under the influence of either *Naturphilosophie* or the school of Helmholtz, so there is no excuse for us not to find the anachronisms in psychoanalytic theory, get rid of them, and reconstruct the theory in an internally consistent, testable form. It would be an enormous job, to be sure. Even the first step—getting a good grasp of the historical development of Freud's ideas—takes a great deal of time and effort. The size of the job is all the more reason for the hope that many research-oriented psychiatrists and clinical psychologists may work together to bring about the needed refurbishing of psychoanalytic theory, with the kind of interdisciplinary cooperation so brilliantly espoused by Murray and exemplified in his successive research teams.

[50] "In 1923, heckled about some contradictions in his early papers by a young member of the Psychoanalytic Society in Vienna, Freud said: 'This problem exists only because thirty years ago I wrote quite candidly, not foreseeing that at some future time every detail would be accepted and made sacrosanct to the last letter.'" Bernfeld, "Freud's Earliest Theories and the School of Helmholtz," *loc. cit.*

17: LEFT AND RIGHT

A Basic Dimension of Ideology and Personality

Silvan Tomkins

By ideology we mean here any organized set of ideas about which human beings are at once both articulate and passionate and about which they are least certain. The foundations of mathematics, the philosophy of science, metaphysics, theology, epistemology, the theory of value, ethics, aesthetics, jurisprudence, government, theory of education, and, finally, theories about child rearing, more recently called socialization—these have all evoked the most coherent and passionate controversy. When the same ideas are firmly established and incorporated into the fabric of a science or tested and found wanting, they cease to constitute an ideology in the sense in which we are using the term. At the growing edge of the frontier of all sciences there necessarily is a maximum of uncertainty, and what is lacking in evidence is filled by passion and faith and by hatred and scorn for the disbelievers. Science will never be free of ideology, though yesterday's ideology is today's fact or fiction. Ideology appears in many domains, but it is found in its purest form in those controversies which are centuries old, which have never ceased to find true believers, whether the issue is joined in mathematics, in aesthetics, or in politics. Over and over again, whether theorists address themselves to one or another of these domains, they appear to become polarized on the same issues.

It is such ideological postures which we would relate to ideo-affective resonance. By "ideo-affective resonance" we mean the engagement of belief and feeling by ideology (as we have defined it) when the ideo-affective postures are sufficiently similar to the ideological posture so that they reinforce and strengthen each other. Ideo-affective resonance to ideology is a love affair of a loosely organized set of feelings and ideas about feelings with a highly organized and articulate set of ideas about anything. As in the case of a love affair, the fit need not at the outset be perfect, so long as there is a similarity between what the individual feels and thinks is desirable and the characteristics of the love object sufficient to set the vibrations between the two entities into sympathetic co-ordination with each other. Once a critical degree of similarity has been reached, a way will be found to heighten the communality. It is possible and indeed common for different individuals to resonate in different manners to the same ideology, just as it is possible for two individuals to fall in love with different aspects of the same person, for different but somewhat similar reasons. A love affair and resonance are relationships between *families* of ideas and feelings. If each family has many similar members, but no two members exactly alike, and if there is as much resemblance between members of one family and another family (e.g. between a grandmother and her grandchild) as between this child and a sibling, then resonance may produce a subset of ideo-affects composed of parts of the original ideo-affects and parts of the ideology which resemble each other more than the members of the total original set of ideo-affects resembled each other, and more than the original members of the ideology resembled each other. By virtue of this new tighter organization the formerly loosely organized personality may become extraordinarily integrated, with varying degrees of exclusion of nonfitting components.

The concept of families of ideo-affects and families of ideas organized into an ideology also enables us to account for many alternative equivalent families. It is like a large family which is married off to another large family, with a common set of ancestors not too far back. The families of such families, if they continue to intermarry, will produce tantalizing communalities, which will be filtered through most conceptual nets except those designed to catch family resemblances. Stated more precisely, if there exists a set of families of ideo-affective postures of the form a, b, c, . . . a_n, b_n, c_n and a set of families of ideological postures of the form A, B, C, . . . A_n, B_n, C_n, then there will be ideo-affective resonances of the following types: (a, b, c, A, B, C,) or (a, b, A, B,) or (a, A, B,) or (a, b, A,), in which all members of one set are mapped on to analogues in the other set, or some are, or some are mapped on to more or less analogues in the other set. Thus one individual exposed primarily to literary controversy might resonate to romanticism rather than classicism, whereas the same kind of person exposed to both politics and literature might resonate to revolutionary ideas in both domains. Further, of three individuals, all romantic in ideo-affective posture, one might resonate to the emphasis on feeling in ideology, another resonate to the emphasis on the unconscious forces within the individual, and the third resonate to the antitraditionalism of the romantic ideology.

Further, there will be resonances of the types (a_1, b_1, c_1, A_2, B_2, C_2) or (a_1, b_2, c_3, A_4, B_4, C_4), in which the fit between the components of the two sets is not as close as it is in other cases. This can happen because of historical accident. If the prevailing ideologies are restricted in range, individuals may resonate to ideologies which are not quite as congenial as another member of the ideological family might have been, had the individual lived a century earlier when this might have been an available alternative. Thus a politically conservative ideology in a democratic society might be much less conservative than the ideology the ideo-affective resonance would have made attractive had the individual lived in a feudal society.

A very special case of such historically produced and limited resonance occurs in the life history of all creative artists and scientists. Ordinarily the artist or scientist as a young man will resonate to that one ideology, among those available, which is closest to the ideology which he will later create to give expression to what is unique in his own ideo-affective posture. At that earlier time he may also graft onto the contemporary organized ideology toward which he is then most resonant certain characteristics that will become the central features of his later ideology.

Not all human beings attain an ideological commitment, nor the same commitment in all the fields where it is represented. Thus many human beings never attain sufficiently intimate acquaintance with the realms of philosophy, art, and science to resonate to one or another ideological posture. Even more, individuals who resonate to one ideological domain fail to do so to another. If our theory is correct, however, it should be possible to predict from the basic ideo-affective postures to what ideological postures the individual would resonate if he were to be sufficiently exposed to these domains. Preliminary evidence suggests that this can be done—that if one knows what an individual believes about the nature of literature, one would also know what he would believe about the nature of mathematics if he were to be confronted with mathematical problems. It also appears on the basis of preliminary evidence that even when an individual is completely innocent of any ideology, if one knows his ideo-affective posture, one can predict what his ideological posture will be if one asks him to consider an ideological question. Thus the completely ideologically innocent layman will not be indifferent to the ideological question in mathematics, "Do you think numbers are real or do you think someone invented them?"

In the foundations of law, mathematics, science, art, or child rearing, theorists who address themselves to one or another of these domains appear to become polarized on the same issues. These issues constitute a polarity extending from the extreme left through a middle of the road position to the extreme right-wing position. These issues are simple enough. Is man the measure, an end in himself, an active, creative, thinking, desiring, loving, force in nature? Or must man realize himself, attain his full stature only through struggle toward, participation in, conformity to, a norm, a measure, an ideal essence basically independent of man?

LEFT AND RIGHT IN VARIOUS IDEOLOGICAL DOMAINS

Let us first examine this polarity as it appears in the foundations of mathematics. For Henri Poincaré and others mathematics is the finest type of human play. Man is most free in this domain because he constructs the entities of mathematics entirely from his imagination. Because of the delight in play Poincaré defends mathematics as an end in itself. "Mathematics for mathematics sake! People have been shocked by this formula, and yet it is as good as life for life's sake, if life is but misery." Courant, among others, equates such a view with childish caprice. It would be a mere game, lacking contact with reality and of interest to no one.

> A serious threat to the very life of science is implied in the assertion that mathematics is nothing but a system of conclusions drawn from definitions and postulates that must be consistent but otherwise may be created by the free will of the mathematician. If this description were accurate, mathematics could not attract any intelligent person. It would be a game with definitions, rules and syllogisms, without motive or goal. The notion that the intellect can create meaningful postulational systems at its whim is a deceptive half-truth. Only under the discipline of responsibility to the organic whole; only guided by intrinsic necessity can the free mind achieve results of scientific value.[1]

The bipolar attitude toward games and play finds its clearest expression in the foundations of mathematics. When everyone was congratulating Lindemann in 1882 over his proof that *pi* is transcendental, Leopold Kronecker said, "Of what value is your beautiful proof, since irrational numbers do not exist? God created the natural numbers; everything else is man's handiwork." Courant's comment is: "In these words Leopold Kronecker pointed out the safe ground on which the structure of mathematics can be built."

E. T. Bell is a representative of the other pole.

> In the older books on geometry, postulates were sometimes called axioms, and it was gratuitously added that "an axiom is a self-evident truth" (which must have puzzled many an intelligent youngster). Modern mathematics is concerned with playing the game according to the rules; (others may inquire into the "truth" of mathematical propositions, provided they think they know what they mean).
>
> The rules of the game are extremely simple. Once and for all the postulates are laid down. These include a statement of all the permissible moves of the "elements" or "pieces." It is just like chess.

[1] R. Courant and H. Robbins, *What Is Mathematics?* (New York: Oxford University Press, 1941), p. 521.

Only a very original philosopher would dream of asking whether a particular game of chess was "true." The sensible question would be, "was the game played according to rules?" Leibniz saw in his binary arithmetic the image of creation. He imagined that unity represented God, and zero the void, that the Supreme Being drew all beings from the void, just as unity and zero express all numbers in his system of numeration.[2]

In an investigation of the determinants of the attraction to mathematics as a career, I have also noted that there is a polarization between right-wing mathematicians, who were attracted as children by its certainty and discipline, by the possibility of knowing what the right answer was and whether they had attained it; and left-wing mathematicians, who were attracted by its novelty and promise of excitement and its "wild, unaccountable spaces."

In the philosophy of science there is the same polarization. On the one hand science is understood as correspondence with reality and facts. Measurement is the most direct route to physical reality, and inference is the danger which must be held in check lest fancy run away with reality. Thus Verplanck, Collier, and Cotlow among many other psychologists reveal, in an aside, their suspicion of inference running wild:

> The sensory, neural, photochemical, or physical processes that have been postulated to generate the observed functions have been inferred from the functions themselves, and have seldom, if ever, been available to direct or collateral observation. Limits have been placed on such inference by information obtained in other disciplines. Physiological, biochemical, and histological evidence, often scanty, have [sic] served to keep in check the variety of inferences drawn.[3]

Most American sciences were governed by such a philosophy until the 1930's when refugee scientists from Europe began to assume a more important role in American thought. Contrast the attitude expressed in the preceding quotation with that of Einstein:

> The formulation of a problem is often more essential than its solution, which may be merely a matter of mathematical or experimental skill. To raise new questions, new possibilities, to regard old problems from a new angle, requires creative imagination and makes a real advance in science. . . . Physical concepts are free creations of the human mind, and are not, however it may seem, uniquely determined by the external world.[4]

The importance of play in science is affirmed by Newton as it was by Poincaré for mathematics. "I do not know what I may appear to the

---

[2] E. T. Bell, *Mathematics* (New York: McGraw-Hill, 1951), p. 437.

[3] W. S. Verplanck, G. H. Collier, and J. W. Cotlow, "Non Independence of Successive Responses in Measurements of the Visual Threshold," *J. Exp. Psychol.*, XLIV (1952), 273–282.

[4] A. Einstein and L. Infeld, *The Evolution of Physics* (New York: Simon and Schuster, 1942), p. 313.

world but to myself I seem to have been only like a boy playing on the seashore, and diverting myself in now and then finding a prettier shell, or a smoother pebble than ordinary, whilst the great ocean of truth lay all undiscovered before me."

Perhaps the classic statements of the extreme left-wing philosophy of science are from Bertrand Russell. In *Our Knowledge of the External World* Russell said, "Things are those series of aspects that obey the laws of physics."

In metaphysics the contrast is between a realistic and an idealistic conception of the relation of man to reality. In the extreme right-wing metaphysics as in Platonism, both man and nature are pale copies of ideas or essences, which exist prior to and independent of man. Man and nature alike owe whatever significance they attain to their participation in, their approximation to, the ideal essences which alone are truly real and important. A less extreme right-wing metaphysics conceives nature as more real, as prior to and independent of man. The extreme left-wing metaphysician conceives the world to be constructed by man or some form of mind. In its extreme form, as in Fichte and in Berkeley, the world is created by mind and is an idea. In its less extreme form, nature is a dull affair, enlivened only by the mind of man. Listen to Whitehead, in *Science and the Modern World*:

> These sensations are projected by the mind so as to clothe appropriate bodies in external nature. Thus the bodies are perceived as with qualities which in reality do not belong to them, qualities which in fact are purely the offspring of the mind. Thus nature gets credit which should in truth be reserved for ourselves: the rose for its scent, the nightingale for his song, and the sun for its radiance. The poets are entirely mistaken. They should address their lyrics to themselves, and should turn them into odes of self congratulation on the excellency of the human mind. Nature is a dull affair, soundless, scentless, colourless; merely the hurrying of material, endlessly, meaninglessly.[5]

In epistemology, reality as grasped immediately by the senses is contrasted with reality as an idea constructed by the perceiving mind. In a second cousin to epistemology, the psychological theory of perception, the contrast is between stimulus-bound theory, such as that of James Gibson, and the constructivist position of Ernst Cassirer or the transactionalist theory of Hadley Cantril and Adelbert Ames.

In ethics, the conflict is between the good defined as happiness and the good defined as self-realization, or perfectionism. In the general theory of value, value defined as any object of any interest is contrasted with value as an external quality of reality.

In the theory of politics, the view of the state as a creation of the

[5] A. Whitehead, *Science and the Modern World* (New York: Macmillan, 1926), p. 296.

people, by the people, for the people is opposed to the view of the state as a superordinate entity through which the people attain such political freedom as is possible. It is the difference between the conservative emphasis on tradition and conformity to the status quo and the progressive's emphasis on change in the interests of the people. In jurisprudence, the contrast is between the interpretation of law as man made and the interpretation of law as transcendental.

In art, there is the recurrent polarity between romanticism and classicism; between conservation of tradition and radical experimentation; between the emphasis on the personal, on the irrational, on human feeling versus the emphasis on control, on restraint, on reason. M. H. Abrams, in his analysis of romantic theory and the critical tradition in *The Mirror and the Lamp,* also finds evidence of a recurrent polarity between the right and left wing:

> The title of the book identifies two common and antithetic metaphors of mind, one comparing the mind to a reflector of external objects, the other to a radiant projector which makes a contribution to the objects it perceives. The first of these was characteristic of much of the thinking from Plato to the eighteenth century; the second typifies the prevailing romantic conception of the poetic mind.[6]

In educational theory, there is a perennial polarity between a left-wing progressive theory, which stresses the wishes of the child, and a more conservative authority-oriented emphasis on moral or achievement norms to be achieved by education.

In our own discipline of psychology the conflict between clinical and experimental psychology is a derivative of philosophies which stress either feeling and thinking or perceiving and acting and which emphasize either theory and observation or experimental control. It is also a conflict between being good (in the achievement or moral sense) and doing good. From the point of view of the authoritarian ideology, God helps those who help themselves. The same phenomenon of revulsion at the "do-gooders" appears among the conservatives in psychology and in politics.

One of the most extraordinary characteristics of this polarity is its apparently almost inevitable appearance even within domains which appear at the outset to be primarily right or left wing in orientation. Thus within the field of clinical diagnosis by the Rorschach method, an essentially left-wing method, we are confronted with the unrelenting antithesis of a free-wheeling Bruno Klopfer and a norm-oriented Samuel Beck.

The same polarity breaks out within psychiatry. Despite the fact that this profession is a left-wing profession in its insistence on the value

[6] M. H. Abrams, *The Mirror and the Lamp* (New York: Norton, 1958), p. 406.

of the individual and on the legitimacy of his claim to be helped rather than rejected, Strupp has shown that there is a radical difference among psychiatrists which is very similar to the general right-wing–left-wing polarity we have postulated. In studying the performance of psychotherapists under comparable controlled conditions, Strupp used a sound film of an initial interview to which subjects responded as vicarious interviewers. The respondents (therapists in the audience) were instructed to behave as if they were interviewing the patient. Strupp found that clinical impressions and therapeutic planning are influenced by attitudinal variables in the therapist. The first group of therapists appeared to be more tolerant, more humane, more permissive, more "democratic" and more "therapeutic." The second group emerged as more directive, disciplinarian, moralistic, and harsh. This contrast suggested the hypothesis that the first group of therapists were "warmer" in their communication to the patient and that "cold," rejecting comments would be less frequent.

> On the one hand, it is a basic attitude of understanding, respect, and compassion—what Albert Schweitzer calls "reverence for life." It is the ability to listen to the patient's story without preconception, prejudgment, or condemnation. It is the ability to pierce the neurotic distortions, the socially unacceptable attitudes and acts, the more unsavory aspects of his personality, and to see behind it a confused, bewildered, and helpless individual trying to shape his destiny, hampered and hindered by his neurotic conflicts and maladaptations. On the other hand, it is an attitude of coldness, calculation, "clinical evaluation," distance, "objectivity," aloofness, moral judgment, and condemnation. It is a readiness to take the neurotic defenses and the patient's character structure at face value, and to react to them with irritation, impatience, annoyance, and anger. It is also an attitude of forming a judgment about the patient's illness, almost from the beginning of the interview, often accompanied by a diagnostic label of "psychopathic," "paranoid," etc.[7]

The analyses also suggested that the empathic as well as the unempathic approach was in part a reflection of the therapist's conscious attitude. That is, to some extent at least, therapists were aware of their positive or negative reaction to the patient and their willingness or unwillingness to enter into a therapeutic relationship.

Finally this same polarity appears in the popular child-rearing literature of America, according to C. B. Stendler. In this literature, there is a polarization between loving and controlling the child. In the child-rearing theory based on Calvinism, methods were consciously related to the type of adult desired—a moral, honest, religious, independent individual who would take his proper place in society. It was assumed that

[7] H. H. Strupp, *Psychotherapists in Action* (New York: Grune and Stratton, 1960), p. 338.

the child was doomed to depravity throughout his life unless given careful and strict guidance by the parents and ultimately saved through Grace. Complete obedience and submission were thus required and achieved by "breaking the will" of the child.

Sooner or later the child would refuse to obey a command, and the issue of "will" was at hand. It was considered fatal to let the child win out. One mother, writing in the *Mother's Magazine* in 1834, described how her sixteen-month-old girl refused to say "dear Mama" at the father's order. She was led into a room alone, where she screamed wildly for ten minutes; then she was commanded again, and again she refused. She was then whipped and asked again. This was kept up for four hours until the child finally obeyed. Parents commonly reported that after one such trial the child became permanently submissive. However, many mothers seemed to find it hard to follow such prescriptions, and the *Mother's Magazine* carried many exhortations to mothers to do their duty toward their children. For parents of this group, indulgence was to be shunned.

Another theory which stressed conformity to a norm, that of achievement and competence, centered on "hardening" the child. Children should become strong, vigorous, unspoiled men, like those in the early days of the country. Cold baths and cold plunges were considered necessary, in the manner of the Indians. The implication derived from Rousseau was that the environment of civilization was dangerous to the child, who therefore required a long period of "training" of an athletic sort.

The other chief competitor for the attention of mothers in the child-rearing literature of the nineteenth century was the delicate-flower theory. If Calvinism hardened the child by first breaking his will to learn submission to God and parents and Rousseauian theory hardened the child to preserve the frontier virtues of stamina and competence, the other theory rejected hardening altogether. As Stendler reports:

> In 1890, "Love, petting and indulgence will not hurt a child if at the same time he is taught to be unselfish and obedient. Love is the mighty solvent," one editor wrote.
>
> Another writer outlined her plan for treating a boy who was labelled lazy, careless, and good-for-nothing; "I thought I would try to win him with love alone, and never strike him. . . . Mothers who have trouble with their children, bring them up the Christian way . . . with a loving and tender heart, and you will surely succeed."

The child was to be led, not driven; persuaded to the right, not commanded. Consistency and firmness are counseled, but with understanding and justice to the child. Corporal punishment was undesirable; the child was likened to an immortal bud just commencing to unfold its spotless leaves, ". . . a beautiful flower opening to the sunshine." The child was ignorant of right rather than bent to wrong.

A verse dating from an earlier day, but often quoted during this period reflects this orientation:

"If a babe sucks his thumb
'Tis an ease to his gum:
A comfort, a boon, a calmer of grief,
A friend in his need affording relief
A solace, a good, a soother of pain
A composer to sleep, a charm and a gain."[8]

As Stendler, in her study of "Sixty Years of Child Training Practices" has shown, there have been regular swings of the pendulum from the tender to the tough-minded treatment of the child. From 1890 to 1900 there was a highly sentimental view. From 1910 to 1930 there was an increasing emphasis on rigid scheduling and disciplinary fervor. From 1940 to the present, the pendulum has swung back again—and there is now appearing evidence for a swing in the other direction again.

The same polarity concerning child rearing is found in the Old and the New Testaments. The difference between the God of love and the God of authority is reflected in the assumed relationship between parent and child. In the Old Testament we find:

He that hateth reproof is brutish.

Proverbs 13:1

The eye that despiseth to obey his mother, the ravens of the valley shall pluck it out.

Proverbs 30:17

He that curseth Father or Mother, let him die the death.

Leviticus 20:9

But in the New Testament:

And ye Fathers provoke not your children to wrath, lest they be discouraged.

Ephesians 6:2 and 3

THE MIDDLE OF THE ROAD

We have thus far considered the extreme left- and right-wing ideologies. What of the middle of the road? This position exists, and indeed one might defend the thesis that the middle of the road represents the most radical ideology rather than a compromise position. This is so because the tension between the right and left wing in ideology has been perennial and a creative synthesis evokes some resonance from both sides. It is not accidental that the most influential modern philosopher, Kant, represents a synthesis of the right and the left and that the giant

[8] Quoted with permission from C. B. Stendler, "Sixty Years of Child Training Practices," *Journal of Pediatrics* [published by The C. V. Mosby Company], XXXVI (1950), 122–134.

of modern music, Beethoven, also achieved a creative synthesis of right- and left-wing musical forms.

Consider Kant. He affirmed both that reality, the *Ding an sich,* exists independent of and prior to man and is forever unknowable and that what man does know he has in large part created—the categories of the mind through which alone nature can be experienced. Kant also achieved the same synthesis in his ethical theory. Let us suppose that Kant was torn between the demands of the right and the left. How could one synthesize a foundation for morality which was personal and subjective and at the same time universal and objective? Kant's solution was extraordinarily creative. It was that one should act in such a way that what one did could be universalized. Be yourself, find morality within, but let it be possible that your morality is capable of serving as a norm for mankind. As in his metaphysics and epistemology, he unites the creative and subjective with the universal and objective. It is an extraordinary *tour de force,* and all philosophy thenceforth has been more or less "critical." In contemporary value theory the word commitment is an analogous synthesis which attempts to avoid both the pitfalls of "caprice" and the harshness of external "demands." It is a modern version of willing the obligatory. Where one would speak of demands or, with a less strident voice, of responsibilities, the modern Kantian speaks of commitment.

In music, Beethoven, like Kant, stands between the classical and romantic styles. Form never becomes an end in itself as in much classical music, and expression never completely overflows form and constraint as in much romanticism. It is because Beethoven, like Kant, struggled to join the right and the left that his interpreters, the conductors, have been able to transform him into a romantic or into a classic composer.

In recent philosophy Whitehead is perhaps the principal representative of the creative synthesis of the right and the left. In his recipe for a viable society he insists that loyalty to tradition must be combined with a willingness to experiment. The revolutionary is like a child with an arrow in his hand, who brings his society to the brink of its destruction, but without whom that society would perish.

ASSUMPTIONS OF IDEOLOGICAL POLARITY

Having examined some representatives of the extreme right-, middle-, and left-wing ideologies, let us now re-examine some of the communalities and more primitive assumptions behind this array of families of ideological components. Can we simplify this somewhat complex set of affirmations? I believe this is possible and I shall present briefly what appear to me to be the major underlying assumptions of this perennial polarity.

The first and most important pair of assumptions which underlies the polarity is: Man is an end in himself versus man is not an end in himself: the valuable exists independent of man. The major assumption from which most of the other forms of the polarity may be derived is this belief of man about man. No question with which man confronts himself engages him more than the question of his own worth. On the left he conceives himself to be an end in himself, to be of ultimate value; he wishes to be himself and to realize the potentialities which are inherent in him. On the right man is at best neutral, without value. There exists a norm, an objective value, independent of him, and he may become valuable by participation in, conformity to, or achievement of this norm. On the left, as a derivative, whatever perpetuates man's existence is valuable and whatever destroys or threatens it is of negative value. On the right, anything which harms or threatens man is neutral. It may be considered positive if it changes his wishes or behavior in the direction of positive values or if it punishes him for seeking negative values or failing to achieve positive value. It will be negative if it changes his wishes or behavior in the direction of negative values or if it punishes him for seeking positive values or rewards him for failing to achieve positive value.

From this basic postulate there are a number of derivatives which are essentially variants of the affirmation or denial of the value of man, or man is good versus man is evil. The first variant on the affirmation of man's value, in general, concerns his moral value. The left-wing ideology not only affirms his general significance but, as a special case, affirms man's inherent goodness in contrast to the extreme right-wing affirmation of man's essential badness. Whereas the left affirms that man must be corrupted to become bad, i.e. to violate his own nature, the right affirms that he must labor by the sweat of his brow to become good. In the more extreme right-wing ideologies man is so bad that he can never completely attain a state of goodness.

Man should be the object of love versus man should be loved if he is worthy. A second derivative concerns the appropriate personal positive affects toward man. The left urges man to love man because he is an end in himself, whereas the right makes love conditional upon his conformity and his achieved value. If he fails to meet the norm, the right urges hate rather than love.

The third derivative is: man should be the object of respect and approbation versus man should be respected if he is respectable. The left urges unconditional glorification and respect and approbation for man as well as unconditional love, whereas the right urges a conditional respect dependent on norm achievement or compliance.

The fourth variant is: unconditional and unlimited versus conditional and limited approbation toward the achievements of man. The left urges unconditional and unlimited respect, not only for man per se, but for all his works. These are the glory of man. The right urges not only an approbation conditional upon norm achievement but an approbation limited by an awareness of the essential discrepancy between man and the norm. Instead of joy, pride, and confidence in future achievement as extensions of glory, the right urges restraint and a temperate enthusiasm for the further achievements of the human race, with a hint of contempt for the inevitable human frailty which may endanger future achievement and with some skepticism about the inherent recalcitrance of nature to man's purposes.

Approbation of man's affects versus disapprobation of man's affects is the fifth derivative. Nowhere is the polarity between the right and left sharper than in the attitudes toward man's affects. The left has positive affects toward affects per se and is at home in the realm of feeling. The right is uneasy about and intolerant of affect per se, lest it endanger norm attainment. Approval of human affect is limited and contingent on its utility in enabling compliance, or as a reward for norm achievement. More often affect is portrayed as intruding and jeopardizing rational control of behavior.

Approbation versus disapprobation of man's reason is the sixth derivative. For the left, reason is another instance of the glory of man for which there should be approbation. In its relationship to the world perceived through the senses, reason guarantees man a certain distance between himself and the potentially excessive pressure of the immediacy of the senses. This is the position of the left. In contrast, the right wing views reason in this same context as overweening and a source of much error, which can be held in check only by the authority of the world external to the individual, the external norm which impresses itself through the senses.

The seventh, and last, derivative of the first major assumption is: disapprobation versus approbation of reason as a restraining force on affects. There is no clearer example of the ambiguity of concepts in ideology than the various roles in which reason has been cast by both the right and the left. Although the left approves of reason when it enhances man's independence of brute empiricism and although the right disapproves of reason when it sets itself in overweening opposition to the weight of authority and tradition as these are communicated over the sensory channels, the left is as hostile to reason as the right is approving when reason is viewed as a function controlling the drives and affects. When reason is viewed as limiting and restraining the feelings and drives, the left views this as a violation of the nature of the human being, but the right under these same conditions views reason as the representative of the norm within the human being and therefore as an object of approbation. This reversal of position between the right and left with respect to reason is evidence for our belief that the underlying assumption in the polarity of the right and left is the acceptance of the human being as an end in himself versus the glorification of a normative realm and the essential derogation of man. When one understands the fundamental role which these oversimplified, strongly positive and negative affects toward man play in the ideological polarity, one can account for a variety of apparent inconsistencies in the status assigned to various of man's functions and characteristics.

The second major assumption underlying the polarity, which is, however, rarely made explicit, is that of the identity of the real and the valuable. The real and the valuable are identical: man is real versus man is unreal. Theoretically it would have been possible to assume that man might be the most important entity in nature, but that he was not as real as the world in which he lived because it existed before him and would continue to exist after there were no men; or that man was insignificant and of no value, but that he was real, as evil is real, and even that he created the world as an idea out of the depths of his willfulness, as his plaything. In fact, however, there appears to be an extraordinary correlation within all ideologies, whether of the left or of the right, that if man is the most valuable phenomenon, he is also the most real entity and that if the norm or essence is the most valuable phenomenon, it is also the entity of greatest reality, in comparison with which, as in Plato, both man and nature are poor copies. Psychologically it is obvious enough that what is important must be real and what is real must be important, but the philosophic generalization of such an assumption is theoretically unwarranted despite its psychological persuasiveness.

The Greek legacy to Western civilization was in fact a double one. First was the left-wing ideology of man as the measure, in the sense of creator, and second was the right-wing ideology of the Platonic essence, independent and prior to man. Historians have emphasized one or the other of these ideologies according to their own ideological postures. In contrast to the emphasis on the significance of the legacy of Platonism, Hadas has stressed the left-wing legacy:

> The most striking single feature of the Homeric ethos is the enormous importance attached to individual prowess, individual pride, individual reputation. . . . The Homeric hero may not compromise loyalty to his own being with loyalty to any other, human or divine. . . . Achilles actually prays for the defeat of his own side in war, to enhance his own glory, and he allows his comrades to die in battle when it is in his power to protect them. . . . He and others like him earn the title of hero because they enlarge mankind by demonstrating man's capacity for greatness, by

endowing the commonplace things of life, food and weapons and clothing, with an aura of glory, by pushing back the boundaries of what is possible to man. . . . His superhuman stature is officially recognized, after his death, and he receives annual offerings on his particular day and his mediation is invoked in realms of activity appropriate to his heroism. . . . The Homeric ideal is summarized in a single line "To strive always for excellence and to surpass all others."[9]

The third major polarity is that values are what man wishes versus values exist independent of man. Inherent in the assumption that man is or is not an end in himself is an implicit definition of the nature of values. For the left wing, a value is a human wish; we would say, a human affect. If what he wishes defines the valuable, man can become an end in himself insofar as man wishes to be himself and loves himself. For the right wing, values are independent of man and therefore men may or may not wish for the good, the true, and the beautiful. Wishing per se cannot make it so, and wishing neither adds nor subtracts from the value or reality of anything. The left wing's theory of value is essentially an affect theory of value. As Ralph Barton Perry defined value, it is any object of any interest. We should generalize his use of the word interest, however, if we wish to describe the typical value theory of the left-wing ideologist, since the latter in fact believes in and defends the entire spectrum of affects.

The fourth polarity is that man should satisfy and maximize his drives and affects—hunger and sex, himself and others, work and play, novelty, risk, and familiarity, intimacy and detachment—versus man should be governed by norms which in turn modulate his drives and affects. The left-wing ideologist urges maximal satisfaction of the full spectrum of the drives and the positive affects. He regards the satisfaction of both sex and hunger as natural and good. As Bertrand Russell, among many others, has expressed it: "The source of all the harm is that the good life has been sought in obedience to a negative imperative, not in broadening and developing the natural desires and instincts."[10]

In contrast, John Locke: "As the strength of the body lies chiefly in being able to endure hardships, so also does that of the mind. And the great principle and foundation of all virtue and worth is placed in this; that a man is able to deny himself his own desires, cross his own inclinations, and purely follow what reason directs as best, though appetite lean the other way."[11]

The right-wing ideologist urges the control of all the drives and the affects by reason, in the interest of some norm. The left-wing ideologist

[9] M. Hadas, *Humanism* (New York: Harper & Brothers, 1960), p. 132.
[10] B. Russell, *On Education* (London: Allen and Unwin, 1930), p. 250.
[11] J. Locke, *Some Thoughts Concerning Education* (New York: Charles Scribner's Sons, 1928), p. 350.

stresses man's natural affective investment in himself as well as in others. He presents man as naturally both self-interested and socially responsive. The right-wing ideologist is more likely to stress man's natural egoism to the disadvantage of his social responsiveness. The latter, he is likely to argue, is a by-product of control of natural egoism by norms, through the exercise of reason. The left-wing theorist portrays man as equally excited by work as by play. The right-wing theorist makes work a more serious, more alien demand upon the human being and rejects play as utterly childish. The left-wing theorist portrays man drawn to novelty and risk and to familiarity, excited by the new and addicted to the old. Thus Camus, in *The Myth of Sisyphus:* "Delicious anguish of being, exquisite proximity of a danger we do not know, it is to live then to run to our death. . . . I have always had the impression that I lived on the high seas, threatened, at the heart of royal happiness."[12]

The quest for the familiar in the novel is more explicit in Fromm:

> There is no innate "drive for progress" in man; it is the contradiction in his existence that makes him proceed in the way he set out. Having lost paradise, the unity with nature, he has become the eternal wanderer (Odysseus, Oedipus, Abraham, Faust); he is impelled to go forward and with everlasting effort to make the unknown known by filling in with answers the blank spaces of his knowledge. He must give account to himself of himself, and of the meaning of his existence. He is driven to overcome this inner split, tormented by a craving for "absoluteness," for another kind of harmony which can lift the curse by which he was separated from nature, from his fellow men, and from himself. . . . This split in man's nature leads to dichotomies which I call existential because they are rooted in the very existence of man: they are contradictions which man cannot annul but to which he can react in various ways, relative to his character and his culture. . . .
>
> If he faces the truth without panic he will recognize that there is no meaning to life except the meaning man gives his life by the unfolding of his powers, by living productively; and that only constant vigilance, activity, and effort can keep us from failing in the one task that matters—the full development of our powers within the limitations set by the laws of our existence. . . .
>
> There is only one solution to his problem: to face the truth, to acknowledge his fundamental aloneness and solitude in a universe indifferent to his fate, to recognize that there is no power transcending him which can solve his problem for him. Man must accept the responsibility for himself and the fact that only by using his powers can he give meaning to his life. But meaning does not imply certainty; indeed the quest for certainty blocks the search for meaning.[13]

The right-wing ideologist is committed neither to novelty and risk,

[12] A. Camus, *The Myth of Sisyphus* (New York: Knopf, 1955), p. 215.
[13] E. Fromm, *Man for Himself* (New York: Holt, Rinehart and Winston, Inc., 1947), pp. 41, 44–45.

nor to familiarity, but to the norm, be it an achievement norm, a norm of morality, or a norm of manners. These may demand that the individual risk his life in the interest of the norm, but they may also demand that he conform to tradition as the carrier of the norm. The fact that human beings are excited by risk and by novelty and that they enjoy the familiar is irrelevant.

Finally, the left-wing ideologist urges both intimacy and detachment as basic human needs. In his stress on intimacy he is captivated by all those modes of knowing in which the distinction between the subject and the object is lost. He believes there is no better way to acquaint oneself with the other than to coalesce with that other, be it human, impersonal, or divine. Even within the doctrine of mysticism there are important variations in the degree of intimacy permitted the subject. Thus in the so-called throne mysticism the worshipper maintains a respectful distance from the object of adoration. At the same time the left-wing theorist urges the importance of detachment, perspective, and rational analysis to understand the object better and to see it in its relatedness to other objects. Thus the left-wing philosopher is likely to be one who spends much of his life in reflection on the value of immediacy. Whether a left-wing ideologist stresses one or the other, as he may do, depends in part on what he takes for granted and what is the most visible enemy. Thus if he lives in an age of superstition, he is apt to glorify rational analysis. If he lives in an age of science he is apt to stress, as do the existentialists today, the value of intimate surrender to the object.

The right-wing ideologist is indifferent about these distinctions, so long as there is norm attainment and compliance. However, he rejects mysticism and too great intimacy, lest it be too orgiastic and too emotional and lest the distinction between the worshipper and the worshipped become too attenuated. In science he is contemptuous of any doctrine of intuition, lest it weaken the demands of rigorous proof. But he is equally suspicious of too great an emphasis on detachment and theoretical activity, for fear that the authority of the real world be undermined or derogated.

The right-wing ideologist in science is likely to urge a middle course, eschewing the Scylla of seduction by the object and the Charybdis of alienation of the object through overweening pride in the power of reason. In contrast, the left-wing ideologist is hostile to a stable marriage between the self and the object, preferring both the passion of a love affair and the detachment of the uncommitted bachelor. In terms of psychoanalytic ideology, left-wing science oscillates between the oceanic communion of the womb, or the oral stage, and the overweening pride of the phallic stage, whereas right-wing science is a derivative of the anal stage, in which the emphasis is on successfully duplicating the directives of the model and, above all, in making no mistakes.

The fifth major polarity is that man should minimize drive dissatisfaction and negative affects—hunger and sex, fear, shame, distress and aggression—versus man should maximize norm conformity and norm realization. The left urges first of all the sanctity of human life. It is an absolute which is not to be surrendered. In the American credo the human being has first of all the right to life, as well as to liberty and happiness. The right-wing thinker is not indifferent to the maintenance of life. He may be troubled by the taking of life, either one's own or another's, but mainly because it is a norm violation or violation of the will of God. He is not, however, troubled by the lives which must be surrendered in the name of the norm, be it God or State.

The left-wing ideologist urges that the frustration of either hunger or sex be minimized, whereas the right-wing ideologist regards them as either neutral or as impediments to the attainment or maintenance of piety, achievement, or whatever the norm that is affirmed. The left urges that the human being has the right to freedom from fear, from being humiliated, from distress, and from reason for anger. He defends however the right of the human being to be angry and to protest. As Camus expressed it in *The Myth of Sisyphus*, revolt is "the impulse that drives an individual to the defense of a dignity common to all men." The right urges control of aggression by the individual but urges its use for the punishment of norm violators. The use of aggression is, however, most often reserved to authority which represents the norm.

Contempt for the norm offender is urged upon all by the right. The left under similar circumstances counsels empathy and understanding and the imposition of negative sanctions only as a last resort in the interests of saving the lives and minimizing the suffering of others. Since the right is concerned only with the maintenance and achievement of norms, any violation of norms is appropriately punished through increasing the suffering of the offender. The right-wing ideologist defends the use of contempt as an agent of social control and is indifferent to the negative consequences of hierarchical relationships. The left-wing ideologist rejects contempt as a technique of social control lest it alienate and jeopardize social solidarity and egalitarian sentiments. All men are born free and equal, and should remain so. Shaming is therefore minimized and no man should bend the knee to another. Nor should anyone be terrorized, according to the ideology of the left. According to the right, beginning with the fear of God, it is appropriate that authority be the object of fear and trembling, particularly if insurrection is at question. According to the left, distress and suffering are to be outlawed and as minimized as humiliation and terror. Life should be made as tolerable as the imagination of man can so contrive it. For the right, offenders should suffer, and whether the pious are distressed is a matter of indifference. It is more often assumed that the way of both the blessed and the sinner are necessarily hard, since there is a permanent gap between the individual and the norm.

In the attitude of the left- and right-wing ideologists of science there is a differential sensitivity to the negative and positive affects. The left urges imagination and the maximizing of excitement and enjoyment in the pursuit of truth. Shame should occur only if the main chance has been missed. The right urges discipline and rigor and the minimizing of error, lest one be the proper object of contempt. Shame should occur if one has been shown to be in error or if one has had overweening pride and overreached himself. One stresses the logic of discovery, whereas the other stresses the logic of verification.

The sixth major polarity is: affect inhibition should be minimized versus affects should be controlled by norms. The left-wing theorist stresses the toxicity of affect control and inhibition, and it therefore becomes a special case of the principle of minimizing negative affect that such control should be kept to a minimum. The left-wing theorist is more alarmed at the cost to the individual of defending himself against the expression of distress, shame, aggression, excitement, or enjoyment than he is at the cost of freely expressing his affects. He is likely to stress the value both to the individual and to society of an openness and tolerance for intrusions of the irrational, of the Dionysian, of the *Weltschmerz,* of the *fin de siècle.* The right-wing ideologist sets himself sternly against such intrusions and argues for the importance of controlling affects in the interests of morality, achievement, piety, or classic beauty. It is not that he is necessarily, in Nietzsche's term, an apologist for the Apollonian rather than the Dionysian. It is rather that he is for some norm, which may require heroic mobilization of affect and energy to achieve or which may require unrelenting hostility against those who challenge the good, the true, or the beautiful. If that challenge is seen to be from within, then the most severe inhibition of the offending affects may be required; and, at the same time that positive affects toward the norm may be demanded, it may also be necessary not to inhibit all negative affects but to direct them against the self.

The seventh major polarity is that power should be maximized in order to maximize positive affects and to minimize negative affects versus power should be maximized to maximize norm compliance and achievement. All ideologists invoke a power postulate in which the ability of the individual to realize values is urged. The difference lies in which values the means-end power should maximize. The left wing is, first of all, an ideology of individualism. Although it does not set the individual into necessary conflict with society (since it urges that man is at once a self-interested and a social animal), nonetheless it has usually set itself against any subordination of the individual to the society, since society is conceived to be a set of individuals rather than the representative of some normative authority. During those historical periods when social and political authority is seen as violating the rights and dignity of man, the left-wing ideologist, as we have seen in the case of the Homeric hero, is apt to set himself in violent opposition to tradition and even to the needs of others with whom he may in large measure identify himself. The same left-wing ideologist, confronted with mass misery, such as that which followed in the wake of the industrial revolution, may reject the robber baron and identify with the masses to such an extent that one may overlook the communality of these two pictures. What is common, first in identification with and glorification of the hero, and then in identification with and glorification of the masses against the exploiting, individualistic capitalist, is the belief in maximizing the power of human beings to control their own destiny, to maximize their positive affect, and to minimize their negative affect. It is a bias in favor of humanity, both the individual human being and groups of human beings. Historical circumstances dictate whether the heroic individual is pitted against society or whether society is pitted against the tyrant.

At another time the power of the creative individual to refuse the cake of custom, the pressures of the group toward conformity, is the message of the left-wing ideology. Whatever limits the power of human beings to maximize their positive affects and to minimize their negative affects—whether this limitation be internal or external, in the masses or in an elite class, in a corrupting or an exploiting individual—that limiting force will be opposed by the left-wing ideologist, depending on where the major threat is seen at the particular historical moment.

The idea of the importance of freedom is a derivative of the idea of power, since it has been supposed that without the freedom for each individual to grow in his own way there could be no development of individuals who differ from each other.

The emphasis on the full development of the human personality has dominated Western ideology since Leonardo. This was the ideal from the Renaissance artists, through the Elizabethans, through Locke, Voltaire, and Rousseau. As Bronowski maintained:

> The vision of the freely developing man, happy in the unfolding of his own gifts is shared by men as different in their conceptions as Thomas Jefferson and Edmund Burke. . . . The Renaissance ideal of man had an element of condottiere brutality, which has lingered on in Western thought; it is perhaps inseparable from the Western admiration for power, over nature and over men. Something of this sense of power, of mastering the tech-

niques and desires of the earthly life, is present in the ideal men of the Reformation—in Calvin's 'new man' and in the Puritan soldiery. . . . A different direction was set by the Tudor ideal of a gentleman and by the seventeenth-century ideal of the virtuoso. This direction leads from the humanist of the sixteenth century to the philosophe of the eighteenth and is seen at its best in the tolerant, rational, free, and yet convinced and single-minded men of English dissent and of the American Revolution.[14]

We agree with Bronowski's affirmation of the continuity of the idea of power as a fulfillment of the potentiality of the human being, but we would stress more than he does what each ideologist thought was the proper use of this power. For the right-wing ideologist it is not to maximize man's enjoyment and excitement and to minimize distress, fear, and shame, but to examine his power to achieve, to be a gentleman, to be virtuous, to be pious, to be perfect, or to amass wealth.

In the interests of power the left-wing ideologist affirms the desirability of power of the self (1) over the self, if and when any part of the self threatens to restrict the freedom of the self as a whole, as in the perpetuation of an infantile conscience or as in the swamping of the self by panic, grief, rage, or humiliation; (2) over other selves, including the state, if and when others threaten to restrict the freedom of the self; (3) over nature, if and when it is recalcitrant to the attainment of human purposes.

The eighth major assumption is the polarity between the principle of pluralism versus the principle of hierarchy. The left ideology assumes that conflict between affects within the individual and between individuals should be minimized. This is a derivative of the more general strategy of maximizing the positive affects and of minimizing the negative affects. Since all satisfactions are desirable, limitation by conflicting satisfactions is to be minimized. The right-wing ideology ordinarily orders all wishes according to a norm and according to the necessity of the particular wish or behavior in furthering maintenance or achievement of the norm. No attempt is made to minimize conflict per se.

The ninth major assumption is the polarity between the principle of selectivity by maximizing positive and minimizing negative affect versus the principle of selectivity by maximizing normative behavior. Not only is there a difference between the strategy of pluralism versus that of hierarchy, in which the left tries to minimize conflict as much as possible, while the right is indifferent to conflict per se; but when restrictions on maximizing strategies cannot be avoided, i.e. when the principle of pluralism breaks down, the left-wing ideology bases the choice between competing interests, either within the individual or between individuals, on the same principle as that which dictated pluralism. Thus

[14] J. Bronowski and B. Mazlish, *The Western Intellectual Tradition* (New York: Harper & Brothers, 1960), p. 522.

if an individual is confronted with the necessity of surrendering one of his satisfactions in the interest of another, according to the left this selectivity should be governed by the general strategy of maximizing positive and minimizing negative affects. Freud's reality principle by which the pleasure principle is governed is a familiar example. The right-wing ideology has another criterion: that should be surrendered which is lower in the normative hierarchy or which will most threaten some higher member of the hierarchy.

In a conflict of interests between men, resolution should be governed by the principle of maximizing wish fulfillment and minimizing wish frustration of every party to the conflict, according to the ideology of the left. According to right-wing ideology, in a conflict of interests between men resolution should be governed by the principle of maximizing norm achievement or conformity. When the norms were those of an aristocratic society, that basic conflict of interests perpetuated in the institution of slavery was solved in favor of the slave owner and rationalized on the grounds that he was the more worthy of the competing human beings and that the slave was a barbarian or in some way inferior.

The tenth major polarity is that of tolerance and amelioration of weakness versus intolerance and punishment of weakness. All ideologies of both the right and left, however much they may glorify man, have also taken notice of man's imperfections and frailties. The left-wing ideologist counsels forgiveness and indulgence and offers nurture. One should try to change the imperfect one by example, by love, and by the lure of identification. For hate return love. Toward those who sin by failure to do something, offer forgiveness, give yet another chance, offer support and inspire by exciting interest. When man is weak he most needs love. If man is not perfect, he is perfectible. Stress his positive qualities.

The right-wing ideologist has a complementary set of injunctions. Towards man's weakness man should be unrelenting, unforgiving, and punitive. If a man is weak, he should not be helped, he should help himself. Toward man's weakness, do not offer love, but demand reform and atonement. Against the will of the offender every pressure should be brought to bear to break that will. The weak should be toughened and the strong-willed should be curbed. Man should never be permitted to forget his imperfection, his sins, and his weaknesses. He is not perfect and there are limits to his perfectibility. For these discrepancies between the ideal and the actual, the appropriate response is to terrorize, to shame, and to distress the offender.

Let us examine Russell and Locke again, on the subject of education. First Russell:

> A thousand ancient fears obstruct the road to happiness and freedom. But love can conquer fear, and if we love our children nothing can make us withhold the great gift which it is in our power to bestow.[15]

Contrast this with Locke:

> Esteem and disgrace are, of all others, the most powerful incentives to the mind, when once it is brought to relish them. If you can once get into children a love of credit and apprehension of shame and disgrace, you have put into them the right principle, which will constantly work and incline them to the right.[16]

Although the right-wing ideologist stresses negative sanctions, such as shame and disgrace for weakness and error, he may also stress positive sanctions as a reward for norm maintenance or achievement. As we see in Locke, the love of right principles is a shield against the shame and disgrace of norm violation. Nonetheless, in response to actual norm violation the primary sanctions urged by right-wing ideologists are negative.

The details of the difference in socialization which ultimately produce resonance to one or the other ideological posture we have considered elsewhere.[17] These concern differences in tolerance for, or intolerance of, the several primary human affects: excitement, enjoyment, surprise, distress, contempt, shame, fear, and anger.[18]

---

[15] B. Russell, *On Education* (London: Allen and Unwin, 1930), p. 250.
[16] *Loc. cit.*
[17] S. S. Tomkins, *Affect, Imagery, Consciousness* (New York: Springer, 1962).
[18] This paper was originally written in honor of Henry A. Murray and delivered at the thirtieth anniversary celebration of the Harvard Psychological Clinic in 1957. This is a revised and expanded account of that address.

18: THE GOLDEN RULE AND
THE CYCLE OF LIFE

Erik H. Erikson

By the bequest of the late Dr. George W. Gay the "advanced or graduating classes" of Harvard Medical School are to hear each year a
lecture "Upon Medical Ethics."[1] The bequest specifies, with increasing
concreteness: ". . . and upon wise and proper methods of conducting
the business of physicians as relates to fees, collections, investments etc."
Over the years, however, Gay Lecturers seem to have found in and between those lines a sanction for ranging over a widening area, from
economic prudence to professional propriety and from medical wisdom
to the ethics of human and international relations. I take advantage of
such leeway by offering a few insights coming from the study of life
histories—a field of study first inspired by a series of physicians (from
Sigmund Freud to William James and Henry A. Murray) who became
psychologists and who created out of the study of cases the study of lives.
The insights to be advanced will, it is hoped, prove to be relevant to
"wise and proper conduct" even though the only kind of ethical investment to be recommended is that of one generation in the next.

THE GOLDEN RULE

My base line is the Golden Rule, which advocates that one should
do (or not do) to another what one wishes another to do (or not do) to
him. A pretty battered base line it is, and obscured with the grime of
hypocrisy. No wonder that systematic students of ethics often indicate a
certain disdain for this all too primitive ancestor of loftier and more
logical principles. Yet, for generation after generation this rule has
marked a mysterious meeting ground between ancient peoples separated
by oceans and eras, a theme hidden in the sayings of great thinkers.

I would like to take the Talmudic version of the Golden Rule for
my opening: "What is hateful to yourself, do not to your fellow-man,"

[1] The present essay was the George W. Gay Lecture Upon Medical Ethics,
presented at Harvard Medical School on May 4, 1962.

the Talmud says, adding, "That is the whole of the Torah and the rest is but commentary. Go and learn it." The rule in this form, as critics have never tired of pointing out, is the rock bottom of moral prudence. But then, the rule was so stated by Rabbi Hillel in answer to an unbeliever's challenge that he be told the whole of the Torah while he stood on one foot. Pressed for brevity, the great rabbi put basic things first. If he added that the rest was but commentary, nobody acquainted with the Jewish way of life would mistake "but commentary" for "merely commentary," for surely sometimes the ongoing commentary is the very life of a rule.

The Golden Rule obviously concerns itself with one of the very basic paradoxes of human existence. Each man calls his own a separate body, a self-conscious individuality, and a personal awareness of the cosmos; and yet he shares this world as a reality also perceived and judged by others and as an *actuality* within which he must commit himself to ceaseless interaction. To identify self-interest and the interest of other selves, the rule alternately employs the method of warning, "Do *not* as you would *not* be done by," and of exhortation, *"Do* as you *would* be done by." For psychological appeal, some versions rely on the minimum of egotistic prudence, while others demand a maximum of altruistic sympathy: it must be admitted that the formula, "Do not to others what if done to you would cause you pain," does not presuppose much more than the mental level of the small child who desists from pinching when he gets pinched in return. On the other hand, mature insight and more are assumed in the saying, "No one is a believer until he loves for his brother what he loves for himself." Of all the versions, however, none commits us so unconditionally as "Love thy neighbor as thyself": it even suggests a true love of ourselves.

I will not (I could not) involve us in comparative religion by tracing the versions of the rule to various religions; no doubt in translation all of them have become somewhat assimilated to our biblical versions. Yet, the basic formula seems to be universal, and it reappears in an astonishing number of the most revered sayings of our civilization, from St. Francis' prayer to Kant's moral imperative and to Lincoln's simple political creed: "As I would not be slave, I would not be master."

The variations of the rule have, of course, provided material for many discussions of ethics weighing the soundness of the logic implied and measuring the degree of ethical nobility reached in each. My field of inquiry, the study of life histories, suggests that I desist from arguing relative logical merit or spiritual worth and instead relate some variations in moral and ethical sensitivity to successive stages in the development of human conscience. In the framework of the cycle of life, the most primitive and the most exalted rules may well prove necessary to each other.

THE DEVELOPMENT OF MORALITY

This lecture is entitled the "Lecture Upon Medical Ethics" and not upon "Medical Morality." The implication is clear: a man who knows what is legal or illegal and what is moral or immoral has not necessarily yet learned what is ethical. Highly moralistic people can do unethical things; whereas an ethical man's involvement in immoral doings becomes by inner necessity an occasion for tragedy. The dictionary, our first refuge from ambiguity, in this case only confounds it; morals and ethics are defined as synonyms *and* antonyms of each other. In other words, they are the same, with a difference—a difference which I intend to emphasize.

I would propose that we consider moral rules of conduct to be based on a fear of threats to be forestalled—outer threats of abandonment, punishment, public exposure; or a threatening inner sense of guilt, shame, or isolation. In contrast, I would consider ethical rules to be based on a love of ideals to be striven for—ideals that hold up to us some highest good, some definition of perfection, and some promise of self-realization. This differentiation is, I think, substantiated by developmental observation, and the developmental principle is the first of those principles which will represent for us the kind of insight which we have gained by the study of life histories.

All that exists layer upon layer in an adult's mind has developed step by step in the growing child's, and the major steps in the comprehension of what is considered good behavior in one's cultural universe are—for better and for worse—related to different stages in individual maturation. The response to a moral tone of voice develops early. The small child, so limited to the intensity of the moment, somehow must learn the boundaries marked by "don't's." Here cultures have a certain leeway in underscoring the goodness of one who does not transgress or the evilness of one who does. But the conclusion is unavoidable that children can be made to feel evil and that adults continue to project evil on one another and on their children, far beyond the call of rational judgment.

Before discussing this early moral sense in more detail, let me mention the later steps which I will differentiate from it: they are the development of an ideological sense in adolescence, and of an ethical sense in young adulthood. The imagery of steps, of course, is useful only where it is to be suggested that one item precedes another in such a way that the earlier one is necessary to the later ones and that each later one is of a higher order. But development is more complex, especially since all manner of step formations take place simultaneously and in not too obvious synchronization.

To return to the moral sense, psychoanalytic observation first established in a systematic fashion what certain Eastern thinkers have always known, namely that the radical division into good and bad can be the sickness of the mind. It has traced the moral scruples and excesses of the adult to the childhood stages in which guilt and shame are ready to be aroused and are easily exploited. It has named and studied the superego, which hovers over the ego as the inner perpetuation of the child's subordination to the restraining will of his elders. Although the voice of the superego is not always cruel and derisive, it is ready to become so whenever the precarious balance which we call a good conscience is upset. At those times the secret weapons of this inner governor are revealed: the brand of shame and the bite of conscience. Are these "caused" or merely accentuated by the pressure of parental and communal methods, by the threat of loss of affection, of corporal punishment, of public shame? Or are they by now a proclivity for self-alienation which has become a part—and, to some extent, a necessary part—of man's evolutionary heritage? All we know for sure is that the moral proclivity in man does not develop without the establishment of some chronic self-doubt and some truly terrible, even if mostly submerged, rage against anybody and anything that reinforces such doubt. The "lowest" in man thus is apt to reappear in the guise of the "highest": irrational and prerational combinations of goodness, doubt, and rage can re-emerge in the adult in those malignant forms of righteousness and prejudice which we may call moralism. In the name of high moral principles it can employ all the vindictiveness of derision, of torture, and of mass-extinction. One surely must come to the conclusion that the Golden Rule was meant to protect man not only against his enemy's open attacks but also against his friends' righteous encroachments.

THE EVOLUTIONARY PRINCIPLE

Lest this view, in spite of the evidence of history, seem too "clinical," we turn to the science of evolution, which in the last few decades has joined psychoanalysis in recognizing the superego as an evolutionary fact—and danger. The developmental principle is thus joined by an evolutionary one. Waddington even goes so far as to say that superego rigidity may be an overspecialization in the human race, like the excessive body armor of the late dinosaurs. In a less grandiose comparison he likens the superego to "the finicky adaptation of certain parasites which fits them to live only on one host animal."[2] In recommending his

[2] C. H. Waddington, *The Ethical Animal* (London: Allen and Unwin, 1960).

book, *The Ethical Animal* (in addition to the works of J. Huxley and G. G. Simpson), I must admit that his terminology contradicts mine. He calls the awakening of morality in childhood a proclivity for "ethicizing," whereas I would prefer to call it moralizing. As many animal psychologists do, he dwells on analogies between the very young child and the young animal, instead of comparing, as I think we must, the young animal with the pre-adult human, including the adolescent.

I cannot dwell here on the new insights into the cognitive and emotional gains of adolescence which enable the young—often only after a severe bout with moralistic regression—to envisage more universal principles of a highest human good. The adolescent learns to grasp the flux of time, to anticipate the future in a coherent way, to perceive ideas and to assent to ideals, to take—in short—an ideological position for which the younger child is cognitively not prepared. In adolescence, then, an ethical view is approximated, but it remains susceptible to an alternation of impulsive judgment and odd rationalization. It is, then, as true for adolescence as it is for childhood, that man's way stations to maturity can become fixed, can become premature end stations or stations for future regression—in one person or in masses of individuals.

The moral sense, in its perfections and its perversions, has been an intrinsic part of man's evolution, whereas the sense of ideological rejuvenation has pervaded his revolutions, both with prophetic idealism and with destructive fanaticism. Adolescent man, in all his sensitivity to the ideal, is easily exploited by promises of counterfeit millennia, easily taken in by the promise of a new and arrogantly exclusive identity.

The true ethical sense of the young adult, at its best, encompasses moral restraint and ideal vision, while insisting on concrete commitments to those intimate relationships and work associations by which man can hope to share a lifetime of productivity and competence. But young adulthood engenders its own dangers. It adds to the moralist's righteousness and to the ideologist's repudiation of all "otherness" the territorial defensiveness of one who has appropriated and staked out his earthly claim and seeks eternal security in the superidentity of organizations. Thus, what the Golden Rule at its highest has attempted to make all-inclusive, tribes and nations, castes and classes, moralities and ideologies have consistently made exclusive again—proudly, superstitiously, and viciously denying the status of reciprocal ethics to those "outside."

If, so far, I have underscored the malignant potentials of man's slow maturation, I have not done so in order to dwell on a kind of dogmatic pessimism which can emerge all too easily from clinical preoccupation, often leading only to new moralistic avoidances. I know that man's moral, ideological, and ethical propensities can find and have found on occasion a sublime integration, in individuals and in groups, who are both tolerant and firm, flexible and strong, wise and obedient. Above all, men have always shown a dim knowledge of their better potentialities by paying homage to those purest leaders who taught the simplest and most inclusive rules for an undivided mankind. But men have also persistently betrayed them, on what passed for moral or ideological grounds, even as they are now preparing a potential betrayal of all of human heritage in the name of science and technology, that is, in the name of what must surely be good merely because it can be made to work—no matter where it leads.

We now see where it may lead. But only in our time, in our generation, have we come to view with a start the obvious fact that throughout history the rule, in whatever form, has comfortably co-existed with warfare. A warrior, armored, spiked and set to do to another what he fully expected the other to be ready to do to him, saw no ethical contradiction between the rule and his military ideology: he could, in fact, grant to his adversary a respect which he hoped to earn in return. This tenuous co-existence of ethics and warfare may outlive itself in our time; the military mind may well come to fear for its historical identity when technical mass annihilation replaces tactical warfare. The Golden Rule of the nuclear age, which is "Do not unto others unless you are sure you can do them in as totally as they can do you in," creates not only an international deadlock but a profoundly ethical one as well.

One wonders, however, whether this deadlock can be broken by even the most courageous protest, the most incisive interpretation, or the most prophetic warning—a warning of catastrophe of such immensity that most men must ignore it, as they ignore certain death and have learned to ignore the monotonous prediction of hell. It seems, instead, that only an ethical orientation, a direction for vigorous co-operation, can free today's energies from their bondage in armed defensiveness. We live at a time in which—for all the species-wide destruction possible—we can think for the first time of a species-wide identity, of a truly universal ethics, such as has been prepared in the world religions, in humanism, and by philosophers. Ethics can not be fabricated; it can only emerge from an informed and inspired search for a more inclusive human identity, which a new technology and a new world image make possible as well as mandatory.

Man's sociogenetic evolution is about to reach a crisis in the full sense of the word: a crossroads offering one path to fatality and one to recovery and further growth. Artful perverter of joy and keen exploiter of strength, man has learned to survive "in a fashion," to multiply without food for the multitudes, to grow up healthily without reaching personal maturity, to live well but without purpose, to invent ingeniously without aim, and to kill grandiosely without need. But the processes of sociogenetic evolution also seem to promise a new humanism, the acceptance by man—as an evolved product as well as a producer and as a self-conscious tool of further evolution—of the obligation to be guided in his planned actions and his chosen self-restraints by his knowledge and his insights. In this endeavor, then, it may be of a certain importance to learn to understand and to master the differences between infantile morality, adolescent ideology, and adult ethics: each necessary to the next, but each effective only if they eventually combine in that wisdom which, as Waddington puts it, "fulfills sufficiently the function of mediating evolutionary advance."

At the point when one is about to end an argument with a global injunction of what we *must* do, it is good to remember Blake's admonition that the common good readily becomes the topic of "the scoundrel, the hypocrite, and the flatterer"; and that anyone who would do some good must do so in "minute particulars." And indeed, I have so far spoken only of the developmental and evolutionary principle, according to which the propensity for ethics grows in the individual as part of an adaptation roughly laid down by evolution. Yet, to grow in the individual, ethics must be generated and regenerated in and by the sequence of generations. This generational principle we must now make more explicit.

THE GENERATIONAL PRINCIPLE

Let me make an altogether new start here; let us look at scientific man in his dealings with animals. Harry Harlow's studies on the development of affection in monkeys are well known. He did some outstanding experimental and photographic work attempting, in the life of laboratory monkeys, to "control the mother variable." He took monkeys from their mothers within a few hours after birth, isolated them, and left them with "mothers" made out of wire, metal, wood, and terry cloth. A rubber nipple somewhere in the middle emitted piped-in milk, and the whole contraption was wired for body warmth. All the "variables" of this mother situation were controlled: the amount of rocking, the degree of "body warmth," and the exact incline of the maternal body necessary to make a scared monkey feel safe and comfortable. Years ago, when this method was presented as a study of the development of affection in monkeys, the clinician could not help wondering whether the object of study was *monkey* affection or a fetishist addiction to inanimate objects. And, indeed, while these laboratory reared monkeys became healthier and healthier and much more trainable in technical know-how than the inferior monkeys brought up by mere monkey mothers, they became at the end what Harlow calls "psychotics."[3] They sit passively, they stare vacantly, and some do something terrifying: when poked they bite themselves and tear at their own flesh until the blood flows. They have not learned to experience "the other," either as a mother, a mate, a child —or enemy. Only a tiny minority of the females produced offspring, and only one of those made an attempt to nurse hers. But science remains a wonderful thing. Now that we have succeeded in producing "psychotic" monkeys experimentally, we can convince ourselves that we have at last given scientific support to severely disturbed mother-child relationships as causative factors in human psychosis.

It speaks for Harry Harlow's methods that what they demonstrate is unforgettable. At the same time, they lead us to that border line where we recognize that the scientific approach toward living beings must be with concepts and methods adequate to the study of ongoing life, not of selective extinction. I have put it this way: one can study the nature of things by doing something *to* them, but one can really learn something about the *essential nature* of *beings* only by doing something *with* them or *for* them. This, of course, is the principle of clinical science. It does not deny that one can learn by dissecting the dead or that animal or man can be motivated to lend circumscribed parts of their beings to an experimental procedure. But for the study of those central transactions which are the carriers of sociogenetic evolution and for which we must take responsibility in the future, the chosen unit of observation must be the generation, not the individual. Whether an animal or a human being partook of the stuff of life can be tested only by the kind of observation which discerns his ability to transmit life—in some essential form—to the next generation.

In contrast, one remembers the work of Konrad Lorenz, and the kind of "interliving" research which he and others have developed, making—in principle—the life cycle of certain selected animals part of the same environment in which the observer lives, studying his own role in it as well as theirs, and taking his chances with what his ingenuity can discern in a setting of sophisticated naturalist inquiry. One remembers also Elsa the Lioness, a foundling who was brought up in the Adamsons' household in Kenya. There, the mother variable was not controlled; it was in control. Mrs. Adamson and her husband even felt responsible for putting grown-up Elsa back among the lions and succeeded in sending her back to the bush, where she mated and had cubs, and yet came back from time to time (accompanied by her cubs) to visit her human foster parents. In our context, we cannot fail to wonder about the

[3] Harry F. Harlow and Margaret K. Harlow, "A Study of Animal Affection," *The Journal of the American Museum of Natural History*, LXX (1961), No. 10.

built-in "moral" sense that made Elsa respond—and respond in very critical situations, indeed—to the words: "No, Elsa, no," *if* the words came from human beings she trusted. Yet, even with this built-in "moral" response and with a lasting trust in her foster parents (which she transmitted to her wild cubs), she was able to live as wild lions do. Her mate, however, never appeared; he apparently was not curious about her folks.

The point of this and similar stories is that our habitual relationship to what we call beasts in nature and ("instinctive" or "instinctual") beastliness in ourselves may be highly distorted by thousands of years of superstition and that there may be resources for peace even in our "animal nature" if we will only learn to nurture nature, as well as to master her. Today we can teach a monkey, in the very words of the Bible, to "eat the flesh of his own arm," even as we can permit "erring leaders" to make of all mankind the "fuel of the fire." Yet, it seems equally plausible that we can let our children grow up to lead "the calf and the young lion and the fatling together"—in nature and in their own nature.

MUTUALITY

To recognize one of man's prime resources, however, we must trace back his individual development to his premoral days, his infancy, marked by basic trust—an over-all attitude integrating those things in the newborn organism that reach out to its caretakers and establish with them what we will now discuss as mutuality. The failure of basic trust and of mutuality has been recognized in psychiatry as the most far-reaching developmental failure, undercutting all development.

I would call mutuality a relationship in which partners depend on each other for the development of their respective strengths. A baby's first responses can be seen as part of an actuality consisting of many details of mutual arousal and response. When the baby initially smiles at a mere configuration resembling the human face, the adult cannot help smiling back, filled with expectations of a "recognition" which he needs to secure from the new being as surely as it needs him. The fact is that the mutuality of adult and baby is the original source of the basic ingredient of all effective as well as ethical human action: hope. As far back as 1895, Freud, in his first outline of a "Psychology for Neurologists," counterpoints to the "helpless" newborn a "helprich" (*hilfreich*) adult and postulates that their mutual understanding is "the primal source of all moral motives."[4] Should we, then, equip the Golden Rule

---

[4] Marie Bonaparte, Anna Freud, and Ernst Kris, eds., *The Origins of Psychoanalysis,* "Letters to Wilhelm Fliess, Drafts and Notes: 1887–1902" (London: Imago, 1954; New York: Basic Books, 1954).

with a principle of mutuality, replacing the reciprocity of prudence and sympathy?

A parent dealing with a child will be strengthened in his vitality, in his sense of identity, and in his readiness for ethical action by the very ministrations by which he secures to the child his vitality, his future sense of identity, and his eventual readiness for ethical action. On this mutuality, then, all ethical potentialities are built—and we know how tragic and deeply pathogenic its absence can be in children and parents who cannot arouse and cannot respond.

But we should avoid making a new Utopia out of the "mother-child relationship." The paradise of early childhood must be abandoned—a fact which man has as yet not learned to accept. The earliest mutuality is only a beginning and leads to more complicated encounters, as both the child and his interaction with a widening cast of persons grow more complicated. I need only point out that the second basic set of vital strengths in childhood (following trust and hope) is autonomy and will, and it must be clear that a situation in which the child's willfulness faces the adult's will is a different proposition from that of the mutuality of instilling hope. Yet any adult who has managed to train a child's will must admit that he has learned much about himself and about will that he never knew before, something that cannot be learned in any other way. Thus each growing individual's developing strength "dovetails" with the strengths of an increasing number of persons arranged about him in the social orders of family, school, community, and society. These orders, in turn, safeguard themselves by formalizing the Golden Rule in a hierarchy of institutions. But all orders and rules are kept alive by those "virtues" of which Shakespeare says (in what appears to me to be *his* passionate version of the rule) that they, "shining upon others heat them and they retort that heat again to the first giver."

With such high encouragement I will try to formulate my amendment to the Golden Rule. I have been reluctant to come to this point; it has taken thousands of years and much linguistic acrobatics to translate this rule from one era to another and from one language into another, and at best one can only confound it again, in a somewhat different way.

It would, at any rate, seem irrelevant to formulate any new or better "do's" or "don't's" than the rule already implies in its classical forms. Rather, I would advocate a general orientation not too narrowly hemmed in by scruples and avoidances and not too exclusively guided by high promises and rewards. This orientation has its center in whatever activity or activities give man the feeling, as William James put it, of being "most deeply and intensely active and alive." In this, so James promises, each one will find his "real me"; but, I would now add, he will also acquire a conviction that truly ethical acts enhance a mutuality between the doer and the other—a mutuality that strengthens the doer even as he strengthens the other. Thus the "doer" and "the other" are one deed. Developmentally, this means that the doer is activated in whatever strength is appropriate to his age, stage, and condition, even as he activates in the other the strength appropriate to his age, stage, and condition.

THE PRINCIPLE OF ACTIVE CHOICE

Our next step is to demonstrate that the inequality of parent and child, or better, the uniqueness of their respective positions which has served as our model so far, has significant analogies in other situations in which uniqueness depends on a divided function. Here, eventually, we may come closer to an application of our amendment of the rule to medical ethics as well.

But there is one more principle which must be added to the developmental one, to mutuality and to the generational principle. I would call it the principle of active choice. It is, I think, most venerably expressed in St. Francis' prayer: "Grant that I may not so much seek to be consoled as to console; to be understood, as to understand; to be loved as to love; for it is in giving that we receive." Such commitment to a decisive initiative in love is, of course, contained in the admonition to "love thy neighbor." It is not in our domain, however, to discuss that religious frontier of existence where man expects to derive his most decisive ethical initiative from a highest grace. Yet I think that we can recognize in these exalted words a psychological verity that only he who approaches an encounter in a (consciously and unconsciously) active and giving attitude, rather than in a demanding and dependent one, will be able to make of that encounter what it can become.

To return to particulars, I will attempt to apply my amendment to the diversity of function in the two sexes. I have not dwelled so far on this most usual subject of a psychoanalytic discourse, sexuality. So much of this otherwise absorbing part of life has, in recent years, become stereotyped; and not the least among the terminological culprits to be blamed for this sorry fact is the psychoanalytic term "love object." For this word object in Freud's theory has been taken too literally by many of his friends and by most of his enemies. (Moralistic critics delight in misrepresenting a man's transitory findings as his ultimate "values.") The fact is that Freud, on purely conceptual grounds and on the basis of his scientific training, pointed out that drives have objects; but he never said, and he certainly never advocated, that men or women should treat one another as objects on which to live out their sexual desires. Instead, his central theory of a mutuality of orgasm which combines strivings of sexuality and of love points, in fact, to one of those basic mutualities in which a partner's potency and potentialities are activated even as he activates the other's potency and potentialities. Freud's theory implies that a man will be more a man to the extent to which he makes a woman more a woman—and vice versa—because only two uniquely different beings can enhance their respective uniqueness for one another. A "genital" person in Freud's sense thus is more likely to act in accordance with Kant's version of the Golden Rule, namely, that one should so act as to treat humanity (whether in his person or in another) "always as an end, and never as only a means." What Freud added, however, is a methodology which opens to our inquiry and to our influence the powerhouse of inner forces which provide the shining heat for our strength—and the smoldering smoke of our weaknesses.

I cannot leave the subject of the two sexes without a word on the uniqueness of women. One may well question whether the oldest versions of the rule meant to acknowledge women as partners in the golden deal; and today's study of lives still leaves obscure the place of women in what is most relevant to men. True, women are being granted equality of political rights and the recognition of a certain sameness in mental and moral equipment. But what they have not begun to earn, partially because they have not cared to ask for it, is the equal right to be effectively unique and to use hard-won rights in the service of what they uniquely represent in human evolution. One senses today the emergence of a new feminism as part of a more inclusive humanism. This coincides with a growing conviction—highly ambivalent, to be sure—that the future of mankind cannot depend on men alone and may well depend on the fate of a mother variable uncontrolled by technological man. The resistance to such a consideration always comes from men and women who are mortally afraid that by emphasizing what is unique, one may tend to re-emphasize what is unequal. The study of life histories certainly confirms a far-reaching sameness in men and women insofar as they express the mathematical architecture of the universe, the organization of logical thought, and the structure of language. But such study also suggests that while men and women can think, act, and talk alike, they naturally do not experience their bodies (and thus the world) alike. One could illustrate this by pointing to sex differences in the structuralization of space in the play of children. But I assume here that a uniqueness of either sex will be granted without proof, and that the *différence* acclaimed by the much-quoted Frenchman is not considered a mere matter of anatomical appointments for mutual sexual enjoyment, but a psychobiological difference central to two great modes of life, the paternal and the maternal modes.

The study of creative men reveals that only a vital struggle makes it possible for them to reconcile in themselves the paternal and the maternal dimensions of all mental productivity. It may well be that there is something in woman's specific creativity which has only waited for a clarification of her relation to masculinity (including her own) in order to assume her share of leadership in human affairs, which so far have been left entirely in the hands of gifted and driven men and often of men whose creativity eventually has yielded to ruthless self-aggrandizement. Mankind now obviously depends on new kinds of social inventions and on institutions which guard and cultivate that which nurses and nourishes, cares and tolerates, includes and preserves. Mere conquest and invention alone and more expansion and organization will make life more exciting but not more livable. And if my amendment to the rule suggests that one sex enhances the uniqueness of the other, it also implies that each, to be really unique, depends on a mutuality with an equally unique partner: only when women dare to assume the motherhood of man, may men be emboldened to overcome the boyhood of history.

MUTUALITY IN PROFESSIONAL ETHICS

By now, one might well have reached the conclusion that my discursiveness was intended to leave me little time for the problem of medical ethics. However, medical ethics can only be a variation of a universal theme, and it was necessary to establish the general context within which I could hope to give a slightly different emphasis to a subject so rich in tradition.

There is a very real and specific inequality in the relationship of doctor and patient in their roles of knower and known, helper and sufferer, practitioner of life and victim of disease and death; for which reason doctors have their own and unique professional oath and strive to live up to a universal ideal of "the doctor." Yet the practice of the healing arts permits of extreme types of practitioners, from the absolute authoritarian over homes and clinics to the harassed servant of demanding mankind, from the sadist of mere proficiency to the effusive lover of all (well, almost all) of his patients. Here, too, Freud has thrown intimate and original light on the workings of a unique relationship. His letters to his friend and mentor Fliess illustrate the singular experience which made him recognize in his patients what he called transference—that is, the patient's wish to exploit sickness and treatment for infantile and regressive ends. But more, Freud recognized a countertransference in the healer's motivation to exploit the patient's transference and to dominate or serve, possess or love him to the disadvantage of his true function. He made systematic insight into transference and countertransference part of the training of the psychoanalytic practitioner. I would think that all of the motivations necessarily entering so vast and so intricate a field could be reconciled in a Golden Rule amended to include a mutuality of divided function. Each specialty and each technique in its own way permit the medical man to develop as a practitioner and as a person, even as the patient is cured as a patient and as a person. For a real cure transcends the transitory stage of patienthood; it is a life experience which enables the cured patient to develop and to transmit to home and neighborhood an attitude toward health which is one of the most essential ingredients of an ethical outlook. This variation on the over-all theme of an amended rule is all I can offer you here.

Beyond this, can the healing arts and sciences contribute to a new ethical outlook? This question, which always recurs in psychoanalysis, is usually disposed of with Freud's answer: The psychoanalyst represents the ethics of scientific truth only and is committed to studying ethics (or morality) in a scientific way. Beyond this, he leaves *Weltanschauungen* (ethical world views) to others.

It seems to me, however, that the clinical arts and sciences, although employing the scientific method, are not defined by it or limited by it. The healer is committed to a highest good, the preservation of life, and the furtherance of well-being. He need not prove scientifically that these are, in fact, the highest good; rather, he is precommitted to this basic proposition while investigating what can be verified by scientific means. This, I think, is the meaning of the Hippocratic oath, which subordinates all medical method to a humanist ethics. True, a man can separate his personal, his professional, and his scientific ethics, seeking fulfilment of needs in personal life; the welfare of others in his profession; and in his research, truths independent of personal preference or service. However, there are psychological limits to the multiplicity of values a man can live by; and, in the end, not only the practitioner, but also his patient and his research, depend on a certain unification in him of temperament, intellect, and ethics: this unification clearly characterizes great clinical teachers. Although it is true, then, that as scientists, we must study ethics objectively, we are, as professional people, committed to a unification of personality, training, and conviction which alone will help us to do our work adequately. At the same time, as transient members of the human race we must record the truest meaning of which the fallible methods of our era and the accidental circumstances of our existence have made us aware. In this sense, there is (and always has been) not only an ethics governing clinical work and a clinical approach to the study of ethics but also a contribution to ethics of the healing orientation. The healer, however, has now committed himself to prevention on a large scale, and he cannot evade the question as to how to assure ethical vitality to all lives saved from morbidity and early mortality.

MUTUALITY AMONG NATIONS

And now a final word on what is and will be for a long time to come, the sinister horizon of the world in which we all study and work: the international situation. Here, too, we cannot afford to live for long with a division of personal, professional, and political ethics—a division endangering the very life which our professions have vowed to keep intact and thus cutting through the very fiber of our personal existence. But again, I can offer you only another variation of the theme, and propose, in all brevity, that what has been said here about the relationships of parent and child, of man and woman, and of doctor and patient, may have some application to the relationship of nations to each other, nations which by definition are units at different stages of political, technological, and economic transformation. I know that it is all too easy for us to believe that nations thus engaged should treat one another (or, at least, that we should treat others) with a superior educative or clinical attitude. This is not what I mean. The point is, again, not one of underscored inequality, but one of respected uniqueness within historical differences. Insofar as a nation thinks of itself as a collective individual, it may well learn to visualize its task as that of maintaining international relations of mutuality. For the only alternative to armed competition seems to be the effort to activate in the historical partner what will strengthen him in his historical development, even as it strengthens the actor in his own development—toward a common future identity. Only thus can we find a common denominator in the rapid change, the rapid unification of technology and history, and transcend the dangerous imagery of victory and defeat, of subjugation and exploitation, which is the heritage of a fragmented past.

Does this sound utopian? I think, on the contrary, that all of what I have said is already known in many ways, is being expressed in many languages, and is being practiced on many levels. At our historical moment it becomes clear in a most practical way that the doer of the Golden Rule and he who is done by, is the same man, *is* man.

Men of clinical background, however, must not lose sight of a dimension which I have taken for granted in what I have said. Although the Golden Rule in its classical versions prods man to strive consciously for a highest good and to avoid mutual harm with a sharpened awareness, our insights assume an *unconscious* substratum of ethical strength and, at the same time, unconscious arsenals of destructive irrationality. The last century traumatically expanded man's awareness of the existence of motivations stemming from his animal ancestry, from his economic history, and from his inner dividedness; but it also created methods of productive self-scrutiny. It will be the task of the next generation to begin to integrate such new awareness with the minute particulars, not only of advancing proficiency, but also of that ongoing mutuality, by which alone man's ready rage is neutralized.

It does not seem easy to speak of ethical subjects without indulging in some moralizing and ideologizing. As an antidote I will repeat the final words of the quotation from the Talmud, with which I began. It does not say: "Here is the rule; go, and act accordingly." It says: "Go, and learn it." Here lies our challenge.

BIBLIOGRAPHY OF HENRY A. MURRAY

1919–1923   Ten publications on physiological research.

1925–1927   Ten publications on research on physiological ontogeny. Summarized in (with Alfred E. Cohn) "Physiological Ontogeny: I. The Present Status of the Problem," *Quarterly Review of Biology,* II, 469–493.

1928   "A Case of Pinealoma with Symptoms Suggestive of Compulsion Neurosis," *Archives of Neurology and Psychiatry,* XIX, 932–945.

1931   (With Herbert Barry, Jr., and Donald W. MacKinnon) "Hypnotizability as a Personality Trait," *Human Biology,* III, 1–36.

1933   "The Effect of Fear upon Estimates of the Maliciousness of Other Personalities," *Journal of Social Psychology,* IV, 310–329.

1934   (With Harold A. Wolff and Carl E. Smith) "The Psychology of Humor," *Journal of Abnormal and Social Psychology,* XXVIII, 341–365.

            "The Psychology of Humor: II. Mirth Responses to Disparagement Jokes as a Manifestation of an Aggressive Disposition," *Journal of Abnormal and Social Psychology,* XXIX, 66–81.

1935   (With Christiana D. Morgan) "A Method of Investigating Fantasies," *Archives of Neurology and Psychiatry,* XXXIV, 289–306.

"Psychology and the University," *Archives of Neurology and Psychiatry*, XXXIV, 803–897.

"The Harvard Psychological Clinic," *Harvard Alumni Bulletin*, October 25.

1936 "Facts Which Support the Concept of Need or Drive," *Journal of Psychology*, III, 27–42.

"Techniques for Systematic Investigation of Fantasy," *Journal of Psychology*, III, 115–143.

"Some Concepts for a Psychology of Personality," *Journal of General Psychology*, XV, 240–268.

(With David R. Wheeler) "A Note on the Possible Clairvoyance of Dreams," *Journal of Psychology*, III, 309–313.

(With Richard Wolf) "An Experiment in Judging Personalities," *Journal of Psychology*, III, 345–365.

1937 "Visceral Manifestations of Personality," *Journal of Abnormal and Social Psychology*, XXXII, 161–184.

1938 (With staff) *Explorations in Personality*. New York: Oxford University Press.

1940 "Sigmund Freud: 1856–1939," *American Journal of Psychology*, LIII, 134–138.

"What Should Psychologists Do about Psychoanalysis?" *Journal of Abnormal and Social Psychology*, XXXV, 150–175.

1943 (With Morris Stein) "Note on the Selection of Combat Officers," *Psychosomatic Medicine*, V, 386–391.

Thematic Apperception Test. Cambridge, Mass.: Harvard University Press.

1945 (With Christiana D. Morgan) "A Clinical Study of Sentiments," *Genetic Psychology Monographs*, XXXII, 3–311.

"Assessment of the Whole Person," *Proceedings of the Meeting of Military Psychologists and Psychiatrists*. College Park, Md.: University of Maryland Press.

1946   (With Donald W. MacKinnon) "Assessment of OSS Personnel," *Journal of Consulting Psychology,* X, 76–80.

1947   "Proposals for Research in Clinical Psychology," *American Journal of Orthopsychiatry,* XVII, 203–210.

            "Time for a Positive Morality," *Survey Graphic,* XXXVI, 195 ff.

1948   "America's Mission," *Survey Graphic,* XXXVII, 411–415. (With staff) *Assessment of Men.* New York: Rinehart & Co.

1949   "Research Planning: A Few Proposals," in S. S. Sargent and M. W. Smith, eds., *Culture and Personality.* Beloit, Wis.: Viking Fund.

            Editor, Herman Meville, *Pierre, or The Ambiguities.* New York: Hendricks House. (With introduction.)

1950   (With Clyde Kluckhohn) *Personality in Nature, Society, and Culture.* New York: Alfred A. Knopf.

1951   "Uses of the TAT," *American Journal of Psychiatry,* CVII, 8.

            "Thematic Apperception Test," *Military Clinical Psychology,* XLV, 54–71.

            "Toward a Classification of Interactions," in T. Parsons and E. A. Shils, eds., *Toward a General Theory of Action.* Cambridge, Mass.: Harvard University Press.

            "In Nomine Diaboli," *New England Quarterly,* XXIV, 435–452.

            "Some Basic Psychological Assumptions and Conceptions," *Dialectica,* V, 266–292.

            "Foreword," Edwin S. Shneidman, *Thematic Test Analysis.* New York: Grune & Stratton.

            "Foreword," Harold H. Anderson and Gladys L. Anderson, *An Introduction to Projective Techniques.* Englewood Cliffs, N.J.: Prentice-Hall.

1952   "Poet of Creative Dissolution: Conrad Aiken," *Wake,* XI, 95–106.

1953   (With Clyde Kluckhohn and David M. Schneider) *Personality in Nature, Society, and Culture.* 2nd ed.; New York: Alfred A. Knopf.

1954   "Science in Two Societies," in *The Contemporary Scene.* New York: Metropolitan Museum of Art.

1955   "Versions of Man," in *Man's Right to Knowledge.* New York: Columbia University Press.

"Introduction," A. Burton and R. E. Harris, *Clinical Studies of Personality,* Vols. I, II. New York: Harper.

"American Icarus," in *Clinical Studies of Personality,* Vol. II.

(With Anthony Davids) "Preliminary Appraisal of an Auditory Projective Technique for Studying Personality and Cognition," *American Journal of Orthopsychiatry,* XXV, 543–544.

1956   "Religion in an Age of Science," *Christian Register,* CXXXV.

"Morton Prince: Sketch of His Life and Work," *Journal of Abnormal and Social Psychology,* CII, 291–295.

"Introduction," G. G. Stern, M. I. Stein, and B. S. Bloom, *Methods in Personality Assessment.* Glencoe, Ill.: The Free Press.

1958   "Drive, Time, Strategy, Measurement, and Our Way of Life," in G. Lindzey, ed., *Assessment of Human Motives.* New York: Rinehart & Co.

"Foreword," Robert N. Wilson, *Man Made Plain.* Cleveland: Howard Allen.

"Individuality: The Meaning and Content of Individuality in Contemporary America," *Daedalus,* LXXXVII, 25–47.

1959   "Introduction to the Issue 'Myth and Mythmaking,'" *Daedalus,* LXXXVIII, 211–222.

"Vicissitudes of Creativity," in H. H. Anderson, ed., *Creativity and Its Cultivation.* New York: Harper.

"Preparations for the Scaffold of a Comprehensive System," in S. Koch, ed., *Psychology*, "A Study of a Science," Vol. III. New York: McGraw-Hill.

(With Hadley Cantril and Mark A. May) "Some Glimpses of Soviet Psychology," *American Psychologist*, XIV, 303–307.

1960   "Two Versions of Man," in H. Shapley, ed., *Science Ponders Religion*. New York: Appleton-Century-Crofts.

"Historical Trends in Personality Research," in H. P. David and J. C. Brengelmann, eds., *Perspectives in Personality Research*. New York: Springer.

"The Possible Nature of a 'Mythology' to Come," in *Myth and Mythmaking*. New York: George Braziller.

Editor, *Myth and Mythmaking*. New York: George Braziller.

1961   "Unprecedented Evolutions," *Daedalus*, XC, 547–570.

"Prospect for Psychology" (Address delivered at the International Congress of Applied Psychology, Copenhagen, Denmark, August 18), *Science*, CXXXVI (1962), 483–488.

"Beyond Yesterday's Idealisms," in *The Fate of Man*. New York: George Braziller.

1962   "The Personality and Career of Satan," *Journal of Social Issues*, XVIII, 36–54.

1963   "Studies of Stressful Interpersonal Disputations," *American Psychologist*, XVIII, 28–36.

INDEX

A

Abasement, 80
Abrams, M. H., 395
Adamson, Joy, 420–421
Adler, A., 179, 283
Aggression: related to interpersonal conflict, 79; in stories of Maugham, 155
Ahab, Captain, 221–227
Albert, Ethel M., 325
Alienation: major themes of, 64–67; roots of, 68–70; study of, 41–70; themes of, interpreted, 60–64
Allen, J., 196
Allport, G. W., 181; on the ego, 251–252; on values, 329–330, 332
Ambiguity: intolerance of, 161–177; and mentally disturbed patients, 168–170; and Navy men, 168–170; and university students, 168–170
Ames, Adelbert, 394
Anxiety, 163
Arsenian, Jean, 140
Artist: and the psychologist, 349–350
Artistic production: and the study of personality, 145
Ascendance, 7, 10–11, 25–27
Asch, Solomon, 341–342
Attitudes: and values, 329–331
Auden, W. H., 242
Auditory Projective Test, 162–165

Authoritarian personality, 157; and tolerance of ambiguity, 161–162
Autobiography: used in case study, 45–49
Azzageddi Test, 162–165

B

Bacon, Francis, 202
Bakan, D., 106
Baldwin, James M., 343
Barron, Frank, 230; on complexity-simplicity, 174–176; study of diffusion, integration, and enduring attention, 235–248
Bateson, G., 171
Beck, Samuel, 395
Bell, E. T., 392–393
Bellak, Leopold, 2, 231; study of stories by Maugham, 143–159
Berdyaev, Nicholas, 243
Bernfeld, S., 369, 371–372, 374, 376
Bloom, Benjamin S., 127
Boss, Medard, 118
Brentano, Franz, 371, 377
Breuer, Josef, 367, 375, 377
Bridgman, Percy W., 207–208
Bromberg, W., 96
Bronowski, J., 408–409
Bruecke, Ernst, 370–372, 374
Bruner, J. S., 326, 330

438   *Index*